NEW YORK CITY BLUES

NEW YORK CITY
BLUES

Postwar Portraits from Harlem to the Village and Beyond

Larry Simon

Edited by John Broven   Photos by Robert Schaffer

University Press of Mississippi / Jackson

The University Press of Mississippi is the scholarly publishing agency of
the Mississippi Institutions of Higher Learning: Alcorn State University,
Delta State University, Jackson State University, Mississippi State University,
Mississippi University for Women, Mississippi Valley State University,
University of Mississippi, and University of Southern Mississippi.

www.upress.state.ms.us

The University Press of Mississippi is a member
of the Association of University Presses.

Photographs by Robert Schaffer unless otherwise credited

First printing 2021
∞

Library of Congress Control Number: 2021939960

Harback ISBN 978-1-4968-3471-3
Trade paperback ISBN 978-1-4968-3499-7
Epub single ISBN 978-1-4968-3472-0
Epub institutional ISBN 978-1-4968-3473-7
PDF single ISBN 978-1-4968-3474-4
PDF institutional ISBN 978-1-4968-3470-6

British Library Cataloging-in-Publication Data available

For my daughter Nell, with all the love and affection
in the universe. And for my parents, Sol and Ethel,
whose creative spirits and warmth are a joy
that lingers well beyond their lives on earth.

—LARRY SIMON

In memory of my dear wife Shelley, who made me a proud,
transplanted New Yorker; Hy Weiss, the wily New York
record man who became a beloved family friend; and popular
music photographer Paul Harris, a valued contributor to this book.

—JOHN BROVEN

Don't forget where blues was born, out of slavery where people are having a hard time. This was a way of people holding themselves together and maybe having hope for the future. Blues and gospel are the same thing basically. It's about hard living, and experiences and hope. The blues had a weird lonesome-type, built-in sound. It varied here and there with the beat, this, that and the other. But the basic thing is there, no matter where they do it. Blues.

—BOBBY ROBINSON
Producer, entrepreneur, record man
Harlem, New York

CONTENTS

Paul Harris Photo Portfolio

Goodbye to a Friend

ACKNOWLEDGMENTS

I wish to thank all of the musicians and producers who gave so generously of their time in granting these interviews—and in a number of cases welcoming me into their homes with warmth and kindness. I give special thanks to John Broven, not only for his brilliant and tireless editorial work but also for his level of commitment and collaboration throughout the project. John's contributions to this book could have just as well made him coauthor, such was the degree of his participation.

John and I both wish to extend our deeply felt gratitude and appreciation to our contributors. Thank you Val Wilmer, Paul Harris, Richard Tapp, Anton Mikofsky, Bob Malenky, and Victor Pearlin.

We have received generous assistance, whenever required, from Cilla Huggins (*Juke Blues* magazine), Matt Barton (the Library of Congress), Bruce Bastin, Chris Bentley (including his booklet to *Down Home Blues*, a three-CD Wienerworld box set centered on New York), Jonas Bernholm, Kyril Bromley, Maxine Brown, Jay Bruder, Tony Collins, Donn Fileti, Todd France, Jimmy Gielbert, Mike Gilroy, Marv Goldberg, Jay Halsey, Rob Hughes, Red Kelly, Dan Kochakian, George Korval, Ruth McFadden, Seamus McGarvey, Opal Louis Nations, Debbi Scott Price (for the wonderful map), Jeff Roth (the *New York Times*), Rob Santos (Sony Music, New York), Gordon Skadburg, Nicolas Teurnier (*Soul Bag* magazine), Russ Wapensky, and Adam White; also, John is appreciative of the transcription work on his interviews by Aja Bain and Tracy Powell.

We express our thanks to the staff of University Press of Mississippi, especially Craig Gill and Carlton McGrone, and also our editor Norman Ware, for their enthusiastic help and guidance throughout.

We would also like to thank the friendly and helpful staff at the Library of Congress in Washington, DC.

—LS

NY CITY
Blues
LOCATIONS

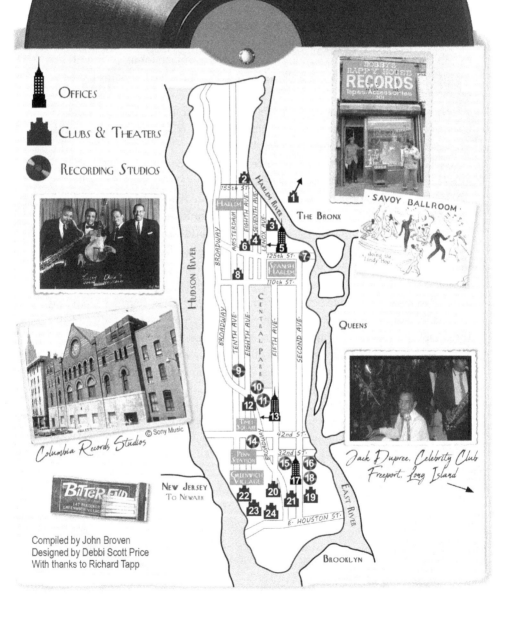

Offices

Clubs & Theaters

Recording Studios

Columbia Records Studios © Sony Music

BITTER END
147 BLEECKER
GREENWICH VILLAGE

BOBBY'S HAPPY HOUSE
RECORDS
Tapes Accessories

SAVOY BALLROOM
doing the Lindy Hop

Jack Dupree, Celebrity Club
Freeport, Long Island

HARLEM

155th ST.
Broadway
Amsterdam
Eighth Ave.
Seventh Ave.
Lenox Ave.
Harlem River
125th ST.
SPANISH HARLEM
110th ST.
The Bronx

CENTRAL PARK

Hudson River
Broadway
Tenth Ave.
Eighth Ave.
Fifth Ave.
Second Ave.

Queens

TIMES SQUARE
42nd ST.
32nd ST.
PENN STATION
GREENWICH VILLAGE
Broadway
East River

New Jersey
To Newark

E. HOUSTON ST.

Brooklyn

Compiled by John Broven
Designed by Debbi Scott Price
With thanks to Richard Tapp

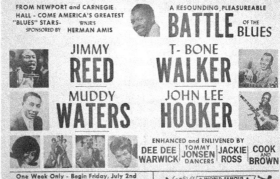

1961   1965

1961

PREFACE

Larry Simon

This book offers a glimpse into New York City blues scene from the post–World War II years through the early 1970s. It was a scene that happily, but briefly, returned with a number of those original players in the late 1980s, lasting through the mid-1990s. Accordingly, I was able to interview many of these great artists who had been generally ignored in their prime by blues researchers.

Like the blues of Chicago, many of New York's blues musicians came north from areas to our south or southeast such as the Carolinas, Florida, or Tennessee, and upon arriving in an urban area plugged in and went electric. Sonny Terry, Brownie McGhee, Sticks "Stick" McGhee, and Champion Jack Dupree were among the most active and well-known figures in New York City. What is not so well known is that before Terry and McGee became international stars of the folk-blues circuit, Brownie was an electric guitarist in New York mixing it up with jump blues in a more urban style. The New York "sound" was varied, not as easy to define as Chicago or the jazzier style of the West Coast. Some players had a very pronounced gospel quality, and, in the style of others, there was a closer connection to the acoustic roots, sometimes merely amplified or mic'd for loudness and distortion, but not as utterly transformed as many of the Chicago or Texas musicians whom we are all familiar with.

Through these interviews and photos, my hope is that the music and musicians will come alive. My goal is that readers will emerge with a strong sense of a number of the major personalities and places, a good idea of the history in the interviewees' words, and a decent introduction to the rich variety of sounds as well as a hunger to hear more and delve deeper into New York City's very own blues culture.

My involvement with these wonderful artists began in an Irish bar in New York City late one afternoon in 1987. Prior to this, I had worked extensively in the downtown New York avant-garde jazz, rock, and new music world, beginning in the gritty days of the late 1970s, playing with artists such as La Monte Young, Lester Bowie, Julius Hemphill, John Zorn, Frank Lowe, and many others, even the radical street musician David Peel. I also had a band that played clubs such as CBGB, Tier 3, the Squat Theatre, the Gas Station, and Arleen Schloss's loft "A's." We had been called by various names (Realpolitik, Fester's Farm); then, as we veered more toward working with blues artists, we settled on Killing Floor NYC. Ironically, it was mostly through the English blues magazine *Juke Blues* and the record store Down Home Music in El Cerrito, California, that I first heard about some of the great but, by 1986, mostly retired artists of New York City's indigenous and unique blues scene. The articles I read in *Juke Blues* led me on my quest to find these musicians and see if I could get them interested in playing out once again. The first musician I searched out was pianist Bob Gaddy, who was in his sixties and was working the late-night shift as a cook in an Irish bar in the Gramercy Park area of Manhattan. When I walked into the bar, I asked if Bob Gaddy, the blues pianist who worked there, was around. The bartender replied that he didn't know anyone by that name. It so happened that a moment later Bob emerged from the kitchen. The bartender said, "Oh, you mean Bobby, the cook?" He didn't have a clue that Bob Gaddy was a brilliant blues artist with a recording career and had been a cornerstone of the original New York City blues scene. I went over to Gaddy, an extremely warm, friendly, and dignified gentleman, and asked if he'd be interested in having my band play behind him and doing some shows. He was very enthusiastic about the idea and said, "Great." Bob very quickly introduced me to his other musical colleagues, and we ended up playing shows up and down the East Coast as well as in Europe. Guitarist/vocalist Larry Dale told me he had played across Europe, Harlem, New Jersey, upstate New York, and areas surrounding New York City, but until he met me he had never played a gig in New York City below 125th Street in Harlem.

One of the musicians to whom Bob Gaddy introduced me was the legendary and, at that time, notoriously reclusive guitarist "Wild" Jimmy Spruill. He happened to be a favorite of the late rock guitarist Robert Quine, an acquaintance of mine. One day walking down Third Avenue I ran into Quine and told him I'd been in touch with Spruill. Quine didn't believe I'd ever be able to get Spruill on stage again. At one point, I was afraid he was right. Our first big show, after a few smaller club dates, was a performance at Washington Square Church on May 6, 1989, sponsored by the wonderful organization the World Music Institute. Along with Gaddy, the show also featured Larry Dale and Rosco Gordon backed by my band Killing Floor NYC. The show received a lot of publicity, including from the *New York Times*, as it drew attention to the fact that we did indeed have our very own blues scene in the metropolitan area, just like Chicago, Los Angeles, or Memphis. Very few New Yorkers knew this. Spruill agreed to perform and was advertised to be there. Despite my pleading, as well as encouragement from Gaddy and Larry Dale, we couldn't persuade him to appear. Hal Paige was also scheduled to perform, but he, too, was a no-show. As a note of historical interest,

Bob Gaddy at the piano, A. J. Johnson (drums) at the Blue Frog, the Bronx, 1993.

guitarist Tiny Grimes was also slated to be on the show but died two months before, on March 4, 1989. Before long, Spruill did start doing shows with us and other musicians in New York City, and even came to Europe for a performance at the prestigious annual Blues Estafette in Utrecht, the Netherlands. It was a revue I put together that I named in honor of Bobby Robinson called the Bobby Robinson Rhythm and Blues Revue. We came to Utrecht with Robinson (as our emcee), Bob Gaddy, Larry Dale, Jimmy Spruill, Dr. Horse (aka Doc Pittman), and Noble "Thin Man" Watts, along with my band playing behind everyone. It was fantastic!

The artists were back out and revved up to be playing for mostly new and extremely enthusiastic audiences, both in New York and abroad. Many in the crowds were unfamiliar with them (and the scene they were part of), or perhaps thought they had long since retired or even passed away. It was a joy and a privilege to have played a part in making this comeback happen.

During this time, I had the idea to interview the various artists and asked my friend, photographer Robert Schaffer, to take pictures. My goal was to compile all this information and publish a book. Life progressed, and the idea fell by the wayside. In the spring of 2016, I finally got back to it and contacted my friend, author/researcher John Broven, hoping that he would contribute his vast knowledge and editing skills to this volume. As work progressed, other musicians, photographers, and authors came aboard. I am so thankful for everyone's contributions.

I sincerely hope that this book brings readers closer to the music and the artists.

NEW YORK CITY BLUES

INTRODUCTION

John Broven

In a first on the subject, this compendium of original interviews and vignettes attempts to validate New York's underappreciated blues tradition. Let's dig deeper. There's no doubt the city's blues scene in the comparative "golden age" from the 1940s through the 1960s, which is the book's main focus, was impacted irrevocably by migratory patterns from the southeastern states. Inevitably, southern rural music origins were absorbed into an urban environment. As a result, there is a distinct New York City blues legacy to celebrate and study.

For the record, New York City comprises five boroughs: Manhattan (including Harlem), the Bronx, Brooklyn, Queens, and Staten Island. Our focus is, of course, primarily on Harlem but also encompasses the Bronx and Brooklyn.

"I know Harlem can't be heaven, 'cause New York is right down here on earth." So sang RCA Victor blues singer and songwriter Doctor Clayton as he captured the area's charms in his 1946 recording of "Angels in Harlem." Harlem! Yet it's a place of contradictions, where some of the best entertainment anywhere rubbed shoulders with the appalling poverty of many of its African American residents.

In the pre–World War II era, Harlem had resonated to the bands of Duke Ellington and Cab Calloway at the Cotton Club. Other lively venues included the Savoy Ballroom and Smalls Paradise. Somehow, the blues didn't fit into this exotic scenario. With the music's low profile, contemporary accounts of the early postwar New York blues scene are hard to find. So, it's illuminating to look back at a 1959 US blues research trip, which started out in New York, by Frenchmen Jacques Demêtre and Marcel Chauvard in a series that first appeared in France's *Jazz Hot*, then in England's *Jazz Journal*. "We were in the land of the blues—a strange country where the irrational rubs shoulders with the bizarre, but where an extraordinary sense of humanity draws together like brothers the bluesmen and those around them," they wrote in their native language, with their native compassion. "As we see it, the bluesman's life is on the same level as that of factory workers and modest employees. Working-class people like blues in general, especially when sung or played by groups consisting of tenor sax, organ, and guitar."

3

The pioneering researchers added, "But this love of blues is hardly at its best in New York, a town which has tasted too many brews for blacks to have remained aloof from other musical forms: cha-cha-chá, pop songs, and modern jazz. And much to the despair of jazz musicians, rock 'n' roll is very popular with the young breed. The situation is all the more complicated as feelings of near-disgust for the blues are expressed by many sophisticated Afro-Americans higher in the social scale."

The Frenchmen, who stayed in Brooklyn with pianist "Champion" Jack Dupree and his wife Lucille, met uptown in Harlem with guitarist Larry Dale at the Central Ballroom, session guitarist Jimmy Spruill at the Apollo Theatre, and artists Tarheel Slim and Little Ann with record man Bobby Robinson at his office. All these music personalities are featured in the pages of this book. Another coincidence is that Demêtre and Chauvard attended a Dupree performance at the all-black Celebrity Club in Freeport, Long Island, a forgotten venue that is remembered by another interviewee, Paul Oscher, and that hosted gigs by Tarheel Slim and Little Ann, as well as Doc Pomus, who is also featured here. Interestingly, the Dupree show was topped by the "exceptionally fine" Solitaires, a hot act for interviewee Hy Weiss's Old Town label. The writers noted that at the club's show "musicians and dancers are as one, a fact that emphasizes the near rituality of the dancing and music."

Jimmy Spruill and Champion Jack Dupree, 125th Street, Harlem, 1959. Photo © Jacques Demêtre/ Soul Bag Archives.

As an aside, here was Champion Jack Dupree, barrelhouse pianist, playing on the same bill as a top vocal group. That doesn't comply with the Caucasian habit of pigeonholing different musical styles, but it may explain why vocal groups and rhythm & blues artists are easily referenced here in a blues book. And just look at the billing on the Apollo Theatre marquee in the 1959 Jimmy Spruill and Dupree photograph: Ella Fitzgerald and Oscar Peterson. In a way, this musical potpourri is representative of the cosmopolitan nature of Harlem and the Big Apple.

Champion Jack Dupree at the Celebrity Club, Freeport, Long Island, 1959. Photo © Jacques Demêtre/Soul Bag Archives.

New York's blues identity problem was hinted at in an article in the *New York Times* by Peter Watrous dated May 5, 1989, announcing a concert masterminded by Larry Simon—author of this book—with his band, Killing Floor NYC, at Washington Square Church. Included on the bill were Larry Dale, Bob Gaddy, and Rosco Gordon, all interviewed here. The headline was accurate: "New York's Cool Blues, with a Hint of Memphis," but in which section of the illustrious newspaper did the story appear? Why, "Pop/Jazz."

Watrous made a brave attempt to explain that "where other blues centers had their big names, New York—fed by the twin sources of North Carolina emigrants and unemployed swing-jazz musicians—had no major figures." Watrous added, quite fairly, that "New York blues has been traditionally overlooked by music fans and historians." That's still the case in 2020. Yet for a while in the 1980s and 1990s, Dale, Gaddy, and Gordon had a second coming in a sort of blues revival, often with Simon's band.

The nearest New York ever had to a blues leader was Brownie McGhee in the 1940s and early 1950s. He played on a novel three-78 rpm Circle album with his brother "Stick" and Dan Burley, manager editor of Harlem's influential *Amsterdam News*, who had been a leading party-piano player in Chicago. The 1946 session, also with New Orleans bass player George "Pops" Foster, was released as "South Side Shake" by Dan Burley and his Skiffle Boys, with the material variously described by label owner/note writer Rudi Blesh as "fast blues rock," "low down" and "real bottom" slow blues, and "good time" party music.

By the mid-1950s, after a searing series of blues releases for Bob and Morty Shad's Jax and Harlem labels, Brownie had been hijacked by the folk-blues movement. In this folkies' world, there were no wailing amplified harmonicas—even with Sonny Terry in support—or thudding backbeats. Instead, there was a predilection for familiar ditties aimed at the white audience. Jack Dupree was also a potential leader, but stylistically he was still more New Orleans than New York, and he relocated to Europe by the end of 1959. Essentially, there was no Big Apple equivalent of style drivers Muddy Waters, Little Walter, Howlin' Wolf, and Jimmy Reed in Chicago—or the immensely popular Chuck Berry and Bo Diddley; John Lee Hooker in Detroit; Lightnin' Hopkins in Houston; B. B. King in Memphis; Fats Domino in New Orleans; and T-Bone Walker (via Texas) or Charles Brown on the West Coast. Yet every New York blues artist was influenced by these national figures one way or another.

The blues, moreover, is the very antithesis of what New York represents. The city has a natural optimistic swagger enhanced by the bright lights and skyscrapers of Broadway, and emboldened by its place as the commercial hub of America. There has been an eye toward the bounties of tomorrow, not a backward look to yesterday.

New York has always been a melting pot, directing and absorbing the latest popular trends in every music form since time immemorial. The Caribbean islands—notably Cuba and Puerto Rico—with Spanish Harlem as a spiritual home, have had a special influence by way of rumba, mambo, cha-cha-chá, boogaloo, salsa, and Latin jazz, even permeating the city's mainstream pop and blues recordings.

Through the decades, the New York roots music scene, to which blues and rhythm & blues belong, has benefited from being home to a number of towering activists, in every sense of the word. Look at their names and some of their achievements: The John and Alan Lomax southern field trips for the Library of Congress, including the discovery of Lead Belly, are in league of their own; John Hammond II, a giant at Columbia Records, presented the landmark *From Spirituals to Swing* concerts in the late 1930s, oversaw the original Robert Johnson reissue, and introduced Bob Dylan and Bruce Springsteen to the world at large; Decca producer Milt Gabler made Louis Jordan the no. 1 "race" seller of the 1940s, and propelled Bill Haley and the Comets into becoming a prime force in international rock 'n' roll in the 1950s and beyond; and Pete Seeger led the left-leaning folk revolution with the Carnegie Hall hootenanny concerts and more.

The jazz age has been served well by historians from the United States and Europe, including George Avakian, Nat Hentoff, Nat Shapiro, Marshall Stearns, Dan Morgenstern, Leonard Feather, Stanley Dance, Gunther Schuller, and Hugues Panassié. Likewise, Donn Fileti, formerly of Relic Records and from Hackensack, New Jersey, and others have done marvelous work in documenting the vocal group scene, known today as doo-wop. New York's blues researchers have included Lawrence "Larry" Cohn, author of *Nothing But the Blues*, who was an executive at CBS/Epic Records and 1991 Grammy winner for his *Robert Johnson: The Complete Recordings* set; photographer and reissue producer Frank Driggs; *Blues Who's Who* author Sheldon Harris; researchers Dan Kochakian and Robert Palmer; and *Blues Research* magazine collaborators Len Kunstadt, Anthony Rotante, and Paul Sheatsley. Special praise goes to Arnold Shaw for his interviews in *Honkers and Shouters: The Golden Years of Rhythm & Blues* (including a large New York section) and to the thoughtful 1950s *Billboard* reporter Bob Rolontz, who went on to head RCA Victor's Groove and Vik labels. As is the case in other regions, the New York gospel scene remains hidden from general view, obscuring the huge influence of the church among the black population.

Now is the moment to explore the city's blues history, with its many Carolina musicians and other southern migrants. Their background has been described expertly by Bruce Bastin in *Red River Blues: The Blues Tradition in the Southeast*. Generally, here was a gentler, more melodic sound contrasting with the gritty blues of Chicago and Detroit that was nurtured mainly by migrants from Mississippi and nearby southern states. A prime New York musical inspiration was North Carolinian Blind Boy Fuller, who directly influenced Brownie McGhee and Tarheel Slim in a style known as Piedmont blues. Bastin, who worked closely with fellow field researcher Pete Lowry, reissued many Eastern Seaboard blues and rhythm & blues recordings on his Flyright (UK) label, including in the early 1970s an ahead-of-the-curve three-LP series of New York country blues, R&B, and city blues (with a personally long-forgotten John Broven note: "What a field for research!" I exclaimed).

For all the laid-back Carolina influences, there was evidence of a tougher emergent New York blues sound verging on black 'n' roll and R&B, starting with Stick McGhee's "Drinkin' Wine Spo-Dee-O-Dee" with brother Brownie (Atlantic, 1949), through Cousin Leroy's down-home releases for RCA Victor's Groove label (1955) and Al Silver's Herald-Ember group (1957), climaxing in 1958 with Champion Jack Dupree's acclaimed drug-themed *Blues from the Gutter* Atlantic LP, and Tarheel Slim's black rocker, "Number 9 Train" (Fury).

At this stage, I ought to explain that when the abbreviated term "R&B" is used, it refers to original rhythm & blues, not the generic modern black music appellation. In other words, rhythm & blues was the natural successor to blues and race music, and was formally named in 1949 by Jerry Wexler of *Billboard* and later Atlantic Records. The term was supplanted by "soul music" in the 1960s before its "contemporary R&B" reincarnation.

My grateful thanks, then, to Brooklyn-born musician Larry Simon in helping to document and preserve New York's blues history by pursuing his quest to publish his interviews from the 1990s, aided by his faithful photographer Robert Schaffer. Not only that, but Simon gave many of the interviewees vital exposure on the bandstand at home and abroad in their twilight years. He asked me to edit the project, while requesting four interviews from my late 1980s New York trips for *Juke Blues* magazine. In addition, we are honored by the presence of my fellow-English friends: Val Wilmer, acclaimed jazz photographer, author, and women's activist; and *Juke Blues* colleagues Paul Harris, veteran photographer of blues, R&B, rock 'n' roll, and more, along with Richard "Dickie" Tapp. A shout-out, too, for the *Juke Blues* editors, Cilla Huggins and her late husband, Mick, who did much to promote the New York blues scene in that most professional and artistic of blues magazines.

I first came into contact with New York R&B by accident in austerity-laden 1950s England, where American movies and music added much-needed color and glamour to our lives. The initial record that registered with me was "Why Do Fools Fall in Love" by Frankie Lymon and the Teenagers, which blasted from an outside speaker at a Woolworth's in Maidstone, Kent, in 1956—just as it would have done, it transpired, at Bobby Robinson's record store in Harlem. Certainly, I had no idea of the importance of the Teenagers' record as a passport for countless young vocal groups on New York's street corners to exit the ghettoes by way of the recording studio, onto radio, and into the theater spotlight. Nor had I any concept of the international hit's Harlem origins, nor of the delights of US regional music variations. It was just newfangled rock 'n' roll. A more serious introduction came through the venerable Atlantic label by way of its English licensee, London American Records, including "Searchin'"/"Young Blood" by the Coasters, "C. C. Rider" and "Betty and Dupree" by Chuck Willis, "Mr. Lee" by the Bobbettes, and also albums by Ray Charles (*Yes Indeed!*) and Champion Jack Dupree (*Blues from the Gutter*). The big US national hits were automatically released in England and included "Kansas City" by Wilbert Harrison (Top Rank), "The Happy Organ" by Dave "Baby" Cortez (London), and "Fannie Mae" by Buster Brown (Melodisc). Little could I know that over the years I would meet many of the personalities behind these recordings.

It's still hard to believe that the first bluesman I ever saw live was Jack Dupree at a London club in late 1959. Performing in front of an audience that could best be described as trad jazz elitists, he was well received for his original

New Orleans barrelhouse piano work and side-splitting humor, which would be judged politically incorrect these days. His then-twenty-year domicile in New York meant nothing to me at the time nor, I suspect, to others in the club. Into the early 1960s, I remember subscribing to Len Kunstadt's Brooklyn-based *Record Research* magazine and winning 78s in his auctions for a dollar or so a time. By then, fellow young British enthusiasts were absorbing the contents of the first two important blues books: *Blues Fell This Morning* by Paul Oliver and *The Country Blues* by Samuel B. Charters (followed by James Baldwin's *The Fire Next Time*).

I was intrigued by Charters's reference to "Number 9 Train" by Tarheel Slim being in the lower reaches of "a 1959 'hit parade' sheet from a Harlem record shop." When I eventually acquired the record, on Bobby Robinson's Fury label, it met all expectations on what I see now as a quintessential New York blues rocker. As already noted, Slim, who also embraced the country blues, gospel, and vocal group traditions, and Robinson are featured in this book, as is the master session guitarist on the record, Jimmy Spruill. Surely that "Harlem record shop" had to be Robinson's?

By 1963 I was writing for *Blues Unlimited* and being mentored by its visionary editors, Mike Leadbitter and Simon Napier. Then New Orleans and South Louisiana called, resulting in my books *Walking to New Orleans* in 1974 (subsequently titled *Rhythm and Blues in New Orleans*), and *South to Louisiana: The Music of the Cajun Bayous* in 1983, both since updated and revised.

In 1985, with *Blues Unlimited* running out of steam, I cofounded *Juke Blues* with Cilla Huggins and Bez Turner. In seeking fresh material, we homed in on the relatively underresearched New York blues scene. And so, in 1986 and 1989, I made trips with magazine secretary Dickie Tapp and photographer Paul Harris, and also future Wynonie Harris biographer Tony Collins, to conduct cassette-recorded interviews with as many of the original participants as we could find. Already, the blues heyday was a quarter-century in the past, eviscerated by soul music and, yes, the British Invasion, funk, disco, hip hop, and the rest. Among the many people we met who were willing to share their stories were record men Bobby Robinson and Jerry Wexler; artists Billy Bland, Larry Dale, Bob Gaddy, and Rosco Gordon; session musicians Billy Butler and Jimmy Spruill; and songwriters Rose Marie McCoy and Doc Pomus. (Larry Simon's interviews here with Robinson, Dale, Gaddy, Gordon, Spruill, and others were conducted independently later.)

A brand new world was awaiting us as we listened to—and pieced together—stories of New York's blues and R&B golden age. It's indicative of the passage of time that not one of those original interviewees is still alive, which makes the interviews even more precious. It was on the 1989 trip that I first met *Juke Blues* reader Simon, who helped with our accommodation arrangements, took us to

Bobby Robinson interviewed by John Broven, Harlem, May 16, 1986. Photo by Paul Harris.

a Rosco Gordon recording session, and made sure we attended that landmark Washington Square Church blues concert.

Incidentally, in 1987 a *Juke Blues* consortium released a 45-rpm single by Larry Dale, "I Got a Brand New Mojo"/"Penny Pincher." Enthusiasm for a follow-up faltered, with the result that Golden Crest Records, my family label, later acquired the master and publishing of a recording produced by Larry Simon featuring Dale with Bob Gaddy, Jimmy Spruill, and drummer Andrew "A. J." Johnson. It's a terrific performance of a song penned by *Juke Blues* writer and reviewer Dave Williams. The title? "New York City Blues." Some things are meant to be.

To round off my personal time capsule, I was retired from my managerial position with Midland Bank (now HSBC) in England, which enabled me to become immersed in the music business as a consultant with Ace Records from 1991 through 2006. Suddenly I was seeing the business from the inside, and I am indebted to the Ace directors—Roger Armstrong, Ted Carroll, and Trevor Churchill—for the sharp-end education. I helped reissue on CD many New York hits in the bestselling Golden Age of American Rock 'n' Roll series with Churchill and Rob Finnis, and compiled releases from New York–based labels such as Atlantic, Clock, Decca, Old Town, Prestige Bluesville, RCA Victor, and the Time-Shad-Brent group. At the time of writing, Ace is preparing a CD compilation to tie in with this book.

While negotiating an Ace license for "Tall Cool One" by the Wailers on Huntington Station's Golden Crest Records for the Golden Age series, I met and later married Shelley Galehouse, daughter of label founder Clark Galehouse. As a result, I relocated in 1995 to the United States, living on Long Island in Cold Spring Harbor and then East Setauket, both within easy range of New York City. At the time there were still active blues clubs in Manhattan, including Chicago Blues, Dan Lynch, Manny's Car Wash, Terra Blues, and Tramps; today only Terra Blues survives. By virtue of my new residence, the way was paved for my book, *Record Makers and Breakers: Voices of the Independent Rock 'n' Roll Pioneers* (2009), which featured many New York interviewees. In effect, that book represented the summation of my time as a collector, researcher, author, record company consultant, and label manager.

Back in the early 1940s, in a familiar story, three events conspired to give lift-off to the modern record industry along with subsequent trends in New York and elsewhere: the formation of Broadcast Music, Inc. (BMI) in 1940, providing opportunities for everyday American songwriters; the US entry into World War II, leading to severe restrictions on shellac, the material used for manufacturing records at the time; and the musicians union recording ban implemented by American Federation of Musicians (AFM) president James C. Petrillo.

With business brought to a shuddering halt by the recording ban and shellac shortage, a pent-up demand for all types of music ensued. The liberation afforded by settlement of the union strike and the end of the war changed the rules of the game. With major labels Columbia, Decca, and RCA Victor preoccupied with their best-selling pop artists, the door was opened for a new wave of independent record labels to record the music of the people. The racially segmented blues and rhythm & blues sectors were big beneficiaries in this male-dominated world, which seemingly comprised ethical and hustling record men in equal measure.

There were just a few record women active, notably New Yorkers Bess Berman (Apollo), Miriam Abramson (Atlantic), and later Bea Kaslin (Mascot and Hull), Zell Sanders (J&S), and Florence Greenberg (Scepter and Wand), as well as booker Ruth Bowen of the Queen agency. Between them, their accomplishments were extraordinary.

It's a fallacy to say that in the 1940s the major record companies ignored blues, hillbilly, and other roots music. These corporate giants were still recording such acts in their city-based recording studios, but they were no longer making field trips with cumbersome recording equipment to makeshift studios throughout the South and elsewhere. As with the pop singers and bandleaders, there was a tendency to rely on a stable of blues artists who were reliable at the sales counter and on the radio and jukeboxes. In the case of New York–based RCA Victor, for example, there was a steady flow of blues releases from its talented roster, mainly guided by Lester Melrose from Chicago, including Big Maceo, Arthur "Big Boy"

Crudup, Jazz Gillum, Tampa Red, Washboard Sam, and Sonny Boy Williamson no. 1 (John Lee Williamson). For years, these artists have been labeled under the "Bluebird beat" banner, a somewhat derogatory reference to the supposedly mechanical nature of their music recorded for the budget Bluebird label, an RCA subsidiary. Yet this unfair dismissal ignores their massive popular influence on a future generation of blues artists everywhere, including New York, and the defining of a Chicago blues sound, especially through Tampa Red and Sonny Boy Williamson no. 1.

New York, by virtue of its place at the center of the record business, had hosted many blues sessions in the pre–World War II era, dating back to 1920 with "Crazy Blues" by Mamie Smith (OKeh). A quick glance at my well-thumbed copy of *Blues and Gospel Records, 1902–1942* by John Godrich and Robert M. W. Dixon reveals New York sessions, among others, by Leroy Carr and Scrapper Blackwell (Vocalion), "Blind Gary" Davis, later known as the Reverend Gary Davis (ARC), Sleepy John Estes (Decca), Blind Boy Fuller (Vocalion), Huddy Leadbelly, later known as Lead Belly (Victor/Bluebird), Brownie McGhee (OKeh), Charley Patton (Vocalion), Bessie Smith (Columbia), and Peetie Wheatstraw (Decca). In those years, which encompassed the Great Depression, New York was effectively a clearinghouse for the blues, not a permanent domicile, with quick artist trips to and from the city for recording sessions.

And so after World War II, the independent record business took hold in the bigger cities throughout the country. Many indie labels were Jewish owned, working closely with distributors servicing the stores, record promoters, radio stations, and jukebox operators. At this juncture, the jukebox market, with its assured bulk sales, was critical to the small labels. So was their core audience, black people, who saw the gramophone record as a prime home-entertainment medium at a time when many venues—clubs, theaters, movie houses—were not accessible to them.

As the years rolled by, pioneering New York labels, like Bess and Ike Berman's Apollo and Herman Lubinsky's Savoy—from nearby Newark, New Jersey—were unable to step up the pace in the rhythm & blues field, unlike their West Coast contemporaries Aladdin, Imperial, Modern, and Specialty. However, both Apollo and Savoy developed strong gospel catalogs, while Savoy had an enviable jazz catalog. The staying power of these two labels was more durable than that of several New York indies from the 1940s that disappeared from view. Who now remembers Beacon, National, Manor, or Derby?

There was another national recording ban called by omnipotent AFM president Petrillo throughout most of 1948 that did the record business everywhere no favors. The irritation was such that Arthur Hays Sulzberger, publisher of the hallowed *New York Times*, felt compelled to pen a private ode—a favorite pastime—on February 27, 1948:

On the branch of a willow sat little tomtit,
Singing "Willow, Titwillow, Titwillow,"
And next to him, silent, another bird sat,
By order of James C. Petrillo.

Atlantic Records, launched just as the ban started in January 1948 by Herb Abramson and Ahmet Ertegun, would stand imperiously above all other independent record companies and still survives to this day, albeit as a corporate entity. The label was sent on its way with a *Billboard* no. 2 blues chart hit in 1949 with "Drinkin' Wine Spo-Dee-O-Dee" by Stick McGee, Brownie's brother. Even so, the Atlantic owners, with their exemplary musical tastes that spilled over into jazz, were forced to look beyond the narrow blues market of the time "because there were no blues players in New York," Ertegun told me in 2006. Before long, Atlantic was hitting big with the rhythm & blues of Ruth Brown, then of the Clovers, to be followed by Big Joe Turner along with Clyde McPhatter and the Drifters.

That New York's approach to black music was more sophisticated at this time is illustrated by an examination of the *Cash Box* "Hot in Harlem" chart toppers for the first part of 1950. The no. 1 records included "For You My Love" by Larry Darnell (Regal), "Forgive and Forget" by the Orioles (Jubilee), "Rag Mop" by Lionel Hampton (Decca), "I Almost Lost My Mind" by Ivory Joe Hunter (MGM), "Easter Parade" by Freddie Mitchell (Derby), "It Isn't Fair" by Dinah Washington (Mercury), and "My Foolish Heart" by Billy Eckstine (MGM). Only Johnny Otis's two hits "Double Crossing Blues" and "Mistrustin' Blues" (Savoy), and Jimmy Witherspoon's "No Rollin' Blues" (Modern), could be said to have a raunchy bluesy edge. In 1951, it took Jackie Brenston's influential blues romper "Rocket '88'" with Ike Turner (Chess) three long months to reach the *Cash Box* "Hot in Harlem" chart after it first broke through in the South and spread to the rest of the country.

Regardless of Atlantic's presence, New York did not have a specialty blues record imprint to match Chess in Chicago or Sun in Memphis. Instead, there were the brave Bobby Robinson labels, first Red Robin in 1951, then Whirlin Disc, Fury, Fire, and Enjoy. Record-store owner Robinson had his ears perpetually to the ground, for which he was sought out by other record label owners, and captured the full range of the sounds of Harlem right through to the advent of hip hop in the 1970s. At this point, local disc jockeys inspired new dance moves by playing an assortment of repeated "break beats" sampled from records, especially those of James Brown. It was a young-generation street phenomenon.

Rightfully, Robinson is a continued presence in this book. Yet his storefront labels were always run on an undercapitalized shoestring, even with a no. 1 million-selling pop hit in 1959 to his credit with "Kansas City" by Wilbert Harrison, which almost overwhelmed him in business terms. This meant that Robinson had to enlist a succession of partners, including his brother Danny from Red Robin to Enjoy, label owner-distributor Jerry Blaine, the mysterious restaurateur Clarence "Fats" Lewis, promo man Marshall Sehorn, and fearsome Morris Levy of Roulette Records. Some partners were more suitable than others, as Robinson's labels came and went into the hip hop era.

Broadly viewed, the New York record industry in the 1940s and 1950s was dominated by the major label giants, with their grand recording studios, seemingly unlimited budgets, and a national/international perspective. As blues matured into rhythm & blues, the majors served this relatively minor market (to them) primarily through their subsidiary labels: Groove and Vik (RCA Victor), Coral (Decca), and OKeh (Columbia). Yet the nimbler independents Atlantic, Apollo, and Savoy, and later Jubilee and Josie, Sittin' In With, Jax, and Harlem; Herald and Ember, Old Town, Gee and Rama, Baton, End and Gone, and Fire and Fury among many others, were able to tap into the local, often untried well of talent. Large or small, the indie labels all had access to the best studios and best session players in town. From an artist's perspective, records served as professional promotional tools to secure live bookings, with the prospect of a big bonus if a hit resulted. For the major labels, records also helped to sell their gramophone players.

Along with the major record companies, the old-guard Tin Pan Alley music publishers were finding it difficult to come to grips with R&B and rock 'n' roll. Accordingly, the indie record labels set up their own firms to publish new songs and provide a vital second source of income. There were also shrewd independent publishers like Hill & Range, owned by the Aberbach brothers, Julian and Jean; and Regent Music, operated by Benny Goodman's brothers, Gene and Harry (who partnered with the thrusting Chess brothers, Leonard and Phil, of Chicago in Arc Music).

Radio, driven by disc jockey Alan Freed of WINS New York, was a crucial promotional adjunct to the record industry, followed by television led by Dick Clark's *American Bandstand*. Technological revolution had arrived in the 1940s with the invention of recording tape, the long-playing album by Columbia, and the 45-rpm single by RCA Victor, which confined the clumsy 78-rpm disc to history. Then came the stereo experience, initially for hi-fi buffs, with brilliant Atlantic Records engineer Tom Dowd at the forefront. The growing influence of teenagers propelled the climate of change.

From the 1940s onward, the New York jazzmen, cool and hip, such as Charlie Parker, Dizzy Gillespie, Coleman Hawkins, Lester Young, and Miles Davis reigned supreme, as did jazz labels Blue Note and Prestige. A strong folk music scene was led by Pete Seeger and Woody Guthrie, also embracing Josh White and Lead Belly, and it continued by way of the Greenwich Village clubs of the

Bob Dylan era. In the early 1960s, folk music crossed over into blues territory in a big way, having already ensnared Brownie McGhee and Sonny Terry. This style manifested itself in a series of "unplugged" acoustic recordings, known as folk blues, by Muddy Waters, Lightnin' Hopkins, John Lee Hooker, and others.

Here was the musical style that initially appealed to a young John Hammond Jr., as told to Larry Simon: "When I was seven years old my dad brought me to hear Big Bill Broonzy, who played a show at Judson [Memorial] Church in Washington Square in the Village. . . . And I just gravitated toward blues ever since then. I became a fan of Sonny Terry and Brownie McGhee, who had played often in the Village." As we've already seen, Terry and McGhee had recorded many strong blues recordings before taking the folk route with Moe Asch's Folkways label in 1955. McGhee even had a no. 2 hit in 1948 with "My Fault" (Savoy) on the *Billboard* "race" charts.

There was also a 1960s country blues revival period highlighted by the rediscovery of pre–World War II artists like Son House, Fred McDowell, and Bukka White, and also the gospel guitarist, the Reverend Gary Davis.

The no-holds-barred electric blues had reasserted itself by the mid-1960s, sparked by European interest through groups like the Rolling Stones, who were enamored with the heavy Chicago blues sound of Chess Records. Bobby Robinson showed how it should be done with his down-home recordings of Elmore James and Lightnin' Hopkins with New York session men.

By then, soul music was taking hold and having a massive local impact by way of artists such as Wilson Pickett, Don Covay, Solomon Burke, and J. D. Bryant. New session men came on the scene, notably guitarists Eric Gale and Cornell Dupree, as well as drummer Bernard Purdie. As Red Kelly told me, "Carolinians like guitarists James Hines (with Roy C), and Sammy Gordon (with his brother Benny), created a style all their own in the mid- to late sixties, I think born out of that same blues tradition." Kelly, known as the Soul Detective, added that Sammy Gordon's funk record "Upstairs on Boston Road" (For The Archives label, 1972) "references a Bronx club, the Boston Road Ballroom, where he had a regular gig, as the New York style evolved into the funk and hip hop that Bobby Robinson also plugged into." There were still plenty of other musical trends in New York, from folk rock to new wave and disco.

The city was privileged to have the premier black music venue in the country, the Apollo Theatre on 125th Street in the heart of Harlem. It formed part of a theater circuit, which also included the Howard in Washington, DC, the Royal in Baltimore, the Earle in Philadelphia, and the Regal in Chicago. While the Apollo attracted national stars, there were opportunities for local hit acts and band musicians to perform, along with budding artists on the weekly amateur night talent shows. Incidentally, for historical reasons, the original anglicized spelling has been used throughout this book to describe the Apollo Theatre, as the spelling "Theater" didn't come into prominence until 1991, when the Apollo Theater Foundation was established.

Another European researcher, Swede Jonas Bernholm—then in his early twenties and later to found Route 66 Records—gave rare firsthand accounts in his online book *Soul Music Odyssey 1968* (2nd ed.) of his June 1968 visits to the Apollo to see the weekly show and amateur night. It was soon after Dr. Martin Luther King Jr. and Robert F. Kennedy had been assassinated. Seated in the cheapest seats in "the gods," Bernholm was enthralled by Jerry Butler's performance, and also by the Jive Five and Jean Wells but not so much by the Delfonics or the Spinners. The keen young Swede enjoyed the knockabout theatrical reaction to the parade of amateurs, none of whom stood out. More seriously, he was not thrilled to find himself alone in Harlem in the late evening after one show when king heroin and the Black Panthers were becoming dominant. (For more on Harlem's cultural, social, and musical upheaval, see Stuart Cosgrove's essential book *Harlem 69: The Future of Soul*.)

Further down the line, there were the smaller clubs in Manhattan and surrounding areas. "Well, there wasn't such a thing called blues clubs," former Muddy Waters harmonica player Paul Oscher told Simon. "There was just black clubs and bars. Chicago maybe was more all blues, you know what I mean? Like some of the places there, you got Pepper's Lounge and Theresa's and some places on the West Side where like Elmore James played and that was just total blues. But in New York or any other city in the United States there were black clubs and the music was some jazz, soul music, some blues. Later on they got the hip hop thing." From the 1940s into the 1960s, many of these clubs were sophisticated venues patronized by blacks, all smartly dressed, looking for "showtime" at weekends before church on Sundays. There were also the working-class juke joints.

This is the world that the interviewees in this book inhabited and influenced. So what glimpses do we glean here of a long-gone New York blues scene that doesn't deserve to be forgotten? We are told of Bobby Robinson's rural beginnings in the Carolinas; Billy Butler playing at the famed Apollo Theatre including amateur night; Billy Bland singing with Buddy Johnson's Orchestra at the Savoy Ballroom; recollections of the swinging Fifty-Second Street jazz clubs by Al "Dr. Horse" Pittman and Doc Pomus; and shows at the Baby Grand club in Harlem with revered comedian Nipsey Russell as emcee.

We learn about the many opportunities given by record men Robinson and Hy Weiss to local bluesmen and vocal groups; the stories behind huge hit records including Billy Butler's timeless guitar solos on Bill Doggett's New York–recorded "Honky Tonk" (King, 1956); and Jimmy Spruill's idiosyncratic guitar work on two national no. 1 records, "The Happy Organ" by Dave "Baby" Cortez (Clock) and "Kansas City" by Wilbert Harrison (Fury), covering three successive weeks in May 1959—a monumental feat. Spruill also soloed on saxophonist Noble "Thin Man" Watts's 1958 Top 50 instrumental hit, "Hard Times" (Baton).

Then there was black radio and its influential deejays such as Dr. Jive (Tommy Smalls), George Hudson, Ramon Bruce, and Jocko Henderson; the unfair 1959 payola pillorying of Alan Freed; memories of recording for those genius producers Jerry Leiber and Mike Stoller, and also for neglected Spivey Records and Prestige; and single-minded young white bluesmen John Hammond Jr., Bob Malenky, and Paul Oscher between them playing with legends such as Muddy Waters, Lightnin' Hopkins, and Sonny Terry, and performing at the lamentably undocumented small clubs of the Bronx, Harlem, Brooklyn, Long Island, and New Jersey. Malenky remembered being told that "blues was really a going thing in the black community" in the 1950s. At the other extreme, there were Pomus and Rose Marie McCoy writing songs at the Brill Building, a glorified song factory, with the prospect of their creative work being taken up by Elvis Presley, the ultimate prize. Up in Harlem, there was the astonishing influence of the Reverend Gary Davis on young guitar practitioners, including 1960s country-blues hope Larry Johnson; the explosive soul era with admired exponents such as James Brown and Joe Tex; and the early rumblings of rap and hip hop. There are even recollections of playing on Broadway. Only in New York.

At the very last minute, we were able to include Val Wilmer's feature on classic woman blues singer Victoria Spivey, who was active with her Spivey label in Brooklyn through the 1960s and into the 1970s. With songwriter McCoy, there are further profiles on feminist champion Rosetta Reitz, and also June Bateman with Noble Watts and Little Ann with Tarheel Slim.

A word about the interviews: It's never easy for an interviewee when you're discussing events that occurred decades ago—especially, I find, with dates and personnel on record sessions. In the heat of the moment, a fact or name can easily be blurred. That's why the interviews here have been modestly edited, and ample explanatory footnotes have been added. As for the interviewer, there are always the questions you wish you had asked. For example, if only I'd quizzed songwriter Doc Pomus, once an unlikely but dedicated young New York blues shouter, on the backstory of his early Chess 78-rpm single, in 1950—the next release to his "Send for the Doctor" (1440) was Muddy Waters's classic "Louisiana Blues." With Billy Bland, while discussing Chuck Berry's "My Ding-a-Ling," I forgot to ask about the personnel of his vocal group, the Bees, who had recorded a 1954 version of Berry's 1972 no. 1 song as "Toy Bell" (Imperial). The full names are still not known.

On the other hand, there were the unexpected surprises, such as when Pomus told me that he played club dates in the mid-1950s with his band featuring King Curtis and Mickey Baker, both of whom were destined to become top session men. Who knew? Or, when Billy Butler said that he once stood in for the popular Ravens vocal group *singing* bass, and also played the dreamy guitar on the Flamingos' all-time classic, "I Only Have Eyes for You" (End, 1960). Just as the manuscript was being delivered, I received confirmation that Calvin Newborn played guitar on Bobby Lewis's 1961 no. 1 hit, "Tossin' and Turnin'," and not Jimmy Spruill as I had believed.

For all the interviews accomplished, there are always the interviewees who escaped. Among those elusive artists, with much regret on *two* occasions, was the fascinating but underappreciated Dave "Baby" Cortez. Henry Glover, such an inspiring producer for King, Glover, and Roulette, could not be torn away from the racetrack, while Decca A&R man Milt Gabler slipped the grasp of the *Juke Blues* team.

Record man Paul Winley would never consent to a taped interview, which was his right, but he was more than happy to discuss parts of his story over entertaining lunches at Sylvia's Restaurant in Harlem. Winley was a longtime 125th Street record man and songwriter who has been rather eclipsed by Bobby Robinson. The brother of Harold Winley of the Clovers, Paul had regional success in the late 1950s with the doo-wop of the Jesters and Paragons on his Winley label and worked closely with Cortez. Later, the wily record man did well in the nascent hip hop arena with Afrika Bambaataa and Tanya Winley, his daughter.

I should point out that the interviewees in this book are but the proverbial tip of the iceberg. There are many more participants who deserve to be featured, the majority sadly never formally interviewed. I'll mention blues artists Clarence Ashe, Cousin Leroy, Leroy Dallas, Lee Roy Little, Long Island's Little Buster and Sam Taylor, Little Red Walter (Rhodes), Alonzo Scales, Square Walton, and Ralph Willis; versatile producers Leroy Kirkland, Clyde Otis, and Sammy Lowe; and writers Otis Blackwell and Rudy Toombs. Then there are other record men and women, disc jockeys, distributors, jukebox operators, promoters, record retailers, club owners, and artist agency owners, who all made up the fabric of the vibrant old-time New York record business.

More than a half century has passed, but the recorded work of the New York blues community, natives or transplants, is still an inspiration. Thanks to the internet medium, the vast majority of recordings discussed in this book are easily heard on YouTube, Apple, Spotify, Pandora, and Amazon. Happily, the Schomburg Center for Research in Black Culture in Harlem is available for further investigation, as is the Performing Arts Division of the New York Public Library.

I make no apologies for readily quoting in the footnotes chart records from *Billboard* and *Cash Box*, important trade magazines whose writers and reviewers were publishing, in effect, the first draft of history. For all the data-collection imperfections, the trades' charts do give an indication of which records were popular at the time, what sold—and what was of influence. There are chart summaries in the appendix (along with lists of recommended records and detailed biographical data). Take a look to see what riches came out of New York's indie recording studios such as Atlantic, Bell Sound, and Beltone, many of them produced by the label owners themselves. The majors' Columbia, Decca, and RCA Victor facilities, with their staff producers, should not be overlooked, either.

Why listen to recordings made all those years ago? History apart, they often sound as good if not better today. That to me is a definition of classical music. I've always said that if any young drummer wants to learn the art, then listen to New Orleanian Earl Palmer's recordings from the 1950s and 1960s. Or, thinking of New York, study Panama Francis's stick work. For blues guitar, look no further than Billy Butler with his all-time classic fretwork on "Honky Tonk" and more, or Jimmy Spruill's accompaniments, or Larry Dale's outstanding licks on Champion Jack Dupree's *Blues from the Gutter* (again), or Tarheel Slim on "Number 9 Train" (again). Then there is the majestic work of Mickey "Guitar" Baker, who, like Butler and Spruill, had a readily identifiable style. Saxophone? The first-call players included King Curtis, Sam "The Man" Taylor, "Big" Al Sears, and Noble Watts. Blues piano? New York had those tasteful exponents Van Walls, Dave "Baby" Cortez, and Bob Gaddy, as well as Dupree.

All these artists and session men contributed to a studio sound that was New York's. If any one person stands out with a predominantly bluesy edge, it is guitarist Jimmy Spruill, from North Carolina, for his driving rhythm work as much as for his solos. The perfect example is Wilbert Harrison's "Kansas City" (Fury). As New Yorker Mike Gilroy told me, "I think in a larger sense that this is a New York sound." There you are, it's that Carolina link again.

The Harrison sequel, "Goodbye Kansas City," with Spruill—and the same rhythms—heavily featured again, was a paean to Harlem, with the singer leaving KC for NYC with his "crazy little baby, and boy she is a pretty one," heading for "the Apollo and we'll dig the crazy show," then "we'll stop in the Baby Grand, dig those cats on the bandstand." Sadly, the song failed miserably in the marketplace.

How to put Spruill's guitar style into words? As it happened, he described it to me during the 1986 research trip, published in *Juke Blues*, no. 6: "My 'scratchin'' style came about because I sat down one day, I didn't know what to play. It really came from 'Kansas City,' that *chicka-chick-chick*. The guy who recorded me [Bobby Robinson] said, 'I don't want that!' I said, 'I'm gonna play what I want to play. If you don't like it, forget about it! I got a name for it: scratchin.'"

Spruill expanded on his rhythmic stamp as "up and down strokes, but I knew how to choke the strings—you had to choke all the way down the neck to get that scratchin' sound. Then I bent the notes, eight notes above from where I started from . . . you know, *eeeow* back down. It's hard if you don't know how to do it [*sighs*], but to me it come natural. It was my own sound." Why isn't Spruill better known, except among the cognoscenti? Possibly because, as I wrote in

Juke Blues, "[d]espite his great potential as a guitar hero, he was a New York session guitarist at a time when studio musicians went uncredited."

Not surprisingly, much of the underlying support elements of the old-time
music scene have been and gone: the variety theaters, music publishing houses,
independent record companies, distributors (mostly on Tenth Avenue), record
stores, recording studios, pressing plants, clubs from Harlem to Greenwich Village and beyond—as well as artists with a genuine reason to have the blues.

For all the changes through the years, it is still possible to admire many of the
venerable musical landmarks in New York City. I'm talking about the still-func-
tioning Apollo Theatre on 125th Street and the Brill Building at 1619 Broadway;
and such sites as the old Atlantic Records offices at 234 West Fifty-Sixth Street,
Decca's studios in the Pythian Temple at 135 West Seventieth Street, Tin Pan
Alley on West Twenty-Eighth Street, Columbia Thirtieth Street Studio (known
as The Church), and RCA Victor's A and B studios at 155 East Twenty-Fourth
Street. Other locations have been eviscerated by time, notably Harlem hotspots
the Savoy Ballroom, Rockland Palace, Smalls Paradise, and the Baby Grand club
(the last two venues are featured, with the Apollo Theatre, in chapter 19: "Legends of New York City"). Let's not forget Bobby Robinson's record shop, also in
Harlem, a victim of gentrification, or Colony Records on Broadway, a victim
of changing retail trends. Collectively, these venues hold colorful histories that
deserve to be remembered.

For its part, Harlem was infested by crime rackets, gangs, pimps, and drugs
for many years. Just take a look at a ten-minute documentary film, *Blind Gary
Davis*, shot in the Harlem of 1963 to see what a different, unglamorous age it
was. The abject social conditions, marked by urban decay, poverty, and little
hope for the future, would spawn the civil rights and Black Power movements.

It was a far cry from the optimism of the 1920s Harlem Renaissance, a time
of artistic, intellectual, literary, and political creativity, when the joint was literally jumping. Or the minirenaissance of the 1950s rhythm & blues era centered
around the Apollo Theatre. Throughout it all, religious institutions retained a
stronghold on Harlem. There was a world apart from a Saturday night show at
the Apollo and Sunday services at the influential Abyssinian Baptist Church on
nearby 138th Street.

Yet through good times and bad, an important blues scene did arise, with
the interviewees here representing an astonishing cross section of personalities
who helped create a niche regional tradition. This book confirms that the New
York City blues people—black and white, male and female—do matter.

LARRY SIMON INTERVIEWS

1

BOB GADDY

Interviewed in Braunau, Austria (with Larry Dale present),
November 17, 1993

Bob Gaddy, a central figure in the New York City blues scene, was born in Vivian, McDowell County, West Virginia, and relocated to Harlem after World War II. Gaddy was a top blues pianist, singer, and songwriter. Aside from recordings under his own name for labels such as Randy Wood's Dot, Bob and Morty Shad's Jax and Harlem imprints, and Hy Weiss's Old Town, he worked with Sonny Terry, Brownie McGhee, Champion Jack Dupree, Larry Dale, Jimmy Spruill, and others.

In the years I spent playing with Bob Gaddy, I found him to be a great bandleader, always kind and respectful, but assertive. Respectful of his audience, too, at all times and all places. It was important to Bob that we look good, with a coat and tie, a suit, something nice, even if we were playing a local dive on an off night. I actually lost out on a few gigs until I upgraded my wardrobe a bit. He had an old-school charm and temperament that won over his audiences as well as his bandmates.

Larry Simon: How did you start playing?

Bob Gaddy: Well, I think it was back in 1939, 1940, I started out playing a lot of gospel, church music. I had no interest in the blues or whatnot. I came from a very religious background. I was raised up in church. I started playing piano when I was fourteen or fifteen years old. I used to go to church, holy sanctified church. They had a piano player that played with the singing. I didn't know nothing about no piano playing, but I liked it and I used to watch him all the time. Sometime during the week I go down to the church and fool around on the piano and play some of the stuff that I saw him do. So one day he came in and found me, he says, "Oh, so you're trying to learn how to play the piano?" I said, "Yes, I'd like to." So he showed me the basic key, the key of C. He showed me the basic changes C–F–C–G. I practiced that for a long time. Finally after five

Bob Gaddy (1924–1997), at the Blue Frog, 3340 Jerome Avenue, the Bronx, 1993.

or six months later he taught me another key. I would go down there every day after that and crawl through the window. Practice until everything was beginning to fall in place. But I was playing only gospel music.

Simon: He didn't show you any blues?

Gaddy: I didn't know nothing about no blues. And then after the war [World War II] broke out I went into the service, the navy, I begin to meet a lot of boys from all over the country that played. They were playing this boogie-woogie. I began to take a notice of the blues and all that type stuff. I began to learn it by watching other people, then I practiced it when I was by myself. So in other words, I'm more or less a self-taught player. And so after I went into the service and went overseas I met all sorts of players, jazz players and blues singers. I could always sing, I sang in church. Every Wednesday night they used to have these talent contests. I won a couple of them by doing some boogie-woogie tunes. Practically every week I would win but I didn't start playing professionally till I came out of the service. The first nightclub I ever played in was in San Francisco before I went overseas. A couple of the boys in my outfit, they knew I could bang on the piano a little bit so we went around to a couple a' nightclubs in Frisco and Oakland, California, and we get to drinkin' and they say, "Hey, Bob, can I ask you to come on over and play a number?" And I was ashamed, you know, I had what you call stage fright. And we get to drinking and I got pretty high. We were in this section of Frisco with a lot of nightclubs, I can't remember what it's called, and we were in this nightclub and I'm dancing with this chick having a party. My friend says, "Hey Bob, why don't you go up there and play a number for us?" They had jazz in the club, they wasn't playing nothing like blues in the club at that time. So I went up and did a boogie-woogie tune and that upset the band because they weren't playing that kind of stuff. And everyone went crazy because I played that "Pinetop's Boogie Woogie" thing[1] and I had just enough drinks in me that I didn't have no stage fright in me then and they liked it so well they asked for another one. From then on I'd go in there every time I was on leave and them guys would get me up there to bang away on the piano. And I went overseas and come back but I hadn't thought nothing about doing it professionally, it was just a hobby. And after two years in the South Pacific I had learned more because a whole lot of guys in our outfit played piano and guitar and I began to get more interested in the professional part of it.

I came back, came out of the service, went home, stayed three or four months in North Carolina. I thought of going to California but got to New York here. I ended up going to Washington, DC, but I only stayed three or four weeks, I didn't like it so I went on to New York. I was going back to California, I just went to New York to visit my uncle. And I got here and got to partying and spending my money. I had to get a job so I had to get my old man to send me some money because mine ran out. I had sent him some money from overseas, and he said this is the last time because you run through all of your money. So I got here and I got stuck in New York. So I went out and got a job and I've been here ever since. That was the spring of 1946 when I first came to New York City. So I started going around to different nightclubs. I didn't meet Brownie McGhee until around 1949 or '50. I was going around to all these clubs but I still wasn't thinking about anything too professional. And then I got my first night club gig. There used to be a bar on 125th Street right next door where Bobby Robinson's record shop used to be, not where it is now [closed in 2008], there used to be a big club they called the Apollo Bar [located upstairs within the Apollo Theatre]. There was a big long bar where you go in. There was nothing but faggots hangin' out in the front. In the back there was a room called the Tiger Room. That's where they had the entertainment. But when you walk in the bar, nothing . . . nothing did bother me. So me and a guy name Ray I had met at the Savoy Ballroom, I used to go dancing a lot at the Savoy Ballroom, took me to the club, me and him and a couple of girls, to see Al King. They had a lot of jazz. At intermission there was a guitar player, Johnny Saunders, playing by himself. Al would have a four-piece band, and during intermission Johnny would entertain, just him singing, just him and the guitar. So we were just sitting there and Ray said "Bob why don't you go out there and play a song?" And I said "No man," and this chick I was with said "you play?" And I said "Oh I fool round a little bit," like that, and they said "Oh, come on," and they called the waiter to ask the bandleader if I could play. At that time all I had were a few boogie-woogie tunes and blues songs I could sing. So the

Bob Gaddy and "Wild" Jimmy Spruill at the Blue Frog, the Bronx, 1993.

waiter went over and asked Johnny Saunders, and he said "Yeah, have him come up and play with me." So I got on the piano behind him, just him and I. We did a boogie-woogie tune, then I sang one or two after that. And the manager he asked where I'm working at, I said downtown. I didn't know what he was talking about. I thought he meant a regular job. He thought maybe I was working in some club. I wasn't working in no club nowhere. I said I'm not working in a nightclub, and he said, "Listen, how would you like to work here Friday and Saturday night?" That was the first job offer I ever had, he said he'd like me to work the intermission with the guitar player. I worked there for about two months. Then there was a place across the street they used to call the Mayfair, right opposite from where the Baby Grand used to be. They changed it to the Top Club, 125th Street and Saint Nicholas Avenue. So I happened to walk in there one night. I think it happened to be the first time I went in there. In the back they had a curtain and I heard a guy back there playing piano and talking and singing and playing the blues, and I said "Man that guy sounds good." And I've never heard of or never seen Jack Dupree before. So I went back there by myself and said I want to see this guy. So I sat down and there was this little short black guy going to town with them blues. I kept going back, but I didn't say anything to him that night. I didn't meet him. So I begin going in there when I would take an intermission with Johnny Saunders over at the Apollo Bar. I'd walk over there and listen for a while. So finally one night after going over there three or four times, I got to meet him. I said "I like the way you're kicking that piano," and I said to myself one of these nights I'm going to go ask him if I could go up there and play. The next time I went by there I spoke to him, I said "My name is Bob Gaddy, I play a little piano." I'd been drinking a little bit, and I guess I had nerve enough to ask him if I can come up and play. He said "Yeah man, what kind of music do you play?" I said "a little boogie-woogie" and he said "Do you sing?" And I said "Yeah, I always could." So I got up there and sang a few tunes, and that's when I first met Jack Dupree. And him and I got to be good friends after that. And I learned a lot from him, a lot of slow blues. Most of the blues I ever did was fast. Very seldom did I ever bother with the slow stuff. This was along about 1949, and I really started getting into this thing. And he introduced me to Brownie McGhee. He was working around at Felton's Lounge [on Lenox Avenue]. It was him and a piano and a guy with a [wash]tub, his name was Bob Harris. One night I met him, and he had a big girl named Tiny who was playing piano. I got up and played with him, and he hired me that night to play with him at Felton's, Thursday, Friday, and Saturday night. And I stayed there with Brownie McGhee for about four or five months. Then some guys from Jersey came in and they liked us, they liked the band. Brownie fired his other piano player, Tiny, that first night when I came on the scene. Brownie and I stayed together until he went on to a Broadway show with Sonny Terry, *Cat on a Hot Tin Roof* [1955]. And these guys come in from Jersey, they had a motorcycle club. They heard the band and hired us to play a gig in Rahway, New Jersey. We went out there and played a dance for them, and I don't know how we got to this place out there called Billy's Tavern, but we left Felton's. After we played that dance, everybody out there in Jersey wanted us. We wound up in Billy's Tavern and stayed there for about two years.

Simon: Was Brownie McGhee playing electric guitar at that time?

Gaddy: Yeah. So they were flocking into Billy's Tavern, and the place wasn't big enough to hold us. So they laid us off for about a year and rebuilt the place to be bigger, Larry [Dale] used to take us out there every night. We didn't have a

Bob Gaddy at the piano,
A. J. Johnson in the
background at the Blue
Frog, the Bronx, 1993.

car. Larry would take us out there every night when he was learning to play guitar. So they reopened it bigger, and we came back and stayed there for about four
years. That was with Brownie. Bob Harris, he got rid of the washtub for a big ol'
upright bass. He never could learn how to play it. Then we added saxophone.
The radio guy, Clint Miller, used to broadcast radio shows over the air, and he
came in and started booking big acts. Me and Brownie was the house band. B. B.
King used to come in there, and Chuck Willis, and all those big artists.

   Simon: Who was playing saxophone in the band?

   Gaddy: We had some alto player, I don't remember his name. He traveled a
lot with the big bands. Then we got a guy named Skinny Brown. We stayed there
until Brownie got hooked up with Sonny Terry and they did *Cat on a Hot Tin
Roof*. Then he left me, and Larry and I got together after that. The first time I
met Larry he came into Felton's Lounge. Brownie came to me and said there's a

fellow here that wants to sit in and play and sing a couple of numbers. That was all right with me. I said "Yeah, OK, good." I say "Does he have a piano player with him?" and he said "No." First night he came in there he got on the guitar. I'm waiting and said "What are you gonna sing, man?" In those days he wasn't doing nothing, but anything B. B. King would do he was trying to do it. And he was doing pretty good at singing, and I was thinking what the heck kind of guitar is this man playing! It was kind of hard for me to figure out what sort of changes he was making, but I didn't say nothing to him. I looked at him. But you'd be surprised. It seems like just a couple of months after that him and I landed a job together. Back in 1954 I started working with him. Larry and I been working together off and on ever since then, except when he left to go with Cootie Williams and I had to get another guitar player.

Simon: How did you start recording?

Gaddy: Brownie McGhee. Me and Brownie McGhee was working at Felton's Lounge, and after three or four months Brownie said, "Would you like to make a record, play on a recording session?" Well I never did this before. He said, "I got a recording date." At that time he recorded for Morty Shad. So I played on the session with them, and they asked me if I wanted to record. They knew I sang,

Neon sign above the Blue Frog, the Bronx, 1993.

but I didn't have no material, and they didn't want to record something somebody else already recorded, so Brownie wrote a couple of tunes for me. That was
the first record I made [in 1952]. I did one instrumental called "Bicycle Boogie," a slow blues, and a few others. I never got any money from those recordings. I never knew what happened to it. But later on Brownie came up with
another recording for Old Town Records for Hy Weiss, that's released on Ace
Records [of London] now. I recorded [twenty-one] numbers for Hy Weiss. He
released "Operator" and "Woe Woe Is Me" [and six other singles]. All that stuff
he [licensed] to Ace Records, and they got it out now on LP and CD.[2] I recorded
for Old Town back in 1956–60.

Simon: Did you write any of those?

Gaddy: I wrote a couple of them, and Jack Dupree wrote some and Brownie
wrote some.

Simon: How did you meet Jimmy Spruill?

Gaddy: Bobby Robinson was having a recording downtown. I don't know
what took me down to that recording session, because I wasn't recording, but I
happened to be there and I was listening to him record. I like the way the guitar
was sounding. Larry [Dale] had gone with Cootie Williams. And I had Joe Ruffin, a guitar player was playing with me at the Sportsman's Lounge in Yonkers.
Larry and I had been playing there for about twenty-four months. That night
when I went down to the studio this guy was playing for Bobby Robinson. I saw
this guy, he look like he just came out of the country somewhere. And it was
Jimmy Spruill. I didn't know him at the time. But I liked the way his guitar was
sounding. It was the middle of the week, Tuesday or Wednesday, or something,
and I was working the Sportsman's Lounge Friday, Saturday, and Sundays. So
after I got to talk, I said "Hey man, I like the way you play that guitar. Where you
working at?" He said "I'm not working anyplace." I said "What are you doing
this weekend?" I said "I'll get rid of Joe Ruffin." He's all right, but I like this guy
better, you know?

At the time I had a white guy playing with me, a white guitar player, saxophone, and drummer. Anyway something happened to those guys, and I got
Emmett Bly on tenor sax and I hired Jimmy Spruill to work with me that night.
I don't remember who we had on drums. We didn't have no bass player, didn't
use one back then. Jimmy was a different guy then than he is now, didn't act so
crazy. He was quiet, dead quiet. Played his ass off. Didn't talk all that crazy stuff.
Anyway the place went crazy over him, he played such a beautiful guitar. Jimmy
stayed on with me for about four or five months until they closed the place
because it was wintertime and they didn't have no heat. Leonard Moreland, he
was the owner, didn't have no heat in there. Sometimes he didn't pay us. Jimmy
Spruill got his own group after that. That was around 1958.

Bob Gaddy with Arno Rocha, owner of the Blue Frog, the Bronx, 1993.

Bob Gaddy with Killing Floor NYC (l. to r., Larry Simon, Bob Gaddy, A. J. Johnson, and Brian Jost), video shoot, midtown Manhattan, 1993.

Simon: Wasn't there another sax player, a guy named Jimmy Wright?

Gaddy: Yeah, Jimmy Wright was with me when Larry left. I was doing a little gig in Peekskill every Wednesday night. Larry was supposed to be coming back after two weeks with Cootie. So I took a guitar player up there in his place, and Jimmy Wright was still with me. Jimmy Wright undermined me for that job. He talked to the boss's wife, wanted to bring his group in there because he wanted to play jazz. He wanted to get away from blues. He had been with me and Larry for a long time then right after Larry left he talked her into hiring his band. So she told me one night, "I thought Larry was coming back." It was Larry's gig. He had gotten the gig, I was just taking over until he came back, but Larry ended up staying with Cootie for damn near two years [1957–1959]. But after two or three weeks Jimmy had gotten behind my back. I had gotten Jimmy Wright into recording sessions with the Cleftones. Me and Larry was on recording sessions with the Cleftones. I got all them recording dates. I took the whole band. I come to find out when the record came out Jimmy had complained the changes weren't right so you couldn't even hear me, they mixed it out, Jimmy Wright did all that. So the boss's wife told me that night Larry isn't coming back. She didn't tell me nothing about Jimmy Wright is going to take over the gig. So I come to find out working there on Wednesday night. Meanwhile, I went down to Tarrytown and found work in another club. Jimmy Wright stayed there for about two

Video shoot, midtown Manhattan, 1993.

A. J. Johnson and Bob Gaddy at the Blue Frog, the Bronx, 1993.

Bob Gaddy at home, Harlem, 1986. Photo
by Paul Harris.

weeks, and she kicked him out. And they closed the place after that, and Jimmy
Wright came to Tarrytown and try to get that gig from me.

Simon: Sounds nasty.

Gaddy: Well he was a nice guy, but he wasn't really a bluesman. He did swing,
jazz type of music.[3] I met him through Brownie McGhee. We was playing out
in Jersey.

Simon: So what was happening for you in the 1960s?

Gaddy: Larry came back from working with Cootie Williams [in 1959], and
him and I got back together. We started working all out through Brooklyn, the
Arlington Inn and the Downbeat Club [with the House Rockers]. I sort of got
out of the business after awhile but Larry he kept the band together and got
away from the nightclub dates, kept doing big dances.

Larry Dale [to Larry Simon]: When you come around to where Bob was
working you got him playing again. You put *him* back in the business.

Gaddy: That brings us to 1987. You [Larry Simon] came by to where I was
working, just as I was leaving. I'd been working there for about fourteen years
[as an all-night cook in an Irish bar].

Simon: Fourteen years! When I asked the guy up front at the bar if you were
there he didn't even know your name, and to me you were famous! I said, "Is
Bob Gaddy working here?" and he said, "Who is Bob Gaddy?"

Gaddy: I haven't been doing too much around then, just hanging around with Larry. Larry had a synthesizer player with him all the time, Chuck Collins.

Simon [to Gaddy]: You used to go around with a Hammond organ sometimes, right?

Gaddy: We used to have to carry it up the stairs, remember the Central Ballroom? [to Larry Dale]: The whole band used to carry it up the stairs. That was the early '60s.

Larry Dale: That thing weighed about 1,500 pounds

Gaddy: I took that same organ up to Port Chester where we were working with Bill Keys, about '64, and I took it up to Bridgeport, Connecticut, too. I kept going until about 1970, and most of those clubs I had been working out of turned over to DJs and they cut the bands out.

Dale: Well, we're back now, baby. I'm ready!

Gaddy: We're brothers.[4]

NOTES

1. Clarence "Pine Top" Smith's "Pine Top's Boogie Woogie" was first released in 1929 by Vocalion and is cited as the formative boogie-woogie record along with Meade Lux Lewis's slightly earlier "Honky Tonk Train Blues" (Paramount, 1927).

2. Ace Records of London released a Bob Gaddy LP, *Rip and Run* (CH 164), in 1986; and a CD, *Harlem Blues Operator* (CDCHD 407), in 1993, both licensed from Hy Weiss's Old Town Records.

3. Jimmy Wright famously played tenor saxophone, with Larry Dale on guitar, on the Frankie Lymon and the Teenagers' international hit "Why Do Fools Fall in Love" (Gee, 1956). Wright and Dale also appeared in the 1956 film *Rock, Rock, Rock!* accompanying LaVern Baker.

4. See chapter 3 (on Larry Dale), endnote 6, for details on latter-day Bob Gaddy recordings with Dale. In 1993, Gaddy also recorded a solo cassette, *Alone with the Blues*, for Paul Oscher's Mo-Jo Productions.

2

"WILD" JIMMY SPRUILL

Interviewed at his home in the Bronx, 1993

A Bronx resident, originally from Washington, Beaufort County, North Carolina, Jimmy Spruill was a prolific studio guitarist in New York City in the 1950s and 1960s, heard on many recordings, most famously Wilbert Harrison's "Kansas City" and "The Happy Organ" by Dave "Baby" Cortez. Spruill had a unique style, widely admired by guitarists in the know.

Jimmy was a remarkably creative individual in whatever he put his mind to, not just his completely original guitar style. On entering his apartment, one encountered his original furniture designs and wall ornaments. His speech pattern even reflected his nonstop flow of ideas, which seemed to outrun his ability to vocalize them. He often spoke so quickly in communicating his thoughts, he seemed to clip the end of words in his enthusiasm to get out the next word.

Jimmy died of a heart attack during a journey on a Greyhound bus returning to New York from Florida, where he had been visiting longtime friend Noble "Thin Man" Watts. He wasn't on the bus when it arrived in the Port Authority Bus Terminal and was missing for nearly a week. I was part of a news segment on WOR-TV, New York City, featuring a number of his colleagues in the music community jamming and talking about him and hoping for news of his whereabouts. This broadcast led to the sad discovery that he had been removed from the bus in Fayetteville, North Carolina, on the way to New York and died before reaching a hospital; he had not been carrying ID, having left his wallet in Florida. Those of us who got to experience Jimmy's playing on his return to the New York club scene are fortunate to have heard him playing at his most brilliant, fiery, and creative level.

Larry Simon: Hy Weiss [of Old Town Records] said to me, "Larry, you are a musician. You've got to protect everything you do, because a guy like me is gonna steal it."

"Wild" Jimmy Spruill (1934–1996), at the Blue Frog, the Bronx, 1993.

Jimmy Spruill: That's right!

Simon: But he says it, he admits it. A businessman.

Spruill: Bobby Robinson is full of shit, too, he's a businessman. I like him, I like Bobby. Me and him get on pretty good. But you got to be like that when you're a businessman, or people are going to walk all over you.

Simon: What first brought you to New York?

Spruill: What brought me the first time was to visit my brother and to see what it was like. I liked it up here, and I thought I could make a living playing music so I stayed up here. I think it was around 1955 or '56 around June 8.

Simon: And you came up from North Carolina. Had you been playing in that area?

Spruill: I was playing Saturday and Friday night gigs—they call them fish fries. All I ever did was play music.

Simon: Did your family play music?

Spruill: No, no!

Simon: So music is something you picked up on yourself?

Spruill: Before I did, I would go to the movies and see Roy Rogers play the guitar and say "I'm going to play the guitar too."

Simon: All by ear?

Spruill: Yeah, but I played trumpet with music. I played first trumpet in high school, marches. But I tell everybody I can't read [*laughs*]. The reason I say that is because they'll put music in front of you, and when you play with music you can't play with no soul, so I tell them I can't read no damn bit.

Simon: You ever play trumpet when you got to New York?

Spruill: No, only in high school. So when I first got here I worked as a super for two months, but then I met Bobby Robinson's brother Danny. He got me my first recording with Charlie Walker, "Driving Home" [in 1956].[1] What happened was, Charlie Walker got drunk during the recording. He got his name on the record but he couldn't play nothing because he was drunk, so I played all the parts. About three parts on there [guitar overdubs]. Next hit record I made was "Hard Times" with Noble Watts.[2] Then I met Bob Gaddy and started recording with Bobby Robinson. Bob Gaddy gave me club dates.

Simon: Bob [Gaddy] told me he had overheard you at a session.

Spruill: Right, right. We had done "Kansas City" [with Wilbert Harrison],[3] and Bob had done something that sounded like "Kansas City," same music but different words. We had met at Beltone Studios in Manhattan in the late '50s.

Simon: Were you doing mostly studio work?

Spruill: I was doing everything; boat rides, studio work, live shows, you name it.

Simon: Do you have your own band?

Spruill: No, I was working with King Curtis and different bands.

Simon: What was it like working with King Curtis?

Spruill: It was fine. He was a nice guy. We did a lot of college gigs.

Jimmy Spruill, with self-modified studio Les Paul guitar, 1993.

Simon: Who was the most demanding person you worked for? Who wanted you to play it exactly a certain way?

Spruill: No one was demanding to me, because they wanted me to play how I feel. They knew how I sounded. But it was probably King Curtis, but he trusted me. He'd say, "Jimmy, do what you can do, show me what you got" but I'd always play what I feel. As long as it comes from me, he knows it's going to be good.

Simon: Did you also record with him as well as play live?

Spruill: I think we did a thing called "Chicken Scratch."[4] I did stuff with so many people I forget who I did things with.

Simon: One of your most famous sessions was, of course, "Kansas City" [Wilbert Harrison].

Spruill: Also, Baby Cortez, "The Happy Organ."[5] I don't see why people said it was so good but people liked it.

Simon: What are your favorite recordings that you are on?

Spruill: I don't know. I don't have any favorites. I don't think any of them are any good [*laughs*]. I don't think I'm a guitar player.[6]

Simon: Why do you say that?

Spruill: I enjoyed myself, but I don't think I'm a guitar player. I am an artist, yes, but not a guitar player. Most of them don't have a feeling. I have a good feeling.

Simon: Do you feel you are stronger at playing rhythm or lead, or are both equal?

Spruill: Oh, both the same. One thing when I'm playing lead, I never know what I'm going to do until I do it. I don't care. I don't work out a solo. Every time it will be something different. It comes to me as I play in an artistic manner. I don't have to rehearse a solo. Most people do.

Simon: I hear a big difference between your soloing and your rhythm playing style. You have a very precise and recognizable rhythm style that is much more controlled and planned than your soloing.

Spruill: Right, but I don't rehearse it. I can hear it a little before we do it, what's supposed to be done.

Simon: Is there something that led you to that kind of chopping sound in your rhythm playing?

Spruill: I'll tell you where that came from. "Kansas City," right, we played that down one time. Bobby Robinson came in and told me "I want to hear something like B. B. King" and I said, "Dammit, play it yourself" and I got mad and I started chopping. It was a mistake, I didn't give a damn [*laughs*]. I felt like, "I'll play what I want to play!" So I did. And when it came time for the solo I took a solo. But that was a mistake. When you get upset, you do any damn thing. No one would have done that kind of chopping.

Simon: What was it like working with Wilbert Harrison?

UK release, courtesy of John Broven.

Spruill: It was OK, I liked him. He did drink a lot but that never bothered me. Anything I wanted or needed he'd get it for me.

Simon: What about Elmore James, what was it like working for him?

Spruill: He was a great guitar player, but he liked his bottle.

Simon: Did he communicate much, or did he just tell you the key and let you do what you want?

Spruill: No, he wanted his music right. If it was not right he would get on your butt right then. On one of his albums you could hear him talking to another guy, "Wait a minute, wait a minute, that ain't right." I think I did two albums with him, with Bobby Robinson.[7]

Simon: When did you put your own group together, the Hellraisers?

Spruill: I'd say around 1960, '61.

Simon: What kind of work are you doing with that band?

Spruill: I'd like to say club dates, boat rides, wedding receptions, recording sessions. Instead of calling Elmore James they'd call me in. The reason they would call me in is because I could play. Elmore James wasn't able to play behind everybody. I guess he could do it. But by himself, oh, he could play more with one finger than I could with all my fingers. But playing with other people he wasn't too good, as far as I could see. Somebody else may see it different. But he could play in more than one style. He could play jazz also. He tuned the guitar differently. Very good, oh man!

Simon: Very few people know he could play jazz.

Spruill: Oh, are you kidding? That man could play circles around B. B. King, anybody else I know. Albert Collins, all those guys, Albert King, couldn't stick it to Elmore James's regular guitar, I'm not talking about the slide thing. He was something else! Nice guy.

Simon: I guess he's one of your favorite musicians.

Spruill: Oh yeah. Nice guy.

Simon: Who are some other people you really admire, respect, and enjoy?

Spruill: All people who play music.

Simon: But what about musicians you listen to yourself?

Spruill: Larry Dale, Bob Gaddy. I like a lot of people, George Benson, I played with him on a recording session. Kenny Burrell, I played with him on a recording session.

Simon: Were you at a session with Miles Davis?

Spruill: Yeah, he was down there but I don't know if he was on the session. He was a crazy man [*laughs*], but I wouldn't say anything about the man. He was a nut, but I know, I'm a nut.

And Chuck Berry, forget about this guy. I did three nights with him in New Jersey. On the first night he said, "What I want you to do, Jimmy, is stay behind me. I don't want you out there jumping around." I said, "Well it's my band. You don't want to play with my band, you can get your long ass back where you came from." So after that night we got on fine. Otherwise he wanted me to stay behind him all the time. I told the man, "I don't have a boss, the only boss I have is God, and you're not God so get the hell out of my face." I don't take no boss stuff, because when you have a boss, you don't have your own mind, somebody's always telling you what to do. That's why I never have a boss. Have somebody you respect, they tell you what to do and get the hell out of your face. A boss is just like a slave driver. So you don't never consider nobody your boss. You do, you're in trouble. They take your mind away from you.

Simon: So it sounds like you didn't get on too well with Chuck Berry on that first night.

Spruill: It wasn't me. It was him jumping on me. So I had to tell him what I thought. If there is something I don't like, I'm going to tell you about it. I don't have to get mad, I just tell you about it and go on to the next thing.

Simon: When was this?

Spruill: Around 1959.

Simon: Now, who was in the Hellraisers?

Spruill: John Robertson (drums), Horace Cooper (piano), Bam Walters (sax) [also Charlie Lucas, second guitar].

Simon: What are some of the clubs you played back in the late '50s and '60s?

Spruill: Smalls Paradise, Renaissance, Rockland Palace, Astoria Manor, downtown at the Hotel Commodore, the Manhattan Hotel, New Yorker Hotel—the Moonies [followers of the Reverend Sun Myung Moon] own it now, lots of hotels.[8]

Simon: Were you treated any differently back in those days at the clubs?

Courtesy of Mike Gilroy.

Spruill: They loved me then and they love me now. Don't like my looks, I get my ass home, I watch my TV, you know. You see I'm not a person who needs one particular job. When you get so you need one particular job, you're in trouble. People gonna kick your ass. I just pack my guitar, put it in the case, and leave. Make the job that night and don't come back anymore.

Simon: So you've always had an attitude that if it doesn't feel right . . . don't do it!

Spruill: I don't have to do it. I don't work for the money, I work because I'm happy. If I'm not happy with something I'm not gonna to do it. Like I took this guitar, I wasn't happy with it so I just saw it off. [Spruill sawed the sides off his Les Paul Studio model—see pictures.]

Simon: You tend to do that sort of thing with your instruments don't you?

Spruill: Yeah, if I don't like it, I do it the way I'm pleased with.

Simon: So it's almost like your philosophy of life?

Spruill: There you go! I don't like it, I just cut it off and go do it the way I want to do it. If it don't work right, change it and do something else, what fits your mind. Make sure you're comfortable with. If you're not comfortable with it, don't bother, even if it's music.

Simon: What are some of the other things besides music that you do?

Spruill: I'm a brick mason, a plumber, an electrician, a carpet layer, an interior decorator. I draw. I can't tell you all the stuff I do.

Simon: At a certain point you stopped playing in public. When was that?

Spruill: Fifteen or eighteen years ago [the interview was in 1993].

Simon: Why did you stop?

Spruill: I stopped because I was fed up with the same thing over and over. I can't stand the blues over and over and over. You see, there is a difference between the blues and blues music. When you play the music, we hear the blues. When you're out in the field picking cotton every day, with your mother, pulling that sack of cotton down that road with a snake crawling over between your legs . . . that's the blues! See what people don't realize is, the blues don't have no changes to it. The way you all play it, it got the chord changes in it. There ain't no chord changes in the blues, "Oh Lord, help me make it through the day" [*sings a bit of a field-style work song*]. The next day she may sing two or three more bars, the same thing, the next two or three weeks. So that were the blues. And she would sing that and she would look up and water'd come out her eyes because she was so sad because she had to pull that damn sack and make a living and pick that cotton and put it on the big truck so they'd weigh it and give her the money. So that were the blues. But later on they come and put changes to it, but that's not the blues. They call it the blues, but it's not the true blues. People say, "Oh you should be proud." Why should I be proud? Blues is a prayer, and people don't realize what blues is. It's sadness, sorrow, complaint, you know. Blues isn't something you should be proud of, you couldn't help it. Who brought the blues on us? Slave masters! Right? So if someone bring something on you, you gonna be proud of it? Isn't it sadness? And everyone you go up to says, "Well, you should be proud of your heritage." Blues! For what? And then I explain it to them. Then they understand.

Simon: So is that feeling about being a bluesman or playing the blues something that didn't feel right to you?

Spruill: See, you're wrong with that. I'm not a bluesman. I play the blues. A bluesman runs around with a bottle of whiskey in his pocket, gets drunk up on stage. That's a rhythm & blues man, he keeps that bottle in his pocket and keep himself pepped up. I'm a man that plays the blues but I'm not a bluesman. I'm not a sad person.

At home with a Teac 4-track home studio, the Bronx, 1993.

Simon: Did you stop playing because it was upsetting to you to keep playing this type of music?

Spruill: No. It's only sad if you accept it like somebody says, "Hey, nigger." If I accept it then I am what that person called me. I don't accept that! You know what I mean? I'm not a blues person, but I'm a person that plays the blues because I'm gonna make some money from that.

Simon: So why did you stop playing blues?

Spruill: I stopped because I couldn't get the right guys. I mean the older guys that play the blues, most of them died. And the young people don't do nothing but rap. And a white fella couldn't play with no feeling. So I stopped! I moved on to playing rock 'n' roll.

Simon: You don't really want to play rock?

Spruill: No, not really, I like playing a lot of classy stuff. I like music, I don't like noise. I do it as a clown. To me it's funny, you know? It's not a big thing to me. Some people take it real serious. It's serious in one way. But in another . . . everybody's raising hell about the blues. Most white people just got into it, I been into it since sixteen years ago. I don't want to hear that shit. Want to hear about somebody killing your people?

Simon: When I first met you, you weren't performing much anymore. But now you are out there again playing.

Spruill: It's not a big thing to play it [blues]. What is it? I mean, you know . . . [*sings a little blues phrase*] all night. And don't nothing ever change. And I'm a person who's got an artistic mind, right? So if I do the same thing over and over, it will drive me nuts! If you've been programmed in life and gonna do the same thing over again, like most people are, it's all right. But I'm a Gemini person, and I've got about fifteen personalities and I wanna use 'em. If I lived a thousand years, I wouldn't be able to do what I want to do.

Simon: So were you feeling limited by blues?

Spruill: I don't know. You can't be limited by blues, because blues always has a different thing you can go into but how much can you change the blues?

Simon: Now, you are also interested in country and church music and a whole variety of styles, correct?

Spruill: Oh yeah.

Simon: Do you go to a church?

Spruill: I don't go to church. Church for what? Do you go to church?

Simon: I don't.

Spruill: What would you go to for if you went?

Simon: If I went, maybe I'd go to share thoughts with other people who think or feel the same way, but I don't think the same way as any large organized spiritual or religious group.

Spruill: Well I don't either! That's why I don't go.

Simon: I have my own spiritual beliefs, but they don't exactly coincide with any organized religion I'm aware of.

Spruill: I believe in God in here [*touches heart*]. I don't want to deal with nobody's belief. Sounds like you got it.

Simon: I've always felt that an organized religion is kind of telling you how to believe.

Spruill: Right. That's why I don't go. That's exactly how I feel about it. It's very smart to think that way. See, people will program you. Or you'll program yourself by thinking that way. You let them do it. You let them in your mind. You gotta be careful, they'll mess it up. I'm not like most people. When you get to know me, you say, "Damn, I didn't know Jimmy's like that, at all." I don't care who's the star. Whoever is playing, I want to enjoy myself. I can back you all night and never take a solo. I'm sixty years old and I been playing professionally since I been twelve years old, so I don't need anything, I don't care about anything. I don't need aggravation. When you've lived as long as I have, you take the rest of your life and enjoy. You don't try and hurt nobody. You try to help people. They don't appreciate it, leave it alone. Don't try to get back at them, leave it alone. A small amount of people are going to hurt each other.

Simon: Do you still spend a lot of time working down in Florida?

Spruill: Yeah. I don't like to do one thing all the time. It bugs me. I don't know about you, but I can't stand it. You're a Capricorn, you got the nervous energy somewhere, nervous energy, Capricorn people!

Jimmy Spruill at the Blue Frog, the Bronx, 1993. Also pictured below with Bobby Robinson at the same venue, 1993.

Simon: When you had your own group together, did anyone sing or did you do all instrumentals?

Spruill: Yeah, Irving Johnson sang.

Simon: Did you do originals or mostly cover tunes?

Spruill: We did some originals sometimes. We did something called "The Rooster" [Enjoy, 1964][9] but we never recorded too many things because Bobby Robinson was handling everything. He'd say, "I'm going to do it," but never finish it. We recorded "Hard Grind" [Fire, 1959].[10]

Courtesy of Victor Pearlin.

Simon: At one time wasn't your group playing between acts at the Apollo Theatre?

Spruill: We were playing a regular show. We played with Wilbert Harrison and the Ramrods. We played between acts for James Brown, Jackie Wilson, Sam Cooke, Fats Domino, John Lee Hooker, Buster Brown. We played at places all around New York.

Simon: Did you know Mickey Baker?

Spruill: Yeah, Mickey and Sylvia.

Simon: Are you still in touch with him?

Spruill: No, he left town and I took all his jobs [in the studio]. When he was here it was me and him. When he left I took all the jobs. We had a different sound. I didn't try to be good. I tried to be different.

Simon: You've had a long association with Noble "Thin Man" Watts.

Spruill: Yeah, since about 1956. He's like a brother.

Simon: What are some labels that you've been on over the years?

Spruill: Fire and Fury, Clock, Atlantic, Vanguard, oh, Columbia, I did some things with that white boy who played harmonica . . . John Hammond, *The Best of John Hammond* [and *Big City Blues* and *Mirrors*, all three LPs on Vanguard].

Also on the session there was Jimmy Lewis, he plays upright bass, also played with King Curtis; Bobby Donaldson on drums; Billy Butler on guitar. Good guitar player. Nice guy! Oh, nice guy, beautiful! You ever meet him?

Simon: I did, recently. He really did seem like a wonderful person. When I met him, he told me his wife was sick and he was staying home a lot to take care of her. Seemed like his career slowed down after his wife became ill and died.

Spruill: That man was beautiful. You ever hear tell of a man named Bill Jennings [a jazz guitarist who recorded for King and Prestige]? Wow! I was playing with a guy the other day, it make me have, uh . . . , stress. Because the guys, they can't play. I've played with some guitar players! I mean musicians! I play with them and record with them. And you go in there [the studio], they run it down one time, they say, "Listen Jimmy, the next time, you gotta play it." Ain't no rehearsing. You play it or they get someone in your place.

Simon: What did you do with Bill Jennings?

Spruill: We did something with a group, the Charts, [on "Deserie" (Everlast, 1957)]. He was a good guitar player, but he was a junkie. Skeeter Best, you know that name? This guy is great![11] He was even better than Bill Jennings. They dominate me, they are all better, and I played with all of them and they all asked me, how do I bend my strings. So they all want to know how I bend my strings but I never want to know what they do. I didn't care what they did. I want to do it my way. I don't care how good you are. I don't want to take what you know and play it. I want to take what I know 'cause I can play it best.

Simon: Did you ever play on any jazz sessions?

Spruill: No, I don't like jazz. Jazz is out of tune. The chords are out of tune. Listen to this [*picks up his guitar and plays an A major chord, then plays an A13 chord*]. The 13th is out of tune. Listen to this [*plays AMa7*]. But people don't realize that. You tell them that, they'll have a fit. "Lord, man, you just don't!" Check it out for yourself. Out of tune! Every chord you make in jazz is mostly out of tune.

Simon: There is a lot of dissonance in the chords.

Spruill: Out of tune! Out of tune with nature. Out of tune with a natural chord. Play a flat with a natural thing it's going to be out of tune. An added flat with a natural, it's going to be out of tune.

Simon: I know what you're talking about, but to me it's a difference in what you will accept.

Spruill: That's what I said about your mind awhile ago, if you accept it. But if you accept it, you have to understand it when you listen to it. Do you understand it when you listen to it? What's this? [*plays a 13th chord on guitar*]. Now do you think that is in tune with nature?

Simon: That sounds good to me.

Spruill: I know it, because you accept that. I accept it, but I know it's not right. With a major chord those notes are not right. But most people are like you.

Jimmy Spruill at the Blue Frog, the Bronx, 1993.

One day when you take it note by note and understand like I do, otherwise you will never understand it. Because you were trained that way, like some people say, "Looka here, look at that nigger." They gonna call you "nigger" because they were trained that way. They can't help it, the way they were brought up. Because when you get something in your mind, it's hard to get it out.

Simon: What would you say to somebody who says they like that sound?

Spruill: I wouldn't say nothin' because they accept it. I wouldn't say they are wrong because I understand it both ways. It's still out of tune. I accept it too but I don't accept that it's in tune. I accept that it's a chord with four notes in tune and two out [of tune].

[This discussion of extended chord tones and their "out-of-tuneness" was quite vague. It is possible he was hearing in a way similar to La Monte Young or Lou Harrison, composers who work with just intonation tunings, hearing tones that are further from the tonic harmonically and more distant from the overtone series, literally more out of tune acoustically. Or possibly complex altered chordal extensions beyond 7th chords and the clash resulting from the resultant dissonant intervals.]

Simon: Have you listened to late John Coltrane or to Cecil Taylor? They don't even play traditional chords, the music is "out."

Spruill: Oh yeah, I've been in the studio with King Curtis when they were there recording in the other room. We'd stop and listen.

Simon: What do you think of that stuff that is really out, without even any chords?

Spruill: That's what I think, "out." What do you think when jazz people have a jam session? Or rock musicians get together and everyone is soloing all at once? I like country and western music to tell you the truth. I like that and I like classical music—a lot of violin and strings. It's good for the mind. You can't think when you have a lot of noise going on.

Simon: Do you like having music in the background when you are doing your other type of work like carpentry? Or does it distract you?

Spruill: Don't need it! I have it in my head. Anything I need to listen to, I turned it on in my head and it comes in. I don't need a radio on. I have my own tunes. You might think, "Damn he must be nutty."

Simon: I studied sitar for a number of years, and my teacher told me something his teacher told him. The highest achievement is not to a imagine music but to hear or listen to music that is present in your mind or soul.

Spruill: Whether it's a tune or something, I hear the music. That's what makes me the way I am.

Simon: That's interesting, you are saying the same thing that a master Indian musician is saying, that you are receiving music.

Spruill: There you go again. Everyone is a master of their own self, or they should be if they're not! If I'm not a master of my own self, I'm in bad shape. You say, "The master says." I am a master! Of my own self. Otherwise, you are telling me they are a master and I am not [*laughs*]. That's not nice [*laughs*]. Go ahead, I'm listening to you.

Simon: Do you like studio or live performance work better?

Spruill: Don't make no difference to me, I just want to enjoy myself.

Simon: I'm getting your philosophy pretty clearly. As long as you have the freedom to be yourself and enjoy what you're doing.

Spruill: I don't care what it is, anything. I'm enjoying myself now. Anything where I enjoy myself I'll do it all day long. If I'm not enjoying myself I'll cut it off, boom! Forget it! I don't care how much money I'm getting. I'm not like most people, I rather make nothing at all than be miserable. I cannot be paid off if I do not want to do anything. It could be a million dollars, I'm like that. Money don't talk to me at all. You talk to me with kindness, with some kind of care and respect. Then I do it!

My grandmother was Cherokee, long black hair. My mother was light complexion. My father was dark. Most of my people was always doing something with their mind. They were always building something, using their artistic mind. I like everything. I like life, period. I like smart people. I don't like talking to a dumb person, can't answer me back or give me something I'm interested in talking about. We can talk but it's wasting my time. That's the reason sometimes when I'm on stage I'm not saying anything or playing anything. I play with a lot of people, sometimes it's just OK. I'm looking around for something that will feed my mind. Something that will do myself some good. If I don't get something that feeds my mind I feel shitty so I'm ready to get off the stage.

Simon: Do you do a lot of recordings by yourself with overdubbing here in your apartment with your own equipment?

Spruill: Yeah, a lot of things.

Simon: You gave me a tape once. It was a very different kind of thing, almost your own completely original style of music that you invented. It had a mix of gospel, country, blues. A lot of different things mixed in [see an example on my website: www.larrysimon-music.com].

Spruill: I got a lot of that. That's the kind of stuff I like. I like music with good chord changes, a feeling and telling a story. If you're not telling a story, I don't need it. You're here every day of your life and if you're not learning something you're wasting your time. We are not here that long. You don't want to waste no time here. You don't know where the hell you're going after here. You know you're here now. Take what you've got and enjoy. I don't have time to get mad at you and stay mad at you. Nobody do. Like black and white always arguing with each other. About what? Enjoy yourself.

Simon: When you say "telling a story" with your music, do you mean an abstract story or a literal story?

Spruill: Well, to you it will mean one thing and to me it would mean something else. It's how you look at the music. I may see one thing in my music that you can't see, and when you're listening to my music, you see something that I can't see. The story may be a different story for you.

Simon: Is the story sometimes a literal story for you or is it a story of emotions or feelings?

Spruill: Both.

Simon: Do you ever write words?

Spruill: Instrumentals. I write words but they are secret, for myself. If I write words people could not understand me. They wouldn't like it because I tell the truth. I tell the truth about everything and people wouldn't like that. People like to hear you tell lies. You try to tell the truth nowadays and they are, "Oh god, you have a problem!" I think everybody should have a right to do what they want to do as long as it don't hurt nobody else. People marry a different race of people. People get mad because a person is black, a person is a white, a person is a Jew, whatever. What the hell, God made us all! Marry who the hell you want to marry! That's my opinion. You know, but most people don't like that. You ever live down South?

Simon: No, I visited but I never lived there.

Spruill: OK, down there they don't like—well it used to be, it's gotten a little better—they don't want the black to mix with the white, but they'll let the black cook for them. Why do you let somebody cook for you but you won't let them mix with you? They were trained that way, they can't help it. To me that's stupid. I just like people in general, as long as they've got some sense. If they ain't got no sense, stay away from me!

Simon: Are there any dreams you have that you still would like to accomplish?

Spruill: Oh yes, a lot of them. I want to get rich and own my own plane and learn how to fly.

Simon: What are you going to do to get rich?

Spruill: I love to play music or do home improvements, but you can't get rich doing that at my age. I'd rather go down to Atlantic City and make some money [gambling]. You can't be messing around here trying to work at my age and hope to get rich. You're not going to get rich by working, no way. You know that. I'd be a fool to tell you I'm going to work and get rich. Maybe the lottery.

Simon: Do you like traveling?

Spruill: Oh, I love to travel and fly too. When my back was messed up, I couldn't do anything.

Simon: When did you get married?
Spruill: In 1961, and I have twin daughters.
Simon: Does your wife or daughter ever come to your shows?
Spruill: They have, but not too often.

[The interview ends talking back and forth about our mutual small tape recorders and the merits of pursuing one's dreams regardless of commercial gain. This is omitted due to the back-and-forth nature—it became a conversation and was no longer an interview.]

NOTES

1. "Driving Home" was a two-part record released in 1957 by Danny Robinson's Holiday label with credits to Charles Walker and Band (guitar – James Spruill).

2. "Hard Times (The Slop)" by Noble "Thin Man" Watts peaked at no. 44 on the *Billboard* Top 100 in early 1958 on Sol Rabinowitz's Baton label. Curiously, it never made the *Cash Box* pop or *Billboard* R&B charts.

3. "Kansas City" by Wilbert Harrison hit the no. 1 spot on the *Billboard* Hot 100 on May 18, 1959, for two weeks; it had been released on Bobby Robinson's Fury label. This meant, with "The Happy Organ" (see note 5 below), Jimmy Spruill was on no. 1 records for three weeks consecutively, an incredible achievement for which he would have probably only received standard union session fees.

4. "The Chicken Scratch" was recorded by the Commandos, featuring saxophonist King Curtis, and released by Juggy Murray's Symbol label in December 1958. Murray was better known as the owner of the successful Sue label with hits by Bobby Hendricks (of the Drifters), Ike and Tina Turner, Baby Washington, Jimmy McGriff, and more.

5. "The Happy Organ" by Dave "Baby" Cortez, on Wally Moody and George Levy's Clock label, hit the no. 1 spot on the *Billboard* Hot 100 on May 11, 1959, for one week. On the *Cash Box* Top 100 chart, it stayed at no. 1 for two weeks.

6. Spruill's other *Billboard* nationwide chart accompaniments include: "Deserie" by the Charts (Everlast, no. 88, 1957); "Bad Motorcycle" by the Storey Sisters (Cameo, no. 45, 1958); "So Much" by Little Anthony and the Imperials (End, no. 87, 1958); "Dedicated to the One I Love" by the Shirelles (Scepter, no. 83 in 1959, no. 3 in 1961); "It's Too Late" by Tarheel Slim and Little Ann (Fire, no. 20 R&B, 1959); "Fannie Mae" by Buster Brown (Fire, no. 38, 1960); and "All in My Mind" by Maxine Brown (Nomar, no. 19, 1960).

7. Spruill may have been referring to Elmore James's Blue Horizon (UK) double-LP, *To Know a Man*, with studio talk and false takes. There were two James LPs, *The Sky Is Crying* and *I Need You*, from Bobby Robinson's Fire masters that appeared on Sphere Sound, a subsidiary of Bell Records, in 1965 and 1967. Spruill was present on at least two Elmore James Fire singles from 1960: "Rollin' and Tumblin'"/"I'm Worried" and "Done Somebody Wrong"/"Fine Little Mama."

8. Spruill also said he played at Central Ballroom and the Baby Grand club in Harlem; and at the Apollo in Harlem (with Wilbert Harrison) and the Howard in Washington, DC (with Noble Watts). See John Broven with Paul Harris and Richard Tapp, "I Was Wild! The Story of Jimmy Spruill," *Juke Blues*, no. 6, 1986.

9. "The Rooster," with vocalist Irving Johnson, was Spruill's final single, released by Bobby Robinson's Enjoy label in 1964.

10. The 1959 instrumental "Hard Grind" is a magnificent example of Spruill's mastery of the guitar.

11. Clifton "Skeeter" Best was a respected jazz guitarist from North Carolina who played and recorded with the likes of Erskine Hawkins, Earl Hines, Ray Charles, Etta Jones, and Harry Belafonte.

Larry Dale (1923–2010), in front of Bobby's Happy House record store, off 125th Street, Harlem, 1993.

3

LARRY DALE

Interviewed at Bobby's Happy House in Harlem
with Bobby Robinson present, September 19, 1993

Larry Dale was one of the finest blues guitarists and vocalists of his time, although not nearly as recognized as his remarkable talents deserved. A soft-spoken and somewhat reserved gentleman, Dale was born in Hungerford, Texas, and spent a good deal of his life residing in the borough of the Bronx, New York City. One of Dale's finest sessions—cited as an influence by Brian Jones of the Rolling Stones— is his playing (under his real name, Ennis Lowery) on Champion Jack Dupree's classic 1958 Atlantic album *Blues from the Gutter*. Aside from own recordings, Dale worked as a sideman with numerous artists including Cootie Williams and Paul "Hucklebuck" Williams, and most notably on Frankie Lymon and the Teenagers' 1956 international hit "Why Do Fools Fall in Love" (Gee). Additionally, Dale can be seen in the 1956 film *Rock, Rock, Rock!* as a sideman with tenor saxophonist Jimmy Wright in the sequence featuring LaVern Baker. He was also an urbane blues singer of underappreciated merit from the Joe Turner school.

I had the great pleasure to work with Larry Dale for a number of years during the 1980s and 1990s. Despite his long career, which included European tours with Cootie Williams and others, I was very surprised when Dale told me I had gotten him his first New York City gigs below 125th Street in his entire career. His East Coast territory covered the Bronx, Harlem, New Jersey, Long Island, and upstate New York, but never before in Manhattan lower than Harlem.

Larry Simon: Did you record for Bobby Robinson in the past?

Larry Dale: Bobby recorded me a long time ago. He knew me before I even played guitar when I was working on cars. I used to work down the street.

Simon: A general question for you both: Is there a particular way you would describe the sound of New York blues that makes it different from, say, Chicago or Los Angeles?

Larry Dale and Bobby Robinson in front of Bobby's Happy House record store, Harlem, 1993.

Bobby Robinson: As far as the blues is concerned some particular place may have a little diversion on it, but blues is basically blues, I don't care where you do it at. If you do something different you ain't doing blues. Blues is basically a sound.

Dale: A southern sound.

Robinson: Yeah, a southern sound. Don't forget where blues was born, out of slavery where people are having a hard time. This was a way of people holding themselves together and maybe having hope for the future. Blues and gospel are the same thing basically. It's about hard living, and experiences and hope. The blues had a weird lonesome-type built-in sound. It varied here and there with the beat, this, that, and the other. But the basic thing is there, no matter where they do it: blues.

Simon: In New York, weren't a lot of the horn players also jazz players? Like in New York there is more jazz going on. In Chicago a horn player might just play blues.

Robinson: Well I'll tell you the truth, in New York there wasn't too much blues done in New York with horns. It was just basically a rhythm thing. The best blues are basic rhythm instruments. It might have a horn here and there.

Simon [to Larry Dale]: You didn't have much in the way of horns, in your music did you?

Dale: No. I think B. B. King started that. I think B. B. King cleaned it up a little bit with all those horns. What Muddy Waters and all them was doing is

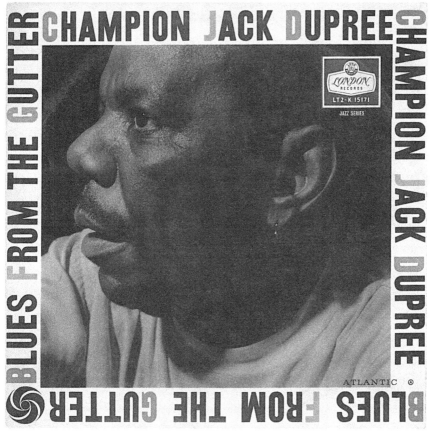

The classic LP featuring Larry Dale, guitar, as Ennis Lowery. UK release, courtesy of John Broven.

what I would call basic black blues, right out of the woods, you know. It was a thing, man. It's different when you put horns and stuff behind you. It cleans it up too much. Europeans like the cornbread. What I mean by cornbread, I mean chitlins, pig feet, I'm talking down to earth. When you make it pretty, it screws up for a lot of people. I made that record "Penny Pincher" [Juke Blues Records, 1987], and they called me from all the way over there and told me when I come to play in Europe they ain't gonna be going for that over there. You know what they asked me to do when I come over there? "Mama, You Got Bad Blood." That's a number Champion Jack Dupree did. They called me all the way from England and they said, "Larry, when you come over, that "Penny Pincher," they ain't gonna to be going for that. It's too clean. It ain't chitlins ["No!" –BR], it ain't pig feet ["No!" –BR], it ain't hog maw ["No!" –BR], you know what I'm talking about! I thought "Penny Pincher" was the best record I've done in a long time. They sent me a tape of Jack Dupree. I know what they want, Dupree [refer-

Larry Dale in front of Bobby's Happy House record store, Harlem, 1993.

(L. to r.), Patrick Grant (cameraman), Larry Dale, A. J. Johnson, and Bob Gaddy at a video shoot, midtown Manhattan, 1993.

ring to Dupree's Atlantic album *Blues from the Gutter* featuring Dale's stunning guitar]. Jack was big over there in Europe. What they want is [for] you [not to] pronounce your words properly, like John Lee Hooker, like chitlins, fatback stuff, and then you get clean and pretty like me [*laughs*]. They want the real basic thing that was done a long time ago.

Robinson: When I was a kid I knew I was going to get a whipping. Saturday night they used to have what they called a frolic. This is as low as they get. Way out in the country a bootlegger he had this thing way out in the cotton field, way in the country there. I was fourteen or fifteen.

Some grown boys come by in a Model A Ford, a Roadster, fifteen guys be on it—three or four in the front seat. There was a rumble seat, guys on the fender with their arms around the lights, and a guy sitting up on the hood and the guy would roll down the windshield and look out the window to drive the car. I'd go down the road apiece from my house after it got dark, and the guys would come and pick me up. This is a dangerous place because the guy is a bootlegger, illegal liquor dealer, and whatnot. And the guy would have three lanterns tied to the porch. There was no light. And you'd walk in the house past where the beds was and just two chairs and two guitar players, that's all that was in the room then you go ahead into the kitchen coming from the living room across the kitchen there was a table, and there was two big women there frying fish and chicken and whatnot all night long. Every time you go you have to buy a piece of fish or chicken or a drink. Man those guys, they got there in the corner facing each other with guitars, acoustic guitars, and they sang the blues, and they get onto dancing and after a while after three or four drinks of that good strong liquor, they were gone. It was like that all night long. I was fascinated with it. Here were people who worked hard on the farms all day long. They went out on a Saturday night with liquor and music and dance and they let their hair down. This was for real. They don't give a fuck about money, they wasn't getting none no how. They didn't worry about money. There weren't no money to be got. I'm talking about the '30s. So they got drunk and danced until day. Two guitars, that was the real blues.

Dale: That was the real stuff. Now when you add three or four horns to the rhythm section and everything behind and violins and shit. They clean the blues up too much. The blues represents a heartache.

Robinson: That's where the blues comes from, heartache and pain. A guy had to find a way to express he had no money, during the depression, no food to eat. A guy had a woman she may be gone, whatever. It was real. They couldn't have all these instruments anyway. Acoustic guitars and harmonica. That was it. Foot stomp was the drums.

I just came back from a music convention in Atlanta, Georgia, I make a point to go down there every year find out who is playing blues. More people are playing blues now that hadn't been two or three years ago. You'd be surprised.

Larry Dale with Killing Floor NYC (l. to r., A. J. Johnson, Larry Dale, and Larry Simon) performing for the World Music Institute NYC blues show, Washington Square Church, Greenwich Village, May 6, 1989.

Simon [to Larry Dale]: You once told me a bit about knowing Mickey Baker and teaching him about getting a blues feel.

Dale: I used to teach Mickey, and Sylvia too. Sylvia was so good looking and everything, it was hard to concentrate. So beautiful at the time.[1] Anyway I used to teach Sylvia chords and I would teach Mickey how to make the strings cry. If you just go to a note it won't cry. If you push it from this note to that, the string would cry. That's what Mickey wanted to know from me.[2] But Mickey was a helluva guitarist, five times better guitar player than me. But you see, all that fingering and stuff, that's not blues. When people play jazz, to me it looks like they are concentrating on how many damn notes they can put in a bar. For me, I ain't never liked it. But the more notes you put in, the more helluva musician you are. But to me the blues is something that's simple, it's something anybody can understand [*sings*]:

> When I woke up this morning and looked outdoors,
> I knew that was my milk cow by the way she lows,
> If you see my milk cow, please drive her on home,
> 'Cause I ain't had no milk and butter since my milk cow been gone.[3]

Some shit like that! Overseas they love that. And down in the woods they love that, right now! But people in cities they're trying to get away from it, especially the black people, they're trying to get away from it. But of course you go to their house and you find a ton of Bo Diddley records underneath the cabinet.

Simon: You've been playing around New York since about 1953. What were some of the big clubs and what was it like playing in them at the time?

Dale: I didn't work in any clubs in the city. The clubs I worked in probably nobody never ever heard of 'em. I worked in Yonkers for twenty-four months [in a club] called the Sportsman's Lounge. Before I worked there it was called the C-Plus Club. I went there one Saturday night when a jazz band was playing. When I took a break me and pianist Bob Gaddy got up there, and the boss came running up and said, "Where are you two working?" Shit, I had never worked nowhere. I said, "We're not working anywhere right now," and he said, "Would you like to work here?" Bob got a tenor player and a drummer. We took the gig, started the following week, and stayed there twenty-four months. I stayed there until I went off with Cootie [Williams]. Then Cootie came up one night and listened to me. Didn't say anything to me that night but he called me the next day and asked if I'd like to join his band. I had my own band with my name up-front but then I got to thinking, "Well, if I join Cootie maybe I'll get known like Cab Calloway." So I turned the gig over to Bob Gaddy. I joined Cootie [during 1957–1959] and we went to Europe, played in Paris [in 1959].

Simon: With Cootie were you playing jazz and blues?

Larry Dale inside Bobby's Happy House
record store, 1993.

Larry Dale inside Bobby's Happy House record store, 1993.

Dale: No, it was up-tempo blues. I did the tunes that Joe Williams had been doing. He went with Duke Ellington and got big. I thought if I went with Cootie I might get big. We did a thing called "It's All in Your Mind" with Wini Brown [RCA Victor, 1957].[4] But nothing happened. Then I did a session for Hy Weiss [in 1960], "What Your Love Means to Me," "Let Your Love Run to Me."[5] Then I did a thing for Atlantic Records [in 1961], "Drinkin' Wine Spo-Dee-O-Dee." All this stuff is out in Europe. They don't tell me nothing and I don't get no money. These teenagers that got all those hits, the Cleftones and the Valentines, Frankie Lymon and the Teenagers they didn't give them no money, just clothes, pretty cars—pretty clothes because they had to work. But it takes a lot of money to promote a record, so I don't mind. Any record I make, give the money away, because I'll make the money on the bandstand.[6]

Larry Dale at Delta 88, New York, circa 1994.

Larry Dale, top, with Larry Simon at Dwyer's Pub, New York, May 1989; at right, in front of the Apollo Theatre, 125th Street, Harlem, May 1986; at bottom, on 125th Street, Harlem, May 1986. Photos by Paul Harris.

Rosco Gordon (l.), Larry Dale (kneeling), with Killing Floor NYC, Celebrate Brooklyn Festival Prospect Park, Brooklyn, July 7, 1990.

Courtesy of John Broven.

NOTES

1. Mickey Baker was New York's no. 1 R&B session guitarist in the 1950s before emigrating to France. With Sylvia Vanderpool (later Robinson) as Mickey and Sylvia, the duo had a hugely influential 1957 hit, "Love Is Strange," for Groove, the RCA Victor subsidiary. The last RCA Victor session by the duo was in January 1965.

2. Dale had recorded in 1954 for Groove as a vocalist for Baker, who was using the stage name Big Red McHouston at the time.

3. Lyrics based on Kokomo Arnold's 1934 Decca recording "Milk Cow Blues." The song was famously recorded as "Milkcow Blues Boogie" by Elvis Presley on Sun Records in late 1954.

4. Dale recorded with Cootie Williams's Savoy Ballroom Orchestra as a vocalist and guitarist in 1957 for RCA Victor; and again on tour in Paris in January and February 1959, resulting in two LPs for French Decca.

5. These 1960 sessions, which also included "Big Muddy" and "Let the Doorbell Ring" with Jimmy Spruill (guitar) and Bob Gaddy (piano), were recorded by veteran producer Henry Glover for his Glover label, distributed by Hy Weiss's Old Town label.

6. Dale also recorded for the following labels: Jax (1952), Groove (1954), Herald and Ember (1955–1956), Vik (with Champion Jack Dupree, 1957), RAM (1968), and Fire (1969). See a full discography with personnel in John Broven, "Larry Dale: The New York Houserocker," *Juke Blues*, no. 9, Summer 1987. Dale's latter-day recordings include "Penny Pincher"/"I Got a Brand New Mojo" (Juke Blues, 1987); *Bob Gaddy, Larry Dale and the House Rockers, Live* (recorded in Austria, 1993); "Big Muddy," "Rock a While," "Baby What You Want Me to Do," and "I Got a Brand New Mojo," recorded live with Bob Gaddy in Austria and backed by the excellent Mojo Blues Band (Styx, Austria, 1999); and a superb "New York City Blues" with Bob Gaddy, Jimmy Spruill, Larry Simon, and drummer A. J. Johnson (Golden Crest/Ace, released 2010), written by British blues writer Dave Williams.

Al Pittman, aka Dr. Horse, aka Doc Pittman (1917–2003), performing at the Cajun Cafe, New York, 1993.

4

"AL" PITTMAN, AKA DOC PITTMAN, AKA DR. HORSE

Interviewed in New York, 1993

Alvergous "Al" Pittman, born in Vienna, Georgia, was a unique stylist who was a singer and also played the cocktail drum, a single handheld sort of elongated bongo. He began performing in New York City in the 1930s and can best be described as a jump blues–style musician, but it was never so easy to neatly categorize him. Pittman also fit into the swing mold and was heard on Fifty-Second Street in New York in the 1930s. Early on he used spoken word as an element in his songwriting, as evidenced in his song "Jack, That Cat Was Clean" (Fire, 1962). Pittman considered himself one of the earliest rap artists. Like most of the performers in this book, he also worked with the great producer Bobby Robinson. From 1967, he sang with assorted Ink Spots groups.

Doc had a wonderful, cheerful demeanor. He was on the scene for a very long time and was a true old-school entertainer. Considering that, he was very aware of the current musical trends and always spoke with excitement about whatever next big project he had in the works.

Larry Simon: Who would you say are your biggest influences?

Dr. Horse: The late Louis Prima, and naturally, Satchmo. And a guy by the name of Tiny Bradshaw. He always had a punch, you know, he really knew how to move and sell, too—he was great people, the late Tiny. And Joe Williams.

Simon: You originally grew up in Florida, right?

Dr. Horse: Right. That's right.

Simon: How did you end up in New York, and how did you start doing music here?

Dr. Horse: I came to New York in 1934, and I happened to see a picture called *The Big Broadcast* [starring Bing Crosby, from 1932]. Remember that? Sometime back, with the Mills Brothers and Cab [Calloway] and everybody was in that. So I decided I wanted to get in the entertainment world. I had a friend of mine that used to play the ukulele, so I decided that I'd get me one and I taught myself to play it. So we used to do little private gigs. Everything we heard Bing Crosby do and the Andrews Sisters, we used to try to do it with the ukulele. And then when I came to the city, I heard about the Apollo Theatre, you had to go on the amateur hour. So that's one of the hardest audiences in the world to work for. But I came in third. I was surprised myself. So after that, here's what happened: I went downtown to see if I could get some kind of connection there because I used to write tunes. I was just feeling my way around. I happened to see some guys playing on the street, and one of the guys, one of the greatest entertainers we ever had, was Slim Gaillard [with Slam Stewart]. Remember Slim and Slam?

Simon: Yeah, of course.

Dr. Horse: Yeah, he was playing on the street and then my other very good friend that we lost, Redd Foxx, he was playing. He had a tub with a string in it and he played it like a bass [*laughing*], you see? So I could see that people were giving him money, I said, "Well that's not too bad, I think I could do that" [*laughing*]. So two days later, that's what I done. I came down and started playing on the street and the people started giving us money. I had another guy with us, he was a dancer, and I happened to see Redd Foxx with the tub and the string, see here's what we got, we got a washboard. The guy got thimbles and a kazoo [*laughing*]. So that's what we were doing, you know? That was our rhythm. Some of the biggest people caught us that liked what we were doing so we started adding. We had a group known as the Tramp Band because we had the kazoo, the washtub, and we used to dress really funny, with funny clothes [*chuckles*].

Simon: What were the guys' names that were in that?

Dr. Horse: Well, we had Jimmy Butts that was on the bass violin. And another guy we caught dancing on the street. He was very funny. We put him in front, and his name was Sausage. So we called him Dr. Sausage, then we named it Dr. Sausage and the [Five] Pork Chops. Yeah, that was the name of the group. So the guy playing the washboard, his name was Al Johnson. And shaking the maracas—we had maracas—his name was Bob Wright. And at the piano was Jimmy Harris. And I was on guitar.

So what happened is we got real lucky there because we went on the *Major Bowes Amateur Hour*. We won that and we went on tour with that show. For thirty-two weeks, we stayed on tour when he had the shows going around, the *Amateur Hour*, and we went to all different cities.

Simon: So this was a tour organized by Major Bowes?

Dr. Horse: That's right. We were playing in a place in Detroit called the Club Plantation. They had a big revue there. Sixteen girls and a twelve-piece band, the Edgar Hayes [Orchestra], and he had with him at that time, was Dizzy Gil-

Dr. Horse playing the cocktail drum,
Cajun Cafe, New York, 1993.

lespie. They had us in there as an extra added attraction. And by the way, Joe Louis, at that time, the fighter—he was living upstairs at the hotel that we were living in. So we used to see the champ every day, because we were working there. So somebody caught us, that owned the Fox Theatre there, one of the biggest in Detroit. We were doubling from the Plantation at the Fox. And then some guy caught us that owned the Onyx on Fifty-Second Street. We followed Stuff Smith, you know, the violinist. That's where all of the biggest played—Coleman Hawkins was on the street, Maxine Sullivan with John Kirby, who had the Biggest Little Band in the Land. Billie Holiday was at the Famous Door, Art Tatum also was on the street. We went there for two weeks and we stayed for sixteen weeks on Fifty-Second Street and you just don't do that.

Simon: What year was this that you were, that you got there to Fifty-Second Street?

Dr. Horse: I think this was '36. With all that talent then, Ben Webster and Lester Young, all the giants were playing on the street at that time. And from there we left and toured the Midwest, went to Chicago there, we did a tour.

Simon: Did you like touring?

Dr. Horse: Yes, I did. You met a lot of different people and you happen to see what the show world was really like there, with the different acts. And at that time, you really had some acts out there. And I'm not kidding you ... it's kind of hard to follow some of them. But we were a novelty, what we were doing.

Simon: Where else did you go?

Dr. Horse: Indiana. And we just played a lot in the city, in New York. And then we played the Howard Theatre in Washington, and naturally the world-famous Apollo Theatre in Harlem.

Simon: What about your time with the latter-day Ink Spots?

Dr. Horse: So then there was an opening for [me in] the Ink Spots, and I stayed with them [from 1967] till 1971.[1] And we toured the country, Florida, Georgia, Texas, and just the whole bit, and also all the way to the International Hotel, at that time, in Las Vegas.

Simon: Did you go to Europe with them?

Dr. Horse: Nope, I didn't go to Europe with them at that time.

Simon: Tell me about the recording you did with people from Count Basie's band and pianist Sammy Price.[2]

Dr. Horse: In fact, I did the last concert with him [Sammy Price]. We were there in Boston. We worked about four or five places, at the colleges. [The album] was kind of heavy: Freddie Green on guitar, with the drummer Sonny Payne and the trombonist was Vic Dickenson—all giants, you know, and they were lovely to work with. We sent the stuff over to Kapp Records. And I was surprised, they called me and said Dave Kapp wants you to do the album. He was a biggie. And so we sent the tape over and he wanted me to do the album [in 1961]. Yeah, it was something else. In fact, that's why I went to Europe the first time, Sam and I, 'cause it took off there. Better audience than the people here sometimes. I mean, it was in every window in the Champs-Élysées [in Paris]. And looked like it was going to take off a bit there. But so far it was very good. I was remembered there. And then I did another thing for Bobby Robinson. In fact, I made the first rap record, "Jack, That Cat Was Clean." That was one of the first that was recorded. Oh, and it took off.[3]

Simon: Where'd you get the idea to speak it?

Dr. Horse: Well, I used to fool around lyric-wise writing. And I was a little ahead of my time! When we cut that I had all these jazz players on the record too. I had Red Prysock on tenor. And I had Billy Butler on guitar. Remember him? He's fabulous, one of the greatest in the business. See, we were in the service together, in World War II. They came around, you know, the company said, "We got any talent? We got to have a talent show pretty soon. You come up to the band room and give the bandmaster your name, we'll see." So I said, well now, I better think of something to go up there with. And then I sat down in the barracks and I wrote a thing called "Count Cadence." That's the way they count, when they're marching, they said, instead of one, two, they said hup, two, three, four. But what happened is, when I went up to the band room now, a fifteen-

Courtesy of Larry Simon.

Dr. Horse and "Wild" Jimmy Spruill at the Blue Frog, the Bronx, March 1993.

piece band, you know who was in the rhythm section? Billy Butler. And Shep Shepherd, he was a drummer with Bill Doggett on "Honky Tonk."

Simon: Oh, OK. Billy Butler . . . He cowrote "Honky Tonk"?

Dr. Horse: I think he did. But you know, Bill [Doggett], naturally, he was a leader so I think his name was on there. See, Billy [Butler] was just fooling around, you know, riffing a little bit, practicing or something. Billy made an unusual riff there on the guitar, when he played the solo there. Guitar players had to take a year to learn that [*laughs*].

Simon: Yeah, everyone has to learn that solo. It's perfect.

Dr. Horse: Yeah, that was something. So Billy said, "I was just fooling round. You know how you do things like that." And so, yeah, I had him on the session ["Jack, That Cat Was Clean"] when I cut for Bobby on Fire Records. And that really took off. The other side had "Salt Pork, West Virginia." The last thing that I recorded [about 1982], for a private company, it's a thing called "Somebody Got to Go." That's a blues thing. That's the last thing I done.[4]

Courtesy of Victor Pearlin.

Simon: When you were on Fifty-Second Street, did other musicians sometimes come by and sit in with you?

Dr. Horse: Oh, they came by to see what was happening, but if you got Art Tatum next door or Billie Holiday and you see these guys in there, what they are doing [*laughing*], you got to laugh yourself. We were doing some funny things. Yeah, like John Kirby, he used to come over to catch us; Charlie Shavers used to watch us work. They'd come in on the break to catch us, you know. They were working next door.

Simon: And who wrote the material that your band did?

Dr. Horse: Oh, we did ourselves. But also things that were out, we used to do things like "Undecided." Remember when Ella [Fitzgerald] was doing that? But

Dr. Horse, Larry Dale, and Bobby Robinson at the Blue Frog, the Bronx, March 1993.

we'd do it our way. We had a kazoo there, you know, plus we had the washboard with the thimbles [*laughs*]. We were noted for a beat that we had, like the Savoy Sultans. See, it was a washboard, the guitar, the maracas, and the piano.

Simon: You also did the recordings "I Think I Know" and "I'm Tired of It" also with Billy Butler and Red Prysock?

Dr. Horse: Yeah, that's right. I did that with Bobby [Robinson, in 1961].

Simon: What do you think of rap music the way it is now? You know, "Jack That Cat Was Clean" is considered one of the earliest rap records. What do you feel about what it sounds like now?

Dr. Horse: I always get that question wherever we play, people come ask me. So I decided I'd sit down and put it into music what I think of rap music today. Yeah, it's called "Crazy Beat": "I ain't no rock 'n' roll fan, but I like to hear that crazy beat. It's just a little something about it that makes me want to tap my feet." So that's the lyrics. And then I did another thing about my mother-in-law, and it was called "Woman! You Talk Too Much."[5]

Simon: Do you enjoy listening to what's on the radio now for rap?

Dr. Horse: Well, it's a little confusing there. You don't hear no tunes, no melody, like you used to. It's like words and rhythm. I wrote a couple of ballads, a thing called "I Had a Dream." That was with the Ink Spots, I was second tenor. That's on the other side of the last thing I done, with the Spots. And the other side is "Somebody Got to Go."[6]

Simon: Have any of your songs that you wrote been published?

Dr. Horse: No. I got to get it with BMI [Broadcast Music, Inc., the performing rights collection agency]. I want to get them all published.

Simon: How did you start playing cocktail drums?

Dr. Horse: Well, [*laughs*] what happened is, when I went with the Spots [Ink Spots in 1967], as a rule, they only had the guitar but they had the big band, the original group, they had that big band behind them. So, with the agent that got me with the group, see, he wanted to send us out with just the piano and you know the guitar like they used to have. But I said, "You can't do that." You got to have some kind of a little rhythm there when you don't have the band. Some cocktail drums, what I'm using now. Because what used to happen is, you'd get a guy with a thousand dollars' worth of drums but he didn't want to bend. You know, they get foolish. So I told them I, I'd like to get some cocktail drums. So he said, what's that? I said, "It's a large tom-tom." "So who's going to play that?" I say, "I'm going to play it" [*laughter*]. So I got it, and I fooled around in my house. You got to have some kind of little movement there, you know? So that's why I started to play the drum.

Simon: Was the Musical Jockeys the name of your band after you had the Tramps group?

Dr. Horse: Yeah, that's right. We were booked in one of the biggest rooms, I mean, biggest houses—that was MCA at 745 Fifth Avenue [formerly the Squibb Building]. The way we happen to get this, I don't know if you ever heard of a guy by the name of [Emmett] "Babe" Wallace. When Chick Webb died [in 1939], Wallace started to front the band there for awhile with Ella [Fitzgerald]. And he's very talented. But we recorded a demo with him. You'd have to send in a dub [demo recording] to get into the big places. You know, they want to know what you're doing. So we backed him up one day at Nola's [recording studio, 111 West Fifty-Seventh Street near] Broadway, doing two of his numbers. And it's a funny thing—the guys that he went to see, when they heard the dub, they wanted to know what group was behind him. So he was nice enough to tell them it was my group. And they sent for me to come down to MCA. And I went down there. And he said—they wanted me—they said, bring the group, and you'll be at 745 Fifth Avenue at two o'clock in the afternoon, so everybody was there, and two guys sittin' in there said, just go through your routine. So we just went through about five numbers. And we started on the sixth number, and we finished. So the guy, he called me over to the table where the two of them were sitting. He says, "I want you to go to Room 7 and pick up the contract, 'cause you open at the Five O'Clock Club in Washington, DC, next week." It was a Monday, I said to myself, "I wonder what he's been drinking?" [*laughs*]. Yeah, I'm telling you, that's one of the prettiest rooms at that time, the Five O'Clock Club in Washington, DC.

Simon: Are we now talking about your group Dr. Horse and the Musical Jockeys?

Dr. Horse at the Blue Frog, the Bronx, March 1993.

Dr. Horse and unidentified bass player, Cajun Cafe, New York, 1993.

Dr. Horse: Yeah, yeah. That's right. But it was just changing the name from the Pork Chops to Dr. Horse and the Musical Jockeys.

Simon: Was anyone else in your family musical, or were you the first one to start doing music?

Dr. Horse: Well, I can only say this here, my old man was a minister, so he was musical when he start preaching. Naturally we sang in church, but not in the choir. We'd sing there. But I mean, we were brought up in church. And that's what you'll hear. That really was rhythm, when the people say rhythm, you hear the sisters. That's right.

Simon: How did you meet Bobby Robinson?

Dr. Horse: Bobby had heard about me, about the Musical Jockeys. One thing I'll always say about him, he can hear, 'cause he had a religious label too, you know [Revelation Records].[7] And so he had to hear, listen to that, plus the R&B and all that. That's why I say, he could hear, and he knows how to record a person. Once he's behind the glass in there, he doesn't distract you from doing what you . . . he can hear. You do two takes: He knows which one he's going to use, instead of doing eight or nine or ten, he could hear, and that's what happened. Everybody can't do that. And I give him credit for that, he can. So, yeah, he can

Dr. Horse with Larry Simon, sound check at the Blue Frog, the Bronx, 1993.

Dr. Horse and band at the Cajun Cafe, New York, 1993.

hear that, that "Jack, That Cat Was Clean." He told me, he said, you know, that's a little different from what I had for a while. [Red] Prysock, at that time he was very hot, you know, and he said, "I think you got a big one here." Billy just laughed when they heard that, you know, Billy Butler.

Simon: So when you did the recording for Bobby Robinson and you used Billy Butler and Red Prysock, those were not guys you were regularly playing with? Were those just guys you did the recordings with?

Dr. Horse: No, that wasn't the guys in the working band.

Simon: OK. So is there anything you would like to say about what plans you have coming up before concluding the interview?

Dr. Horse: Well, one thing I'd like to say, that I was lucky enough to work with some of the finest people in the show world. But all in all, to do something that I never, never could do—I really think I can. And that's write a musical. In fact, I did do one, but my partner Edgar Hayes, the pianist that played "Stardust" . . . so what happened is, I told him before, I said I'm writing a musical here. I said I think we might have a shot with it. And I said I want to open with Basie and I want six of the best comics and twenty-three chorus girls. And he said, you couldn't do it—how you gonna do that? They wouldn't buy that. I said, no, listen, and I kept going with it. And about a month later, I didn't know they were rehearsing, but when I showed them that I had written down was the same thing as *Sophisticated Ladies* [Broadway, 1981]. You understand what I'm saying? They had the same thing, with the star Gregory Hines, the same idea that I had with the big band, but I was gonna use not quite as big a name as they had. Like Irene Reid, did you ever hear of her? I was going to use her. Because when I first heard her, I was thinking she was always underrated as a star. But he [Hayes] called me, says, you know, you had that idea, why didn't you stick with it until it was finished? I said, now you tell me! So that was that.

NOTES

1. According to Marv Goldberg, author of *More Than Words Can Say: The Ink Spots and Their Music* (Lanham, MD: Scarecrow Press, 1998), Al Pittman worked with several Ink Spots groups, including those led by Charles Ward and Jim Nabbie. Goldberg added, "From June 1968 until sometime in late 1970, those Ink Spots were Jimmie Nabbie (first tenor), Johnny Taylor (second tenor), King Drake (baritone), Doc Pittman (bass). By November 1970, Taylor had been replaced by second tenor George Smith (from the 1963 group)." For a short while in 1970, Sonny Til, the famous lead singer of the Orioles, was a member of the Ink Spots.

2. The Kapp LP *The Blues Ain't Nothin' but a Good Man Feelin' Bad!* is credited to Sammy Price and his Bluesicians featuring Doc Horse (1961).

3. As Dr. Horse, he had two singles for Bobby Robinson's Fire label: "I'm Tired of It"/"Think I Know (1961) and "Jack, That Cat Was Clean"/"Salt Pork, West Virginia" (1962). The latter song was a huge hit for Louis Jordan back in 1946.

4. "Somebody Got to Go," in the name of the Original "Doc" Pittman and the Unforgettable Ink Spots, arranged by Leroy Kirkland, was released as a 12-inch single on the J. J. label in 1982. Before that, the Unforgettable Ink Spots had a mid-1970s single on the GP label (with "Mark My Words" vocalized and written by Pittman).

5. Pittman recorded "Crazy Beat"/"Woman! You Talk Too Much" in the name of Al (Dr. Horse) Pittman with the Musical Jockeys for the Clown label of Brooklyn in 1960.

6. See note 4 above. The J. J. release on Discogs.com has "Stardust" on the B side, not "I Had a Dream."

7. Revelation Records was run by Bobby Robinson with John Bowden and Clarence "Fats" Lewis between 1959 and 1962 from the Fire-Fury group offices at 271 West 125th Street, Harlem, New York.

5

NOBLE "THIN MAN" WATTS AND JUNE BATEMAN

Interviewed at Watts's apartment in Brooklyn, New York,
with his wife, singer June Bateman, present, November 1993

NOBLE WATTS

Noble "Thin Man" Watts, from DeLand, Florida, was a blues, jump blues tenor sax player. Watts had a history of playing across a variety of styles and had a national hit in 1958 with "Hard Times" (Baton). He worked with such luminaries as Lionel Hampton, Cannonball Adderley, the Griffin Brothers, Dinah Washington, and many of the artists interviewed in this book, among countless others. Noble Watts loomed large on the New York blues scene in the 1950s and 1960s. He died in DeLand, his birthplace, in 2004. His wife was the singer June Bateman.

JUNE BATEMAN

June Bateman (birth name Marian June Batemon) was born on November 17, 1939, in Schulenburg, Texas, and moved to Chappaqua, New York, at an early age. After meeting Noble Watts in New York City, her professional career took off with 45-rpm recordings on Bobby Robinson's Fury and Enjoy labels, Danny Robinson's Holiday and Everlast labels, and others. She relocated to Florida in 1984 and died in DeLand in 2016.

When I interviewed June and Noble Watts I was invited to their very nice apartment in Brooklyn. Noble would travel between his place in Florida and Brooklyn to be with June. They were both very gracious. June was extremely kind and often tried to fill in some remarks on behalf of Noble. His nature was much

Noble "Thin Man" Watts (1926–2004) and June Bateman (1939–2016), at their apartment, Brooklyn, New York, November 1993.

more introverted. He was open to being interviewed but seemed somewhat awkward talking about himself. He really lit up when I asked him about artists he liked and were influential to him. As we went along, he loosened up and became more excited about recalling his experiences. June, at the time, had a job working for the state of New York. Noble was still playing but was concerned about upcoming medical issues curtailing his work.

Larry Simon: Tell me a bit about where you were born and how you started in the business.

Noble Watts: I was always in love with music, so, in the little town that I grew up in, in Florida, it's named DeLand, there never was much of anything going on there. I came up in there and it was during the 1920s and '30s. And it was really racially upset, two sides of the tracks. I was in love with music. I used to hear a band downtown, a commercial band, a community band, rehearse, and I would run downtown and sit in a tree and watch them. My first big musical trip was on the piano. I had a lady, there was a schoolteacher there, our little school, she was on the other side of the tracks—our school. It was in the days of segregation and I learned the basics.

She agreed to teach me the basics. I thought I was going to be able to do what I wanted with that. So I began to get a little tired of going to lessons. My daddy knew I was in love with music and I always tried to follow music, so he had heard of Stetson University, in DeLand, and there was a violinist on the musical staff. He agreed to give me violin lessons. In return I would clean his yard for him. So I agreed to take violin, not that I was in love with the violin, but I wanted anything musical I could get. So I took violin for about a year, and there was a band, in Daytona, which is about seventeen miles away, Daytona Beach it was much more of an aggressive town than my town. They had a black high school band over there, I guess about forty, fifty [kids], and a very, very good dance band. I thought that was the most wonderful thing I had ever seen in my life, the young kids playing jazz. So that's when I was attracted to the brass. I was a trumpet player for ten years. And I met up with Cannonball Adderley.

Simon: In Florida?

Watts: Yeah, that's where he's from. Tallahassee. He was born in Tampa, but he was reared in Tallahassee.[1] His parents would allow him to go and play during the summer when school was out, so I was allowed to do just about the same thing. But I was getting ready to go astray and quit school, but I kept on, but I could play. They were fast company, they always were fast company [*chuckling*], but they wanted me to come to college at A&M.[2] And that got me to the point where I wanted to go to college. So I did go back to the school where I was, at high school in DeLand, and then I went on to A&M College. That's where we became the thirteen original members of the Florida A&M band—thirteen members was the dance band. I participated in so many of the different musical

Noble Watts, Brooklyn, November 1993.

groups and activities. I was playing trumpet until I lost control of the muscle. And I couldn't play the trumpet no more. I liked the sax anyway from the beginning but I was afraid, so many keys. From there I jumped on, I had to learn something—I was also interested in playing around with horns, the clarinet. So I picked up the saxophone and I liked to play saxophone. I got on the wagon and I been on the wagon ever since.

Simon: So you started off all your work in Florida but then you ended up in New York.

Watts: Yeah, well, yeah. Played with all the dance bands all through Florida, and a couple of other groups. One of them was called Charlie Brantley and [his Original] Honey Dippers. They were out in Tampa and we had six, maybe seven pieces. It was a rhythm & blues group in the style of Louis Jordan.[3] Billy Eckstine wanted the group so bad he had to bring us to New York but the leader [Brantley] wouldn't go for it because he thought he would lose the top billing. That would have been the biggest billing he'd ever have had in his life anyway if he would have had a billing with Billy Eckstine. But he was kind of an older guy. We was young guys, and he was an old guy, but he was the show. He was carrying on all this kind of foolishness like Louis Armstrong and a fool clown, and he had gotten to be big in the area. We just spread it out. It was going to be a great band, but he wouldn't go for coming to New York. Billy Eckstine came down [to Florida] to do that when he was real hot.[4] And they booked us to play behind him. And when we got to the place where we were playing, which was the biggest black club in the Florida, in this area, it was the Two Spot, in Jacksonville,[5] he heard the band and he ran back out and got his horn and he played all night long with the band. He did the whole show with the band, and he was a great big star doing that. So many different adventures that I could talk about.

Simon: How did you up end in New York?

Watts: The way I got to New York, I was ready to get the hell out of Florida. The money wasn't like it is today. You can get up and go. So when one of the boys with one of the most popular bands come through Florida and they had a record out, they was on jukeboxes—that was your ticket. I left with a group out of Norfolk, Virginia, was called the Griffin Brothers. And that came in 1951, and they had a hit record with Margie Day, "Little Red Rooster."[6] And I joined the band in Tampa, Florida. I left the Honey Dippers and went with them. During the time Dot Records recorded all the white boys.[7] We was the first black band they really recorded, the Griffin Brothers. We had to do something to follow up "Little Red Rooster," and they hired me in Florida and we went back and we did an instrumental called "Shuffle Bug," and that made the charts.[8] Ever heard of Daddy Grace's church uptown [in Norfolk, Virginia]? Yeah, well all right, Daddy Grace had bands in his church, and these two boys was in his band at one time, the Griffin Brothers, grew up in that religion, and one of them [Buddy] was a pretty good musician, a pianist, he finished Juilliard [School of Music, New York]. I think it was about five or six of us in the band. So I worked the Apollo Theatre, I came with them to New York. They was based out of Norfolk, Virginia. And we'd go on tour. Irvin Feld, he used to bring the [Ringling Bros. and Barnum & Bailey] circus downtown, one of the biggest producers—he started putting these things together and calling them packages, putting different black groups, sending them out on these shows. So we would go out and play—we would have maybe twenty-five engagements throughout the states of North and South Carolina. We had two or three different bands, whatever, maybe a singer. I remember I ran into Paul Williams. We was booked in with Paul Williams, and I liked his band—"The Huckle-Buck" [Williams's 1949 no. 1 R&B hit song].[9] Larry Dale was with him for a while also. So that's how I got to New York.

Simon: And then you [referring to June Bateman] both met in New York City?

June Bateman: Yes, much, much later.

Simon: When did you both meet?

Bateman: We met in New York when Noble had his hit record, "Hard Times." Jimmy Spruill was with him. So I met him in about [early 1958]. Yes.

Simon: And were you singing with another group?

Courtesy of Victor Pearlin.

Bateman: Well, you know, as a youngster, I was with the doo-wops, and Jimmy Spruill, he introduced me to Noble. He said I want you to hear this girl, she sings the blues. Which at the time Noble was really jazz, so I don't think he really cared that much who June Bateman was. It worked out in the long run.

Simon: So you were primarily with jazz groups.

Watts: Lionel Hampton. But I was always one of the jazz artists, yeah. Bill Doggett, Tiny Bradshaw.

Paul Williams in his office
at home in Harlem, 1986.
Photos by Paul Harris.

Simon: On the King label?

Watts: That's right, King, that's right.

Simon [to June Bateman]: So then you recorded together once you met, doing blues or R&B oriented material?

Bateman: Well, at the time I was, I'd been working with four fellas, doo-wop, called the Marquis at the time.[10] And I went as a soloist. So when I would go around, you know, as a kid you're starry eyed, big time. "Hey, I'm with the guy who played 'Hard Times.'" And I did a few dates with Noble, including Sugar Ray Robinson, so it sort of caught on and he learnt me about my timing and so forth, which I didn't know at that time.

Simon: Because some of those records are still available now, being reissued.

Bateman: Yes. In fact we've been able to get quite a few of them. Some we had forgotten about. Yeah, I got a hold of a few that Noble was on with the Baton label.

Simon: That was in New York that label wasn't it?

Bateman: Yes.

Bateman: Yes, Sol Rabinowitz ran the label.[11]

Watts: Big [i.e., tall] man. Now he's in Greece running labels over in that area.

Simon: And you started putting your own bands together at a certain point, right?

Watts: Yeah, yeah, in 1957.

Simon: And what was your first recording that you had with your own band?

Watts: "Pig Ears and Rice"[12] [*chuckles*]. And it didn't do anything. And the [third] was "Hard Times" [Baton], that was top [50].[13] It's still, right now, it's a classic.

Simon: Another popular tune you wrote was "Jookin" [for Bobby Robinson's Enjoy label in late 1962].

Watts: [June] woke me up one morning when I was sleeping, humming something to me like that, oh yeah.

Bateman: Yeah. It was just something that came in my mind, I woke him up.

June Bateman at home,
Brooklyn, November 1993.

Simon: So that's your idea?

Watts: Uh huh.

Bateman: Yeah, "Jookin" was originally my idea.

Watts: She gets credit, she gets credit for it.

Bateman: The flip side of it, Noble and I did a duo on "What Ya Gonna Do."

Simon: So you knew Jimmy before you knew Noble even.

Bateman: Yes, in fact Jimmy and I used to record with King Curtis, and so we did a lot of things together before I met Noble. He's my godbrother. Yeah, we're extremely close. That's family. We stay in touch.

Simon [to Watts]: Do you have a favorite recording of your own, a recording that you wrote that's your favorite?

Watts: All of them that sold anything.

Simon: And who are your favorite musicians to listen to, that influenced you?

Watts: Actually I like Gene Ammons.

Bateman: His favorite, I must say.

Watts: Sonny Stitt.

Bateman: Stanley . . .

Watts: Stanley Turrentine. And he used to love me, but Stanley got better than me. Yeah, I like him. I really like Dexter Gordon, all of those guys. That's the days I come from.

Simon: Do you know Bob Gaddy and Larry Dale? They did some stuff on Hy Weiss's Old Town label.

Bateman: Larry is one of my homeboys. He's from Texas. I'm originally from Texas. King Curtis, I think he was from Fort Worth [he was].

Simon: So now you work for New York State?

Bateman: Yes, I'm a travel promotion agent for the state. Travel consultant. Yeah, we promote the Island of New York program.

Simon: So the ads on TV for vacationing in New York, is that from your department?

Bateman: Yeah. In fact I'm on the way now to the National Tourism Convention in Atlantic City in the morning.

Simon: And how come you stopped doing music?

Bateman: One-nighters. I thought that one [referring to Noble] in the business was enough. At one point it was OK but then we started going out on one-nighters with big shows, Jackie Wilson, Brook Benton, so I said one night, "Noble, this is it. I'll go back to New York." I didn't mind the clubs but the one-nighters had gotten a little much for me.

Simon [to Watts]: And you also went to school with Nat Adderley, right?[14]

Watts: Yeah. We was classmates: Nat and Cannonball.

Simon: Who else came out of it, of the A&M marching band from the time you were in it?

Noble Watts, Brooklyn,
November 1993.

Noble "Thin Man" Watts
and "Wild" Jimmy Spruill,
rehearsal at the Blues
Estafette, Utrecht, the
Netherlands, November 20,
1993. Photo by Paul Harris.

Watts: Well, all thirteen of the boys that came out of the band were good musicians. Leonard Spearman, he's ambassador to Africa now [ambassador to Rwanda, 1988–1990; ambassador to Lesotho, 1991–1993]. Leonard Spearman, he was a trumpeter. William Wheeler, he went and got his doctorate in music, then he decided to go back to school in law.

Simon: Are you doing any recording projects that you're in the middle of now or do you have any that are planned coming up?

Watts: Not right now.

Simon: You want to get your medical stuff taken care of?

Watts: Well that's what I'm gonna see about, yeah. Gotta figure out what I'm gonna be able to do.[15]

Courtesy of Victor Pearlin.

NOTES

1. Julian "Cannonball" Adderley, the jazz alto saxophonist, was born on September 15, 1928, in Tampa, Florida, and died on August 8, 1975, in Gary, Indiana.

2. Now known as Florida A&M University in Tallahassee, at one time the school was called Florida Agricultural and Mechanical College for Negroes, then Florida A&M College.

3. For more on Charlie Brantley, an influential territorial bandleader but not very well known today, see the website www.tampabaymusichistory.com/charlie-brantley-and-his-original-honey-dippers.php. Ray Charles played piano in the band in 1947.

4. Billy Eckstine had a string of hit pop records for National and MGM between 1945 and 1951.

5. For more on the Two Spot club in Jacksonville, see: www.jaxhistory.org/portfolio-items/two-spot/.

6. "Little Red Rooster" by Margie Day with the Griffin Brothers (Dot) was a no. 5 *Billboard* R&B hit in early 1951.

7. Noble Watts was referring to the later pop success of Randy Wood's Dot label—first of Gallatin, Tennessee, then of Hollywood—with artists such as Pat Boone, the Hilltoppers, and Gale Storm. In fact, among the early Dot blues artists were Brownie McGhee and Bob Gaddy.

8. "Shuffle Bug," an instrumental featuring the saxophone of Watts, was actually the flip side of a no. 1 *Billboard* R&B hit by the Griffin Brothers featuring Tommy Brown, "Weepin' and Cryin'" (Dot), in January 1952.

9. Watts recorded with Paul Williams for Vee-Jay Records, of Chicago, in December 1956, resulting in two singles.

10. June Bateman was featured as lead with the Marquis on "Bohemian Daddy"/"Hope He's True" (for Jerry Winston's Onyx label) in late 1956 in the popular style of Frankie Lymon and the Teenagers. The Marquis, from central Harlem, also comprised Lloyd Lomelino, Ronnie "Rocco" Mack (who wrote the Chiffons' 1963 no. 1 hit, "He's So Fine"), Robert "Babe" Stowers, and unknown (Charlie?). Bateman's first solo single was cut for Danny Robinson's Holiday label about June 1957, with Jimmy Spruill taking the guitar honors. Her "Believe Me, Darling" (Fury, 1960), written by Spruill and featuring his immaculate guitar, is a favorite soulful blues record.

11. See John Broven with Richard Tapp, "Sol Rabinowitz's Baton Records," *Juke Blues*, no. 72, 2012. In 1961, Rabinowitz joined the Epic Records subsidiary of Columbia and relaunched OKeh Records before joining CBS International. Prior to retiring in 1986, he spent his last ten years with CBS starting up a successful division in Greece, as Watts stated.

12. "Pig Ears and Rice" coupled with "Mashing Potatoes" was Watts's very first release, in the name of the Noble Watts Quintet, for De Luxe Records, the King subsidiary, in December 1954.

13. "Hard Times," released originally as "The Slop" with the tag line "The New Teen-Age Dance Sensation," made no. 44 in the *Billboard* Top 100 in early 1958. Credited to Noble "Thin Man" Watts and his Rhythm Sparks, the instrumental featured Jimmy Spruill on guitar.

14. In 1990, Watts recorded an LP with Nat Adderley, *Noble & Nat*, for Bob Greenlee's King Snake Records of Sanford, Florida. Previously for King Snake, Watts had cut the *Return of the Thin Man* LP in 1987, reissued by Alligator in 1990.

15. Just after this interview, Watts recorded in 1994 as a guest soloist on *Goin' Back to Daytona* by Floyd Miles (King Snake CD). Watts's last solo recording from 1993, done just prior to this interview, was the *King of the Boogie Sax* CD (Wild Dog Records, a subsidiary of Ichiban).

6

BOBBY ROBINSON

Interviewed at Bobby Robinson's record store,
Bobby's Happy House, Harlem, September 19, 1993

Morgan "Bobby" Robinson, born in Union, South Carolina, was a crucial figure in the New York blues scene. A major producer and owner of important
independent labels including Fire, Fury, and Enjoy, he also was a songwriter
and talent scout. Over the course of his career, Robinson had a no. 1 pop hit
in 1959 with Wilbert Harrison's "Kansas City," a magnificent achievement, and
recorded well-known R&B and blues artists such as Gladys Knight, King Curtis, Elmore James, Champion Jack Dupree, Lightnin' Hopkins, and Arthur "Big
Boy" Crudup. Robinson also recorded doo-wop, soul, and some of the earliest
rap artists, including Grandmaster Flash, Spoonie Gee, and Doug E. Fresh. The
majority of the artists in this book worked with Mr. Robinson, a true legend.

In 1946, Bobby Robinson opened his famous record store that became
known as Bobby's Happy House. In the course of speaking to John Broven for
Juke Blues magazine in 1986, Robinson related how he'd come to open his small
shop combined with a shoeshine parlor, which according to him was the first
black-owned enterprise on 125th Street. There was a small, high-end hat shop
that was no longer doing such good trade, and he made an offer to take over
the lease. The elderly owners had been planning on retiring, so a deal was made.
Bobby bought four electric shoeshine machines that were in the front part of
the store, with a tiny record section in the back. At first his shoeshine business
was bringing in more money, but eventually, due in large part to the store's prox-
imity to the Apollo Theatre, the Baby Grand club, Frank's Steakhouse, and the
Theresa Hotel, where the Apollo artists stayed, his store became popular, and the
music won out. Musicians, as well as those at the business end such as Ahmet
Ertegun of Atlantic Records, Leonard Chess, and the Bihari brothers of Modern
Records, would all stop by to see how their records were selling and to see what
advice Bobby could impart on buying trends. He had broken a barrier. At that

Bobby Robinson (1917–2011), in front of Bobby's Happy House record store, 125th Street, Harlem, September 19, 1993.

time, the shops on 125th Street might have had African American employees but were not generally black owned. This was a truly important and indelible part of Bobby Robinson's remarkable legacy. Latterly, his shop was a popular tourist destination, but it closed in 2008, a victim of Harlem's escalating gentrification. At the age of ninety, Robinson never fully recovered from this devastating blow.

To offer a personal note, I consider myself fortunate to have known Bobby. He was a very friendly and outgoing gentleman. Full of fascinating stories, he had enormous energy and enthusiasm looking ahead to new projects. And he always took a minute to ask after one's family. When I was touring overseas, he'd check in with my wife—my daughter had just been born—and give a call to make sure all was well. I never forgot that; it was so thoughtful.

This interview shows how Bobby Robinson came from a poor farming background in the South, was influenced by early gospel choirs, and took every opportunity to spot and create hit records emanating from the streets of Harlem. Bobby was an inveterate storyteller; some of his tales were occasionally on the taller side, but those quoted here are corroborated by the use of extensive footnotes.

Larry Simon: You had an early label with your brother Danny?
Bobby Robinson: Yeah, Red Robin Records.[1] Yeah, he got out of it. Like I told him, he's not a real dyed-in-the-wool music man, you know. He's still in

the music business, but he's a wholesaler. He's a wholesale jobber—been that for years. Worked out of the Bronx, worked out of his house [*laughs*]. A one-man operation. He got stores all down here and there, and the Bronx and Westchester, and whatnot.[2]

Simon: I'm curious to know, what are some of the recordings you've done that are your favorites, your personal favorites?

Robinson: Oh . . . I got so many I don't know. I cut my first record in [1951]. And I've been recording ever since. And I did a lot of things. I had about ten labels I recorded on.[3]

Simon: So there's just hundreds of things?

Robinson: Yeah, and so I got two or three books of songs I did. Let's see. Well, I got to say, "Kansas City" by Wilbert Harrison, "Soul Twist" by King Curtis, "There's Something on Your Mind" by Bobby Marchan, "It's Too Late" by Tarheel Slim and Little Ann, "Fannie Mae" by Buster Brown. These were all big, big records. And Gladys Knight and the Pips, "Every Beat of My Heart,"[4] and a couple of other things I did on them.

Courtesy of Victor Pearlin.

Larry Dale and Bobby Robinson
in front of Bobby's Happy House
record store, 125th Street, Harlem,
September 19, 1993.

Courtesy of the *Juke Blues* archive.

I was at the Rock and Roll Hall of Fame awards in 1992 at the Waldorf Astoria in New York City. I made an acceptance speech on behalf of Elmore James, he was my artist.[5] I've been trying for two years to get a videotape copy of my speech. I finally got it yesterday, it's terrific, man! It was in the Grand Ballroom. I didn't have anything written out, I figured what the hell, I know everything about him, I just went out there and got a standing ovation. I was Elmore James's manager and producer, so I accepted the award on his behalf.

Simon: I heard you first met Elmore James when you were driving around Chicago?

Robinson: Elmore James first recorded in Jackson, Mississippi, where he was living.[6] He was a radio repair man so the lady [Lillian McMurry of Trumpet Records] who ran [the Record Mart furniture and record store] decided she wanted to cut records with some artists she had there. So she asked Elmore just to be one of the two guitar players who played behind the guy singing. So she got there and the guy [Sonny Boy Williamson no. 2 (Rice Miller)] did some sides and finished. And she said, "Elmore, why don't you do another one?" And he said, "I don't know, I just do other people's songs." She said, "Go ahead and sing one from when you work nightclubs." They kept after him, he didn't want to do it at all. So he did a standard blues thing they did on gigs ["Dust My Broom"]. The guys backed him up and that's all he did, one side. This was 1951.[7] So she put out the record with Elmore on one side and someone else on the other [Bobo Thomas].

I used to get records in to review in my record shop [on 125th Street] that used to be around the corner from this one [Bobby's Happy House]. I listen to this and I said, "Goddamn!" I was struck by his authenticity and sound. So I couldn't wait till the next day came. I called down to Mississippi. I called the company and spoke to the lady and she said she hadn't seen Elmore in months, he just disappeared. So I started to search for him. I called some blues guys I knew in New Orleans and other places. He went out west and did some things in California.[8] Finally, this was years later, he had a heart attack, I didn't know about that. I was in Chicago promoting another hit record I had, a record called "Fannie Mae" by Buster Brown [in late 1959]. So, in the evening like I usually do, I got in my car. Chicago was full of nightclubs, blues everywhere you go. I just want to see what I could find, you know, so I was just driving around: a club over here, a club over there, and there was this club, you can hardly see it, had a lattice on the wall like a yard, two steps down, then you are in the club. There was a sign hanging on the lattice that said, "Elmore James here tonight." I saw that and stopped, put on my brakes, backed up and looked at it again. I had given up, I didn't know where to find him. I pulled over and parked my car. I went in and there were three guys sitting at the long bar, and then you step up two steps and there was another section at the end of the bar. There were three guys: a drummer, bass player, and this guy with a guitar in his lap. I had never seen a picture of Elmore James; I didn't know what he looked like, nothing. So I approached them and I said, "Who is Elmore James in this crowd?" He said, "That's me." I said, "Are you the original Elmore James?" He said, "The one and only." I said, "I'm going to sit here at the end of this bar and get a drink. When you guys start to play and the minute you open your mouth I'll know if you are the man I'm looking for. If you are, I'm buying the drinks and the drinks are Scotch. If you're not, the drinks are beer." They started and I knew that was him, nobody else sounds like him and I was so excited. He had just come to Chicago that same day! And I was looking for him for years! I recorded him the next day [in November 1959]. When he finished in the club I didn't let him out of my sight. We went out and had dinner and talked till daybreak. He was living over somewhere around Forty-Fifth Street in a big house with a lady and I went home with him. We were sitting in the living room and it started to rain. It was pouring down rain the next morning. I had stayed there all night. I had found out he had no recording contract. He had that heart attack. For three years he's been down on the farm in Mississippi there, foolin' around doin' nothin'. So we got up the next day, called three or four guys over, the two guys he had plus a saxophone player and a piano player that he knew. All the boys were originally from Mississippi. When he come to Chicago to play he didn't need to bring a band 'cause all his homeboys were here, just get together and back him up. So we got these guys over there and were sitting around. Elmore and I went by the window and we was looking out in the street and it was pouring down, floods of rain. He said it looks like the sky is crying. So I said, "What did you say?" He said, "Looks like the sky is crying, water looks like tears rolling down the street." And when he said that I said, "Come over here, man, sit down." I got a pencil and pad and I say, "Strike me a lonely weird sound." And he did it and the bass came behind. And I sat there and wrote it out. And he put in a word or two here and there and in a few minutes' time we had "The Sky Is Crying."[9] And they got to playin' it. And just what he was doing, all the band fill in with that. And we ran that down seven or eight times. We had nothing written. I was afraid overnight we go back home some guy would go to sleep and forget what he did. So we did it seven or eight times until I was satisfied we had captured it, we had a sound. Everyone had it down. I didn't have a tape recorder there. And I said, "Rain or no rain, I'm afraid to let the guys go home." We had nothing written, some guy would forget. I wanted to capture this identical sound. I said, "Suppose we rent a studio and cut it right now?" I got on the phone and called a studio in downtown Chicago and set up for seven o'clock. Got into two cars, soaking wet, we got in there. I was sure if we hadn't done it that night after working on it three or four hours, the next day it would've been some different thing. I was so excited about it we had nothing else to do, he had no other song. I said, "Oh shit, what are we gonna put on the other side?" He said, "I got a little instrumental thing

I do at dances when I play around; everyone seems to like it, they request it, I got no name for it. I'll tell you what I'm going to do, if you like it we'll call it, "Bobby's Rock."[10] I said, "OK, let me hear it." So he showed the band, it was a nice little funky thing. I said, "OK, good, do that." So we left there and the next time I brought him into the studio, that was in New York. He came alone and I had a fifteen-piece band, big horn section, four or five horns. I handpicked the guys.[11]

Simon: What label of yours is that on?

Robinson: That was on Fire Records. We did a big session that night, all night long, we started 8:00 p.m. I got a case of beer and sandwiches. We had a party there, the place was full of people and we did about ten sides or twelve sides that night.

Courtesy of Victor Pearlin.

Simon: What about arrangements for the band?

Robinson: No arrangements, nothing I did for him was arranged.

Simon: With fifteen guys, how did everyone know what to play?

Robinson: I had the guy who did "The Huckle-Buck" in charge of the horns, that was Paul Williams. He would tell the guys what to play. He would tell the guitar player or the drummer do this here, do this there, work it out like that. Every time we get ready to do another thing we'd do it like that all night long. Never had a written thing. Elmore James was very easy to follow.

Simon: Not like someone like Lightnin' Hopkins?

Robinson: I gave Lightnin' Hopkins the biggest record he ever had [in 1961]. And guess what? We only had a drummer with brushes [Delmar Donnell]. Hopkins had an acoustic guitar so I had the guy put a mic stand right in front and set him on a high chair with the mic right between his legs and another mic by his guitar. And he recorded nine sides for me, and the drummer was just following him. I'd say put a fill here and there. And I got the biggest record he ever had, "Mojo Hand."[12]

Simon: Did he have to do a lot of takes?

Robinson: No, I just run it down and the drummer would follow him wherever he would go.

Lightnin' Hopkins, Hunter College, New York, 1974. Photo © by Anton Mikofsky, used with permission.

Simon: What about Elmore James, same thing, one take?

Robinson: Yeah.

Simon: What is your approach as producer? Some producers like to get involved with arranging and getting their own stamp on it. Other producers like to let the artist's vision be primary.

Robinson: Well, I get my stamp on it because Paul Williams was directing the horns, but I made changes here and there; do this here, bring this in here. So I had my stamp on it. Even though I wasn't a musician as such, I would tell him and all the guys why don't you do this and do that, or right here I want the full sound of the horns and we would work it out. Then maybe we would run it down again with just the guitar, bass, drums, and piano. And keep running it until I'm satisfied.

Simon: So you would give him directions and shape it up?

Robinson: When we got the sound where I wanted it we would cut it.

Simon: Did you find it easy to communicate with someone like Lightnin' Hopkins?

Robinson: Yeah, I could communicate with him. I cut him in Texas, and I cut him in New York. He was in a club in the Village—that's where I met him. I listened to him play for two or three hours then went back to the dressing room. That's how I first met him and he agreed to do a few things for me. I said, "How will we work it?" He said, "I don't know, let's do six or seven things. I have to fly back tomorrow evening. Let's record tomorrow, give me $400. I got no musicians with me." "So I'll get a drummer, that's all." So he said, "Give me $400 and you got it. I don't want no royalties, just give me $400 and I'm gone." He wouldn't sign with nobody. He recorded with about fifteen labels.[13] He just put the money in his pocket and he was gone.

Simon: When you write material do you generally come up with the ideas for the lyrics or do you also help with the ideas for the melodies and the lyrics?

Robinson: Everything.

Simon: Like when you did the song with Lee Dorsey?

Robinson: "Ya Ya?" I wrote that sitting in a bar in New Orleans [about June 1961]. I asked the barmaid for a sheet of paper. She handed me a little tablet with red lines she had over by the register. I had a pencil and I got a thing down here, see how you like that, see if she could feel this [*sings*] "Sitting here la la, waiting for my ya ya." "La la," that's just like a song, and "ya ya," that means a girl. The fact that you're sitting there waiting means that she's not there, she's late. Then I said, "May sound funny but I don't believe she's coming." Dorsey said, "Yeah." Then people started coming around and looking at us. We worked the whole thing out right at the bar in around thirty minutes. I knew it was a hit record, I just knew it. We worked it out just like that. I would run down a few lines. I'd say to Lee, "Let me hear you do it," I'd say, "that's it." Then he come up with a few lines, we'd fit it in here and there. So the next morning, I didn't know Allen Toussaint, he was hot then in New Orleans. "We'll get Toussaint to make an arrangement." Lee met me that morning and we went over to Allen Toussaint; we sang it for him, the two of us sang for him. And he was over on the piano [*Robinson sings what Toussaint played*]. And I said, "Man, I want you to do this for me." And he said, "I can't, I just signed with the record company exclusively.[14] I get a percentage of everything whether I do it or not, a percentage of everything they put out. They got me exclusively, I can't." That broke my heart. I said, "Man can you squeeze in one last session?" He said, "No, but I'll tell you what I'm going to do. I got a man arranges the same as I do." And I said, "Oh, shit, I don't want nobody else. This is your kind of a thing." He said, "You'll be satisfied." So he called Harold Battiste.[15] Harold came over to Allen's house and Lee had a little tape recorder with the piano part Allen had played and we gave him that. Lee and I sang for him and Harold made notes, that's all. It was simple. So he took his notes and the tape. The next afternoon he called and said, "Listen, you ready to come in at five o'clock? I got all the guys, I got it together." And Toussaint also gave us one of his songs.[16] We went in at five o'clock.[17] I had never seen the musicians before. He ran it down with the band for me to hear and I knew that was it! There was a little guy on piano [Marcel Richardson] that he got off a street corner. It was a funny thing, a little ol' skinny freckle-face guy and I never seen him before or since. And he had a little round hat he wore [on] his head. He wore it so much when he took it off the print of the hat was on his head; just got him off the street. Everybody in New Orleans is a musician. Everybody there damn near plays something. Everybody.

Simon: You're based here in New York. How did you hook up with his musicians in New Orleans?

Robinson: I was a very busy man back then. Here's what happened: a girlfriend of mine worked at ABC-Paramount Records [in New York]. And Lee Dorsey had done a song that was popular that they played in New Orleans during the [1961] carnival. There was a record company man from ABC down there who thought he might be able to get some action on it and he may be able to get him a deal and they pressed it. I always get copies of them sent to me here for my store. All the companies send me a lot of 45s. At night when it's kind of quiet I'm listening with a pencil and pad, the ones I like. I make notes, this one and that, the ones I want to order. I go on down the line. And I put this one on, I looked at it, Lee Dorsey. I had never heard of him.[18] I put it on and I listen to this thing, you know, damn this guy's got an odd sound. He sounded very odd, he didn't sound white, he didn't sound black, he was like in-between. So I got on the phone and called this girl Pearl Woods, this was my girl [at ABC-Paramount] and said, "Listen I got a couple of records from your people today and I played a thing by Lee Dorsey." She said, "Ain't it a bitch?" That's the first thing she said. She said, "That's an odd-sounding son of a bitch." She said, "Well, I've got news for you. They don't have him, ain't nobody have him, got no contract; they are trying out a record, seeing what happens to it. I don't know where he lives, but I know he's somewhere in New Orleans." She said, "I listen to that record, it's a bitch!" She was a songwriter, too, she was a funny girl.[19] I said New Orleans, all right, let me see if I can find him. I had been to New Orleans. I recorded a guy Bobby Marchan, he was also from New Orleans and I did a session on him down there the year before [with the Tick Tocks]. So I called this guy, he managed a lot of groups, I figured he'd know a lot of people,[20] and I said, "Listen, I got a record here from a guy in New Orleans named Lee Dorsey." He said "Yeah, yeah, ain't he good?" I said, "You know him?" He said, "Yeah, he lives right down the street here." I said, "Lay the phone down right now, don't touch it. Go get him!" He put his phone down and ran out and got him. That was amazing, because New Orleans is a big city, and the chances are the guy wouldn't know

FANNIE MAE ● SINCERELY ● GOING ON A PICNIC ● ST. LOUIS BLUES ● CORENA
IS YOU IS OR IS YOU AIN'T ● I'M GOING BUT I'LL BE BACK ● JOHN HENRY
MADISON SHUFFLE ● DON'T DOG YOUR WOMAN ● LOST IN A DREAM

FLP 102

FIRE
HIGH-FIDELITY RECORDS

BUSTER
BROWN
THE
NEW
KING
OF THE
BLUES

The Fire LP by Buster Brown, who had a big 1960 hit with "Fannie Mae." Courtesy of John Broven.

who the hell he is. So the guy came back and put him on the phone and I say, "You Lee Dorsey?" He said, "Yeah, that's me." I said, "I understand you don't have a contract, the people down at ABC told me." He said, "No, I'm not recording for nobody. I'm an automobile body and fender man, repair man. I just did that for the festival." I said, "Would you like to do some things, you have an odd sound, we can get something going on you." He said, "Yeah, I'll take a shot at it." I said, "I'll tell you what I'm gonna do, I'll be down there next week. I'm going to a convention in Miami. When I leave the convention, I'll go to New Orleans and look you up when I get there, and we'll see if we can put something together when I get there." So I went to Miami for the convention, then caught a plane to New Orleans. I got in at night and called him up. He lived way down in the Ninth Ward. Way down in the country, like. I went down there and we were sitting in his house, sitting with his wife, and he had three or four kids. It was so far out there down these country roads, outside of town; there were no lights on the porch and the kids were on the swing on the porch of the wooden house, swinging and making noise. We sat down in the living room and started talking. He said, "I'm not really a singer, I just like singing. I used to be a lightweight fighter." While we were talking, his wife was sitting there with me and another guy. He was talking to the kids on the porch saying, "Sitting on the la la, yeah yeah," and the kids would respond "ha, ha" and clap. I said, "What are those kids doing out there?" I said, "Have those kids come in here," and they came in grinning and I said, "What's that song you all singing out there, what's that little thing?" And they start grinning. And I said, "Let me hear you do it." So they all look at each other [*Robinson sings and claps like the kids singing*]. I said, "You got anything else more?" They said, "We ain't got anymore," so I said, "OK, go ahead out." So I said to Lee, "Come on let's go to town and get a drink, and let's see if we can cook up something."

Simon: So that's what ended up with you and him sitting there with the yellow pad in the bar and writing "Ya Ya"?

Robinson: Went to town, went to the bar, got the pad.

Simon: With Bobby Marchan was that a similar thing? You were sent records by him . . .

Robinson: Well Bobby Marchan was in a group Huey Smith and the Clowns, and they had a couple of records.[21] And he left them and went out west to that Mormon town, Utah, Salt Lake City, yeah. I still don't know how he got way out there. And he got into a club, he was doing a female act, he was a faggot, you know, he dressed like a female and sang like a female and he was working this club and he knew about me from somewhere. Maybe he heard about me from the "Kansas City" [Wilbert Harrison] recording, that's probably what it was. So he called me up one day and said he was with Huey Smith and he's in Salt Lake City and he's got a thing out there, it's a record done by Big Jay McNeely, a thing called "There Is Something on Your Mind," he had a pretty good record, I got a different version of it.[22] He said, "I do talking on one side, a monologue to the music and on the other side I sing. The people out here just flipped over it. I'd like to cut it with you." I said, "I tell you what we're going to do, you know any place around there where they got a Playland?" There was a lot of places then, Playland, you go in and play little game things, and they had a little thing you go in and make a record for fifty cents. He said, "Yeah, there is a Playland down here in town. I think they got a place you can make a record out there, make a little demo." I said, "That's all right, I don't care about no music. Go out there and sing it. Just what you do in a club. Record it with just your voice and send it to me right away and let me listen to it before I leave for Chicago for a convention next week. Send it airmail special delivery. I'll get it and call you back, and

Bobby Robinson in front of Bobby's Happy House record store, 125th Street, Harlem, September 19, 1993.

if we can do something I'll arrange for you to meet to be in Chicago and we'll cut it in Chicago." So he sent it to me and I sat down and listened to it: "After you can't stand it no more, you're going downtown to the pawnshop and get yourself a pistol, and then you make it back up on the scene, where your loved one and your best friend are now together,"[23] all this talk. And I listened, played it over and over one night, and I said, "What the hell is that?" I listened to it carefully and I said, "This could be a hit!" Picked up the phone and called him. He said, "I'll tell you the truth. I just had to send some money home, I don't got no money." I said, "I'm going to get you a room in a hotel in Chicago, I'm leaving for Chicago tomorrow. When I get to Chicago I will call you and we'll do it, we'll take a shot at it." I spoke to my distributor in Chicago [George or Ernest Leaner of United Record Distributors] and said, "We need a good fucking blues band with a bass and a guitar player." He said, "I got just the man for you, Lefty Bates." I called him up and went over to his house. We sat and talked and I played that demo for him. I told him I just want three or four guys, no horns or nothing. He said, "I got a good rhythm section." I said, "All right, bring them down." I got on the phone and set it up with the studio for eight o'clock that night.[24] I had the musicians meet me there. Bobby Marchan met me there. We got the band set up. There was no music for this, just follow him. I got to set it up. I got the engineer in the booth and the guys are set up. He's singing and the guys start to back him up. They got the feel and follow him right down the line and they did it all the way through. I said practice it one more time all the way through. They did it again exactly the same way, he did his talking. I said, "Do it the same way, let's cut it, do it right now just like you did it." And they cut it in one take. Smash hit!

Simon: Is he still alive?

Robinson: He's doing the same thing. He's doing a female impersonation down in New Orleans. He's in charge of a big club. He hires the entertainment, groups, bands and singers, and other people too.[25]

Simon: I understand the first business you owned was a shoeshine store near to the Apollo and you went on from there with a record department in the back. And being near to the Apollo Theatre you met all these musicians. But were there also clubs around that you were going to?

Robinson: Oh, yeah.

Simon: Tell me about some of the clubs, the names of them.

Robinson: Well, back in those days there were clubs all over, everywhere. You know, that was before drugs got in here, everybody was drinking liquor. Sugar Ray Robinson had a club right over on 124th Street.

Simon: Was that jazz or blues or everything?

Robinson: Just blues singers and whatnot. And there were jazz clubs too. There was a couple of jazz clubs around, you know, different places. And there was Well's [restaurant, on 132nd Street], was open all night—jazz musicians in there. And there's Smalls Paradise, up there they had different singers, different groups coming in seven nights a week. And right across the street over there on the other side, all over, see. So I was in and out of clubs all the time. And this

Bobby Robinson inside his office in Bobby's Happy House record store, 125th Street, Harlem, 1993.

club, that club, you know, like Top Club was right over on 125th Street, one block and a half away from here. And they had a lot of different acts come in there. I was everywhere, you know, in and out of this place and that place. And I was recording. I recorded a lot of stuff.

Simon: There's a guitar player I'm curious about on your CD that came out on Capricorn,[26] on the Willis "Gator" Jackson recording ["Good to the Bone," Fire, 1959], a guitar player named Bill Jennings.

Robinson: Terrific. Terrific. It's a shame. I did a couple of things on him.

Simon: You still have unreleased tracks?

Robinson: Never did . . . yeah, never did put them out. Had them for years.

Simon: You still have them?

Robinson: Yeah. I don't know what condition the tapes are in.

Simon: 'Cause that's something people would like to hear I bet, he's good.

Robinson: He was a hell of a guitar—left-handed guitar player. Old guy [about forty at the time].

Simon: So he was old even back when you were recording that stuff?

Robinson: Yeah, he'd been around for years. Way back—Depression. He'd been around a long time. But he was a hell of a player.

Simon: Mostly worked as a sideman, or did he have his own band?

Robinson: Sideman [and leader]. With different bands and things. And hell of a player. He wrote a few things too. And he played with his left hand, you know, left-handed player: Bill Jennings. So I cut Willis Jackson [who was married to Ruth Brown]. Willis Jackson was with Cootie Williams. Cootie Williams picked him up out of Florida, and he created a lot of excitement. He played horn, all wild, you know. So anyway, I got him and Bill Jennings and then a couple more guys with him. And we did three or four things. I did this thing with Bill Jennings, a part 1 and part 2. And then after that, they went out of town, and this and that and the other. I had so many acts.

Simon: And how about Skeeter Best, you know him, guitar player?

Robinson: Yeah.

Simon: Is he around still or what?

Robinson: No, he died [in 1985]. Skeeter Best. Great guitar player.

Simon: Did you ever record him?

Robinson: No, only . . . he backed up quite a few of my artists.

Simon: And Billy Butler is another great guitarist that you used. He was with King Curtis.

Robinson: Yeah, King Curtis. Terrific player. Bill was a great guy.

Simon: He died about two years ago . . . and his wife was very sickly, so he was staying home a lot to take care of his wife. He wasn't touring, because he wanted to be home for his wife. And his wife died. And then he died like two years after that [in 1991]. Did you ever study music or it's all your ear?

Robinson: All by ear.

Simon: Earlier I asked what you thought were some of your favorite recordings that you had produced. Now, what was your biggest published song?

Robinson: Percy Sledge did a song on Atlantic Records, one of my biggest songs. I did it with Joe Haywood first [for Enjoy]. And Percy Sledge heard it. "When a Man Loves a Woman," was a no. 1 hit for Percy Sledge [in 1966]. And coming off of that he was searching for something else to do, that he could make a big record off of. And in the meantime, while he had that out, I put out "Warm and Tender Love." My artist was unknown, but he did a terrific job on it. He was just, just breaking on that record, just starting. But Percy Sledge had a no. 1 record, "When a Man Loves a Woman." And he called me up from Alabama, said, "Bobby, I just heard this record, I got to do this record. Man, I know you got it out, man, but I'm looking for something that I can make another no. 1 off, and I hear in this record, it's the only thing I know that I can do it on. I'm coming to New York next week. Three days from now I'll be in New York. Let's sit down, let's do something and let me do that song." So he came to New York and did the song. He had a no. 1 hit [actually no. 17 pop, no. 5 R&B in *Billboard*]. I collected for a three-month period $10,000 off of that . . . and I had to give part of that song away. They had put pressure on. But you know, this boy was very hot. Atlantic, and his manager, they wanted to give him a piece of the song and so and so. So I did a three-way cut on the song. I gave part of it away to get him to do it, you know. But it still was probably a good thing. Because my artist was unknown, even though he might have had a pretty big record.[27] But it wouldn't have lasted twenty-five years. I still draw royalties off it every three months. And like this was a big surprise. I [might have gotten] $4,000, $3,000, you know? But to get $10,000? Oh, I was really shocked, man. I thought it was a mistake [*laughs*]. But that shows you. I made over $100,000. The last check was about a couple of years ago. Thirty-five records on that song—worldwide, every language. And that's, that's my biggest song moneywise. But I did a lot of other things that I like, you know. I did some doo-wop things.[28]

Simon: Is there any particular song that you really love that never made it big, something that you always felt should have but never did?

Robinson: Yeah, I had a few things like that. I don't remember right offhand so much now. But there were a few things I felt really should have made it. Some things I released when I had maybe three hits going. I had maybe another three, four records out—seven records, eight records out. And I didn't concentrate, I had so much going—this is a bad time for them to be released. But they should have made it. They would have made it probably, you know.

Simon: If the timing was different?

Robinson: Yeah. There were some certain records like it. I had some good things that didn't really make it real big. Maybe it was because I was so busy with

(L. to r.), Dr. Horse, Larry Dale, Bobby Robinson, and Jimmy Spruill (on the floor), at the Blue Frog, the Bronx, March 1993.

other things. I had big things at the time, and I was wheeling dealing worldwide, radio stations and whatnot. Wilbert Harrison, radio stations all over the country. I went with him to, oh, fifteen, twenty cities.

Simon: So you traveled around with him to promote it? You did everything? It wasn't like you hired somebody to take it around. You discovered the artists. You produced them in the studio. You take the record all over the country. You did everything.

Robinson: I placed it on radio, produced the record, did the promoting, deal with this guy and that guy—it was basically a one-man operation. It really is.[29] Yeah, I had other people packing stuff and taking it to the post office.

Simon: But the big stuff was all you doing it.

Robinson: All, all me, all me.

Simon: You're talking about maybe recording some of that old gospel stuff?

Robinson: Yeah. And it's gonna disappear because in the church now, the church is modernized. We lived out in the country. It was a country church there. And I lived right near the church. It was the next house. And all the preachers come stay for the weekend and preachers from different cities, they'd always stay at my house. My grandfather was a preacher, and they knew him. But they all spent [time at] my house, one block to the church. And I got to talk to a lot of preachers. So anyway, I go back every year, every summer to a revival. Had one week where every night they had preaching and whatnot. And I met these people years ago. And this one choir from another church, an old man—he must be pushing eighty—tall, skinny black man with a little white hair around his head, eyeglasses. And he's the leader of this choir. And another is an old woman. And I'd say she's about sixty-five, seventy. She leads a choir called the St. Louis Baptist Choir. And they don't bother with no music. They got their handclap [*claps hands*]. And they do that, and sing. And they got that down. Everybody's in syncopation and they sing, and it's like something you never heard. I heard this since I was a little kid, this kind of singing. And they got it down. They know how to sing. Like I had to stand up and listen! The church is going there singing, I have to listen. And the world never really heard the old gospel songs and the real singing, when people didn't have no instruments. They were forced to create syncopation and hand clapping and foot stomping and synchronizing to make it fit in. They had nothing else. I grew up in a church, we never had an organ in the church when I was there. They got it now. All the music was a cappella. We never knew nothing else, you know. And I grew up with that, the real thing. So I listen to them singing. And [the old man] did about four, five songs. And old people, you know, been singing all their life. They come through the hard times. They were there through the Depression. And they got the real thing. They lived it, and they feel it and they sing it. They got it, boy. I'm telling you. You listen to that [*laughs*]. So I'm going to go down there. And I got a young guy down there, he's a deacon of a church. And he goes around, he makes it his business to visit about fifteen churches, two or three counties around, and back and forth. And he's with a group. They sing here and there. So he gets together, it's about eight or ten groups. They have a general rehearsal once a month, at one place. So I'm going to speak to him, and have him gather together about a dozen, from two or three counties, of the top groups one night. I'm gonna fly down there and have one Saturday night when I have a whole church full of groups, and I'm gonna let this group do two or three numbers, that group do three numbers. And I'll talk to them, explain, whatnot. And they'll be anxious, they want to get on record or CD or something like that. You know, what the hell. And I'll work out a thing with them to donate whatever amount to the church. I'm sure that'll be satisfactory with them. And I'll cut them for nothing—no money. I'll pay the expenses. We'll figure out royalties, whatever the percentage, and I'll give it to whoever they say. And I'll work it out right there. And I'm gonna cut some real authentic country gospel, the real thing, before it dies out. I've wanted to do that. I'll put it on a video machine in the window, and I'll feature it, get a few stores to feature this for me, you know, start hitting other cities with it. I just want to do it to save it, have it for people to see and hear. It's so real, you know. And I remember when, even when these people was young and when it was being created, when it was made, and what it meant. It held people together. You know? Like in the Depression, you didn't know if you was gonna eat or not [*laughs*]. I think about some of those days. Most people lived in the country. I was lucky, and my grandfather, 1892 he got this land. We still have it today, so it's a hundred years. And since we own our own land, during the Depression we were on the farm, all worked on the farm, raised up on the farm. Practically everything you eat, we raised. That was an advantage. People who didn't have their own farm, sharecroppers on the other farm, they didn't have none of their own, but it was given to them and whatever. You know? And people around town did little odd jobs, whatever they could get. So we raised potatoes, enough to last all year—big patch of sweet potatoes. Well, cotton was the main crop. So sales hit rock bottom—seven cents a pound instead of thirty-five cents a pound. So you didn't make money off it. You just paid bills, couple of bills. But potatoes, fruit—my grandfather had a fruit orchard all around the house. We had about twenty-five peach trees, about a dozen apple trees, and a long rear fence he built up with grapes, in the middle of the street. Grapes, peaches, pears, all that. My grandmother and my mother in fall and summer canned all that fruit, and kept a closet full, top to bottom, pears, peaches, canned fruits. You know? And we had, outside, we had potato banks. We'd have three or four banks of potatoes— enough to eat, enough to sell in town. And we had a garden with tomatoes, beans and okra and everything you could mention—big garden full. And we'd gather all those fruit, those vegetables and things. We'd either can them or find some way to sell. So we had things all the time. And my dad raised corn and wheat. And the cornmill, or wheat mill, up from us there, a few miles away on a riverbank. I remember there was a very small guy, I went with my daddy, and we'd get this wheat—six or seven great big sacks of wheat—on a wagon. And we'd go up there, and the guy would run you five gallons or six gallons of meal, put the corn in, run you six gallons, and he'd take the seventh gallon. Six gallons; he'd take the seventh gallon, like that. And we'd take all this here, and he got his part. And we'd load them and go home. So we had meal, cornbread and whatnot, all the winter. And also we had flour, wheat, cut that and go do the same thing. I've never been hungry in my life other than, you know, just before time to go to eat. I mean, hungry where I go to bed and don't know where it's going to come from—don't know if I'm going to have anything tomorrow. And I knew plenty of people who did. We used to give stuff to people. We had about four cows, butter, milk, all that, all through. So actually, coming up as a small kid, the recession never hit me hard where I missed meals like other people.

Bobby Robinson, in the doorway of the original Bobby's Happy House, 301 West 125th Street, Harlem, May 16, 1986. Photo by Paul Harris.

See, my grandfather [*knocks on wood*], he was dead but he left that farm there [for us]. So we had that farm, and it's everything. See, we could raise what we want to. We could do what we wanted. And that was very rare.

Simon: Yeah, that's lucky.

Robinson: Very, very lucky. Especially black farms, there was only two or three in the whole county that I knew. Everybody else worked sharecropping. And the guy who owned the land, he put everything in his barn, everything, you had nothing in your house where you stayed. In hard times, in the wintertime, there was nothing doing and whatnot. Things are hard. People are in the house, sit by the fire and go to bed; children cry sometimes, nothing to eat. Down there they got no work for them to do, so he'd give them something, maybe . . . you know?

And we had a family across the road from us apiece. Mother would cook eggs and give them some cornbread and some milk. They had nothing to eat, give it to them. And my mother would do that, time after time. And so, that's what you call real hard times, man. You know? I come through it, but I was lucky. I was lucky, you know. I never had a hungry day in my life. See, when I came along, farming was a big thing in the South. Everybody's on a farm. And when the war broke out, '39, '40, '41, and so many thousands of people went overseas and scattered from cities, and that farm was never the same no more.

I know in Detroit, I know damn near everybody in my town went to Detroit and the automobile industry. Thousands of them, you know, all over. And New York, Chicago, Cleveland, St. Louis, Philadelphia. Everybody had a farm. The whole countryside was white with cotton fields, miles and miles. Almost hurt your eyes, everywhere you go down the road, you know . . . whole white world of cotton. I go down there now, you never see cotton. You could see, look for days, you don't see a piece of cotton, no more, no more cotton. All where there was cotton fields, there's houses, and the town is coming out now out to my house. It was five miles out of town. Now my brother has electric lights, running water, and everything. You know, you wouldn't think it's the same place. Two cars in a yard, he sits on the front porch in the morning and waits for the mailman to come by and drop the mail inside and, the sunlight comes in the afternoon. And he's sitting around all day. And he got the big lawns, and they ride all around the big lawn on these mowers. I tell him, I said, "Well, you got a good life, boy." My father was old, and the old people when they get old they don't know what they're gonna do. Wasn't no money coming from nowhere. The younger crowd had to care for them. And when they got too old to work and whatnot, sit around, there was no money coming from nowhere. You know? Had to fix it, stuff they had to eat. Was no homes to put the old people in and just no homes. That was home, where they died. So they was treated like everybody else. No difference. You know? That's the great thing, to have a family where you get old and sick, and can't work and whatnot, and you don't feel you're imposing. Sit down, everybody laugh and talk, and everybody's free as everybody else. That's a great thing!

Simon: What are you working on now [in 1993]?

Robinson: I haven't done anything in about four years [this is aside from running his record store]. I just kind of took off. But I've got three or four artists I just signed. I'll be operating two labels. I reactivated Fire and Fury Records[30] and I have Enjoy Records. That was another thing I had a big push on in the '70s. I was kind of quiet for a long period of time. And rap came out, I jumped on that. I got probably the best catalog of original rap there is in the country. I had Grandmaster Flash and the Furious Five, the Funky Four Plus One More, Kool Moe Dee with the Treacherous Three, Spoonie Gee, and Doug E. Fresh.

Simon: So you have an ear for that also, what you think's going to be [the next big thing]?

Robinson: Yeah, yeah.

Simon: But you don't listen to them much. Whenever I'm in the store I don't hear it.

Robinson: No, no.

Simon: But you know what other people want to hear.

Robinson: I know, I know. And then this is the beginning, the Sugar Hill Gang was the first group—I had the second record out. And so rap had just started. And everybody ran to me. They was coming to me right and left, you know. And I did about fifteen artists. And I had some big records, rap records, you know. But the kids got too wild. And you got five or six, a dozen rap artists, and every time you look around, and there's something happening. I had a bunch of guys one time came to me for the first royalty—a three-month royalty. I had set a meeting with them: Grandmaster Flash and the Furious Five, six guys all together. They stopped by a motorcycle place in the Bronx and picked out six motorcycles and parked them till they come down and get their money. Six motorcycles! They come down and, you know, I said, "Man, listen, we just got started on a thing here. I got—let's see what it was—oh, probably about $15,000 dollars for them, you know? They'd drawn money right and left. They got clothes and they'd drawn money for this and for that. I don't mean just uniforms. They got regular clothes every time I look around. So they had about $15,000 dollars left, you know, with deductions and things. And they had a fit, man. They raised hell: "What are we gonna do now? We got motorcycles, man." I said, "What do you think, you put out a record and you make a million dollars on it the first three months?" You know? Oh, they got very upset. They raised hell. It was stupid—you know, when kids first come out, they think it's a whole new thing, they think that, bam, you're rich overnight. That's what they thought. You know?

Simon: There's guys who've been playing around the city . . .

Robinson: . . . for years!!!

Simon: Yeah, and they just come up with their rent money, maybe.

Robinson: Yeah. So, you know, it got to be too much for me. I would have had probably the biggest rap business in the country. But I wasn't gonna face that with these teenagers. So I cut about ten groups all together. And the original things, I cut. Eventually I released them guys, let them go. But I cut the first things on them. And things I have now is probably the best catalog of what you call first-generation rap.

[For more on Bobby Robinson and other record industry characters, see John Broven, *Record Makers and Breakers: The Voices of the Independent Rock 'n' Roll Pioneers* (Urbana: University of Illinois Press, 2009).]

Bobby Robinson, in front of Bobby's Happy House record store, 125th Street, Harlem, September 19, 1993.

NOTES

1. Red Robin, originally Robin, was founded by Bobby and Danny Robinson at 301 125th Street in Harlem, and ran from 1951 through 1956. Artists included Champion Jack Dupree, Sonny Terry, Brownie McGhee, Allen Bunn (Tarheel Slim), Red Prysock, Tiny Grimes, the Vocaleers, and the Scarlets. There were no major hits.

2. Danny Robinson later operated the Holiday, Everlast, and Vest labels and partnered with Bobby at Enjoy for a while in the 1960s. In his many interviews, Bobby never went into great detail about his brother's activities, as in this interview. Donn Fileti, in his booklet note to *The*

Golden Era of Doowops: Holiday Records (Relic), wrote that Danny was "far more pragmatic than his older (by twelve years) brother . . . [and] became a solid businessman. After a long run on 125th Street in Harlem with his Danny's Record Shop, he operated his Hit Town one-stop." In 1991, "he still sells the latest R&B/rap records to wholesale accounts from his home in the Bronx," as Bobby indicated. Danny Robinson died in 1996.

3. Bobby Robinson's record labels, some in partnership with others (see note 29 below), included Robin, Red Robin, Whirlin Disc, Fury, Fire, Revelation, Enjoy, Blue Soul, Front Page, Bobby Robinson, and Fire & Fury.

4. Those records quoted are literally Bobby Robinson's greatest hits, but see the appendix for more comprehensive lists of his pop and R&B chart records.

5. The Elmore James 1992 Rock and Roll Hall of Fame induction was made by Robbie Robertson of The Band.

6. Elmore James lived and worked his day job in nearby Canton, Mississippi.

7. "Dust My Broom," a Robert Johnson song, was recorded by Elmore James in Jackson, Mississippi, on August 5, 1951, with Sonny Boy Williamson no. 2 (Rice Miller) on harmonica, and it made no. 9 R&B in *Billboard*.

8. Elmore James recorded between 1952 and 1956 for the West Coast–based Bihari brothers' labels, Flair and Modern, and also Checker and Lester Bihari's Meteor of Memphis.

9. "The Sky Is Crying" was recorded November 3 or 4, 1959, with an all-star Chicago band of J. T. Brown (tenor sax), Johnny Jones (piano), Homesick James Williamson (bass-guitar), Odie Payne (drums), and possibly Boyd Atkins (tenor sax). The song was rerecorded as "The Sun Is Shining" for Chess in April 1960, after which Elmore James stayed with Fire Records until his death on May 24, 1963.

10. Actually, "Bobby's Rock" was Elmore James's first Fire single, in December 1959, coupled with "Make My Dreams Come True," dubbed from the original 1953 Flair recording produced by Joe Bihari for Flair. "The Sky Is Crying" was the second Fire release in March 1960. With the excellent sound, it's possible that the studio was Bill Putnam's Universal Recording Corp.

11. Bobby Robinson is in fact referring to the second New York session, with the big band, in February–March 1961. The arrangements were by saxophonist Paul Williams, who had scored a huge no. 1 R&B hit with "The Huckle-Buck" for Savoy in 1949. The first New York session was held on May 23–24, 1960, at Beltone Studios with Jimmy Spruill (rhythm guitar) and Belton Evans (drums).

12. Although Lightnin' Hopkins's "Mojo Hand" charted for five weeks in *Cash Box*'s "Top 50 in R&B Locations" in 1961, peaking at a creditable no. 26, he had bigger hits from 1949 to 1952. There were sufficient Fire tracks to make up an excellent LP, *Mojo Hand* (1962). Robinson also recorded old-time RCA Victor blues star Arthur "Big Boy" Crudup in 1962 for two Fire singles and the *Mean Ol' Frisco* LP but without the same success, artistically or saleswise, as with Hopkins and Elmore James.

13. In a lengthy recording career from 1946 through 1981, Lightnin' Hopkins recorded for many well-known labels, including Aladdin, Gold Star, RPM, Specialty, Sittin' In With, Mercury, Decca, TNT, Herald, Prestige Bluesville, Candid, Arhoolie, and Vee-Jay.

14. At the time, in summer 1961, young Allen Toussaint had just produced a no. 1 *Billboard* pop hit, "Mother-in-Law" by Ernie K-Doe (Minit), followed by "I Like It Like That" by Chris Kenner (Instant), a no. 2 hit. The Minit and Instant labels were founded by New Orleans distributor Joe Banashak. Toussaint went on to have a glittering career as a producer, artist, and songwriter.

15. Harold Battiste was another successful New Orleans producer and arranger, and an AFO label co-owner. His biggest hits, along with "Ya Ya," were "You Talk Too Much" (Joe Jones, 1960),

"I Know" (Barbara George, 1961), and, biggest of all on the West Coast, Sonny and Cher's "I Got You Babe" (1965) and "The Beat Goes On" (1967). Battiste also conceived the Dr. John character for Mac Rebennack.

16. Robinson is referring to Toussaint's song "Give Me You," the B side of "Ya Ya." Toussaint wrote other songs for Dorsey in this period: "Messed Around," "Hoodlum Joe," and "When I Meet My Baby."

17. The Lee Dorsey session was held at Cosimo Matassa's Cosimo Recording Studios at 521 Governor Nicholls Street in the New Orleans French Quarter. Elmore James would record a Fire session there a little later in August 1961.

18. Lee Dorsey's ABC-Paramount release, in March 1961, was "Lottie-Moe"/"Lover of Love," acquired from the Valiant label of New Orleans for national distribution; Valiant soon became Instant Records. According to Jeff Hannusch in *I Hear You Knockin': The Sound of New Orleans Rhythm and Blues*, "Lottie-Moe" was first heard by Bobby Robinson's then–promo man, Marshall Sehorn, who would have a close future relationship with Dorsey and Allen Toussaint.

19. Pearl Woods has 136 songs registered with BMI, including "Party across the Hall" (Yvonne Baker and the Sensations) and "Stop the Wedding" (Etta James). Many of Woods's songs were cowritten with noted New York producer Leroy Kirkland.

20. This is possibly the famed New Orleans promoter Percy Stovall of the Continental Booking Agency.

21. Huey "Piano" Smith and the Clowns had two big hits, "Rockin' Pneumonia and the Boogie Woogie Flu" (1957) and "Don't You Just Know It" (1958), for Johnny Vincent's Ace label of Jackson, Mississippi.

22. "There Is Something on Your Mind" by saxophone virtuoso Big Jay McNeely, with vocalist Little Sonny Warner, made no. 44 pop and no. 5 R&B in *Billboard* on the Swingin' label in 1959.

23. The lyrics were slightly misquoted by Robinson but are corrected here.

24. As with the Elmore James session, it is likely that the Chicago studio was Bill Putnam's Universal Recording Corp.

25. Bobby Marchan died on December 5, 1999, in Gretna, Louisiana, at the age of sixty-nine. Toward the end of his life, he was promoting young New Orleans hip hop artists.

26. Capricorn Records Presents the Fire/Fury Records Story, a 2-CD box set (1992).

27. For the full story of Joe Haywood, from Spartanburg, South Carolina, including evidence that he wrote "Warm and Tender Love"—and not Bobby Robinson—see Red Kelly's Soul Detective website: http://souldetective.blogspot.com/2012/06/update-project-case-one-joe-haywood.html.

28. Bobby Robinson was expert at recording the New York vocal group sound with groups such as the Velvets, the Channels, Lewis Lymon and the Teenchords, the Kodaks with Pearl McKinnon, and Jackie and the Starlites.

29. For all his friendly, talkative nature Bobby Robinson was never effusive in conversation about his partners through the years. The fact that he had to seek outside help indicated he was often cash strapped. Among his partners-investors, some silent, were brother Danny (at Red Robin and, later, Enjoy), Cosnat distributor/Jubilee and Josie label owner Jerry Blaine (at Whirlin Disc), Clarence "Fats" Lewis, Marshall Sehorn, Morris Levy of Roulette Records (at the Fire-Fury group), and John Bowden (at Revelation, a gospel imprint).

30. The original Fire and Fury labels collapsed in early 1963, and the rights, with master tapes, were acquired in early 1965 by Larry Uttal's Bell Records, now part of Sony Music, New York.

7

HYMAN "HY" WEISS

Interviewed at the Weiss home in Woodbury,
Long Island, New York, December 5, 1993

Hy Weiss, born in Romania, was raised in the Bronx. He was a label owner, producer, and constant player in New York's independent recording scene of the 1950s and 1960s. He also had involvement in songwriting and is even cocredited on the Velvet Underground's title "Foggy Notion." As with Bobby Robinson, just about all the artists in this book knew him and worked with him. Weiss is best known for his Old Town label and his large catalog of doo-wop and blues recordings. He is almost as well known for his impact as a hustling independent record man as his attitude toward payola, the not-uncommon practice that was a staple in the record industry in the late 1950s of paying to get your record played on the radio. Unrepentant till the day he died, Mr. Weiss loved to recount, with glee, how much he'd rather engage in the "$50 handshake" (he is reputed to have originated) to get his records on the air rather than spend the time schmoozing with a bunch of unsympathetic radio executives. He is, in fact, so well known for this approach that he was mentioned by Bobby Cannavale's character in this regard on the 2016 HBO-TV series *Vinyl*. Weiss sold his Old Town masters and Maureen Music publishing to Music Sales in 1999.

I interviewed Hy Weiss at his Long Island home. Aside from arriving with photographer Bob Schaffer, I was accompanied by my (then) wife, Theresa, who was pregnant with our daughter Nell. I can't really recall how Theresa came to be there; probably Hy had asked if I was married and said, "Why don't you bring your wife along?" or something like that. Immediately upon arrival, rather than feeling like I was engaging in a formal sort of meeting, I felt like I was just visiting a dear old aunt and uncle for a happy gathering. Hy's wife, Rosalyn, started right in chatting with my wife and made lunch for everyone. When we finished up, Hy insisted that we come back soon. I write this to show another side of Hy

Hyman "Hy" Weiss (1923–2007), at his home in Woodbury, Long Island, New York, December 5, 1993.

Weiss that may be unfamiliar to those who know him only as a very flamboyant and somewhat controversial individual in the old-time record business.

Larry Simon: Where were you from originally?

Hy Weiss: I was born in Romania ... We came over here because they were killin' the Jews ... we stopped in Romania and that's where I was born ... My mother came from Russia. I came here as a young boy ... the pogrom.

Simon: How did you first become involved in the record industry? How and when?

Weiss: Back in [1947] I was a bartender ... I finally got a job—I was a bum! I came outta the service ... And I finally got a job with a bar called the White Rose on Thirty-Fourth Street and Third Avenue. And my brother Sam was working for a company called Runyon Sales, who were distributing records in Manhattan ... also with, the jukeboxes, and he heard that there was a job opening with a ... black record company—the first one, by the way: Exclusive Records, who had Herb Jeffries, Johnny Moore and the Three Blazers, Joe Liggins. Do you remember these names?[1]

Simon: Yeah, sure! I love Johnny Moore.

Weiss: Okay, but in any case, he told me there was a job open and I went up to Exclusive Records in their office, and I met a fellow by the name of Johnny Halonka who was the sales manager, and he gave me a job selling up in Harlem. Then, as time went on, I was selling records and getting acquainted with everybody uptown, and, there was a break for a while where I was supposed to get distribution on Modern Records, too, at the time.[2] They promised me that, and we left. Then I opened up my own distribution, BHS Distributing, in which we distributed Apollo Records and a few other labels. There was another distributor of Apollo Records in the same building. Ike Berman who owned Apollo Records hated this guy, so he gave me the line to sell too, and put me right next to him and we used to play Hindu records to drive the guy crazy! This guy was goin' nuts! Then one time, Ike Berman says to me, "Meet me at six o'clock in the morning," a Saturday morning. I says, "What for?" His wife was Bess Berman, they were the originators of Apollo Records.[3] They had the Larks, Mahalia Jackson. And I was responsible for the Larks doing a cover on a Sonny Boy Williamson no. 2 record called "Eyesight to the Blind," which was their biggest hit. So I met [Ike] at six o'clock in the morning, on a Saturday, and he says, "C'mon! We gonna get a can of gas." I says, "What for?" He said, "We're gonna burn the joint down!" I says, "Ike . . . you're crazy and I'm nuts, for comin' in at six in the morning. Goodbye, I'm goin' home!" [*laughter*]. All right?[4] Then I left that and then we, BHS Distributing, didn't do too well, so I went out and I got a job with a guy called [Jerry Blaine] at Cosnat Distributing. He had all the major [indie] labels at the time.[5] And I became top salesman in the joint. Joint sounds like a prison, right? And one day while we were waiting for a business meeting on a Monday night, a [black vocal] group came walkin' down the street and I said, "Who are you guys?" And they said, "We're with Rainbow Records but we left." And I says, "Waddya mean ya left?" "But we're lookin' for a label and we wanna go with Jerry Blaine," who had Jubilee Records—he had the Orioles and all that stuff. In fact, I'm responsible for the Orioles doin' a record called "Crying in the Chapel" which came off of a little country record that we were distributing[6] and I told Jerry. I saved his life by the way—he gave me twenty-five dollars for my wedding years later . . . but it was all right. So this black group [the 5 Crowns], I said, "I'll tell you what, you don't need him [Jerry Blaine], I mean, you're comin' with me! I'll open up a company." So they said, "All right," and I took 'em to a studio. I didn't know what the hell I was doin' and I cut a song called "You Could Be My Love." And that was my first entry into the record business per se as a manufacturer.[7]

Simon: Did you call your label Old Town at that point?

Weiss: Well, at that time my brother [Sam] was workin' for a company called Old Town Carbon Paper which was in Brooklyn. So I said, "Now I got stationery with Old Town on top," right? So I used the name Old Town Records because of the stationery. And then, a few years later, I got big enough where I had an office with a telephone on the wall. I used to take all collect calls but it was a public telephone. You see, I would get all collect calls until the telephone company wised up and they pulled that telephone. But Old Town Records, that's the way

Old Town Records started and we used to sell the same record, "You Could Be My Love" by the 5 Crowns. I must have sold the same three hundred records every month for about a year. Of course Jerry Blaine said, "You have a big record here!" Every week three hundred goes out, which was a lot of records at the time, 78s. Boy, did I have a deal with the guy at Woolworth's. I'd bring him the three hundred, he'd mark 'em down. I'd give him a dime a record and I'd pick up the records and bring 'em back to Jerry. He'd say, "We got another order from Woolworth's." I kept goin' to Woolworth's and back to Jerry—it was the same three hundred! Ya got the picture [with returns] on that one?

Courtesy of Victor Pearlin.

Simon: Yeah. And you would be in the sound booth, tell 'em if it sounds right?

Weiss: Yeah, I didn't know what I was doin' but I was there. I thought I didn't know what I was doin' but I made some great records throughout my career. In fact, today, I'm askin' myself questions: "Did you know what you were doin'?" And I say "no" to myself.

Simon: Now, on one of the Ace Records [UK] reissues, "Let the Doorbell Ring."

Weiss: Yeah, with Larry Dale.

Simon: They released it so you could hear you on it, talking to Dale.

Weiss: Oh yeah? I didn't know that.

Simon: Like all these false starts where he's starting the guitar and plays the *duh duh duh de dah* opening lick.[8]

Weiss: Well, I produced all the records I made except for one or two that I got from somebody else.

Simon: So you had a good ear, not just a good business sense.

Hy Weiss at his Long Island
home, 1993.

Weiss: I don't know whether I had a good business sense. I may have become a millionaire. Jerry Moss, that worked for me, became A&M Records. Berry Gordy, whom I told to leave his job and forget about being with United Artists: "Open up your own record company." He's a multimillionaire, everybody I knew became millionaires. But I don't care! I had my fun.

Simon: But you must have a very good ear for music also, to handle all the producing and everything.

Weiss: Yeah, pretty good! Yeah, now my kid [Barry] is doin' it.[9]

Simon: Did you write any songs?

Weiss: I'm a writer but I didn't write. Wherever there was an arrangement or something—everything was head arrangements—so I interjected what I thought would be good and I changed the songs around a little bit. And for that I'm entitled to be a writer. I shoulda been a writer on every song I ever made.

Simon: You had a lotta input in it.

Weiss: Yeah, yeah, every one of 'em! In fact "Life Is But a Dream" by the Harptones. The guy that wrote it with me [Raoul Cita] doesn't even know where he got it from. He says he got it from another song and I told him he got it from "You Could Be My Love" by the 5 Crowns, which is where it was stolen from. In fact, if I'd have been a good businessman, I woulda sued Atlantic on "Sh-Boom" and beat them out of a major song,[10] but I didn't do it. I happened to like Jerry Wexler and Ahmet [Ertegun], you know?

Simon: You worked mostly with black artists, right? What was it like for you?

Weiss: It was very normal. I felt more at home up in Harlem than I did in my own house. In fact, somebody called me from a jazz magazine and asked me how it was, if I had any problems. And I said, "Hell no!" I said I just loved being up there. I spent my life up there! It was twenty years of my life that I spent on 125th Street and on 116th Street and I knew everybody in Harlem there was to know.

Simon: You didn't have an office there? Or did you?

Weiss: Yeah, we had . . . at the beginning, we had a little office in a theater. A friend of mine had a [movie] theater on [165 East] 125th Street and we used to see groups there.

Simon: What theater was that? Do you remember?

Weiss: The Triboro Theatre, it was off Second Avenue and 125th Street. This guy Friedman owned it. I gave him a few dollars every month and I'd have all the groups come in and watch shows and see motion pictures and I'd listen to 'em.

Simon: Did you know Bobby Robinson back then?

Weiss: Yeah, I knew Bobby Robinson 'cause I was sellin' him records at Rainbow Records.

Simon: And he would sell them in his store?

Weiss: That's right. Bobby and I got very, very friendly and in fact, I'm still friendly with Bobby [in 1993], Bobby and Danny [Bobby Robinson's brother]. I like 'em both. I can still out-dance 'em, by the way . . . with the hairdo he's got on? He's a very nice guy.

Simon: What kind of music did you specialize in?

Weiss: All kinds! It never entered my mind that I was doin' something. I liked blues.

Simon: And blues, you didn't think it would make that much money?

Weiss: No! I just did it because I liked it. I recorded Arthur Prysock, not because I knew he'd sell records, it was because I liked it. I thought I'd build a star. Whatever stardom he got, he got through me anyhow.[11]

Simon: Who were some of the blues artists that you recall working with?

Weiss: Brownie McGhee, Sonny Terry, Bob Gaddy, Larry Dale I had at the time. Then I got all those musicians, old musicians in there—and Jack Dupree.

Arthur Prysock at his home in Searington, Long Island, September 1989. Photo by Paul Harris.

Larry Simon and Hy Weiss, at Weiss's Long Island home, 1993.

Simon: What about Billy Bland? Do you know him?

Weiss: Yeah, I'm lookin' for him now! He's up there in Harlem, he's got a store, a restaurant. I love 'im! He was one of my favorites. I just loved the hell out of him!

Simon: Did you also record jazz artists?

Weiss: Yeah! It's a funny bit about that one. I cut an album that became a top 10 album in Japan; in fact, it was so good I went to Europe about two, three months ago. I went to a couple of stores and I saw they bootlegged it—the jazz album that I had—Ted Curson [a trumpeter].

Simon: Ted Curson . . . yeah, that's very progressive kind of jazz.

Weiss: Yeah, yeah . . . I like that! I like Teddy, and we're still good friends. Uh, I'm in touch with everybody.

Simon: What other jazz players did you record?

Weiss: Then I had *In the Purple Grotto* [1961 LP] with Jazzbo Collins, then I did Stan Free. I was gonna go into jazz heavy, then, I said, "No, I'll go somewhere else."

Simon: What do you do now, mostly keep track of your old recordings? Or are you doing new projects?

Weiss: I got some ideas. There's a girl I have called Ruthie McFadden who did a record when she was seventeen, she did "Darling, Listen to the Words of This Song." She can outsing any singer. She can take Anita Baker and put her in the garbage can! All right? This girl can sing! And I told her, yesterday, "I'm gonna make you a star again." And she's working in a [lawyers' office], she's great! What I'm doing is taking Arthur [Prysock's vocals] off of the 24-track tape and just using her.

Courtesy of Victor Pearlin.

Simon: Who was your biggest artist, what records that you did sold the best?

Weiss: You know something? I was a one-man operation.

Simon: And you did distributing, producing, everything?

Weiss: Yeah, and when I got a hit record, I would lay out, I chilled out for about six, seven months. I didn't wanna kill myself. And you know what happened when I moved out here [to Long Island]. When I moved out here, I started to go to New York five days a week; then traffic started to get to me. I went to three days, then two days, and finally, I said, "The hell with it! I'm not goin' to New York at all!" Then I kept an office, and then I closed it and I just drifted away from the record business per se.

Simon: So is there a recording that is your favorite?

Weiss: Yeah, "Life Is But a Dream" [the Harptones] is one of my favorites. "We Belong Together" [Robert and Johnny, that is Robert Carr and Johnny Mitchell from the Bronx] is another one of my favorites. I'm a part writer on that, too. And you saw the picture *Goodfellas* [1990]? They used "Life Is But a Dream" in it for the wedding scene. "Remember Then" [the Earls] is a good song of mine.[12] But hidden in all of these things is a song that I own that's one of the best songs in the world, and it makes a lotta money in Europe, a thing called "My Special Prayer." I did it with Arthur [Prysock] and Joe Simon. It went to no. 2 and it sold four, five million records with a German artist. It was no. 1 in the Netherlands, that's no. 1 in Holland—in different languages—and the song is earning with the Percy Sledge record of it in Europe. And the woman who wrote it [Wini Scott] is seventy-six years old and she's in a nursing home—she's a lovely, lovely lady. I call her every week or every day practically. If she doesn't hear from me, she goes crazy.[13]

Simon: You mentioned when you were recording blues records, you did it 'cause you loved the music.

Weiss: Yeah! I had a big record with—well, not a big record—I made a record with Bob Gaddy called "Operator" [in 1956]. It says, "Operator, operator, please dial that number again." I forgot the number ["129"], but if that number had hit, it woulda broke every numbers man in Harlem 'cause as soon as it went on the air, everybody was playin' that number. It was unbelievable!

Simon: And back then, the blues records were listened mostly to by a black audience, unlike today, right?

Weiss: In order to sell blues, that's what caused my trips into the South, 'cause blues records would sell in the South. See here [in New York] we were starting to develop a market for doo-wop stuff. Doo-wop never sold in the South, blues records sold in the South. It didn't sell big but you could always get off of the "schneid" [break a scoreless streak]. See, like Larry Dale's records that only sold in Houston. "Operator" [Bob Gaddy] sold in Detroit, believe it or not. See, Detroit was like being in the South. Chicago, where Muddy Waters was with

Hy Weiss, at his home in Long Island, 1993.

Leonard Chess, was like being in the South. I knew Willie Dixon real well, in fact, I own two of his songs.

Simon: How did you promote your albums when you put 'em out?

Weiss: I went around and I knew all the jocks. Whatever it took.

Simon: Uh huh ... take 'em out to lunch or something.

Weiss: No, I'm not a lunch kind of a guy.

Simon: [*laughter*].

Weiss: In fact there was a write-up about me, it was the *New Yorker*. It tells about the time the FBI came up because of payola, and I told the FBI, I says, "Listen, lemme ask you a question, would you want me to go out with a guy I don't wanna bother with? I don't wanna spend any time with. I'd rather give him the fuckin' money and tell him to fuck off! All right? And play the records." And I didn't have to waste any time [*laughs*]. That was funny but the funny bit is, I made great relationships. Even the jocks that are around today, I get calls every week. And in fact, Tommy Smalls [Dr. Jive] was a big DJ, he died, I'm in touch with his family. And Jockey Jack [Joseph Deighton Gibson Jr.], I'm in touch with him in Atlanta. I knew all of these guys.

Simon: Did you know any of the guys at WDIA in Memphis?

Weiss: Everybody!

Simon: That station still has a blues show on Sundays.

Weiss: Oh yeah? Well, they have to. That's the blood over there. You know where the blues came from, don't ya? From gospel. You know where gospel came from?

See, gospel's not gospel the way you know it—there's gospel and then there's different phases of gospel music. Jubilee is a different kind of gospel music; spiritual is a different kind of gospel. And the gospel music that engendered itself to different portions of the country brought out a certain form of change in the blues, which would become significantly different in different places. Like in Detroit, the blues were completely different than the blues that were sung in Houston, in Dallas. The blues in Georgia and Chicago—Chicago was a conglomeration of everybody's blues! Chicago was like the midsection of the world as far as blues was concerned. Chess Records had most of 'em and Vee-Jay. Willie Dixon was producing.

Simon: The people from New York seemed to have a slightly different sound to their blues.

Weiss: That is [what] a lot of people are surprised at sometimes. I made it authentic, I made my stuff like it came . . . I used the old, old guys.

Simon: I listen to those records of Bob Gaddy.

Weiss: Yeah, right! And people say, "That was made in New York?" I said, "Yeah." I'll never forget, funny bit, one day I'm recording Bob Gaddy and there's a knock on the door. I'm at Bell Sound. Knock on the door, downstairs, union. I said, "Uh oh! We got a problem here." So a guy, Buchbinder, who was part of the union, comes walkin' in, he says, "Hy, I caught you!" I said, "Waddya mean, you caught me?" He says, "You're recording a nonunion date." I says, "You're right." I says, "You're absolutely right. Look at those guys standing in there." And there were six or seven of 'em standing up in front of a mic. I say, "These guys are doin' a cappella." I said, "You don't see any musicians—and who the fuck are you, Buchbinder! Are you breakin' my chops?" He started to laugh and these guys, Bob Gaddy, make the most discordant sounds you've ever heard in your life! I says, "Are you ready to go? Goodbye!! You're wastin' my time!" They put down their instruments, doin' a cappella. That was my idea of standup. Oh, what a funny night. That's one I shoulda put in a book. Let me tell you something about musicians, they're not as bad as they are in California. I recorded Arthur [Prysock] out in California. Each one of them would have a stopwatch on their knee and I'm saying go ahead, go into overtime, who cares—I didn't have the money in the first place. First I'd make the records then worry about paying for it later. It was unbelievable. I had more balls than anyone you know.

Simon: Do you remember how you actually met like these guys, Jimmy Spruill, Larry Dale, and Bob Gaddy?

Weiss: Jimmy Spruill was a sideman—he wasn't that important to me. But Larry Dale and Bob Gaddy, and we'd bring in Jack Dupree, he played piano. I knew all these guys—I was on 125th, 113th Street. Brownie McGhee came up and recorded for me, we recorded an album with Brownie. It's now out on Ace Records [UK].[14] They're the only ones I allow [to license from me]. Anybody else is bootleggin' me.

Courtesy of Victor Pearlin.

Simon: Yeah, you mentioned you were havin' some trouble with bootleggers.

Weiss: Yeah, I go after 'em, that's what gave me my ulcer. I caught a guy in Japan bootlegged my Ted Curson album. That Ted Curson album, goin' back to it, you were talkin' about jazz. That was a steady seller for ten years in Japan. Every time we got a dollar and I sent half of it to Teddy. I happen to like him. Not everybody got that treatment.

Simon: And what about James Wayne?

Weiss: I got James Wayne. Lemme tell ya about that one, James Wayne's the funniest bit in the world! I was in a bar at 125th Street at the [Baby] Grand, where Nipsey Russell used to play. And a guy walks in and says, "I'm James Wayne." I says to him, "You're fulla shit!" He's got an army uniform, he says, "Here, look!" I say, "Gee, ah . . . sing me 'Tend to Your Business.'" That was his big record. So he sings the song for me. So I says, "Oh! let's go!" So we're gettin' in the car, I call my brother, and I called Jimmy Lewis—he used to work for Atlantic, a guitar player who was arrested for dope and everything else years later. But he was a great guitar player, "Baby Face" Jimmy Lewis, and he got me a bunch of musicians. And I went into Beltone Studios and recorded 'til seven in the morning—I didn't have five cents! And they were asking me for money. I said, "You have to wait until I go home and get some checks." I was out, right? Oy, there was nearly a riot in the streets of New York, over there on Thirty-Third Street. Oh god! They were gonna kill me, right? I said, "Fuck off!" I don't give a shit about money, you know. I said, "You're gonna get straight." And then I went and I got money and I paid everybody the next day. And I had four sides of James Wayne.[15]

And then, it was all of a sudden, I spoke to Randy [Stewart] who was with me all his life practically, and he wound up with the Fiestas and he gave me the Gypsies, the girl group I had, which were pretty good.[16] And he says, "I got twenty-five records that I found in my basement . . . the Commanders." I said, "You gotta be kiddin'!" You know who was playin' guitar on that? Jimi Hendrix. I said, "Get me a copy real fast" and I sent it out to Ace. I hope they use it.[17] I like Ace Records, I let them import to the States. I got a bunch of stuff in the back of the house here [in 1993] and in the basement they haven't gotten to. I don't know how good they are, there may be a bunch missing, too.

Simon: Mickey Baker, did you work with him?

Weiss: Of course, I worked with Mickey Baker. Mickey was a great guitarist! Mickey and Sylvia . . . yeah! He's living in Paris [died in 2012]. Yeah, he worked on a lotta sessions for me.

Simon: What about guitarist Kenny Burrell?

Weiss: Kenny Burrell worked on the Ted Curson album.

Simon: People may not know that Kenny Burrell did a lot of bluesy and R&B stuff, as a session man.

Weiss: I used Kenny Burrell. And then, of course, [drummers] Panama Francis, Bernard Purdie. Yeah, I was the first one to use Bernie. I used top musicians for the Arthur Prysock dates. Billy Butler, Jerome Richardson, and all those guys—Jerome was a fantastic saxophonist.

Simon: What do you like to listen to now? Any artists out there that you really enjoy?

Weiss: No! I only like my own. I'm one-sided, isn't that terrible?

[At this point, I had turned off my recorder to end the interview, and Hy Weiss asked that I turn it on again so that he could add the following:]

Weiss: This industry owes a vote of thanks to four people, or maybe five, that were absolutely responsible for black music selling anywhere in the country [from 1947 through 1973]. And these people are Hoss Allen, Herman Grizzard—well, these were four disc jockeys on WLAC Nashville, Tennessee, which covered thirty-five states and was absolutely the forerunner of black music and broke black music into white areas with constant airplay—John Richbourg [John R.], and Gene Nobles, he was a carney. WLAC in Nashville, Tennessee. And because of what they played on the radio, those four people were the ones responsible for bringin' black music into vogue—the only ones. Everybody else—Alan Freed and all the disc jockeys, whoever came later—were not as responsible as WLAC. And these four people that were the jockeys, and if anybody ever wants to do a documentary—if anybody wants to do a write-up, anybody ever wants to do anything—they oughta dig down into Nashville, Tennessee. Meet Mister Hoss Allen and find out where it really was at, 'cause this was the innovator of blues music [on the radio]. Unbelievable asset to America, OK?

Larry Simon and Hy Weiss, at Weiss's Long Island home, 1993.

[For more on Hy Weiss and other record industry characters, see John Broven, *Record Makers and Breakers: The Voices of the Independent Rock 'n' Roll Pioneers* (Urbana: University of Illinois Press, 2009)].

NOTES

1. Hollywood-based Exclusive Records, one of the first important independent labels of the post–World War II era, was operated by songwriter Leon René between 1944 and 1949. Big hits included Joe Liggins's "The Honeydripper," Herb Jeffries's "Left a Good Deal in Mobile," Ivory Joe Hunter's "Blues at Sunrise" (1945), and Johnny Moore and the Three Blazers' "Merry Christmas, Baby" (1947). Later, René owned Class Records, which had national hits by Bobby Day including "Rockin' Robin" in 1958.

2. Modern Records, owned by Jules, Saul, and Joe Bihari, was founded in Los Angeles in 1945. A New York office was set up in July 1948 by Joe Bihari, with Hy and Sam Weiss as salesmen with Lester Sill. "Hy was a darned good salesman," Joe said. The office closed in February 1949 when Bihari returned to California (Broven, *Record Makers and Breakers*).

3. It is possible that BHS Distributing was named after "Bess, Hy, and Sam" or "Berman, Hy, and Sam."

4. For more on "Eyesight to the Blind" by the Larks, see chapter 14 on Tarheel Slim. The "burning the joint down" story relates to a lower Manhattan pressing plant that was allegedly bootlegging Apollo records (Broven, *Record Makers and Breakers*).

5. Cosnat Distributing, owned by Jerry and Elliott Blaine, grew to become one of the biggest independent record distributors in the United States. Their hot lines included Atlantic, Herald, and Chess. Jerry Blaine also headed Jubilee and Josie Records.

6. Hy Weiss was referring to Darrell Glenn's 1953 original of "Crying in the Chapel," a top 10 pop and country hit for the tiny Valley label of Knoxville, Tennessee. The Orioles' cover on Jubilee, now considered a doo-wop classic, stayed at no. 1 on *Billboard*'s R&B chart for five weeks in August–September 1953.

7. Old Town Records was launched by Hy Weiss and his brother Sam in August 1953 from an office in the Triboro movie theater at 165 East 125th Street, Harlem. The 5 Crowns were members of the large Drifters family tree. In June 1957, Sam split from Old Town to form the Superior Record Sales Company, a distributor, and then Win Records, a major one-stop operation. Hy continued Old Town alone but with vital distribution and promotional support from Sam.

8. Larry Dale recorded two singles in January 1960 for Glover Records, a subsidiary of Old Town operated by veteran A&R man Henry Glover, formerly with King Records (see chapter 16 on Billy Butler, note 12). The false starts on "Let the Doorbell Ring" are heard on the 1986 Ace Records LP, *Old Town Blues*, vol. 1.

9. Barry Weiss, Hy's son, enjoyed enormous success as president of Clive Calder's Jive Records from 1995 through 2010 with R. Kelly, Britney Spears, the Backstreet Boys, Justin Timberlake, NSYNC, and Chris Brown. Barry Weiss also had spells as head of the RCA/Jive Label Group and Universal Music Group, and was still active in the business in 2020.

10. "Sh-Boom" by the Chords was a big no. 5 pop and no. 2 R&B hit on Cat, an Atlantic subsidiary label, in 1954, and the song became a massive no. 1 crossover pop hit by the Crew-Cuts (Mercury). Despite Weiss bringing a 5 Crowns song into the argument, the "Sh-Boom" subtitle, "Life Could Be a Dream," was clearly the inspiration for "Life Is But a Dream" by the Harptones. With a Willie Winfield lead, the Harptones record was released on Paradise, an Old Town subsidiary, in July 1955.

11. Throughout the 1960s, Weiss did his best to break Arthur Prysock, who made his name as a heartthrob baritone balladeer, having started as a stand-up singer with the Buddy Johnson Orchestra in the 1940s. Prysock's biggest of several minor Old Town hits was "It's Too Late, Baby Too Late" (no. 56 pop, no. 11 R&B in *Billboard*) in summer 1965. Weiss even contracted an album on Prysock with the Count Basie Orchestra for Verve Records later in 1965. Prysock went on to have modest success in the 1970s disco era on a revived Old Town label.

12. Hy Weiss's biggest hits on the *Billboard* charts were:

- 1958: "We Belong Together," Robert and Johnny (no. 32 pop, no. 12 R&B)
- 1959: "So Fine," the Fiestas (no. 11 pop, no. 3 R&B)
- 1960: "Let the Little Girl Dance," Billy Bland (no. 7 pop, no. 11 R&B)
- 1961: "There's a Moon Out Tonight," the Capris (no. 3 pop, no. 11 R&B); "Rama Lama Ding Dong," the Edsels (no. 21 pop on the Twin subsidiary)
- 1962: "Dear One," Larry Finnegan (no. 11 pop)
- 1963: "Remember Then," the Earls (no. 24 pop, no. 29 R&B)

In 1957, "Walking Along" by the Solitaires was a big local regional hit but curiously didn't break into the national charts. The song did make the top 30 when covered by the Diamonds in late 1958, giving Weiss's Maureen Music—named after his eldest daughter—a publishing bonus.

13. Weiss is referring to the publishing of "My Special Prayer," written by Wini Scott, by Maureen Music. The Arthur Prysock original was released by Old Town in 1963 but did not chart. The Joe Simon version was released in 1967 by Sound Stage 7, making no. 87 on *Billboard*'s pop chart, no. 17 R&B, whereas the Percy Sledge cover hit no. 93 pop, no. 44 R&B for Atlantic in 1969. It is not possible to verify the European chart claims.

14. Weiss was making reference to the 1986 Ace Records (UK) LP, *Old Town Blues*, vol. 1, which featured eleven tracks by Sonny Terry and Brownie McGhee with the rest of the album

made up by four tracks from the unknown "Little Willie" and Larry Dale's "Let the Doorbell Ring." See also note 8 above.

15. James Wayne had a big no. 2 *Billboard* R&B hit with "Tend to Your Business" in 1951 for Bob Shad's Sittin' In With label. Wayne recorded for Old Town in 1954 with guitarist Jimmy "Baby Face" Lewis, but the four sides were not released until 1987 on the Ace Records LP *Harlem Hit Parade: Old Town Blues*, vol. 2, with other tracks by Hal Paige, Ursula Reed, Bob Gaddy, and Larry Dale.

16. The Gypsies had five singles on Old Town, 1964–1966, and after moving to the United Kingdom became popular as the Flirtations.

17. The Nashville recording of "I'm So Glad"/"I'm Sorry for You" by Frank Howard and the Commanders was released on the Barry subsidiary in August 1966, probably through WLAC disc jockey Hoss Allen's Rogana production company. There is reliable evidence that Jimi Hendrix played rhythm guitar on the record. "I'm So Glad" was featured on the *Old Town and Barry Soul Stirrers* CD on Kent (UK), an Ace subsidiary, in 1994.

8

ROSCO GORDON

Interviewed in Portsmouth, New Hampshire, February 7, 2002

Rosco Gordon was born in Memphis, Tennessee. Although listed as "Roscoe" on several record releases in the 1950s, he insisted in conversation that his real first name was spelled "Rosco." He was one of the earliest R&B artists recorded by Sam Phillips at his new Memphis Recording Service studio, launched in 1950 before Sun Records was founded. Rosco had a unique, off-beat rhythmic feel to his music, so much so in fact that Phillips called it "Rosco's Rhythm." Gordon had a no. 1 *Billboard* R&B hit with "Booted" (Chess and RPM, 1952), and no. 2 R&B hits with "No More Doggin'" (RPM, 1952) and "Just a Little Bit" (Vee-Jay, 1960). Recordings of Rosco's music made their way to Jamaica in the 1950s, and he toured there early in his career. Gordon is widely cited as a major influence in the development of ska. In Memphis, Rosco was a contemporary of influential artists such as Johnny Ace, Bobby Bland, Junior Parker, and B. B. King. Rosco moved to Queens, New York, in 1962, running a dry cleaning business with his wife, Barbara Kerr. After a quiet period in the 1970s, he saw a welcome revival in his fortunes including starring in the 1982 Memphis Blues Festival, organized by Hank Davis; trips to Europe including the Blues Estafette in Utrecht, the Netherlands; regular club dates in New York; and new recording sessions.

Gordon performed until his death. He was literally on the way out the door of his apartment heading to the airport to get to a performance when he died of a heart attack. Although Rosco Gordon is rightly associated closely with Memphis, he is included in this book because, as noted, he moved to New York City in 1962, where he spent most of his life, ran his own label, recorded for New York–based labels, and was an active performer. Thus, he was as much a New York artist as a Memphian.

I was Rosco's bandleader for close to ten years, starting in the late 1980s, although he did work with others. Rosco, unlike many artists I've worked with, liked rehearsing, never shied away from it. Though a funny thing is, typically he

Rosco Gordon (1928–2002), House of Blues, Boston, May 1995.

never played a tune the way we rehearsed it, even if we practiced just the day before the show. He rarely played a song the same way more than once. You really had to be on your toes and listen carefully. He never stopped composing, either. He'd say, "This is it, this one's gonna be my next hit."

Over the course of the time I knew him, I grew very close to Rosco, not just as a bandmate but personally, too. He stayed at my house a few times for gigs when I relocated from New York and also got to know my wife and daughter. On a 2019 visit with my daughter Nell to Sun Studio in Memphis, I mentioned to a staff member that I had been Rosco's bandleader. There was much excitement. He has major fans working there to this day. All these years later, I think of Rosco often and miss him deeply.

Rosco Gordon: I was working over at WDIA. Every day I had a fifteen- or thirty-minute show. You know they had shows there, B. B. King, Earl Forest, Johnny Ace, Joe Hill Louis the One Man Band. Well anyway we had a show there and the station manager, David James Mattis,[1] he set up an appointment with Sam Phillips to record me. So I go over there and I played some of my stuff for Sam, and he liked my voice, and he said "I got a thing here I'd like you to do called 'Booted.'" I like strange things, strange tunes, and that was a strange tune. "Booted" was a strange thing. I had a three-piece band, every day on the radio. We recorded the thing but he [Sam Phillips] said you need another side. I wrote the other side. I wrote "Love You 'til the Day I Die." That is the very first one.[2]

Larry Simon: Was that the flipside to "Booted"?

Gordon: Right, and we thought that was gonna be the tune but it wasn't. "Booted" was the tune. It stayed no. 1 for thirteen weeks.[3] Phillips gave me $100! No royalties, no nothing, just $100. After that Ike Turner and his gang came to

Courtesy of Victor Pearlin.

town. That was behind "Booted." They wanted me to record "Booted" for the Bihari brothers. What do I know about business? I'm fifteen years old [actually twenty-three], what the hell do I know about the business? So I recorded the same song for the Bihari brothers.[4] I didn't know any better, I was just in it for the fun. That was a fun time, music then. When school was out I always went to the cotton field and pick cotton. I would sing all day, and when the bus would stop, everybody would flock to me because everybody knew I would entertain them. This is before I won the amateur show.[5]

Simon: What kind of stuff were you singing?

Gordon: Nat King Cole, Ivory Joe Hunter, Charles Brown [*sings* "Black night is falling"],[6] that kind of thing, I love these things. So the Bihari brothers came to town, and Ike Turner, he was the front man, he would go and find the talent and record them. So I had wrote this thing called "No More Doggin." See I have a girlfriend, and I met another girl named Peggy. I had a three-piece band, and we were playing at a club. I was there with Peggy, but my girlfriend showed up anyway. When she came, see Peggy was already with me, that's right when I started singing, "No more doggin', foolin' around with you." Her time was over, you understand? Still sung today, it's a big song today—still being played. It's in a movie in Hungary, *Romeo and Juliet.* So that's how I got into this wild and wacky business, but I love it, hey![7]

Simon: What was life like for you before you started doing music, back when you were a kid in Memphis in the very early '50s?

Gordon: Well I was going to school and I was trying to make money honest. I had a shoeshine stand in front of my door, a two-footer, in front of my parents home, and I would shine shoes on Friday nights, Saturday and Sunday. I started making money too early. I had no business making money at that age. I had a lawn business. I had eight lawnmowers. I would set it up and I would send this one here and this one there. I was making money.

Simon: Were you hanging out in any music clubs?

Gordon: I would be invited to Club Handy. When I would go to Club Handy and they would announce that I was in the house all the musicians would leave the stage, everybody, the drummer, he would have to go to the bathroom, and somebody else he would have to go and eat. So I ended up playing the piano myself. See, my music is unorthodox. What I mean is, it's not 12 bars, it's not 8 bars, it's not 16 bars. It's 11 bars, 9 bars, 6 bars, 5 bars, 13 bars, it's whatever I feel. Well I'm still doing the same thing now. I'll add a bar in a minute because that's what I feel. If I feel like I should add another bar to fit my feeling, I'll add the other bar, but not 2 bars. I'll always add 1 bar or delete 1 bar. Hey nobody is going to play stuff for you but you. Now I was in the studio, Elvis Presley, when he came in, he wanted me to play behind him. Sam Phillips said, "Rosco can't play that kind of stuff." Now what kind of musician can't play 12 bars? Any musician

Rosco Gordon and Killing Floor NYC with Roland Alphonso and Lester Sterling of the Skatalites. (L. to r.), Alphonso, Larry Simon, Gordon, John Errico, and Sterling, House of Blues, Boston, May 1995.

Roland Alphonso (l.), Rosco Gordon, House of Blues, Boston, May 1995.

that calls himself a musician can play 12 bars. But see, I was a big act back then, I had a lot of hits out. Elvis Presley would come down to my rehearsals. I don't know how he would find out. Ninety percent of the time when I was rehearsing, you would see him sitting in the audience with his legs crossed then you turn your head and he's gone. But if you listen to a lot of his early recordings he used a lot of my phrases, you know, before he established himself.

Simon: Was he a friendly sort of guy back then?

Gordon: We weren't social friends.

Simon: Just colleagues on the musical scene?

Gordon: Yeah, and we spoke to each other. But other than that, no, we weren't socializing.

Simon: There was a musical family around Memphis at that time, the New-borns. The father [Phineas Newborn Sr.] had a band, right?

Gordon: Yeah, but his two sons was in the band. And one of his sons' wives[8] was, she was also singing in it.

Simon: The two sons were Phineas Jr. and Calvin?

Gordon: Yeah.

Simon: Did you ever work with either of them?

Gordon: I worked with Calvin just this past Labor Day weekend [2001]. Hank Crawford arranged an LP for me, and Calvin plays guitar on that. We recorded it in New York, this was "a hundred years ago."[9]

Simon: And sax player George Coleman also played with you a long time ago, correct?

Gordon: See when I was young I was a prankster. If you went to sleep, I did you some kind of damage. My drummer, he went to sleep one night in the car, and I put matches around his foot and set them on fire. George Coleman, he would sleep with his mouth open, so I dropped some cigarette butts in his mouth. George hates me for that till this day.

Simon: We did that show at the Brooklyn Museum [August 16, 1992] and it seemed very cordial. So let's go back and talk about the very beginning of your career. When you first started touring did you buy a van to travel with your band?

Gordon: I bought a Dodge station wagon. It was my first car outside of a Cadillac. I believed in the Cadillac. I had eighteen Cadillacs during my life. So, anyway, I bought a station wagon. We went all over the country in that station wagon. When we got to California, the engine was crisped. You could take your finger and break a piece of the engine off. I had all these musicians in the car, six musicians. But now I'm in my Cadillac. I had a Ford but I got rid of it when Billy Shaw from the Shaw Agency in New York came and signed me up and gave me some money. That's when I bought my first Cadillac. I bought a 1952 Cadillac, brand new. And I could've paid cash for it, and wouldn't. And when things went bad the finance company came and put my car up on the back of a truck and hauled it off. And after that, anytime I buy anything if I can't pay cash for something, I leave it there.

Simon: Were there acts you toured with at that time, like a package show, or were you touring on your own?

Gordon: I had such a great band during that time. See, I recorded with my home band, but my road band was a better band. So everybody wanted to work my band. You know, like Big Joe Turner, he wanted to work with my band. Roscoe Shelton, Gene Allison, the Platters, Larry Birdsong, the Clovers. They all wanted to work with my band.

Simon: Who do you remember that was in the band?

Gordon: I have some of the names, but I have trouble remembering all the names. Billy "Red" Love, he played piano and he was also a singer on Sun Records.[10] Now Billy was my piano player and bandleader, and Harvey Simmons was my tenor player. And Jeff Jefferson, that was my sister's husband, he also played tenor in the band; Chico Chism, he played drums in the band. That's about all the names I can remember.

Simon: When you were playing in the clubs back then, were the clubs segregated, just for all white audiences or all black audiences?

Gordon: It wasn't mixed. You were playing for all blacks or you didn't play. Now the concerts, like I played with Stan Getz, Fats Domino, and Lloyd Price, I played with them. This was an auditorium in California, so it was a mixed audience. But I always got a good response. The hundred years I've been in the business I've never been booed.

Simon: How did Butch [Rosco's chicken] enter into it all?

Gordon: I had the record out called "The Chicken."[11] It was a funny kind of record. Butch was my chicken. Butch came in with the record. My nephew said, "Uncle Rosco you got the record 'The Chicken,' I'll sell you my chicken for thirty dollars." Well, I accepted the chicken, but he never got paid. See, the chicken was a pet. He would run around in the house just like we would. I was working in Dallas, Texas.

I had forty-one one-nighters so when I got the plane to go to Dallas, I had him in a crate. When we got on the plane I let him out of the crate. He walked up and down the aisle. Everybody wanted to touch him because he was a beautiful chicken. He had a big ol' comb on his head as big as your hand. It was so big it leaned his head over. He was white as snow. I kept him clean. So anyway, the people on the plane they were playing with him. When I had my wardrobe made, I have a suit made for him just like mine. So when we would go on stage I would put his suit on him. So now I'm working with [Paul] "Hucklebuck" Williams. We were at the Fillmore Auditorium [probably San Francisco], and I put the suit and bowtie on him. He would shake his head and back up five steps, then walk back up the same five steps. Paul said, "Man, that chicken is trying to dance! Why don't the two of you try and work out an act?" So when I get back to the hotel I put the bowtie on him, he shake his head and back up five steps, I back up with him. I found out later why he was shaking his head. He was trying to get that damn bowtie off his neck. Didn't want that bowtie on him, man. He hated the bowtie. It turned into a real big paying act. I had a valet. Two big lights. I like to work the clubs, because that's where the money was. So when you put the lights on him, he would walk from table to table with a cup around his neck. You take the lights off him, he would stop. During the time we were working on stage he would walk from table to table getting that cup full of money, not dollars, people would put in fives, tens, twenties, fifties! They put in everything. He made more money than I did. So I bought him a pink Cadillac. This was his Cadillac. My '57 Cadillac, that was his Cadillac! I had sheets and blankets so he could walk all over the car.

Courtesy of Victor Pearlin.

Simon: How long was he with you in his little lifetime?
Gordon: He lived a year and a half. I think the Scotch is what did him in.
Simon: Scotch?
Gordon: Yeah, every night on stage I had a small bottle of Scotch. Don't give him no water if we're gonna work that night, until we got on stage. He got any kind of liquid in front of him he's gonna drink it. So what I would do, I would open a brand new bottle of Scotch every night and I would pour him a topful. And he would drink that topful. People on the street would say "Here comes Rosco and that drunk chicken." The band blew taps over him, and we buried him in my mother's backyard. Put him in a shoebox and buried him.
Simon: You never found another one like him?

Rosco Gordon, in the background,
speaking to the crowd at House of
Blues, Boston, May 1995.

Gordon: I tried and tried. There was never another Butch. I gave up. The last
Butch I had, I went to South America. The promoter said "What is the chicken
going to do?" I said "This is a dancing chicken." You put that suit on him, and he
would just lay down. So I gave that Butch to the first person who wanted him. I
think they had him for dinner.

Simon: In the movie that you are in, *Rock Baby Rock It* [1957], that's the original Butch?

Gordon: That's right.

Simon: How did that movie come about?

Gordon: Tiger Jones was in Dallas, Texas, and they were doing the movie
already. He caught my show and wanted me to be in the movie.

Simon: Was he the director?

Gordon: He was the producer.[12] I was invited to be in the movie, never paid
me. Same old story.

Simon: Did you know any of the other acts that were in the movie?

Gordon: Let's see . . . I knew the Five Stars and Preacher Smith, the one who
played piano and tried to emulate me. You see, he caught my show before he did

his. He wanted to stand up and play the piano like I did, but it didn't work. He would try standing up, but then he would have to sit right back down.[13]

Simon: Tell me a little bit about your friendship with Johnny Ace and the group the Beale Streeters. Was that a real thing?

Gordon: That was a myth! There was no such thing as the Beale Streeters.

Simon: Who was it supposed to be?

Gordon: It was supposed to be all of us, you know, all the Memphis musicians, B. B. King, Bobby Bland, Johnny Ace, Earl Forest, and myself. We were supposed to be the Beale Streeters, but there was no such thing. Don Robey of Houston Texas,[14] I think he started that myth that we were all in one band together at some point. I only worked with Bobby Bland. At that time I didn't have a car and Bobby Bland took us to the gig. Bobby was singing on the way to the gig. I was thinking, this is backward, I should be his chauffeur, not him chauffeuring me! We were working in Arkansas, and I put Bobby on stage. He sang all that night and I shot dice. I knew he had it.

Simon: What about B. B. King?

Gordon: I never worked with B. B.

Simon: Didn't he sit in with you not too long ago at a club in London?

Gordon: At the 100 Club in London he was just sitting in.[15] But that's the only time I've ever been on the stage with B. B.

Simon: You must have been on some of the same shows back in those days. Did you listen to them?

Gordon: I don't know if he came on first or I came on first [referring to B. B. King's radio show and Rosco's radio appearances on WDIA, Memphis]. Either I would listen to him going to the radio station or on the way back from the station, WDIA. But now, as far as us doing a paying gig together, no, we never worked together. Now we recorded at Tuff Green's house in Memphis, when I recorded "No More Doggin'," and he recorded "Three O'Clock in the Morning" ["3 O'Clock Blues"] at the same time.[16] Now the strangest thing happened here. When I recorded "No More Doggin'" with my band, we were working in Arkansas that particular night, I go to look for the musicians, I can't find them! I called the tenor player's house, his wife said Ike Turner came and got all the musicians and said they hadn't finished recording. So I go back over there, and I hear my band in there, and I hear this strange voice singing "No More Doggin'." That's Ike Turner in there. He's singing my "No More Doggin'"! I say "Hey man, what is this?" After I almost tear Tuff Green's door down getting in there. I said to my band, "What's going on here, we got to work tonight." They said Ike Turner wants to do that particular song. He was gonna steal my "No More Doggin'." After that Ike Turner and I, we were never friends. Before that we were friends, you know, Jackie Brenston and a lot of guys in the band, I knew.

Simon: In the early days of your career was the scene kind of rough, people carrying weapons and stuff?

Rosco Gordon at the Blues Estafette, Utrecht, the Netherlands, 1994.

Gordon: Yeah, it was pretty rough. My first drummer Charles,[17] he got killed. Like I told you, I would shoot dice with anyone, anywhere. We were shooting dice with this guy, and he lost all his money to us. So he upped this .38 and wanted his money back. So I gave him the money I had. I turned my pockets out. But I had my little pocket up here [touched shirt pocket] packed full, but I turned all my other pockets out to him to show I had no money. So he asked Charles, "Give me my money." So Charles says, "The only way you getting my money . . ." *Pow!* [*makes gunshot noise*]. Shot him right there on the spot . . . I took off man.

Simon: Did you know T-Bone Walker?

Gordon: Yeah, we were friends. He loved shooting dice too. But the only one I gambled with was [another blues guitarist, Clarence] Gatemouth Brown. I kept him broke.

Courtesy of Victor Pearlin.

[Rosco Gordon, as stated, is considered a primary influence on the early development of Jamaican ska and reggae. The very unique shuffle feel, dubbed "Rosco's Rhythm" by producer Sam Phillips and heard on "No More Doggin'," is a primary example.]

Simon: My understanding is the outdoor speakers in Jamaica, that were all over the place, were broadcasting your music and you toured there in the late '50s.

Gordon: Also San Juan, Rio de Janeiro, Trinidad for one night. I was frightened out of my wits. It's raining. And I'm in the cab on the wrong side of the highway and, man, I look up and see headlights coming at me from the wrong side of the highway and I start screaming, you know!

Simon: When did you first go to Jamaica?

Gordon: In '57 and '58.

Simon: I heard that people in the Caribbean first got to know your music because they heard it coming from a radio station in Texas that had a very powerful signal that was picked up over there.

Gordon: Yes, that's true.

Simon: And why do you think you in particular? Do you think it was because of what Sam Phillips called "Rosco's Rhythm"? That was a feel very similar to the feel of the music people were listening to in Jamaica?

Gordon: That was it. A lot of the musicians over there recorded a whole bunch of my songs. And of course, later on in New York Roland Alphonso and Lester Sterling from the Skatalites did some shows with us. A weird thing happened when I was there. I was playing for a beauty contest in Kingston, Jamaica, and all the lights went out. But my band kept playing during the blackout. The next day my picture was in every newspaper, wherever you went. I saved the day playing through the blackout.

Simon: Do you think you were one of the first American pop musicians to tour down there?

Gordon: No. Fats Domino, they loved him too.[18]

Simon: But it seems even though he was well loved he didn't have the influence you had. The guys who were working on the documentary on you [never completed], Ken Gerber and Hugh Gilmour, were very interested to speak, for example, to the producer Coxsone Dodd[19] . . . and the musicians themselves like Lester Sterling and Roland Alphonso, said you were the guy that inspired the beginning of ska, which led to reggae.

Gordon: I don't know how this came about. I didn't find out until twenty years later. I was in business in New York. I was supposed to be dead. They gave me up for dead. I disappeared. I disappeared when I got married because I wanted to raise my family like my family raised me, like a human being. But when they grew up and got married I went right back to work.

Rosco Gordon (over Lester Sterling's shoulder), as an unknown fan appears to be praying to Sterling, of Skatalite fame. Boston's House of Blues, May 1995.

Simon: So are we talking about the reggae radio show *The Midnight Ravers* on New York radio station WBAI? They thought you had died but learned you were alive. What happened then?

Gordon: I now have a three-hour show there, twice a year, one in December and one in June.

Simon: I was listening the first time you were on and I heard them promoting it by saying "You have heard about the roots of reggae, well now we have the seed, Rosco Gordon."

[During the broadcast, Jamaican listeners in New York City, who were fans of Gordon's from their youth in Jamaica, called in, delighted and astounded to hear Rosco Gordon. One caller even said that he had named his child Rosco.]

Simon: What were some of the labels you recorded for over the years? You mentioned Sun Records.

Gordon: I first recorded for Sam Phillips, Sun Records, and then I recorded for Modern, the Bihari brothers, in California. Now, I'm recording for all these people at the same time because I didn't know any better. Then I recorded for Duke Records out of Houston, Texas, that was owned by Don Robey. See, they didn't pay you no royalties, and the upfront money was such a small amount. So what you did was take the upfront money, since you weren't going to get any other money anyway. I also recorded for Columbia Records, ABC-Paramount, Rae-Cox, Calla, Vee-Jay, Old Town, you name it. I recorded for everybody, about fourteen different labels.[20]

Courtesy of Larry Simon.

Simon: Who were you with the longest?

Gordon: Sam Phillips. I was with him the longest, 1951 through '57. But he wouldn't pay me. He got all this money coming from every different angle.

Simon: Did he at least try to promote you, get you on the radio, get you shows?

Gordon: He got me on the radio in Memphis because his "brother" was on WHBQ in Memphis.[21]

Simon: Say you could put together a fantasy band with anyone in it you want, alive or dead, who would it be?

Gordon: I would have Pat Hare on guitar; Richard Sanders on baritone—he didn't have a good sense of time, worse than mine, but he had such a great tone; and Willie Wilkes and Billy Duncan on tenor. On the piano I would get Billy Love.

Simon: Instead of you on piano?

Gordon: I learned most of my stuff from Billy and my sister. See, my sister was taking lessons, and when she would come and sit down at the piano, I would sit right beside her. She would make a chord with three fingers and I would do five. I would make the same chord she made but I would add notes to it. And Billy, I think he was one of the greatest piano players I heard in my life. Jeff Greyer on drums from Memphis, he's still there [in 2002]. He's great. And there was another guitar player by the name of Thomas Harwell, he passed away also.

Simon: What about Calvin Newborn? Would he be on in your fantasy band?

Lester Sterling and Rosco Gordon, May 1995.

Rosco Gordon at Boston's House of
Blues, May 1995.

Larry Dale, Rosco Gordon, and Bob Gaddy, video shoot, midtown Manhattan, 1993.

Gordon: Well Calvin, he played jazz. So he wasn't exactly the right style. But I worked with him.

Simon: So tell me about more modern times. You had retired from music. What happened, you won a dry cleaning shop [in Queens, New York] in a poker game?

Gordon: Yeah, I was in the dry cleaning business for seventeen years. I made a good living. I was home with my family every night. That meant more to me than all the money in the world and the fame. My family.

Simon: Then what happened, the kids grew up and you went back to performing?

Gordon: That's right.

Simon: Did you ever pursue your own publishing company or your own record label?

Gordon: Yes, I got my own record label, it was established in 1969: Bab-Roc Records.

Simon: Where did the name come from?

Gordon: The "Bab" came from my wife Barbara [Kerr]'s name and the "Roc" out of mine. Bab-Roc Records, Bab-Roc Music, Bab-Roc Publishing, Bab-Roc Agency, Bab-Roc Production, Bab-Roc everything! Anyway it is still active [in 2002, although his wife Barbara died in 1984]. I've been beat and now I'm wise. People are still trying to take advantage of me, but I know how to protect myself now.

Simon: How did you protect yourself back in the old days? For instance, I heard that Albert King always carried a gun on him so if there was ever a con-

Rosco Gordon at Dwyer's Pub, New York, May 12, 1989. Photo by Paul Harris.

tract dispute, he would just show them his gun and settle things [*Rosco laughing*]. Did anything like that ever go on around you?

Gordon: I only showed my gun once. It was about me playing the piano. Don Robey didn't want me to play the piano. It went on about seven or eight minutes. We were going through this discussion. I let him know I was ready for him. "The very foot you kick me with, that's the one I'll put a bullet in." I said, "I'm not going to kill you. I'm going to put a bullet right in that same foot you kick me with." So we had no more dealings. My whole life has been an adventure. I could go on and on and on and on.

NOTES

1. David James Mattis, previously a disc jockey of hillbilly music, was program director of WDIA Radio, Memphis, who formed Duke Records in April 1952 with distributor Bill Fitzgerald. The second release was Rosco Gordon's "Hey Fat Girl"/"Tell Daddy." By April 1953, Duke had been taken over by Don Robey of Peacock Records of Houston. Duke and Peacock, under Robey, would develop into leading R&B, soul, and gospel labels.

2. Rosco Gordon's first recordings were cut by Sam Phillips for the Bihari brothers' RPM label in February 1951. Gordon had a minor R&B hit with "Saddled the Cow (and Milked the Horse)" at no. 9 on the *Billboard* R&B chart in fall 1951. "Booted," a no. 1 R&B hit, first appeared controversially on Chess and was backed by "Love You 'til the Day I Die" with a Bobby Bland vocal.

3. According to *Billboard*, "Booted" was no. 1 R&B for one week only, March 15, 1952, and stayed on the chart for a total of thirteen weeks.

4. "Booted" was promptly rerecorded by RPM, and both this release and the Chess versions made the charts, according to *Billboard*.

5. The amateur show was held at the Palace Theatre, Beale Street, Memphis, probably in 1950.

6. "Black Night" by Charles Brown (Aladdin) was a massive *Billboard* no. 1 R&B hit for fourteen weeks in early 1951.

7. "No More Doggin'" made no. 2 on *Billboard*'s R&B chart in spring–early summer 1952 on RPM.

8. Calvin Newborn's wife was Wanda, known as "Miss Fine."

9. There are no references in the standard blues discographies to this recording.

10. Billy "Red" Love started out recording for Chess, produced by Sam Phillips, before signing for Sun.

11. Rosco Gordon recorded "The Chicken" for Flip, a Sun subsidiary. Although it was featured in the film *Rock Baby Rock It* (1957) and became well known in later years, it never made the national charts at the time. However, it was a territorial hit in Philadelphia in fall 1956.

12. The producer of *Rock Baby Rock It* was J. G. Tiger, with Murray Douglas Sporup the director.

13. Apart from Rosco Gordon, the Five Stars, and Preacher Smith, other artists featured in this low-budget movie were the Bellew Twins, Johnny Carroll, Cell Block 7, and Don Coats.

14. The Beale Streeters never existed in reality, as Rosco Gordon said, but are credited as the backing band on the early Duke releases, 1952 through mid-1953, by Johnny Ace, Bobby Bland, Earl Forest, and Rosco Gordon.

15. B. B. King did indeed sit in at a Rosco Gordon gig, in a warm reunion, at London's 100 Club in May 1982 after B. B.'s own concert performance at the Hammersmith Odeon.

16. B. B. King's "3 O'Clock Blues" was recorded at the black YMCA in Memphis by Joe Bihari about September 1951; the "No More Doggin'" session was held a little later. Bihari also used Tuff Green's house as a recording location after he and his brothers had fallen out with Sam Phillips due to a contractual dispute with Chess Records.

17. The full name of the deceased drummer is not known.

18. Along with "Blueberry Hill" (1956), Fats Domino's breakthrough record on the sound systems in Jamaica was "Be My Guest" (1959), which with its heavy offbeat was at the root of ska.

19. Coxsone Dodd, a pioneering Jamaican ska and reggae producer, later moved to Brooklyn and recorded Rosco Gordon's *Let's Get It On!* album on Dodd's Studio One label, reputedly in the early 1980s (no date is given on the LP or CD releases).

20. Gordon recorded for the following labels from 1951 through 2002: RPM, Chess, Duke, Flip, Sun, Vee-Jay, Columbia, ABC-Paramount, Old Town, Jomada, Rae-Cox, Calla, Bab-Roc, JSP (UK), Studio One, OSA (with Larry Simon's Killing Floor NYC), Stony Plain (Canada), and Dualtone.

21. Rosco Gordon was referring to the influential disc jockey Dewey Phillips of WHBQ Radio, Memphis, who actually was not Sam Phillips's brother but worked closely with the Sun Records man.

9

PAUL OSCHER

Interviewed at Paul Oscher's home, Austin, Texas, April 30, 2018

Like Doc Pomus, Paul Oscher was born in Brooklyn and, also like Pomus, began his career as a blues musician performing in the long-gone scene of black blues clubs in Brooklyn and Long Island with occasional trips to Harlem and New Jersey. In the late 1960s, Paul moved to Chicago, where he became Muddy Waters's harmonica player and even lived in Muddy's basement, sharing the space with pianist Otis Spann. Paul recorded on albums with Muddy for Chess Records. Paul also worked with T-Bone Walker, Otis Spann, John Lee Hooker, Buddy Guy, Johnny Copeland, Big Joe Turner, Louisiana Red, Big Mama Thornton, Victoria Spivey, and many others. Eventually Paul returned to Brooklyn during the 1980s before moving to California and then Austin, Texas. Tragically, he died April 18, 2021. (Sharron Clare, producer of Oscher's album *Cool Cat* on Blues Fidelity [2018], contributed to this interview.)

Larry Simon: OK, Paul, where were you born?
Paul Oscher: In New York.
Simon: Brooklyn?
Oscher: Yeah.
Simon: Did you ever get any lessons or was there anyone you consider your teacher?
Oscher: OK. Well my first instrument was accordion and that was when I was a kid. My father had a friend that was an Italian guy that played accordion. My father told me . . . I wanted a guitar, right, because Elvis was out there like '58 or something like that, you know, and he says, "No, get an accordion." He says if you play the accordion, you'll never want for a job. You know what a definition of an optimist is? An accordion player with a beeper! OK, so he tells me an accordion can sound like any instrument, right. So, he takes me over to his friend's house who plays the accordion and he shows me all the switches:

Paul Oscher (1947–2021), at C-Boy's Heart and Soul club, Austin, Texas, March 2018. Photo Larry Simon.

clarinet, piccolo, bass, bassoon. Still sounds like an accordion, so I took a few lessons from his friend and I learned like "Merrily We Roll Along." This kind of really bullshit stuff. Couldn't stand it because I had to practice an hour a day and all the kids were outside playing punchball and stuff in the street, stickball. I couldn't stand it so I just took the thing. It was a rental, 12-bass [piano] accordion. I took it and I just threw it on the ground and it broke open. Well, I got in trouble for that, but the reed plate in there, it's like a harmonica! I picked it up

Oscher with his former wife, Pulitzer Prize–winning playwright Suzan-Lori Parks. Photo by Todd France/Corbis.

and just played into it where the bellows would send the air, so that was like my first harmonica.

Simon: So, you actually blew into it?

Oscher: Yeah, I blew into it. Sounded like a bass harmonica, actually, the reeds, you know.

Simon: What part of Brooklyn was it that you were a kid?

Oscher: East Flatbush. So, you know, that was it, and then that was over and then I tried to get into the glee club in sixth grade and the teacher said you should never become a musician. You're tone deaf. Same as my ex-wife [Pulitzer Prize–winning playwright Suzan-Lori Parks], they told her she should never be a writer because she can't spell. So, anyway, that was my thing with music. My parents were not at all into jazz or black music. You know, my father was like in his fifties when I was born. He was born in 1896 and his father was an American citizen before that and so that family went back a long time. So, anyway he liked Sigmund Romberg operettas, *The Student Prince*, and also he had 12-inch records. I mean, that heavy-duty stuff and he liked *Madame Butterfly* and stuff like that. My mother liked *My Fair Lady* and those kind of show tunes. They both liked *The Lawrence Welk Show*.

Simon: Who doesn't? [*laughs*].

Oscher: Yeah, right, and Guy Lombardo and his orchestra. It had nothing to do with blues or jazz or anything. I had an Uncle Sammy who played stride piano. He'd take me on the subway, and he played air piano and whistled the melody. People be looking at him like he's crazy. He's playing like this and whistling and I'm sitting right next to him. And so that was my experience of being around a real musician because he actually played stride piano and stuff.

Simon: Did he ever play professionally or just at home?

Oscher: I don't know. He had a plate in his head from World War I, so that was Sammy. So anyway I had a friend that played the guitar and I used to go over to his house and I would look at his book, and learn how to play the chords. I learned a little bit of strumming stuff, you know, like that. Then I worked in a grocery store after school when I was twelve years old and my uncle, the same Uncle Sammy, had given me a [Hohner] Marine Band harmonica. And I used to deliver groceries on a bicycle and I'm playing harmonica like [*hums* "Oh! Susanna"] reading from the little paper that came with the harp. And a black guy, Jimmy Johnson, that worked in the grocery store, too, he was like twenty-eight years old, gold teeth, process hairdo, dark skin, he says, "Hey kid, let me see that whistle you got." So, I give him the harp and he made like he couldn't play it. Then all of a sudden [*hums blues melody*] I never heard such big sounds come out a little bitty instrument. Then he took it and started playing [*sings*] and he could tap dance to it at the same time. This guy played in Georgia, in medicine shows down South. He could sing like Junior Parker. His tone on the harp was somewhere between Big Walter Horton and Howlin' Wolf. He'd keep that tension in the harp. He showed me my first pointers on the harp and told me what records to listen to, who to listen to like, Little Walter and Howlin' Wolf, and so I went out, any record I could find I bought. There was a record store not far from my house and this guy had all Chess records and 45s and I would buy them up. I bought all that stuff so by the time I was like fifteen, I was already really pretty well indoctrinated into what the blues was, but I had never played out of an amplifier. I didn't know how they was getting that sound. So, I was walking down a street one day and there's a black club called the Nitecap and I'm playing the harp [*hums*]. This guy's standing in the doorway and the guy said, "Hey kid, where you working at?" I said, "I ain't working." He said, "Why don't you come in here and play for people?" So I looked in the club and the people looked like Ike Turner with the process hairdo and the women all looked like the Supremes and this guy was dressed to the nines. His name was Smilin' Pretty Eddie. He was the emcee in the club.

Simon: It's in Flatbush?

Oscher: Yeah, right. It's the Nitecap Lounge and it was near Flatbush and Rutland Road between Rutland Road and Midwood Street. There was two black clubs there, the Seville and the Nitecap. The only black clubs are all on Flatbush Avenue except maybe on the other side of [Prospect Park], down farther, but anyway, this is where a lot of country black people went to these clubs. Now it's like all West Indian, but then it was like country black people like from North Carolina to East Coast black people. So, I went up there and he says, "You just take that harp and blow it into the mic," so he had one of those Elvis Presley mics. You know, those big Shure mics and the sound system was a Bogen public address system with speakers in the club. And I hit that one note, man. It just blew my mind because I never heard an amplified harp. I didn't know what it would sound like. I never played through an amp, but I had learned Little Walter's "Juke" and "Sad Hours" from the records. But I was trying to get that sound acoustically, so my tone was huge. I mean my volume was huge because that's what I was looking for. I didn't realize it came from an amplifier. So, I played those two songs, "Juke" and "Sad Hours," and Pretty Eddie says, "Ladies and gentlemen, put your hands together for a little blue-eyed soul brother," and the place went fuckin' nuts.

Simon: You're like fifteen?

Oscher: Right. OK, so I get off the bandstand, I'm walking toward the bathroom and there's a shake dancer. She's a black girl around nineteen years old with huge false eyelashes and a wig and made up. She's putting pasties on her titties and one titty is bare and I'm fifteen, my knees are like shaking and she looks up at me through her eyelashes. She says, "Hi, baby." I said to myself, "Right, this is my life. That's it. I'm not going back!" I used go there like every weekend, I'd hang out there and they'd get me up on a stage. Then I started going next door to a place called the Seville and there was a guy named Little Jimmy May, who played guitar and he was like the house band at the Nitecap. He had a car and we used to go around to places in Long Island and play in Hempstead and we'd sit in on shows and people would throw tips at us. At that time there was shows in the clubs. There was like maybe a comedian, a vocal group or like a doo-wop-type group. There was a singer that was singing like Sam Cooke or something like that, some soul music and there was a blues player.

Simon: So, we're talking about 1965?

Oscher: Yeah around that, '65.

Simon: And these are like all black clubs in Long Island?

Oscher: All black clubs. There was a club in Great Neck a club called the St. James Hotel. This is where the housekeepers, when they got off it was like a Thursday or something like that and they would go to these clubs and all the black guys would come to meet them. They had black housekeepers in Great Neck in the fancy houses. They would meet there, so we played there. Then we would play in a place called the Showplace Lounge in Freeport, with a guy named Elmore Parker and the Nightlighters—he was a blues singer. There was Club Ruby in Jamaica. It's a pretty big place and there was a place in Riverhead, Long Island, called the Bluebird Lounge, which was all potato pickers, migrant workers. I remember going into that place, they had a big counter and everybody's eating like bowls of chitterlings and hot sauce and I went to the bathroom, here's a guy that's checking his revolver, loaded it, and put it in his pocket. So, that was my first experience of seeing somebody with a gun in New York. So, then we used to play in Bedford-Stuyvesant, the 521 Club, the Baby Grand.

Simon: Baby Grand in Harlem?

Oscher: There was a Baby Grand on Nostrand and Fulton [Brooklyn], too. There's a Brooklyn Baby Grand and a Baby Grand in Harlem. Then there was Club Quarter, M&M Lounge on East New York Avenue and like Pennsylvania Avenue. There's a place called Soul Discotheque. Well, that was later on, that was like in the '70s, Soul Discotheque. Then there's the Platinum Lounge on Fulton Street. There's a lot of places and there's also a black piano player, Jimmy Hill, blind guy. He's still around, he still plays some.

Simon: So, this time in the mid-'60s, blues was still popular music. People danced to it and enjoyed it.

Oscher: For the southern black people.

Simon: It was still enjoyable, like pop music?

Oscher: Yeah, but it wasn't much different than soul music because on every soul show in every black club, somebody would be singing at least one blues. "Sweet Sixteen," "Jelly Jelly," "Stormy Monday." You know, those songs, some Bobby Bland stuff. Blues, jazz, and soul music was together. It's black music. You know, what I mean, it wasn't like there was blues clubs.

Simon: It's a different thing for, like, the white college students where it's almost like going to some kind of special museum or something. I saw B. B. King at the Apollo Theatre years ago and the audience was all middle-aged and older black people. It was almost like going to see a current popular entertainer.

Oscher: You're the only white person there?

Simon: Pretty much. Yeah and there was such a different feel like going to see a pop show rather than an esoteric blues show.

Oscher: Well, there wasn't such a thing called blues clubs. There was just black clubs and bars. Chicago, maybe more all blues, you know what I mean. Like some of the places you got Pepper's Lounge and Theresa's and some places on the West Side where like Elmore James played and that was just total blues. But in New York or any other city in the United States there were black clubs and the music was some jazz, soul music, some blues. Later on they got the hip hop thing. I was playing a club in Brooklyn called Cliff's Pink Pussycat and we played there every Wednesday and when I finished playing, they opened up the back room and a DJ came and this is in '71 or '72. They stayed there till early in the morning. And that's when rap started because the DJ would be there talking shit on his mic and I heard somebody else from the crowd would come up and talk shit. That's how the rap started and then that's also how the musicians started losing their jobs. I was playing this black club in 1974 called Barbara's Club My Way. It's a big black club and this girl come up to me and she put two hundred dollars in my pocket. She said, "I want you all to play at my party and I got another two hundred dollars when you get there." So, it was on Simpson Street in the Bronx, right, and it turned out that this was the headquarters of the Savage Skulls gang in the Bronx, a street gang in the Bronx. We're supposed to play from nine o'clock to twelve thirty or one o'clock. They didn't get there

Paul Oscher, 1979. Photo © by Anton Mikofsky, used with permission.

until one o'clock in the morning and we couldn't leave until seven o'clock in the morning because these guys were really dangerous so we had to play all through the night. But the Bronx really . . . that Simpson Street, it was really a tough area. Whenever I go to Bronx I get lost, but I used to play in the Comet Lounge on 168th Street. There was a guy named Charles Brown that played there [not the famous West Coast pianist], but he was a guitar player from North Carolina. It was 168th Street on Grand Concourse, that's where it was, right on the corner I think—well, maybe like one street in from Grand Concourse. I went up there with a guy from Brooklyn called Les Cooper, he made a record called "Wiggle Wobble,"[1] and then right around the corner from me where I lived in Brooklyn was a guy named Al Browne and he wrote "Bad Motorcycle."[2] So, I used to go on these bus trips with him and play blues, play a harmonica and melodica. On bus trips like to the Peg Leg Bates [Country Club] in the Catskills, it was a black club in the Catskills and people from New York would take three buses.

Simon: That was the name of the club?

Oscher: The club was Peg Leg Bates,[3] Bob Gaddy knows that. There was no white people around in these clubs, I'm the only white guy.

Simon: Did people fuss about that in any way?

Oscher: Not at all. I never had any negativity.

Simon: Or even any consciousness. You were just playing and there was nothing about it?

Oscher: They were just digging it, man, they're digging it. And also it was unusual to find somebody playing harmonica like that in New York at that time. There wasn't too many people that played harmonica.

Simon: So, people just couldn't care one way or the other.

Oscher: No, no. If I could play "Fannie Mae" like Buster Brown, those records were hits at that time. I played Slim Harpo's "Baby Scratch My Back," man, that was big when he made that in '66[4] and this guy Jimmy Myre could sing Little Walter, so he could sing like "Blues with a Feeling" and some stuff like that. I could blow the harp, people would just come up, put money to your head, stick it on your sweating brow, and then throw money at you and women would put money in your pocket and feel your ass at the same time. It's very cool.

Simon: Then you get up and go to school in the morning, or did that fade away?

Oscher: Yeah school kind of . . . when I graduated school I had "50" in every subject.

Simon: But you got through.

Oscher: Yeah I did, yeah. A "50" but that just shows you, like, where my brain was at that time. So, that's what the clubs were like and it was just great, man. I was just surrounded by people, I just loved everything about the music, the people, the scene, the excitement, the women, the sex, the sex was all . . . so much different than going to a white bar. I mean you go to a white bar, you got TV, sports TVs on, the bartender if he doesn't know you he goes, "What do you want it to be, Mac?" That kind of shit. In a black bar the girl says, "Hi baby, what can I do for you?" and then she bends over, she's got a low-cut thing and her cleavage is right there. She bends over and gets you the beer. It's a whole different world than the white clubs—black clubs are just cool.

Simon: So, you weren't doing much work say below 125th Street, like downtown Manhattan?

Oscher: No, no, no. This guy Harmonica Slim though, that guy that took me to Harlem, he lived in the Village, he lived in the basement of a store owned by a guy named Duv, and he got his water out in the back of the toilet.

Simon: In the tank [*laughs*]?

Oscher: Yeah, in the tank. And he cooked with a hot plate and we used to go around the Village and play for tips on the street. He drank Italian Swiss Colony port. This is before I ever got with Muddy [Waters] then he'd go off to a place on the Bowery, which really stunk and it was all winos in there. We'd play and we'd get nickels enough to get another pint, fifty-one cents a pint. But when we played at Eighth Avenue and Forty-Eighth Street, I used to play in a church up there, and the woman that ran the church played the accordion. She called that area the devil's playground and all her clients were like prostitutes and kids of prostitutes and, I mean, people that went to the church. So, Slim, me and him were pretty tight. So, one time we were in the Village and these guys from NYU [New York University] were having a party, so they invited us to play for their party, so I got up there, I'm playing and all of a sudden Slim disappears . . . where the fuck did this guy go, man? I found him in the bathtub. He'd taken one of the bottles of booze into the bathtub and closed the curtain and drank half the bottle and passed out. Harmonica Slim, Andrew Parsons was his name, and that was my first record that I ever made, maybe 1967, at Moe Asch's Folkways Studios on Forty-Seventh Street.

Simon: Who did you do it with?

Oscher: Slim. He brought me up there to make the record with him, but it never got released. I got paid seventy-five dollars for that record.[5]

Simon: I bet the tapes are somewhere.

Oscher: I have the demo from it, 12-inch demo.

Simon: What was the next record?

Oscher: I think it was probably with Muddy Waters. I met Muddy at the Apollo Theatre, it was a big show in July 1965:[6] T-Bone Walker, John Lee Hooker, Bobby "Blue" Bland, Muddy Waters, and Jimmy Reed. It was an all-star blues show. And in the back of the theater where the stage entrance is they have those like fire escape stairs, right? So, I got up on the stairs blowing the harp before the show because I was trying to get in from the back . . . sneak in. So, Luther

"Georgia Boy"–"Snake" Johnson was playing bass with Muddy at the time and he heard me play and he brought Muddy to hear me and they both gave me really good compliments. And when Muddy came to New York in 1967, Snake called me and I sat in with the band. I was hired, so it was pretty cool.[7]

Sharron Clare: So when you were playing at the Apollo Theatre, was that a black [audience] or was it black and white?

Oscher: All black.

Clare: When you played at the church, what kind of music were you playing?

Oscher: Gospel. I played in another gospel church in Brooklyn and it was in Bedford-Stuyvesant, a Sanctified Church and there was a woman . . . I worked in this music store and it was on Brooklyn Avenue and Church Avenue, Milton Arfin Music, and all the pastors and people from the gospel groups used to buy their equipment there. There was a Sam Ash near Union Street and Utica Avenue but they went to Arfin because Milton Arfin Music would give them deals on PAs and stuff for churches. So I met this guy that played the guitar and he played in the church so he brought me down there with him and I noticed right away his shit sounds like blues when he came into the store to play and it was, like, blues. He was squeezing the strings and everything. So, there's a woman at the church about seventy years old, her name Mother Dodds and I said to her, "Mother Dodds, what's the difference between the blues and the gospel music?" She said, "Son, it's the same music, it's the same music, but when you make that turn around like you do in the blues, you are turnin' around to the devil." That's what she said.

Simon: It's the words really, right? [*laughs*].

Oscher: Yeah, it's the words, instead of "Rock Me Jesus" it's "Rock Me Mama."

Simon: Let's talk about some of the strictly New York people.

Oscher: There was a girl Rose Melody, she was from Alabama, she sang with my band, she was a big part of the black scene. She sang on my Spivey single, "Stormy Monday"/"Driving Wheel" by Paul Oscher's Chicago Breakdown Blues Band, in 1976.[8] It's the only 45 ever issued by Spivey, only two hundred were pressed. And there was another girl that used to play in the black clubs, Naomi Davis. Now she uses the name Naomi Shelton and she just sings gospel music. This was in New York in the '60s. And this guy Smilin' Pretty Eddie. He used to book dances, so I used to go with him. Sometimes we played on the dances and he was notorious for, like, trying to beat the band out of the money by leaving after he collected all the money. That's the kind of guy he was, hustler—he used to be a pimp. The thing about him, his eyes never smiled. Like a phony hostess that greets you, big smile like this, but his eyes never smiled, never smiled. You know, what I mean. He was a pimp and he had a protégé, his name was Teddy Walker and he used to sing, like, a lot of Sam Cooke songs. He used to wear clear glasses, just to look cool—not prescriptions, just glasses. You'd see ads for those

Muddy Waters and Victoria
Spivey at the Bottom Line,
New York City, October 3, 1976.
Photo © by Anton Mikofsky,
used with permission.

in the back of *Jet* magazine just to give you a different look—you know, there was ads for wigs and different stuff. Muddy bought a wig in South Central LA, the one where he's got the big pompadour in those pictures. That's the way he looked when I started in the band. And he bought that wig and we were playing in a place called the Burning Spear in Chicago, the old Club DeLisa. Freddy King was the opening act. I had this thing called a flashpot to put flash paper and gunpowder in it. Muddy used to sing, "Got my mojo working, but it ..." I'd hit that thing, be flames and smoke, then he sang, "... just don't work on you" [*laughs*]. It had a great effect. This one night I got too close to his wig ... singed the whole side of it, that's when he went to the natural wig. He loved that wig, man, he would look into the mirror when he's getting ready for the gig, say to himself out loud, "You a real pretty black motherfucker."

Simon: When did you first start meeting people like Jimmy Spruill, Bob Gaddy, Larry Dale?

Oscher: That was through [drummer] Candy McDonald when he was playing, it was about 1971, after I'd left Muddy's band.

Simon: So, you came from Chicago back to New York?

Oscher: Yeah, and then I started playing under the name Brooklyn Slim, not Paul Oscher because I was playing such dumps. I didn't want people to know

(L. to r.), Mickey Baker, Paul Oscher, Champion Jack Dupree, and Louisiana Red, Paris, 1976. Courtesy of Paul Oscher.

Paul Oscher was playing these little places. I was playing this one place every Sunday for about a year called the Fugue on Sixteenth Street and First Avenue [New York]. Lots of people came down there. Joe Turner was there, Doc Pomus, that's where Johnny Copeland came when he first came to New York. I had a gig every Sunday and at first I had it with Ola Dixon on the drums. She was playing drums and then I saw Candy playing somewhere and I told him come on down to my gig, and Candy was just this wonderful drummer, man. He'd take a solo and then stand up and go up on the cymbals and stuff, and at the end of the solo [*sings African-chant style*] like [Babatunde] Olatunji. Hit the tom-toms and shit, and get over every time.[9] So, Candy knew Bob Gaddy and Jimmy Spruill and Larry Dale, and Candy would take me to those gigs. That's how I know them.

   Simon: OK. So, sometimes you played with them?

   Oscher: Yeah, that was pretty cool.

   Simon: Tell me about your experience with Mickey Baker.

   Oscher: Mickey Baker, I met him in Paris. I was over there with Louisiana Red in 1976 on tour. Actually the tour was . . . they really fucked me on this. Red had a manager and the manager said, "Man you want to go on a tour?" And I said, "Yeah." He said you're only going to be over there for a week and we're paying you

$600. I get everything in order, but the day before going on this tour, somehow I remember we was on a rooftop somewhere, he says to me, "Man, you know the way those people over there talk. You know, you can hardly understand 'em. It's not one week, it's six weeks for $200 a week. So, the numbers got juxtaposed and we're only giving you, like, one meal a day, you get breakfast." But I wanted to do it anyway. So I was over there with Red for six weeks, but what I didn't know, we was taking the place of Sonny Terry and Brownie McGhee. So, they put a Red thing over the poster that had originally said, "Sonny Terry and Brownie McGhee." So now it said, "Louisiana Red and Paul Oscher." That was kind of a disappointment for a lot of the audiences because I wasn't Sonny Terry and Red wasn't Brownie McGhee. So, I was over there and that's when I hung out with Jack Dupree and Mickey Baker. Mickey Baker saw me play and invited me to stay in his house in Paris. He lived right near the Bastille and I stayed in his apartment for about two weeks. I remember he cooked some fried eggs with red peppers that I really liked. I found out later that this lick from Mickey and Sylvia's "Love Is Strange," that was really Jody Williams's lick.[10] So, Mickey really stole it.

Simon: Did you do any playing with Mickey when you were at his house?

Oscher: No, we were really just sitting around. He was trying to play slide, but he didn't know how to play slide. He didn't know how to mute the string so it didn't sound scratchy and stuff.

Simon: Larry Dale spoke really highly of Mickey Baker.

Oscher: He's a very nice guy [referring to Dale].

Simon: And Larry Dale said he taught Mickey stuff. Larry said Mickey Baker didn't have a real blues sound, so Larry was teaching Mickey Baker blues.

Oscher: Mickey Baker was trying to get me to teach him blues too, because Mickey Baker was doing shows in Europe as a bluesman, but he wasn't really a blues player. He wasn't like a B. B. King, or T-Bone Walker, that kind of stuff. Mickey Baker was a pop and studio player, but he appreciated the blues when he heard it so that's why he invited me over there so he could try to learn some slide stuff.

Simon: And Jack Dupree is the guy that Bob Gaddy said was his, like, idol and mentor in New York. Dupree lived up in Harlem and was a real seminal figure in the New York scene.

Oscher: He's a little deeper than Gaddy.

Simon: And Larry Dale is the guitarist on one of Jack Dupree's great recordings *Blues from the Gutter* [Atlantic, 1958] under his real name and Ennis Lowery, that's Larry Dale.

Oscher: That's a great record, that *Blues from the Gutter*. That whole crowd, Sticks McGhee, Jack Dupree, Bob Gaddy, Larry Dale, they hung out together.

Simon: Do you think the old guys, what I think of as the original kernel of the New York players like Gaddy and Spruill that were there from the late '40s on, do you hear any difference in their style than like ...?

Oscher: Chicago? Yeah, definitely.

Simon: Can you put it into words?

Oscher: More sophisticated. Larry Dale was a bluesman. I mean there is no real Chicago blues, it's southern blues, then they moved to Chicago. You know, what I mean? There's no West Side blues, no South Side blues [in Chicago]. Just southerners that came from Mississippi, Alabama, Texas, Louisiana, Georgia, Florida—that moved to these places. There's white people, they're the ones that called it Chicago blues. I mean if you ask Buddy Guy what he plays, he'd say, "Blues"; Junior Wells, "We play the blues." You know, they don't play South Side blues or West Side blues. The reason why this happened was because the distribution companies, the record companies had rules of distribution. So, all of the Chess stuff really remained in the Midwest and the South and the Deep South, whereas other companies had the East Coast. So, that's why you see all these styles: West Coast sound, the Midwest-Chicago sound, and the East Coast sound was because of the distribution of the record companies. Because they heard what was played on the radio and they weren't playing Muddy Waters in Virginia. Although maybe Little Walter's "Juke" was a national hit [no. 1 *Billboard* R&B for eight weeks in late 1952], but that's how the styles kind of remained in a certain area. And the New York blues players were from the South originally anyway. I mean Gaddy could also play big band shit and he could play Joe Turner stuff, "Shake, Rattle and Roll," he played a lot of stuff like that. Chicago players didn't play that much of that stuff. Larry Dale could play the B. B. King shit and all that stuff.

Simon: Absolutely. When he would comp instead of playing chords, Larry Dale would very often play almost like what a horn player would play. Instead of chords he would play licks.

Oscher: That's the blues style. What I mean, you know, [*singing*] a repetitive lick. Jimmy Spruill was an interesting player, though, because he would always change up his patterns while he's playing. He wouldn't keep the same pattern all the time.

Simon: He told me he never wanted to be bored so that's probably part of it, he wanted to keep himself interested in what he is doing.

Oscher: He'd always change up stuff, he was really dynamite. I always noticed that about him, he changed the in-between patterns.

Simon: Super creative guy. What do you have to tell me about Doc Pomus, your encounters with him?

Oscher: OK. Well, Doc was coming to my shows since 1975, that was when I first met him, I think. I played Gerde's Folk City in New York. The place was sold out every night. There was an ad, a little ad in the *Village Voice*, "Paul Oscher Blues Band," and I think we got, like, for a whole week something like fifty dollars a man because there's a little tiny guy calculated the shit. I got a fine from the union for that because I was playing in the place and my bass player, his name was Chris Wright, he used to sing with the Swan Silvertones and he could also sing Al Green stuff and sing B. B. King. He was my bass player at the time, he said, "Man, I need to bust a cap in your head." He thought I was ripping him off, but that's the way we got paid. It wasn't me. No, that's what we got, fifty dollars. Place was packed every night. Doc Pomus was there every night, and then he was at my gig at the Fugue. He'd bring Joe Turner down there, and there was a lot of people there: Little Mike, Joe Berson, Ronnie Horvath—that's Ronnie Earl, he was in the front row every weekend, he was with Roomful of Blues. I had definitely a head start among any white players in New York. Doc Pomus used to sing in black clubs like years before me. He knew some of the places that I played at on Fulton Street and he was really respected in black music [circles]. He was going to produce an album with me, but instead he did it with Duke Robillard because I didn't want to sing that Joe Turner song: "She's my TV mama, the one with the big wide screen."

Simon: He wanted, like, jump blues kind of stuff?

Oscher: Yeah, yeah. He really liked Joe Turner.

Simon: I have a kind of philosophical question. Let me throw this one out to you.

Oscher: Let me see what it is first before I [respond] . . . philosophy scares the shit out of me.

Simon: Do you have a musical philosophy or goal? For example, some musicians just see themselves as an entertainer whose goal is to do a great show and make people happy. Others, like Coltrane, have a very complex relationship involving a spiritual path through music.

Oscher: [*long pause*] I don't know if I have any complex path like a spiritual path like Coltrane. Coltrane was also on heroin.

Simon: But his philosophical and spiritual path is what he came to when he got off of it.

Oscher: Oh, OK. You know, I never put too much thought . . . I'll tell you what, I'm happy when I'm playing and nothing goes wrong except sometimes I get cramps in my hands now. I'm just happy I get through the night and I'm happy if I'm kind of free. Like some of the songs I did last night [a weekly gig at C-Boy's, Austin] was very free, like "Blues and Trouble."

Simon: When did you leave New York?

Oscher: I didn't leave New York, I left LA to come here [Austin].

Simon: You were in New York of course. You were born there, then left New York to go to Chicago?

Oscher: Yeah, I lived in Muddy Waters's house there for about four years, five years, and came back to New York and then fucked around New York for a long time.

Simon: And became Brooklyn Slim.

Oscher: Yeah, that was my drinking period. I burned bridges with lots of people and stuff. Then I got married to my wife, and after she won the Pulitzer, she got offered a job at CalArts [California Institute of the Arts in the LA suburb of Valencia]. So, we went out there. My wife was Suzan-Lori Parks.[11] So, we went out there and I stayed out there from 2000 until 2012, but we got divorced in 2011.

Simon: Then you came here to Austin.

Oscher: Austin, yeah, but what I did do in California that was cool, I learned how to do a solo show. So for almost twelve years I was doing solo shows. And I worked up all my shows on the boardwalk. I used to go there at ten o'clock in the morning when the other musicians weren't there so I could just play and hear myself, but I still have an audience going by because you always play better in front of somebody than you do alone in the house. So, that's where I learned my solo show. The funny thing was, I'd go out there and maybe sell a couple of CDs and work up the show. I could play the same song all day until I got it right because people were walking by. But the most money I made on the boardwalk was this film crew was coming in to shoot an ad and didn't have a permit. They had a truck and like twenty people, cameras and everything; they were supposed to get permits, but I guess they had to do it in a hurry, too short a time to get the permit you know. So the guy comes over to me says, "Hey man, would you mind not playing?" "Man, this is where I make my living!" So he reaches in his pocket and he peels off five hundred-dollar bills. And he says, "How about this?" I said, "You got it brother!" [*laughs*]. That's the most money I ever made on the boardwalk. But the best thing the boardwalk ever did for me was [I developed a] solo show and that's when I learned to do the harp and the guitar better. Sometimes I'm playing in unison with the harp. I wanted to set a niche for myself that was different than the harmonica/microphone bandleaders. What I do, there is nobody doing that shit and I still get that tone. So that's the best thing that happened to me. Then when I came to Austin, James Cotton was living three doors down. I went over to this barbecue place, Railroad Bar-B-Cue in Manchaca near Austin that's torn down now, to have dinner with him and his wife, and I said to the woman there, "You have any music in here?" And she said, "What do you play, baby?" So I said, "I play blues." "Well, come on down!" So, the next night, I go over there and they set me up. I had a little crate amplifier that I used for boardwalk blues stuff and I set up there. They sent me in front of a TV, but they shut the TV off, that was nice. They had about four people in the place and I played in the corner, then played for like two hours and didn't make any money or anything. But I hadn't played in like almost a year. After my divorce I did a few gigs somewhere in Canada and some other places. So, I played there and the next day I saw an ad for a stage on Craigslist or something. It was on the East Side in Austin and I went over there and it was like a twenty-foot by ten-foot stage. I had no way of carrying this stage, so I cut it in half and this guy with a pickup truck helped me bring it. I put it in the club and painted it black and I put one half on top of the other so my stage was about twelve inches high. Then I had a nice thing. So, I started this solo show. All I did was say, "Live blues every Tuesday," and some people in Austin found out that one of Muddy Waters's band members was playing there. Then all of a sudden, man, that place got hot like a motherfucker. All the best musicians in Austin was coming down there to see me, the best blues musicians. Then that lasted about four or five months. Then the guy that owned the place, well he leased it, and the people that owned the land got an offer from a developer. So, he had to tear it down, and that was the end of that. Then this guy, Steve Wertheimer, he also owns the Continental Club together with C-Boy's. He asked me to come down there and do my show. I got down there and it just was not the same as this Railroad Bar-B-Cue. That was a real cool place, all wooden floors, wooden ceilings and people were eating barbecue. It was a blues and barbecue place. It was packed and the sound was real good in there. I got over there to C-Boy's and it was like a bar, people drinking and talking and stuff. I was telling stories with my show, you know what I mean . . . of my life and the blues and stuff, you know stories like the story I told you about the Freddy King/Muddy show, or the first time I met Little Walter, things like that. People are really interested in that. So I got down there and I played two weeks, solo and I said, "This is ridiculous." People are drinking. They don't want to see this. So, I told the guy, "Man I need to play with a band here." So, he said, "OK." So, I did that, but the only thing that I regret is that I made myself too accessible. So, it's hard for me to get a big price if people can come see me for five bucks. But what's good about it, it keeps my chops up and keeps a band together. That's more important than the money, but if we go outside Austin, I make pretty good money.

Simon: How did the New York scene change over the years in terms of musicians, the clubs, and the audience?

Oscher: Well, the rock musicians started jumping on the blues bandwagon in the '80s, just because I guess Clapton was popular, they knew Clapton stuff. They started running the blues jams, right, and they started bringing in their rock friends as an audience. And that's when I heard that club owner say, "I can't hire Jimmy Rogers or Pinetop [Perkins] anymore because my audiences don't dig their energy." That's when the blues changed. That's when the blues really got a bad name. I mean as far as I'm concerned, it became not the blues. It changed over with a lot of Hendrix stuff in it.

Simon: And Stevie Ray Vaughan?

Oscher: Stevie Ray Vaughan is a little later, but Stevie Ray Vaughan was more blues-oriented than the stuff I'm talking about. I'm talking about a girl singing "Stormy Monday" and sings, "When Sunday comes, I get down!" [*yells*]. The song is, "When Sunday comes, I get down on my knees and I pray," right? She sings, "When Sunday comes, I get down, I get down, I get down, I get down" [*yelling again*] and then the band goes into this wild solo. That ain't the blues, you know what I mean. So what happened was, they reinvented the blues based on the music they were playing and called it the blues. And that's what changed the whole thing. The people that were into it didn't have any idea where black people came from in the blues. They didn't know that stuff. They just came right out of the back door of Led Zeppelin and the Rolling Stones and groups like Eric Clapton. Groups like that were how they got into the blues. So, these are people that really just didn't understand the blues. They thought just anything can go into 12 bars and anything doesn't go—the blues is a language with a bunch of different dialects. Every blues musician is . . . and remember you quote me on this, this is not you saying this: Every blues musician is a composer and they have their own rules—Muddy Waters, Jimmy Reed, Howlin' Wolf, T-Bone Walker, B. B. King. And you don't mix their styles within the same 12-bar structure. It's like people speaking all different languages at the same time. You go to a blues jam today. You hear somebody play like T-Bone, somebody's playing like Clapton, somebody's playing that Jimi Hendrix, somebody's playing like Robert Johnson. It's like the Babylon, Babel, whatever that was. It's all different languages and they don't go together. When in Chicago, when you went to Pepper's Lounge on a Blue Monday, which is a jam session, they have musicians. If Junior Wells got up there, the musicians played like Junior Wells music. If Otis Rush got up there, they played it like Otis Rush's music. If Otis Spann got up there, they played like Otis Spann. They knew the languages, you know what I mean, and that's the big difference, and a sense of rhythm. So, my music, the thing that I've come to say, I'm not interested in trying to cut my peers. You know what I mean? I'm just happy if I can play better than I did last night, today . . . if things are moving along. So I have a saying, "Don't try to play better than your peers, just try to play better than yourself." That's my theory. That's my, I guess, philosophy, and keep your ego out of shit because, man, you could be playing a great solo and if you say to yourself, "Man that's fucking great," you're going to be right out of the zone. Just go with the flow with the music. Don't worry about making mistakes. Pinetop [Perkins] told me, he said, "Man, when you make a mistake, just do it twice, they'll never know the difference." You should try to get some practice in. [Cellist] Pablo Casals said, "If I don't practice for one day, my friends know it. If I don't practice for two days, my fans know. If I don't practice for three days, everybody knows it" [*laughs*]. But that's what's good about having a steady gig—a once-a-week gig. Yeah, and it also keeps the band together. A great thing about Austin is, if your bass player can't make it, there's six other bass players just as good. If your guitar player can't make it, there's six guitar players that are just as good. They got tons of great musicians here. And the thing

Paul Oscher at C-Boy's Heart and Soul club, Austin, Texas, March 2018. In back, Mike Keller (guitar) and Sarah Brown (bass). Photo by Larry Simon.

about the musicians in Austin, they're not just blues players—they can play any genre because they have to, because of the economy. See, I can't play no country music. I just don't know it and I don't want to know it. And I can't play rock or anything, kind of stuff like that, yeah, but all of the musicians in my band can play any genre and they play well, everyone. Mike Keller, guitar ... he used to be with Kim Wilson's band; the bass guitar player, Sarah Brown, was a big figure in Austin blues scene in the '70s, '80s.

Simon: In closing, would you say there was a favorite time and place in your career?

Oscher: It had to be the time in Chicago, playing with Muddy. My music is from Little Walter, Otis Spann, and Muddy Waters, basically. I mean I do different stuff my way, you know what I mean. I don't do note-for-note covers, which

I always believe that you have to do. But the problem is with white musicians, they don't do anything like this so, like, you'll see black musicians start off B. B. King's "Sweet Sixteen" [*sings opening guitar lick*]. They'll throw that in at least. The whole thing about the blues is telling a story and the music has to go with the story. It's not just the music and it's not just the story. Today, the people don't listen to the words of the story. Black clubs, they listen! When you sing something, you hear black people shouting. Somebody would shout out, "Yeah man, tell it like it is, sing the song." "Man, that sounds like my woman!" You know what I mean, this communication, it's like the church almost. That doesn't happen in the white clubs. They're not listening to the words. They're just looking for some flash and guitar stuff. But I always think that blues is a story. That's what Muddy said, "Blues is a story. You got to tell the story in the blues, and you can't take the blues too far up the road. Otherwise it ain't blues no more." That's what he said.

NOTES

1. Pianist Les Cooper and the Soul Rockers had a big hit with the sax-led instrumental "Wiggle Wobble" for Danny Robinson's Everlast label in early 1963, produced with Bobby Robinson (no. 22 pop, no. 12 R&B on the *Billboard* charts).

2. "Bad Motorcycle," written by Al Browne and Frederick Williams, was a no. 45 *Billboard* pop hit for the Storey Sisters (Cameo) in 1958. The record was originally released by Peak in the name of the Twinkles. Browne, from Brooklyn, was a pianist, bandleader, and producer who worked closely with the popular Heartbeats and songwriter Billy Dawn Smith at Hull Records in 1955–1956. He was *not* the Al Brown who had a top 30 hit in 1960 with "The Madison" (Amy) in the name of Al Brown's Tunetoppers.

3. The Peg Leg Bates Country Club was owned and operated by dancer Clayton "Peg Leg" Bates with his wife Alice in Kerhonkson, Ulster County, in the Catskill Mountains from 1951 to 1987.

4. "Baby Scratch My Back" by swamp-blues harmonica player Slim Harpo (Excello) was one of the biggest R&B hits of 1966, making no. 1 R&B and no. 16 pop in the *Billboard* charts.

5. Harmonica Slim (Andrew Parsons) is listed in *The Blues Discography, 1943–1970* (by Les Fancourt and Bob McGrath; West Vancouver, BC, Canada: Eyeball Productions, 2019) as having recorded unissued titles for Spivey Records in 1967 and having one song released from a 1969 New York session for Mike Vernon's Blue Horizon (UK) label.

6. The handbill for this 1965 Apollo Theatre show describes it as a "A Resounding, Pleasureable [sic] Battle of the Blues," for one week only from Friday, July 2 (see image, page xiii).

7. Oscher followed in the illustrious steps of Little Walter, James Cotton, George Smith, and Mojo Buford in holding the harmonica spot in Muddy Waters's outfit, possibly the best blues band ever. Oscher played with Waters from 1967 through 1971, including recording sessions for Chess, his favorite being the *Muddy Waters "Live" (at Mr. Kelly's)* LP.

8. See also chapter 12 on Victoria Spivey.

9. Candy McDonald played drums on three tracks of Johnny Copeland's W. C. Handy Award–winning LP *Copeland Special* (Rounder), recorded in 1981 at Blank Tapes, 37 West Twentieth Street, New York.

10. "Love Is Strange" by Mickey (Baker) and Sylvia (Vanderpool/Robinson) was a major 1957 *Billboard* hit (no. 11 pop, no. 1 R&B) on Groove, the RCA Victor subsidiary, and is a durable classic. It is generally acknowledged that Baker's ear-catching guitar figures were derived from the Jody Williams licks first heard on Billy Stewart's "Billy's Blues" (Chess, 1956). "Love Is Strange" was allegedly written by Bo Diddley and was actually recorded by him in 1956 but unreleased by Checker at the time. The 2020 BMI registration for the song shows the writers as "Mickey Baker–Ellas McDaniel [Bo Diddley]–Sylvia Robinson."

11. Paul Oscher's former wife, Suzan-Lori Parks, won the Pulitzer Prize for drama in 2002 for her play *Topdog/Underdog.*

John Hammond Jr. (1942–), Courtesy of Two Hands Management, Paul Babin.

10

JOHN HAMMOND JR.

Interviewed September 10, 2019, by Larry Simon,
including questions submitted by John Broven

John Hammond Jr. was born in the heart of New York City's Greenwich Village, on Sullivan Street. He began his career in the early 1960s. Hammond, a singer, guitarist, harmonica player, and songwriter, is known for keeping alive the traditional acoustic blues style as well as working in creative new directions with collaborators such as Tom Waits. Over the years John has played with an enormous number of important and influential artists such as Sonny Terry and Brownie McGhee, Michael Bloomfield, Eric Clapton, Jimi Hendrix, The Band, Muddy Waters, Howlin' Wolf, Dr. John, John Lee Hooker, and many more. John Hammond Jr. has won various awards, including a 1984 Grammy.

Larry Simon: Before we go back and explore your past and the music of that time that you were involved with, I would like to ask you about a particular recording you did that has the guitar player Jimmy Spruill on it. Do you remember your album *Big City Blues*?

John Hammond Jr.: Yes, I do. I remember it well.

Simon: It's such a wonderful recording. It has Jimmy Spruill on it as well as Billy Butler and Jimmy Lewis and Bobby Donaldson. Can you tell me anything about how that session came together?

Hammond: OK. I had signed up with Vanguard Records in 1962, and recorded an album solo, just called *John Hammond*. And it was recorded at the Brooklyn Masonic Temple. It was my first recording, my debut on the scene. When I began playing I was a big fan of country blues—Robert Johnson and Blind Boy Fuller, Blind Willie McTell and Lightnin' Hopkins, and other artists I'd heard on recordings. And I was also a big fan of Howlin' Wolf and Little Walter, and Muddy Waters. So I had these visions of recording Chicago-style as well as country blues, old style. And I made my first record and it was successful

UK release, courtesy of John Broven.

and well reviewed. Vanguard knew a producer named Herb Korsak who worked for Island Records. And they asked him to put together an electric band that would back me up on the second album that I did for Vanguard. I wanted to do Chicago style and my own interpretations of country blues with electric instruments. And he put together Billy Butler, who appeared on "Honky Tonk"—I just loved his playing. I didn't know Jimmy Spruill, but he brought him in. He had played on "Kansas City" [Wilbert Harrison] and lot of other R&B and blues-type recordings. So he was there, and I was twenty years old, and I was a little bit intimidated [*laughs*]. And Jimmy Lewis and Bobby Donaldson made up the whole backup band. I was trying to put across what I wanted to do and they backed me up the best they could. We didn't have a lot of time to record it, so it was done pretty much in about three days I think. It came out the way it did. I was hoping for more of this Chicago-style sound, but I was happy with what we did. I think it was 1963 [released in 1964]. And so it was kind of pre the younger

Chicago artists like, [Paul] Butterfield and [Michael] Bloomfield and so forth. Which is before they released their first recordings. Yeah, Jimmy Spruill was very dynamic and right out there.

Simon: Did you ever end up working with any of those guys again?

Hammond: I worked a gig with Bobby Donaldson on drums and a guitar player, Eric Gale. We did this trio gig at the Village Gate in 1964 for a week. And the Rolling Stones were in New York and they came to hear me play. That was the only band gig that I had with any of those guys. Then I went on to record with a band up in Toronto called Levon [Helm] and the Hawks, for my next Vanguard project, and that was called *So Many Roads* [1965].

Simon: How did that happen? How did you hook up with them in Toronto?

Hammond: Well, I played a lot of gigs up in Canada, in Montreal, Ottawa, and Toronto. In Toronto I was introduced to Levon and the Hawks and we became really good friends. They came to my shows, and I went to their shows, and I sat in with them a bunch of times. They were in New York trying to get a demo session together. And they weren't having a lot of luck and I said "Listen, I record for Vanguard and maybe you guys could record with me on a tune or two?" And it turned into a whole session. We made this album that I thought very dynamic and more in the direction of what I was trying to do with *Big City Blues*. Also, I had spent some time in Chicago, and I met Michael Bloomfield and Charlie Musselwhite, Elvin Bishop and a lot of the young Chicago guys that were just starting out. And Charlie and Michael were in New York at that time and I asked them if they wanted to be part of the project. So Charlie played harmonica on the album and as a result of that, Vanguard signed him up for his own projects.

Simon: Before we leave the topic of the recording session for *Big City Blues*, I'd like to ask if you could say anything about the personalities or style, in the studio, of any of the guys on the session, like Spruill or Billy Butler. What the session actually was like in the studio with them.

Hammond: Well, they were so professional and they had obviously recorded many times. They knew what they were doing. They knew how to do retakes and overdubs and stuff like that, that I didn't know anything about. I was very intimidated by their professionalism and so forth, but I did the best I could. Billy Butler was, I just admired him so much. I was very impressed. He could really play. Jimmy Spruill was like very dynamic. He was trying to do ultra lead licks—and that was also pretty impressive. I was very impressed with their professionalism and I did the best I could.

Simon: Getting back to what you were saying, you ended up working with Bloomfield and those Chicago players. Did they come to New York or you went to Chicago to record?

Hammond: No, they came to New York. I was based in New York even though I traveled extensively and I'd been to Chicago and all over.

Simon: And you, of course, were living in New York.

Hammond: Yes, I was born in Greenwich Village.

Simon: What street?

Hammond: I was born in Sullivan Street. When I was five we moved to Mac-Dougal Street. And this was in the heart of the Village back in 1942.

Simon: So when you started playing the clubs, I imagine your earliest club dates were the ones in the Village, is that right?

Hammond: My earliest club dates were in California. I went as far away from home as I could get. And I started playing in the Los Angeles area. I got my thing together there and came back to New York in December of '62. And I got a gig in a club called Gerde's Folk City [at 11 West Fourth Street in Greenwich Village]. That was my first New York professional date. Before I had gone to California I had played little basket houses, you know, where you go in and play a twenty-minute set and pass your hat at the end of the show. I use to hang out with the New York scene guys. At that time Dave Van Ronk was the reigning blues guy and playing in clubs for money. And I knew that this is what I wanted to do big time. There was a trio from Minneapolis that were playing in New York called Koerner, Ray & Glover and they played acoustic county blues. They did lot of Lead Belly songs and Blind Boy Fuller Piedmont-style blues. They were really good and I really enjoyed hanging out with them. But I used to go to the basket houses with Bob Dylan and Richie Havens, José Feliciano, John Sebastian. We were all of the same generation and hanging out in the Village. There was a real scene at the Village.

Simon: Of course. And you were always doing strictly blues?

Hammond: Yes. That's all I've ever wanted to do.

Simon: And how did that happen for you? Was it just something in your DNA? What do you think about that?

Hammond: I don't know. I just was always attracted to the blues music. When I was seven years old my dad [John Hammond II] brought me to hear Big Bill Broonzy, who played a show at Judson [Memorial] Church, in Washington Square in the Village. And then after the show I was introduced to him, he was a friend of my father. And I just gravitated toward blues ever since then. I became a fan of Sonny Terry and Brownie McGhee, who had played often in the Village. I started buying records and I never thought that I would just play blues. But, I was a big fan. I got a guitar in 1960 and started to play blues myself. In 1962 I started playing professionally.

Simon: That was a pretty quick advance.

Hammond: Yes. I knew all the songs, it was just a matter of being able to put enough guitar together to back up the songs I loved.

Simon: Did you ever do any playing with Sonny Terry and Brownie McGhee?

Hammond: Yes, I did. In fact, I recorded with them, backing them up when I was out on the West Coast.[1] It was very exciting for me. I was a big fan of theirs.

Sonny Terry and Brownie McGhee at the Jazz Expo '67 concert, Hammersmith Odeon, London, October 26, 1967. Photo by Val Wilmer.

Simon: Who would you say are your teachers? Either literally that taught you or by listening to them or to their recordings?

Hammond: Well I didn't have . . . you know, I was still embarrassed to ask anybody to show me stuff. But I used to watch guys play and sort of figured it out of myself. When I was in school in Ohio I had a roommate who had a twelve-string guitar. I was very impressed. His name was Russell Avery. I used to watch him play, and he could play folk-style guitar. There was another guy named Bob Silverman who also played guitar and I used to watch him. And then there was the reigning blues guy. This was at Antioch College in Ohio and his name was Ian Buchanan. He's a New Yorker. And he actually played professional gigs in New York, in the Village. Ian was a friend, or a student of Reverend Gary Davis. So he did lot of that Piedmont-style blues. And he had a student named, they called him at that time, Jerry Kaukonen who turned out to be Jorma Kaukonen. I used to watch them play, and that was very impressive. It impressed me to the point where I thought, gee, I could do that. So, I got my first guitar after that and just drove everybody nuts playing all the time. When I left school, I was in New York, I started hanging out with the guys I mentioned before, Richie Havens and José [Feliciano] and Dylan and John Sebastian. Anyway, I just got to the point where I had to do it. I was little intimidated by New York so I went as far away as I could get and wound up in Los Angeles. Started to play out there.

Simon: And then came back to New York, and settled in, or you stayed in LA?

Hammond: Yeah, I came back to New York and said "Well I got my stuff together now. Let's see what happens." And then I auditioned at Gerde's Folk City. I got the gig and I shared the bill with Phil Ochs for a weekend. We were held over for a week and we both got signed up to Vanguard Records.

Simon: Did you get the sense that audiences at that time were interested in blues, that it was a growing interest at that time?

Hammond: Yeah, you know the folk scene included blues. Sonny Terry and Brownie McGhee, Lead Belly. They were artists that fit into the folk scene because they played acoustic, you know? And they could play in the little clubs like the Gaslight and [Gerde's] Folk City and the Bitter End and other clubs in the city that weren't large enough to have the big bands and stuff, the loud rock 'n' roll stuff. So anyway, the blues was included in the folk scene and there were enough artists that were emerging playing blues that were accepted by the folk crowd. And then, it expanded into the blues fanatics.

Simon: In the early part of your career were you playing equally with electric bands and solo acoustic shows?

Hammond: I would say 90 percent of my gigs were acoustic. I would sit in sometimes with groups that had begun by playing electric. When I was in Chicago we were hanging out with Michael Bloomfield, Charlie Musselwhite, Elvin Bishop, Paul Butterfield, and so forth. I would sit in occasionally with them. I wasn't unfamiliar with electric-style playing. But I was more of the acoustic style. When I was in Toronto, when I met Levon Helm and Robbie Robertson and the guys in their band [the Hawks, predecessors of The Band], I would sit in with them. So I didn't feel unfamiliar. When I made the *Big City Blues* album I knew I was capable of playing electric in that style. Michael Bloomfield put a little band together for me and sent them from Chicago to New York and we played some gigs in New York, Philadelphia, and Boston. That was over about a two-week, three-week span. It was Johnny Littlejohn on guitar, Roosevelt Broomfield on bass, and Billy Bolden on drums. And these guys were right out of Chicago and they couldn't figure me out. Anyway we had these bizarre gigs. I played electric guitar and did the best I could. I put my own little band together in 1966. And for about five years, on and off, I had that little trio together. There was a guy named Charles Otis, drummer from New Orleans, who had come up to New York with [Jerry] Leiber and [Mike] Stoller, and became their studio drummer, and played behind the Coasters and the Drifters, and a lot of the R&B out of New Orleans, for Red Bird Records.[2] And I did an album for Red Bird called *I Can Tell*. It was released on Atlantic a year later.

Simon: And you also did a recording for Red Bird called "I Wish You Would," right?

Hammond: Yeah, that was the B side of the single "I Can Tell."[3] Then we had all this extra time in the studio and we went on to record an album's worth of songs.

Simon: Who were the players on those Red Bird sessions?

Hammond: It was myself on guitar and harmonica, Robbie Robertson on guitar, Charles Otis on drums, and Artie Butler on the keyboards. The bass player was Bill Wyman of the Stones, who I had gotten to know when the Stones saw me playing in New York at the Village Gate.

Simon: And those sessions were produced by Leiber and Stoller?

Hammond: Yes, they were.

Simon: When Leiber and Stoller were producing you, were they trying to go after a British R&B or blues sound, maybe like the early Stones or Yardbirds? Was that a conscious direction in those sessions?

Hammond: No, it was me doing what I wanted to do and then saying, "Gee, that sounds great," and they got behind it. The fact that Bill Wyman was playing bass, I don't think they were even that familiar with him. This was in 1965. I had gone to England in '65 and did a bunch of gigs over there. I had met up with guys like Eric Clapton and John Mayall and Stevie Winwood and the whole cast of characters that were playing blues over there. I was familiar that they were into the same thing that I was. There was a guy named Alexis Korner, [a guitarist] who was the father of British blues, they said. And there were a lot of disciples of his, and he had his own radio show. He was a blues guru there. I met him and so many other really great players.

Simon: There is a harmonica player from Brooklyn. I'm wondering if you ever crossed paths with Paul Oscher?

Hammond: Yeah, man. What a great player! I met Paul when he was playing with Muddy Waters and we were on some gigs together in Canada. I was always impressed with him. He's a terrific player. He called himself Brooklyn Slim.

Simon: Yeah, when he came back to Brooklyn and was doing smaller club dates, kind of incognito. Do you have any perspective on the development of the New York blues scene from the 1940s through the '50s and '60s? And this would be the New York musicians like Sonny Terry and Brownie McGhee. Even though they came up from Georgia and Tennessee, they pretty much settled in New York along with Sticks McGhee [Brownie's brother] and Jack Dupree, also Doc Pomus. I'm talking about Harlem, the Bronx, and Brooklyn.

Hammond: In the late '30s there was a club in Greenwich Village called Café Society [1938–1948; Hammond's father, John II, was a musical adviser for this racially integrated and politically progressive nightclub]. It was run by guy named Barney Josephson. And he booked a lot of artists, mostly jazz, but he also had blues artists there as well. Josh White had a scene going in New York for a while. I was actually on some gigs with Josh White. And when the Village Gate [158 Bleecker Street] opened [in 1958], it incorporated a lot of the philosophy of Café Society. It was a large enough venue so that they could have a big crowd and they could pay the artists. And they had blues artists as well as jazz and folk artists. Art D'Lugoff was the founder and an amazing guy. This guy named Mike Porco opened Gerde's Folk City in New York [original location, 11 West Fourth Street]. It was just called Gerdes when he opened it. He had a place in the Bronx, where he booked a lot of blues artists. This is in the '50s. He booked Roosevelt Sykes and Lightnin' Hopkins and John Lee Hooker. Real blues guys. When he opened his bar in the Village, this is probably late '50s, because it was in the Village, a lot of the Village guys would come and hang out. And it was a large enough room. A guy named Israel Young, who had a place called the Folklore Center on MacDougal Street, went in there and approached Mike Porco and said, "I know you have a place in the Bronx, where you have music. If we could book your room [on West Fourth] on the weekends and have folk acts in there, would that be OK with you?" And Mike said, "OK." And so, they would charge a door charge for the audience who wanted to hear the folk music and Mike would make [money from] the bar. And it became so successful that Mike said, "Listen, I think I can do this myself." So he turned it into Gerdes Folk City [first Gerdes, then Gerde's] and he booked all kinds of artists there, from Joan Baez to bluegrass bands to blues and folk artists, and it became Gerde's Folk City. That's how that scene happened.

From what I'm told, in the '40s, West Third Street, in the Village, was the home of a lot of, either jazz clubs or strip joints, where they had live bands.

And, I remember when I was a kid walking down Third Street, there were a lot of clubs and they had jazz and blues. I was too young to get in. Eddie Condon had a joint there [47 West Third Street—opened in 1945, before moving to Fifty-Second Street]. The Village was always a wide-open scene, it was very bohemian. The racism and the segregation of that era was very oppressive so if there was a place like the Village, where black and white audiences could be together and hear music that was racially mixed, it was a haven for that. And so, the Village became known as a place that blues and black and white artists could play together and not be stigmatized.

I got to know Willie Dixon and he told me stories of coming to New York with Memphis Slim and playing gigs at the Village Gate and recording in New York—and knowing that New York was a scene. Chicago was always a blues scene, but it was limited to, you know, a certain record label type of mentality[4] that didn't include a lot of traveling and so forth so. To come to New York and to be in a bigger venue, it was a big deal. [Willie Dixon] told me a story of how [Dixon and Memphis Slim] were on the train from Chicago to New York, and he had this idea to just sort of rewrite all these county blues tunes that he had learned as a kid and make them into his own songs. And, you know, that was the beginning of his career, I guess, as a songwriter and a collaborator with Slim and all these other great Chicago artists like Howlin' Wolf and Muddy Waters and Little Walter. But it was on a trip to New York on the train, he said that.[5]

Simon: Do you have any thoughts on why New York never became known as a blues city like Chicago, Memphis, or LA?

Hammond: I think New York was the jazz capital and that's where all the hip, cool jazz guys played. And it was also a folk mecca. Greenwich Village and Peter Seeger and the Weavers and all the great folk artists sort of established themselves. There was always a blues scene in New York, but less . . . I mean, like for blues [it was] Chicago; folk, New York—and jazz. Jazz artists always sort of looked down on blues artists. Well that was my impression anyway.

Simon: After *Big City Blues* for Vanguard in 1964 and your Red Bird recordings, did you then go on to record for Atlantic and Columbia? Is that the sequence?

Hammond: Yes, exactly. I made this single for Red Bird and in the can they had about twelve other songs. So the owner of the label, George Goldner, bought out Leiber and Stoller [in April 1966], they were no longer involved with Red Bird [which soon folded]. When I signed with Atlantic, with Jerry Wexler in 1967, they bought the tapes and released the album on Atlantic [*I Can Tell*], which was everything I had done for Red Bird, as much I can tell. And then I went into the studio and recorded an album for [Atlantic] called *Sooner or Later*. And then I went on to record one more album for them in 1969 called *Southern Fried*. And they never really did much promotion on those records.

Simon: That was with the Muscle Shoals people?

Hammond: Yes, exactly. Duane Allman was playing lead guitar on some of it. But that was the Muscle Shoals [Sound Studio] band: Spooner Oldham [keyboards], Roger Hawkins [drums], and David Hood [bass], Eddie Hinton, Jimmy Johnson [guitars]. This was their scene.

Simon: That's a really good record. How do you feel about it?

Hammond: Yes, it's a good record.

Simon: Indeed, yeah. When you think of all of your recordings, are there a couple that stand out that you are particularly proud of?

Hammond: Oh! There's several that I feel very good, that came out the way I had hoped they might. I made some albums with J. J. Cale producing, *Got Love if You Want It* [1992], *Found True Love* [1996]. *Trouble No More* [1994] was a good one, too, with Charles Brown playing piano on that. J. J. Cale was an amazing guy, yeah. But that's the '90s.

Simon: Did you ever do any work with Mickey Baker?

Hammond: Mickey Baker, no, but I was a fan of his. Great player.

Simon: Did your dad influence your career in any way?

Hammond: Actually I didn't grow up with my father. My parents were divorced when I was five. But he would take me to recording studios, you know, that's the work that he did. So I was not unfamiliar with the scene. I never thought that I would ever be involved in anything like that, when I was a kid. But, when I got my own passion for blues and got into playing, I wanted to be professional. I think he was a little worried for me [*laughs*]. He said, "This is a big mistake." And I said, "Well I don't care, this is what I'm gonna do." And so, I just went out and did it. And I think he was proud that I went my own way and did it in my own way.[6]

NOTES

1. John Hammond Jr. recorded the track "Walkin' My Blues Away" for the Sonny Terry and Brownie McGhee A&M LP, *Sonny & Brownie*, cut in Hollywood in 1972.

2. Charles "Honeyboy" Otis started out playing drums with Professor Longhair in New Orleans and recorded with him for Federal in December 1951. Otis came to New York with the Joe Jones band for the 1964 World's Fair and stayed, becoming a fixture on the New York scene. Otis had one cult single for Red Bird in 1964 as the Honeyman: "Brother Bill (The Last Clean Shirt)"/"James Junior," produced by Leiber and Stoller. Otis also accompanied Hammond on his *Source Point* Columbia LP (1971), with New Orleans R&B pianist Esquerita on one track. Otis was inducted into the Blues Hall of Fame in 2011, and he died in 2015.

3. Hammond's "I Wish You Would"/"I Can Tell" was released by Red Bird in December 1965. Both songs were from the classic Chicago blues school, written and recorded by Billy Boy Arnold and Bo Diddley, respectively.

4. Hammond is referring to the dominance of the Chess and Vee-Jay record labels in Chicago in the 1950s and early 1960s.

5. Bass player Willie Dixon came to New York with veteran pianist Memphis Slim to record for Prestige Bluesville in December 1959. Dixon was already established by then as a producer and songwriter for the Chess and Cobra labels, and was a major figure behind the Chuck Berry and Bo Diddley hits of the era.

6. It is hard to overestimate the massive impact that Hammond's father, John II, had in elevating jazz, blues, and rock in New York and throughout the world during his lifetime and beyond.

RICHARD TAPP INTERVIEW

Sonny Terry and Bob Malenky (1943–) at a photo session for the Terry album *Robbin' the Grave* (1974). Photo by Kyril Bromley.

11

BOB MALENKY'S
NEW YORK MEMORIES

New York guitarist Bob Malenky offers fascinating insights into his early blues influences growing up in New York. These in turn led to his involvement in the city's blues scene in the early 1970s, working with Bill Dicey, Charles Walker, and Sonny Terry, and at Spivey Records with Len Kunstadt and Victoria Spivey.

Born on March 3, 1943, in Borough Park, Brooklyn, Malenky's first musical experience was listening to his parents' records of the Almanac Singers, a New York folk music group active between 1940 and 1943 that included Woody Guthrie and Pete Seeger. However, when he was about twelve years old, Malenky started to be attracted to blues and jazz, this when he began listening to black radio stations. He recalled, "By far the bluesiest station was WNJR, which broadcast from Newark across the Hudson River. They had a disc jockey by the name of George Hudson who played a great variety of blues records including then-popular pieces by B. B. King, Junior Parker, and Jimmy Reed as well as the more down-home blues of Muddy [Waters], [Howlin'] Wolf, and Sonny Boy Williamson [Rice Miller]. Hudson even reached back playing Lil Green and Jazz Gillum."

There were other radio stations, too, that young Malenky listened to. He remembered Ramon Bruce (of Philadelphia) on WHAT: "He would play rock 'n' roll but would always throw in really interesting blues." Another was WWRL, which featured Dr. Jive, a disc jockey whose real name was Tommy Smalls. But as the 1950s went on, the blues steadily yielded to teenage vocal groups, although individual DJs had more freedom to play what they wanted: "It was still possible to hear Jimmy Reed, even Lil' Son Jackson or Robert Nighthawk stuck in among the endless doo-wops." Instrumentals, usually blues, were often used at the beginning or end of programs, so were rarely heard right through. One instrumental with particular memories is "Gravy Train" by Riff Ruffin on

Bobby Robinson's Fire label in 1960. It was a record with special significance, as Ruffin was the first blues artist whom Malenky encountered.

RIFF RUFFIN/LIGHTNIN' HOPKINS/MUDDY WATERS

"I was in my first year at Hunter College and during the week between Christmas and New Year 1960 there was a large party at an apartment on New York's Lower East Side, a fundraiser for the civil rights movement. I had taken along my battered steel-string acoustic guitar on which I had begun to play rudimentary blues and [at one point in the evening] a short black man was playing my guitar and singing 'There Is Something on Your Mind,' the Big Jay McNeely hit [Swingin', 1959], which had recently been remade by Bobby Marchan [on Fire]. It was Riff Ruffin. When he had done playing, we introduced ourselves and started to talk about music. I brought up the name Muddy Waters and Ruffin said that he'd known Muddy—'we used to get drunk together in Chicago.' However, in the years since that chance meeting, I've heard little from or about Ruffin, although I've played with and spoken to various blues musicians who were at one time associated with the New York scene, but I'll always remember my first meeting with a working blues musician."

Malenky continued his academic education, which culminated in a master's degree in musicology at the City College of New York. Along the way, there were two other memorable encounters with blues artists: "There was another DJ on WNJR, Pat Connell, who was doing a commercial for a record store in Newark [almost certainly Essex Record Shop], he said: 'They have the real down-home blues—Muddy Waters, Howlin' Wolf, and Lightnin' Hopkins.' I found used 45s of Wolf and Muddy Waters, but not Hopkins. But when the folkies rediscovered Hopkins and started doing his riffs, I began listening to his records.[1] His standard riff isn't hard to do, I picked it up and it was a jumping-off point for a lot of my guitar playing. Anything I play has some reference to Hopkins. In the spring of 1962 he came down to Washington Square Park, where a lot of musicians gathered, late one afternoon and he started to play, hoping to make some money, but nobody was giving him any at the time, although I did get to jam with him a little bit. Then later on, a friend of mine lent him a twelve-string guitar for a gig at the Village Gate, and we went up to the Albert Hotel on Tenth Street to collect the guitar and we sat around jamming with him for a couple of hours or so and I was able to watch him close up. He played mainly at the Village Gate and sometimes in concert. I went to see him as often as I could. His was a white audience but the folkies were really not as much interested in Hopkins as they were in the prewar players like Mississippi John Hurt. Hopkins was a very charismatic guy, a kind and gentle man but he drank a lot and the alcohol sometimes interfered with his personality. He always wanted 'cash on the barrel.' He spent it as fast as he made it. When he came down to Washington Square on that Sunday, I'm sure he had been paid at the Village Gate on Saturday night but had nothing left."

Then in the summer of 1966 Malenky met up with Muddy Waters: "My sister-in-law had gone up to Cambridge, Massachusetts, and Muddy Waters was playing at the famous Club 47 [in Harvard Square], that was the main venue of the folk world of the Boston area at the time. She just made friends with some of the musicians who said: 'We're going to be recording in New York, we're going to be making an album with Otis Spann.' It was the one which came out on Bluesway. They wanted to simulate a live audience, so we went down there and there I am, and Muddy Waters, my all-time hero is pouring me bourbon whiskey.[2] Over the next couple of years, every local blues guy was hanging around with Muddy Waters, but I was one of the earlier ones and he gave me a little lesson in Delta blues playing. It wasn't easy but I picked up a lot of his riffs."

BILL DICEY AND WASHBOARD BILL'S NEW ORLEANS TRIO

It was Bill Dicey who gave Malenky his introduction to the local New York blues scene around 1970. Bob remembered that Dicey had been down in Atlanta, where he had played with Buddy Moss, whom Bob did get to know: "He was a very bitter guy, he had a lot of bad breaks, but there was a warm side to him. Moss never lived in New York, but I heard him here twice: once at the Electric Circus in St. Mark's Place [in 1969] and at a festival in Tompkins Square Park in the East Village in summer '70. I've read in Bruce Bastin's book, *Red River Blues*, that Moss had recorded in New York in the '30s with Blind Willie McTell and Curley Weaver." Dicey had moved up to New York, first to the Bronx, looking to make it in the blues world. However, by the time Malenky met Dicey, the window of opportunity had passed: "Muddy Waters [had] offered him opportunities to play with his band but he [Dicey] wouldn't take it, he wanted to be the main guy." Bob first saw Dicey in action when he was playing with Luther "Snake Boy" Johnson's band at Columbia University: "Luther introduced me to this guy: 'This is my harp player.' Later on a friend of mine in City College who played guitar was playing with Bill Dicey down at [Gerde's] Folk City on [130] West Third Street. Jerome Arnold, Billy Boy's brother, would come down sometimes and play bass. That was the first time I played with Bill Dicey." Malenky remembered Dicey fondly: "He was a really good harmonica player. He could play a lot of different styles. He could do Little Walter style to a T."

It was in the fall of 1970, when Bob was married with two children and working as a music teacher at a private school, that Dicey said to him: "You gotta

Mickey and Sylvia recording session information, with Washboard Bill Cook on "No Good Lover."
Courtesy of Sony Music Archives.

come down hear these guys, they're playing at a place on Ninety-Sixth Street
and Second Avenue. There's a whole blues band down there."

Malenky continued: "We went down and the band was Washboard Bill and
his New Orleans Trio, even though there was nobody from New Orleans.[3]
Washboard Bill had a long history. He had played with King Curtis and Mickey
Baker for King [Records] and was on Mickey and Sylvia's recording of 'No

Good Lover." The trio consisted of Washboard Bill Cooke, who was wearing a white coat with tails and a top hat and playing the washboard—two washboards screwed together on top of a stool; this guy Charles Walker [guitar] of whom I'd never heard; and Sugar Blue [harmonica]. Sugar Blue wore a derby hat, a very young handsome guy at the time.[4] So there they were, this trio, and we sat in with them and they offered us a regular gig." However, the gig didn't last long. It involved playing until four o'clock in the morning four days a week. Malenky was teaching, and it was all too much, although Bob remembered that Dicey had no limitations even though he had a full-time job and children at home: "He thought he was superman."

The bar was called Sports Corner, and it was run by Jimmy Archer, who had been a boxer. People from the Metropolitan Hospital, which was right across the street, came by, and they were the audience. Some nights the bar was dead, but on others there would be a large contingent of local people. The trio also had an entourage of female followers. One was Ola Dixon, who also sang at times with two girlfriends as a vocal trio. Dixon was a musician and sometimes played drums in the band.[5] They played mainly blues standards with Bill Dicey playing harmonica, as did Sugar Blue, but in two very different styles. Sugar Blue was very much influenced by Sonny Boy Williamson (Rice Miller) and played in a

Bobby Bennett (aka Bobby King, Professor Six Million) and Sterling Magee (aka Mr. Satan), 125th Street, Harlem, 1982. Photo by Val Wilmer.

very melodic style, while Dicey played more in a powerhouse style. The band was stable for a while, but there were conflicts, as Walker was an argumentative character. He had a feud with Sugar Blue, who left the band. Walker also didn't hit it off with Washboard Bill, who was a gentle sort of guy and stopped coming along to the gig. Other musicians filled the breach. One was Bobby Bennett.

Washtub bass player Professor Six Million (Bobby Bennett) was one of the musicians who gigged at the Sports Corner bar with Charles Walker and Bob Malenky. Sterling Magee, the guitarist later pictured with Bennett [see page 191], had a couple of excellent rhythm & blues singles on Ray Charles's Tangerine label in 1967. Magee later adopted the name Satan and in the early 1980s was discovered performing as a one-man band on the streets of Harlem by Adam Gussow, a white New York harmonica player. The pair teamed up and enjoyed considerable success as Satan and Adam, recording three albums and touring both nationally and internationally, before Magee suffered a nervous breakdown in 1998, which halted the partnership.

CHARLES WALKER

Charles Walker was born in 1922 in Macon, Georgia,[6] and like many blues musicians moved north up the East Coast to the New York area. He didn't talk much to Bob Malenky about his formative years, although he did say that his father had been a blues singer, "Bo Weevil" Walker, who had never recorded. The son's own career as a blues singer and guitarist started in 1955 in clubs in Newark, with his debut on record coming after he'd moved to Harlem. This was on Danny Robinson's Holiday label with the two-part instrumental "Driving Home," released in 1956. Maurice Simon was the tenor sax player and is credited on the label, while the label also carries a credit "Guitar – James Spruill," with the single seemingly marking Jimmy Spruill's first appearance on wax. Walker's second record followed three years later and again was for Danny Robinson, this time on the Vest label, coupling the instrumental "Charles Walker Slop" with "It Ain't Right." A 1964 session for Atlas Records produced two singles before Bobby Robinson worked his magic with Walker in 1971: "You Know It Ain't Right" (a remake of "It Ain't Right") released on Bobby's Fury label was Walker's best outing on record. The single romps along with some fine harmonica from Larry Johnson and driving piano work courtesy of Lee Roy Little.

Although he is not on the session, it was at the time of the Fury recording that Bob Malenky was a regular member of Walker's band. Following on from meeting Walker at Sports Corner, he worked with him through New Year's Eve 1972. Bob took up the story: "Charles was a heavy guy by the time; he was in his fifties and in bad shape. He had emphysema so you could hardly understand him when he spoke, he had to stop for breath every two words. He could play a bit of lead guitar but rarely did, usually rhythm in the fashion of Jimmy Reed and sang. He played a lot of Elmore James material; 'The Sky Is Crying' was one of his specialty numbers, as was Muddy's 'Forty Days and Forty Nights.' There wasn't much original material, although he did talk about 'Driving Home'— he actually played drums on that session, he was a rudimentary drummer as well. Charles Walker was pretty much living at what had been Bobby Robinson's studio on 125th Street and Eighth Avenue. We would go over there to rehearse on Saturdays. It was a shambles but you could see there was an office, a control room, also a piano and a Wollensak tape recorder. Bobby Bennett would point to this and say: 'It was on here that "Fannie Mae" [by Buster Brown] was recorded.' Bobby Robinson had the keys so we were always running into him. In the summer of 1971 Walker had a session with Herb Abramson who had a studio in the Seventy-Sixth Street area.[7] We went over there to record and Charles was drunk. He was yelling and screaming and playing the guitar too loud, and they didn't get any usable takes. This was Charles Walker's big break and he completely blew it! Also around 1971 he had this guy Peter Brown who was interested in Walker who he saw had some commercial possibilities. We did release four recordings which came out on P&P Records."[8]

"Driving Home," courtesy of Richard Tapp; "40 Days–40 Nights," courtesy of Victor Pearlin.

Courtesy of Larry Simon.

Bob Malenky recalled some of the club gigs he played: "We would usually be a four piece: Charles Walker, me, Dicey, and some kind of percussion. Walker would sing his specialty Elmore James and Muddy Waters numbers and a lot of Jimmy Reed songs; Dicey's specialty was Slim Harpo's 'Baby Scratch My Back' while I played Chuck Berry things like 'Johnny B. Goode.' But we didn't get many gigs; we played Roslyn [Long Island] and got out to Jersey City. Walker found most of the gigs, they were black venues. We never drew a white audience, but not many people came to see us. These were places he had played in the '50s when blues was really a going thing in the black community. He was [still] sure he was going to be a star but was remembering things from fifteen years before. We played this place in the South Bronx, which had been a nightclub. We played in the basement but sneaked up to what had been the nightclub. It was deserted but on the tables there were still beer coasters with Jimmy Reed and Big Maybelle advertising Rheingold beer. You could imagine what it must have been like when it was a going concern."

Things came to an end on New Year's Eve in 1972: "We were playing out in Long Island at Wyandanch, which is a black community. We were playing blues and the crowd didn't want to hear us at all, they wanted dance music—James Brown. [Afterward] we were being driven back to New York and the car broke down on the Northern State Parkway. We waited for hours for someone to come and get us, and I walked into my home at about ten o'clock in the morning. I'm sure my wife thought I was fooling around but I wasn't. I was really stuck. So I just decided I didn't want to work with Walker anymore. After that gig I just didn't want to have much to do with him. He wanted us to go out to the Colonial House club at Huntington Station to play for the door. If we were out there in Long Island at two o'clock in the morning, how would we get home? Neither Dicey nor I wanted to do it. There was no guarantee of any money. We'd had enough. I had a wife and family and wanted to be responsible."

After this parting of the ways, Walker had one last chance to feature on wax. This was when local musician Tom Pomposello recorded Walker and Lee Roy Little in a series of sessions held in 1973 and 1974 with the resulting tracks appearing on the *Blues from the Apple* LP. Bill Dicey and Ola Dixon can also be heard on the album, which was released on Pomposello's Oblivion label.[9]

Then in June 1975 came the news of Walker's passing. Malenky remembered: "I received a phone call from Sugar Blue to say that Charles had died. I went to the funeral up in Harlem, which was an unusual affair. He had written into his will that there were to be no spirituals and no religious content in the service, which made things awkward for the pastor conducting the service, although he did perform the final committal."

VICTORIA SPIVEY AND LEONARD KUNSTADT, SPIVEY RECORDS

"Inevitably any blues players in New York would come in contact with Victoria Spivey and Len Kundstadt,"[10] Malensky said. "I first met them backstage at a Muddy Waters concert. Kunstadt called her 'the Queen of the Blues' and supposedly they were married. They lived together in an apartment in Crown Heights in Brooklyn, which was kind of a center for blues activity. It was amazing some of the local blues people Spivey [Records] found, some of them very good. I can't remember too many of the names but one was this guy who claimed to be Smokey Hogg.[11] But Len was the mover and shaker behind everything. He set up the record label and I think he had more tapes in the closet than anything he ever released; I think some are better than the stuff he put out."

Spivey Records, owned by Victoria Spivey and Leonard Kunstadt, was effectively one step above a vanity label, concentrating on blues albums recorded with a "live" ambience. Starting out as Queen Vee Records, all told the label released about forty LPs from 1962 through the mid-1980s.

Victoria Spivey hailed from the classic female blues era of Bessie Smith and Ma Rainey, and recorded regularly for OKeh, Victor, Decca, and Vocalion from 1926 through 1937. Spivey was born on October 15, 1906, in Houston and died on October 3, 1976, in New York. Kunstadt, before cofounding Spivey Records with Victoria Spivey, was editor and publisher of *Record Research* and *Blues Research* magazines—the latter with Anthony Rotante and Paul Sheatsley—which were early and esteemed discographical vehicles. Kunstadt was born in Brooklyn on May 15, 1925, and died on April 23, 1996. His research papers are lodged with the Institute of Jazz Studies, Rutgers University Libraries.

Malenky had the opportunity to record for Spivey Records on several occasions. This is one example: "In January of 1970 on a Friday afternoon, Len called me up and invited Dicey and me over, I didn't know what it was for. I was playing flute at the time and Lenny said: 'Come on over Monday afternoon and bring your flute.' I went over and it turned out it was going to be a session with Roosevelt Sykes. First in comes Bill Dicey, and then John Hammond. Dicey asked if I'd ever met Roosevelt Sykes which I hadn't and Dicey assured me: 'He's a prince of a fellow.' That's the first I heard that Sykes was going to be there! I played flute. The Sykes session was in a basement studio in Brooklyn. It was owned by a guy named Manny.[12] Len did a lot of recording at his home on a reel-to-reel tape recorder. We did some recording at Dicey's house in Connecticut."

Bob also recalled a Charles Walker gig involving Spivey: "We played down at a place in Brooklyn, I think it was called Parkside Lounge, it was near Prospect Park. We played there a Friday and Saturday night and Victoria Spivey was there. She and Walker absolutely didn't get along. At some point on the Saturday night Walker was playing drums on a little bandstand, a foot off the ground, and the bass drum kept sliding over. Right in the middle of her vocal it fell off the stand and onto the ground. She got angry and the music stopped. Then Dicey had a bout of gastroenteritis and we took him to hospital. That was the way that evening ended up! However, despite Charles Walker and Victoria Spivey not being the easiest of people, I feel privileged to have been associated with both of them."

SONNY TERRY

Bob Malenky first heard Sonny Terry on a folk program with Jerry Silverman and Pete Seeger at Carnegie Hall in 1957 ("Sonny performed a blues about himself and Huddie Ledbetter [Lead Belly] being the 'Best of Friends'"), and then had the chance to sit in with Terry at a show at City College. However, in 1974 came the chance to tour with Terry: "Sonny and Brownie McGhee had some gigs lined up but Brownie McGhee's wife died so he just went back to Oak-

SONNY TERRY
ROBBIN' THE GRAVE

a
collection
of new
songs
with
Sonny
Terry
accompanied
by piano
& guitar

BLUE
LABOR

BLUE LABOR   STEREO   BL 101

Courtesy of Larry Simon.

land. He didn't tell Sonny who showed up [for the tour] but Brownie wasn't there. Well, I had recorded with Sonny for a guy, Kent Cooper, who produced this album *Robbin' the Grave*,[13] so they called me in. At the time Sonny and Brownie had the album on A&M which included Randy Newman's 'Sail Away' so he [Sonny] sang that every show.[14] Sonny picked up things from all over the place; we always did 'Walkin' My Blues Away,' 'Cornbread, Peas and Black Molasses,' 'Midnight Special,' and Chuck Willis's 'What Am I Living For.'" By this time McGhee and Terry's audience was white, and the duo were playing on the folk-blues circuit, but Malenky recalled how Sonny could sometimes play powerful amplified harmonica in the style of the rhythm & blues records they made for a black audience in the early 1950s: "We played this blues club, My Father's Place, out in Roslyn, Long Island, and he was cupping the mic saying: 'Brownie's going to be surprised to hear this!' Also on the 1974 tour we played in Nashville during

a big DJ convention in October. They had the country music awards and everyone was in town hanging around the Martin guitar people. We were playing at
this place, the EXIT/IN. They had a lot of people coming by and it was a real
center of the music world in Nashville. The opening act was Asleep at the Wheel.
The Pointer Sisters were in the audience and they were singing along with us.
On reflection that was my crack at the big time and my chance to make it as a
professional musician. I really thought it might lead somewhere, but I was going
through a difficult time and it wasn't to be."

Malenky had another opportunity to play with Sonny Terry in 1978, and for
a period sat in with Muddy Waters on just about every occasion Muddy played
New York, including the time at the Bottom Line in Greenwich Village when
Bob Dylan turned up for the show. This continued until Muddy started playing the bigger venues in the Johnny Winter era. In September 1980, Bob started
working for Carl Fischer Music publishers in Manhattan and shortly afterward
became involved with the New York Pinewoods Folk Music Society, which gave
the opportunity for a lot of local performances. Malenky also worked with harmonica player Lester Schultz. They called themselves Sleepy Lester and Brother
Bob, the partnership lasting until Schultz's death around 2007. The duo played
at the Greenwich Village Bistro and participated in the MTA subway program,
Music under New York. Bob has kept "learning at the guitar," and to this day he
performs whenever possible, gigging and playing frequently in various styles
and formats, including more recently with local traditional jazz musicians.

NOTES

1. Lightnin' Hopkins had several R&B hits in 1949–1952 on the Modern, Gold Star, Aladdin,
and Sittin' In With labels, but as already noted had a surprise 1961 hit with "Mojo Hand" for
Bobby Robinson's Fire label, which made no. 109 in the *Cash Box* Looking Ahead chart in
February–March in a solid seven-week stay, and also no. 26 in the R&B chart.

2. Otis Spann's first Bluesway album, *The Blues Is Where It's At*, was recorded at Capitol
Studios, 151 West Forty-Sixth Street, on August 30, 1966. Spann (vocal and piano) was accompanied by the Muddy Waters band: George Smith (harmonica); Muddy Waters, Sammy Lawhorn,
and Luther "Georgia Boy"–"Snake"–"Snake Boy" Johnson (guitar); Mac Arnold (bass); and
Francis Clay (drums). Producer Bob Thiele used a live audience to create a party atmosphere.
At the time, Spann and the Muddy Waters band were playing with John Lee Hooker (who also
recorded for Bluesway) at the Cafe Au Go Go on Bleeker Street, Greenwich Village.

3. William "Washboard Bill" Cooke was born in Dupont, Florida, on July 4, 1905, and died
in 2003. He moved back to Florida in 1973 to live in West Palm Beach. This is the Washboard
Bill who recorded with King Curtis and Mickey Baker for King Records (1956–1957) in his own
name, and he was on Mickey and Sylvia's storming "No Good Lover" (Groove, 1956), according
to an RCA Victor session sheet. Frustratingly, Cooke's "Washboard Bill" is shown incorrectly in
blues discographies under Billy Valentine or Billy Vee. In 1992, Cooke received the Florida Folk
Heritage Award for keeping alive the traditional art of washboard playing.

4. Sugar Blue was born James Joshua "Jimmie" Whiting in Harlem, December 16, 1949, and used to see shows at the Apollo Theatre, remembering Little Stevie Wonder in particular. Blue played harmonica on the Rolling Stones' "Miss You" (no. 1 in the *Billboard* pop chart, 1978) and toured with the Stones, and also with Louisiana Red. Sugar Blue won a Grammy Award in 1985 with *Blues Explosion*, an Atlantic compilation album, and he has recorded regularly since those heady times. He was still playing in 2020.

5. Ola Dixon was born in Marion, South Carolina, on February 14, 1943, and moved to New York in the 1960s. She started in the local blues scene as a singer with Charles Walker before playing drums. Later, she recorded for Spivey with Paul Oscher in 1975 and Severn with Jimmy Vivino in 1998–1999. Since then, she has mostly devoted herself to the church.

6. Charles Walker, born on July 26, 1922, died in New York on June 24, 1975.

7. When Bob Malenky mentioned the Abramson session to Bobby Robinson in the early 2000s, Robinson didn't remember it. Abramson was a cofounder of Atlantic Records in 1947. After leaving the label in 1958, he set up A-1 Sound Studios in the early 1960s at the old Atlantic studios at 234 West Fifty-Sixth Street before moving to Seventy-Sixth Street around 1969.

8. One P&P single is credited to Walker: "40 Days–40 Nights"/"My Babe," with Bill Dicey (harmonica), Bob Malenky (guitar), and Bobby King (drums). The other is credited to Bill Dicey and the Blues' All Stars: "Hookie Koochie Man"/"Juke."

9. Tom Pomposello, who once played bass guitar with Fred McDowell, founded Oblivion Records (1972–1976) with Fred Seibert and Dick Pennington, and later made his name in the advertising and marketing business. He was born on July 17, 1949, and died on January 25, 1999.

10. See also chapter 12 on Victoria Spivey.

11. This "Smokey Hogg" was guitarist Willie Anderson Hogg, a Spivey artist. When he arrived on the scene, he was portrayed erroneously as the original Smokey Hogg, who was a good seller for Modern Records between 1948 and 1950.

12. Two tracks by Roosevelt Sykes with Bob Malenky on flute from 1970 appear on the Spivey LP *Victoria Spivey Presents the All Stars Blues World of Spivey Records in Stereo*.

13. The *Robbin' the Grave* Blue Labor LP by Sonny Terry was recorded at Al Weintraub's Bell Sound studio at 237 West Fifty-Fourth Street and Eighth Avenue, New York, April 25, 1974.

14. The 1972 Hollywood-recorded A&M LP *Sonny & Brownie* also featured Sugarcane Harris, Arlo Guthrie, John Hammond, and John Mayall.

BIBLIOGRAPHY

Malenky, Bob. Interviewed by Richard Tapp with John Broven and Larry Simon, East Setauket, Long Island, July 7, 2017.

Malenky, Bob. "New York Memories: Riff Ruffin and the Black Radio Stations." *Juke Blues*, no. 24, Autumn–Winter 1991.

Mikofsky, Anton. Charles Walker obituary. *Living Blues*, no. 23, September–October 1975.

Pomposello, Tom. "Charles Walker: Blues from the Big Apple." *Living Blues*, no. 18, Autumn 1974.

VAL WILMER INTERVIEWS

12

VICTORIA SPIVEY

This chapter was first published in *Melody Maker*, September 13, 1975.

Victoria Spivey had two storied careers: as an original classic woman blues singer in the 1920s and 1930s, and as a Brooklyn-based record label owner with Leonard Kunstadt in the 1960s and 1970s.

Spivey Records, almost a boutique-cum-vanity label, released about forty blues albums by artists known and unknown, black and white, between 1962 and 1985.[1]

In 1975 she was interviewed by Val Wilmer, the renowned British jazz photographer and author, who was on a trip to the United States. At that time, New York, to paraphrase one of Wilmer's articles, was full of "mean streets."

Spivey and Wilmer had first met, with Kunstadt, at a reception for artists on the very popular 1963 American Folk Blues Festival tour of Europe at the Marquee Club, Oxford Street, London.[2]

Besides Spivey, Wilmer interviewed New York–area bluesmen Larry Johnson and Tarheel Slim for *Melody Maker*, the famed British weekly music paper. All three articles are reprinted, with permission, in this book, with new endnotes.

"VICTORIA: THE BLACK QUEEN WITH CLASS" BY VAL WILMER

July was the month in 1975 when Bob Dylan came out of hiding and was seen all over New York—sitting in here and there, greeting old friends, and socializing. One of the friends was Victoria Spivey, "the Black Queen of the Blues," propri-

Victoria Spivey (1906–1976) at home in Brooklyn, 1975. Photo by Val Wilmer.

etor of the Spivey record label and, like Dylan, a legend herself ever since she recorded "Black Snake Blues" almost fifty years ago.[3]

Dylan and Spivey coincided on a visit to hear Muddy Waters at the Bottom Line.[4] They sat together holding hands, and later that night, Dylan and friends accompanied the Queen back to the Brooklyn apartment from where she runs her record label.

"He sat here right where you're sitting now till 7:30 in the morning," she said. "People were all sitting out there in the corridor—following Bob Dylan, you know.

"He said 'Ma, if you need $1 million I'll give it to you—I made $5 million last year,'" Victoria related with a twinkle in her eye. "I told him 'no.' Though, of course, I would have liked a million pennies but I wouldn't take nothing from him."

Dylan, who appears on the Spivey album *Three Kings and the Queen*, singing backup vocals and playing harmonica alongside Big Joe Williams[5]—the other "Kings" are Roosevelt Sykes and Lonnie Johnson—has always held Victoria Spivey in the highest regard. He thinks of her as the person responsible for his discovery.

When she was appearing at Gerde's Folk City [at 11 West Fourth Street] in 1961 after emerging from a long period of retirement, she always made a point of inviting the young Dylan up to sing with her.

Dylan returned the compliment by reproducing a photograph from the *Three Kings* session—his second date, incidentally—on the back of his *New Morning* album in 1970. Intentionally he left off any credit so that, for some time after, the Columbia phones rang with people who wanted to know the identity of the stylish black woman seated at the piano beside the youthful Dylan.

Victoria got a lot of publicity out of the singer's action. Not surprisingly she defends him against any abuse. When a woman stooped to kiss him at the Bottom Line, she drove her off, saying, "Keep away from my son!"

When she heard of A. J. Weberman's obsessive interest in the contents of Dylan's dustbins, she threatened to beat him up. "What right has a guy to go through my guy's garbage?" she demanded. Knocking seventy though she may be, Victoria is more than capable of fulfilling her threats.

Another offshoot of the reunion with Dylan was running into a British film crew headed by Tony Palmer [film director and author]. Two days later the cameras pursued her to Brooklyn for an interview. With typical British pedantry, she was asked, "How do you feel about being one of the classic blues singers?" Victoria chose not to explain. She looked the interviewer dead in the eye: "Oh, I always was a classy blues singer!"

The Queen carries her class well. A closet bulging with gowns includes a little number adorned with black snakes, alligators, and spiders—all of which creatures she has immortalized in song. Autographed portraits sit on the piano— one from Joan Crawford, another from Louis Armstrong: "To Lovely Victoria Spivey from Ol' Satchmo." And the chest of drawers is spray-painted with the legend: "Victoria, the Black Queen." It's definitely the home of a somebody.

Paul Oscher, the fine white harp player who used to be part of Muddy Waters's band, is playing the piano when I arrived; another young man strokes the guitar. The Queen's home is always filled with young musicians—black and white—with an interest in the blues. And she and Len Kunstadt, editor of *Record Research* and her right-hand man, are constantly taping all the talent on hand.

"Play her the tapes of my latest find," the Queen ordered. The voice of Rose Melody flooded out of the tape recorder. Oscher was the pianist on the date, and Victoria took great pride in pointing out the drummer was also a woman.[6] "Victoria finds someone just about every week and records them," said Kunstadt.

"I won't do nothing I don't want to," confided Victoria. "There's a young generation coming up, they can take care of it. Mama ain't gonna work but four days out of a month, but I'll drag my band around and headline them any time. I call it Spivey and Her Blues Power. I tore up those festivals in New York and Philadelphia—I really rocked 'em!"

Her affection for young talent is evenly divided between the races. Otis Spann was always her "son" and she still finds his death [in 1970] hard to accept. She played a tape they made together when the pianist knew he had not long

Leonard Kunstadt, Victoria Spivey, and Derrick Stewart-Baxter, British blues critic, at the Marquee Club, Oxford Street, London, October 1963. Photo by Val Wilmer.

to live; it was almost too moving in its intensity. "I took that boy to all the best doctors but it wasn't no good," she said. And her affection for Paul Oscher and his compadres is obvious. "I ain't got nothing but young boys around me," she said. "They keep me young."

Earlier, while driving to Brooklyn, Lenny Kunstadt spoke of Victoria as "a real poet," a woman who will sit down and write a blues at the drop of a hat. And the Queen can lay claim to over 1,500 songs. "I hear them all the time," she said. "Got blues on my goddamn mind."

In 1927 as staff writer for the St. Louis Publishing Co., she penned material that turned up on many an early recording. Her "T-B Blues" (OKeh), made the same year, was one of the first songs to register protest at the way blacks were treated; TB was then the prevalent disease among them.

"Dope Head Blues," with Lonnie Johnson on guitar, was an early song to appear that dealt with cocaine. She worked for a spell with Blind Lemon Jefferson, who made three versions of her "Black Snake Blues" under the title of "Black Snake Moan,"[7] and her material has been recorded by countless performers. At one time [1930–1931] she led a band called Hunters Serenaders in which Jo Jones was the drummer and Ben Webster played saxophone.

"You get up at five in the morning and write your songs," she told me. "The doctor told them to hide all the paper, pens, and pencils from me because I was cracking up from writing too much. Well, I went over to my sister's house, grabbed a brown paper bag and an eyebrow pencil, and went out and sat on the Brooklyn Bridge!"

Victoria Spivey is the classic example of the good woman who can't be held down. Once she puts her mind to something, she'll carry on through. At one point in the proceedings, she cussed out the faithful Kunstadt for playing the wrong tape. He backed away from her in mock abeyance. "OK, boss!" he said. She beckoned me closer: "He's only jealous of me—I'm a hundred years old!"

Suddenly the Queen switched to another bag. "Hey!" she shouted. "Let's all get drunk and be somebody!" We did.

NOTES

1. Spivey Records artists included such well-known blues names as the Muddy Waters band, Lonnie Johnson, Big Joe Williams, and Willie Dixon as well as Spivey herself. The label also encouraged younger talent such as Sugar Blue (James Joshua Whiting), Bill Dicey, John Hammond, Bob Malenky, and Paul Oscher. See the website www.wirz.de/music/spivey.htm for discographical details.

2. The American Folk Blues Festival lineup on its second annual tour (1963) was a dream come true for young blues fans in Britain and Europe. With Victoria Spivey were Muddy Waters, Otis Spann, Sonny Boy Williamson no. 2, Memphis Slim, Willie Dixon, Big Joe Williams, and Lonnie Johnson, with Leonard Kunstadt as manager. The tour did much to stoke the blues movement throughout Europe and also introduced Spivey and Kunstadt to many established blues artists. For comprehensive AFBF details, see the website www.wirz.de/music/afbf.htm.

3. Victoria Spivey was born in Houston on October 15, 1906, and died in New York City on October 3, 1976, at age sixty-nine. She recorded "Black Snake Blues" for OKeh in St. Louis, May 1926.

4. The Bottom Line, located at 15 West Fourth Street, was a major Greenwich Village music venue from 1974 through 2004.

5. Bob Dylan accompanied Big Joe Williams on two tracks, recorded on March 2, 1962, for the 1964 *Three Kings and the Queen* album (Spivey LP 1004): "Sitting on Top of the World" and "Wichita." Two Dylan accompaniments also appeared on *Kings and the Queen*, vol. 2 (LP 1014, 1970).

6. In 1975, Rose Melody appeared on the *New York Really Has the "Blues Stars"* LP (Spivey 1018) with Paul Oscher's Chicago Breakdown Blues Band and vocalist/drummer Ola Dixon, and she sang on Oscher's 1976 Spivey single. See also chapter 9 on Oscher.

7. Blind Lemon Jefferson first recorded "That Black Snake Moan" for Paramount about October 1926, after which it was known as "Black Snake Moan."

13

LARRY JOHNSON AND GARY DAVIS

LARRY JOHNSON

Personal Introduction by Val Wilmer

Larry Johnson was one of those individuals who made an impression on me that went beyond the music. We met in New York in 1972. He was playing a gig in a little bar on Second Avenue, and we got together shortly afterward to do an interview for *Melody Maker*.[1] We hit it off and I introduced him to the friend with whom I was staying. She cooked dinner for him and I went back to England, having kindled a relationship between the two of them.

For Larry, as he explained at a subsequent meeting, it was easy for him "to do the white girl thing" and live a relatively deracinated lifestyle downtown. But this was the 1970s, when talk of black liberation and black autonomy was a constant, and Larry got tired of "that downtown thing" and went back to Harlem.

Despite his anger over matters of inequality and race, Larry seemed to have time for me, perhaps because I was not American. Most white Americans just would not go to Harlem in that period, so he tested me. He told me to meet him in Thomforde's, an old-style soda fountain on 125th Street at Saint Nicholas Avenue, then took me to meet the legendary Bobby Robinson at his record shop.

That was in 1976. Eventually Larry arranged an interview with Robinson. We met late at night, again at Thomforde's, and spent a couple of hours in fascinating conversation. On the way back, we encountered an elderly man staggering around the subway platform, shouting, whooping, slipping, and sliding. "Don't look at him!" Larry ordered, "Listen to what he's singing. Most people would say

The Reverend Gary Davis (1896–1972), Fairfield Halls, Croydon, Surrey, England, 1964. Photo by Val Wilmer.

Larry Johnson (1938–2016), Washington Square Church, 135 West Fourth Street, New York, May 6, 1970. Photo © by Anton Mikofsky, used with permission.

Larry Johnson and Bobby Robinson, 125th Street, Harlem, 1976. Photo by Val Wilmer.

he was drunk or crazy, but listen to that *sound*! What he's doing goes back to slavery days, the whoops and the hollers and everything. That old man is living history." You never forget a lesson like that.

My interview with Bobby Robinson was not published until 1978, two years after that initial meeting. When I saw Larry again, he was in impoverished circumstances and living in one of the meanest hotel rooms I've ever encountered. His anger, and the frustration he felt from his relative lack of success, spilled over into our friendship and damaged it. I never saw him again, but I'll always remember the lesson he taught me on the subway and those one-o'clock-in-the-morning blues.

Biographical Introduction

Larry Johnson, country blues guitarist, singer, and harmonica player, was born in Wrightsville, Georgia. As a child he was inspired by the recordings of Blind Boy Fuller. After his time in the navy in the mid-1950s, Larry relocated to New York City. He quickly became involved in the New York blues scene and met artists including Big Joe Williams, Sonny Terry, and Brownie and Sticks McGhee. Johnson recorded an impressive East Coast blues debut album, with Hank Adkins, for Prestige in 1965, followed by a first single, "Cat Fish Blues" backed with "So Sweet," for Bobby Robinson's Blue Soul label in 1966. Three years later, recordings from this session appeared on a Blue Horizon (UK) album in an era when the LP was taking over from the 45-rpm single. Johnson made numerous recordings, solo and with other well-known blues musicians such as Big Joe Williams and John Hammond Jr. A milestone in Larry Johnson's life was meeting the Reverend Gary Davis, with whom he became close friends, both studying and performing with him. Johnson, although greatly influenced by Davis, advanced very much in his own unique direction.

"JOHNSON'S CHANGING IMAGE" BY VAL WILMER

"*Good* morning and how are you doing?" The ecstatic sound of the gospel message was well in evidence behind the southern-tinged voice on the telephone. I told Larry Johnson I was doing all right and mentioned that he seemed to be having quite a revival meeting there. "Oh, I got to have my spirituals every morning!" he said.

If you know anything about the young bluesman, his reply was typical. Born in Georgia in 1938, Johnson has made his home in New York for the past few years.

He is unique in that he prefers to deal with the music of an earlier generation or has done up to now, that is. Currently [1972] he is working on a new album where he'll be playing harmonica and singing in a style akin to, he claims, Bobby "Blue" Bland.[2]

This may shock the purists who were delighted to discover a young man singing and playing the country blues, but really it's none of their business. Larry Johnson has to satisfy his own self.

"I feel that I have already set an image as a country blues guitar player," he said. "Now I just want to show today's time people that I can do their thing, too.

"That's mainly because ever since I've been in this thing my audience has been white. I haven't got anything against that but I feel that I should also have a black audience. That is one of my beliefs now.

"If I can do this, I feel that I will reach the world in music and I'll be happy."

Johnson's life in music began in New York in 1961 when he met the Reverend Gary Davis, but, as he put it, "the feel of it began in the South."

His mother had died when he was only two years old, and so his father raised him in a small Georgia country town called Wrightsville. There, he grew up in the days when Blind Boy Fuller records were still to be heard on the local jukebox.

"I can remember when you'd pay a nickel to hear 'Step It Up and Go,'" he said.

He'd come to New York well steeped in the country blues, and met the Reverend Gary Davis at a time when both of them were low: Johnson was an alcoholic hanging out in the Harlem streets, and Davis was a lonely old man whose wife had to scrub floors to maintain them.

"There was no question of age difference because I knew what I was talking about when it comes to blues," he said. "That erased all age. And they knew what they were talking about so that erased all age with me."

By "they," Johnson referred to the other bluesmen from the Carolinas whom he met in New York: Sonny Terry, Brownie and Sticks McGhee, and the late Alec Seward.[3]

"It more or less became like a father and son thing with all of 'em, but more so with Gary because he was sitting up there in the Bronx all day by himself. When we met it seemed like we needed each other. Everybody that was kin to me was in the South or I had broke away from them, and then I met Gary. There he was, sitting there, an old man with nobody young to say nothing to him."

Then and there began a thirteen-year friendship that only ended with Rev. Gary's death on May 5 this year [1972]. Johnson played me some tapes made when the two men were hanging out together—Davis playing guitar and making no other sound apart from the occasional grunt, Johnson laughing out loud in delight at the old man's amazing execution of tricky runs. Their rapport was plain.

"I never had any trouble relating to him or the others, because I was out of the South just like they were. I knew how this country is and they knew how this country is so we didn't have no problems."

Johnson feels that the old-time country blues has shaped his life, and that there was something like destiny implicit in the way the guitar came easily to him.

"And I think I'm the only one ever that studied under the reverend, including Blind Boy Fuller, to come up with a style of playing. See, Fuller played well, he played damn well, but he leaned mostly on Gary. You can hear more of Gary in Fuller's playing than you can hear in my playing.

"So when that happened, I felt—and Gary felt—that I would never play like him. He called me an original and that made me feel good. And it became like, I would say, a personal thing to me. It was something I enjoyed doing. I enjoyed it then and I enjoy it now. Other music just never did interest me to play. I'll listen to it but so far as me getting off on it, I just don't dig it."

According to Johnson, whites are about twenty years behind in their musical tastes. "If they had been interested twenty years ago in the blues, they'd have been up to date. Now they're behind the times and blacks are up ahead, if you want to look at it that way. But what I want to do is remind the black people of their heritage and show the white people that I can combine the two, and bring it all up to date once again and see what happens. If you know anything about harmonica playing, it was modernized by Little Walter. Sonny Boy Williamson[4] and the rest of those guys, they done fine, but Little Walter came along and modernized the whole thing and made it sound beautiful. Now I want to come along and take that a step further. Like in this blues thing, by me being young, that's a step further along."

Johnson and his mentor, the Reverend Gary Davis, stayed close until the day he died, and the loss that the younger man feels is plain. Three days after Davis's death, they had been set to start work on a filmed conversation together, but, in spite of the tragedy, filmmaker Lionel Rogosin decided to carry on with Johnson and Mrs. Davis instead.

The format is simple—they're sitting together and discussing how they each met the legendary reverend and comparing their lives. Johnson tells me the movie says it all. Look out for it—it's called *Brother Davis*.[5]

THE REVEREND GARY DAVIS

Gary Davis, blind since infancy, was born in Laurens County, South Carolina, part of the Piedmont region. In the 1920s he moved to Durham, North Carolina. Then, in the 1940s, Davis relocated to New York City, where he often performed on the streets of Harlem. Davis was influential as both a performer and a teacher. His students included Dave Van Ronk, Stefan Grossman, Bob Weir, Jorma Kaukonen, John Sebastian, and many others. Davis, a singer of mainly spirituals but the occasional blues, was a virtuoso acoustic guitarist, using only the thumb and index finger of the right hand for his intricate picking. His influence is incalculable, extending to Bob Dylan, the Rolling Stones, Peter, Paul and Mary, Keb' Mo', the Grateful Dead, Ry Cooder, Taj Mahal, and more. Of the older generation of bluesmen, Davis impacted Blind Boy Fuller, Bull City Red, Brownie McGhee, Alec Seward, Tarheel Slim, and Larry Johnson.

The Reverend Gary Davis and Larry Johnson: Reflections by Bob Malenky

New York was home to two significant artists from the Southeast: the Reverend Gary Davis, originally from South Carolina, and Larry Johnson from Georgia. Although some forty years apart in age, both carried the musical traditions of their respective origins to an audience that welcomed the real thing. Davis was a dazzling guitarist whose influence is very much with us today. Larry Johnson was less widely known and deserved more attention than he received. Here are my recollections of two important musicians who touched my life.

The Reverend Gary Davis was a musical phenomenon who settled in New York in the 1940s. He was embraced by the folk music community, which was largely white and middle class. His guitar playing was complex and his singing passionate. Davis had a huge impact on guitar players, and many people went to the hovel he and his wife Annie lived in. This was located in the South Bronx,

The Reverend Gary Davis, Fairfield Halls, Croydon, Surrey, England, 1964. Photo by Val Wilmer.

known as one of the poorest and most dangerous areas of New York or any other city.

Davis charged five dollars for a lesson, and many of his students stayed for lengthy jam sessions, ate dinner, and even spent several days with Gary and Annie. Except for his 1935 sessions produced by J. B. Long,[6] Davis didn't record much until the mid-1950s,[7] and his music was ignored by the black public who listened to groups like the Dixie Hummingbirds or singers like Clara Ward. It was the Greenwich Village folkies who formed his fan base. He was very influential on Dave Van Ronk, who was in turn influential on the folk scene.

I admired the reverend; I heard his records and attended his concerts, but I never studied with him, nor did I know him personally. Davis played on the streets in New York and often played at the Gaslight, a Village coffee house. According to Ian Zack's fine biography *Say No to the Devil: The Life and Genius of Rev. Gary Davis* (2015), he hung around Eddie Bell's guitar shop on Forty-Seventh Street.

It is through Davis's students that I heard numerous stories and anecdotes. Through my experience playing with Sonny Terry, I got a feeling for the personality of this amazing artist. Sonny had known Davis from Durham, North Carolina, when they were in the circle of musicians that formed around Blind Boy Fuller and included Brownie McGhee.

By way of Larry Johnson, I got some idea of Davis's life in the black community. Larry was one of the few black musicians who studied with Davis, and his story is interesting. I first heard Larry Johnson live, opening a concert for Howlin' Wolf [in 1973].[8] He already had an album on Prestige with Hank Adkins[9] and was playing in the Village in folk venues. In 1974 or 1975, I attended a Rev. Gary Davis tribute concert at the Harlem Museum with Larry, Sugar Blue, and Rev. Frederick Douglas Kirkpatrick, which was attended by Annie Davis. Anton Mikofsky was instrumental in organizing the event and later managed a trio consisting of Larry, Sugar, and Bobby Bennett (aka Professor Six Million). The group sounded great, but didn't last long. In the following years, it seems Larry played out of town a lot; at least I wasn't aware of him playing locally often.

Larry Johnson came from a town called Wrightsville, Georgia, and settled in New York after being discharged from the navy. At that time, he was playing mostly harmonica and did at least one session for Bobby Robinson with Charles Walker.[10] Larry met Gary Davis when he was hanging out with Brownie McGhee in Harlem, which inspired the young bluesman to concentrate on guitar. At that time, he played acoustic guitar using thumb and index finger on the right hand, as Davis played.

Johnson had a checkered career, and I heard about him once in a while. He was working as a cook at Dan Lynch's establishment on Second Avenue near Fourteenth Street in the early 1980s when Bill Dicey was running weekly blues jams there. Years went by in which I heard nothing of Larry and found mention of him in Bruce Bastin's *Red River Blues* (1986).[11] At that time I found a copy of an album with Larry Johnson and Nat Riddles, a great harmonica player, on Spivey.[12]

In the early 1990s I heard Larry was playing at a pub on Third Street near NYU, and I attended and brought an acoustic Gibson guitar. Larry was playing a Washburn acoustic/electric and had trouble with the pickup, so he used my Gibson J-50 acoustically for the gig. He started off solo but was joined by a band later in the set. From that point I began a friendship with Larry Johnson. Larry had been playing in Europe and had returned to the States. He had a pension from the navy and got gigs mostly at Terra Blues on Bleecker Street. On Friday nights Larry would attract a group of blues lovers, which often included Len Kunstadt. Several times I was invited to sit in, and felt honored.

Larry's repertoire included original songs that had a strong flavor of the finger-style Piedmont blues tradition. He did not like the slow, mournful "deep" blues favored by Muddy Waters and Lightnin' Hopkins. When I played with him we did up-tempo songs like Fats Domino's "All by Myself" (based on a Big Bill Broonzy song) or Joe Turner's "Boogie Woogie Country Girl." I remember doing "Step It Up and Go" with him. After a major falling out with Terra Blues, Larry played sporadically in the New York area. He often played at outdoor programs at Lincoln Center, once at a tribute concert for Bobby Robinson with Doc Pittman (aka Dr. Horse).

While Larry is best remembered as a bluesman, his repertoire included "The Crawdad Song," several of the Reverend Gary Davis's songs, and "Cab Driver," learned from the Mills Brothers [a 1968 top 30 pop hit]. He was a deeply religious man, although he rarely performed spirituals. Few of his songs are done by other performers, but Andy Cohen, a great guitarist and Davis disciple, sings "Where Did You Learn to Cook": "Tell me baby, where did you learn to cook? It must not have been out your mama's cookbook."

I often ran into Larry on 125th Street. The last time I saw him was in the spring of 2014. He was showing signs of mental confusion, but I did get his phone number. He called me suggesting we work together, which I would have loved, but I didn't know of any venues. In our last conversation I told him he was mentioned in Zack's biography of Gary Davis, and he expressed interest but didn't seem very excited. I also mentioned that Andy Cohen was performing "Where Did You Learn to Cook," but he didn't remember the song.

To say Larry Johnson didn't get the recognition he deserved is an understatement. He was not a flamboyant performer, and was relaxed and genuine on stage. He told me that when he opened for Howlin' Wolf, Wolf called him over and thanked Larry for not trying to upstage him. As if anyone could upstage the mighty Wolf. I remember Larry Johnson with love and respect. Many of Davis's students went on to greater fame and fortune, but Larry carried a bit of the feeling and wisdom of the reverend as well as the sound.

NOTES

1. This article by Val Wilmer was first published in *Melody Maker*, November 4, 1972.

2. There is no Bobby Bland–type LP listed in the blues discographies for Larry Johnson. Still, he did record with the Willie Dixon band in 1973 for Spivey Records. See www.wirz.de/music/johnsdsc.htm for an illustrated Johnson discography.

3. Alec Seward, a guitarist, was born in Charles City County, Virginia, on March 16, 1901, and died in New York City on May 11, 1972. He recorded for various New York labels from 1947 to 1949, quit music in 1957, but made a comeback in 1965, recording for Prestige Bluesville with Larry Johnson and also Blue Labor a year later at a party with Brownie McGhee and Sonny Terry.

4. Johnson was almost certainly referring to Sonny Boy Williamson no. 2 (Rice Miller), as he would have been too young to remember Sonny Boy Williamson no. 1 (John Lee Williamson). However, Sonny Boy no. 1 (1914–1948) was the premier and most influential blues harmonica player before the arrival of Little Walter with "Juke" in 1952.

5. It seems that the *Brother Davis* movie was never finished due to Davis's death. However, director Lionel Rogosin did make a 1970 film, *Black Roots*, including Davis and Johnson. Before that, Ian Zack, in his book *Say No to the Devil: The Life and Genius of Rev. Gary Davis* (Chicago: University of Chicago Press, 2015), reported that a Harold Becker documentary short, *Blind Gary Davis*, premiered at the Murray Hill Cinema, New York, on June 27, 1963. The black-and-white film has a poignant air, shot in pregentrification Harlem. Another Davis movie was released in 2014, *Harlem Street Singer: The Reverend Gary Davis Story*, directed by Trevor Laurence and Simeon Hutner. It won several film festival awards and is available on DVD.

6. The Reverend Gary Davis was discovered by North Carolinian talent scout, store manager, and store owner J. B. Long, who also gave recording opportunities to Blind Boy Fuller, Bull City Red (George Washington), and Brownie McGhee. As for Davis, he played in three New York sessions for the American Record Corporation (ARC) in July 1935 in the name of Blind Gary of mainly spirituals, except for one blues 78-rpm cut at the very first session. Fuller and Bull City Red also recorded on the same trip.

7. From the 1950s, Davis recorded for labels such as Folkways, Riverside, Prestige Bluesville, Vanguard, and a host of minor record companies.

8. Larry Johnson opened for Howlin' Wolf from May 30 through June 4, 1973, at Max's Kansas City club, 213 Park Avenue South, New York.

9. The fine Prestige LP *Larry & Hank: The Blues/A New Generation*, with Larry Johnson and Hank Adkins, both guitars, was recorded in New York on November 25, 1965, with notes by Sam Charters.

10. This is the excellent Charles Walker Fury single, "You Know It Ain't Right"/"Rock Me Mama" (1971), with outstanding harmonica by Larry Johnson.

11. Bruce Bastin, *Red River Blues: The Blues Tradition in the Southeast* (Urbana: University of Illinois Press, 1986).

12. The Spivey LP *Larry Johnson and Nat Riddles Featuring the Doctor's Basin Free* was recorded in New York on May 2, 1983.

14

TARHEEL SLIM
WITH LITTLE ANN

This chapter was first published in *Melody Maker*, December 1, 1973.

Tarheel Slim was born Allen Rathel Bunn in Bailey, North Carolina, in 1923 and settled in New York City in 1951. A tasteful, melodic East Coast guitarist and singer who performed in a variety of styles ranging from blues and gospel to R&B and doo-wop, Bunn recorded for Bobby Robinson's Red Robin, Fury, Fire, and Enjoy labels as well as Apollo, Lamp, and Atco among others, and in the 1970s cut a country blues album for Pete Lowry's Trix label. As well, Tarheel Slim sang with the Four Barons, Larks, and Wheels vocal groups. His most popular recordings, "Darling It's Wonderful" (Lamp, 1957) and "It's Too Late" (Fire, 1959), were made with wife, Anna Sandford (1935–2004), performing respectively as the Lovers, and Tarheel Slim and Little Ann. Bunn worked with fellow New York blues artists such as Big Chief Ellis, Jimmy Spruill, and Sonny Terry.

"TARHEEL SLIM: A MAN FOR ALL SEASONS" BY VAL WILMER

It was summer in New York, and Pete Lowry and I had sat sweltering in the Bronx apartment for two hours, waiting for Tarheel Slim.

It was getting to the point where even the beer wasn't cold enough and I was wondering whether meeting the singer would be worth all the fuss.

He'd been out to a party the night before and not returned. Even his wife, the former Little Ann from their singing days together as the Lovers, was starting to get anxious.

Tarheel Slim (Allen Bunn)
[1923–1977] the Bronx,
New York, 1973. Photo by
Val Wilmer.

Then the door burst open and in ambled a tall, laughing man wearing Bermuda shorts and sneakers.

Slim was still hung over from the night before, but during the general carousing, he'd managed—God only knows how—to get his head shaven. Both Pete and Ann roared at the sight before them, but Slim couldn't care less. He threw himself down into a chair and proceeded to charm the pants off everyone in the room.

It's the same with music.

On *No Time at All*, an album recorded by Lowry and shortly to be released on his Trix label, there's a very unusual kind of blues ballad, "Weeping Willow," which is an absolute charmer.[1] It rubs shoulders with several other originals, some Blind Boy Fuller numbers, and other songs traditional to North Carolina, colloquially known as the Tar Heel State.

Tarheel Slim was born Allen—or Alden—Bunn[2] some [fifty] years ago near the North Carolina town of Wilson.

He grew up around church songs—he remembers "Nearer My God to Thee"— and he would copy his mother's way of singing them. "I would take my guitar and try to find this note, and then, if my mother'd come in maybe after a beer or two on a Saturday night, if she wanted to sing 'Red River Valley,' I would find that, too.

"So I came along with both. I learned to play spirituals, blues, rock 'n' roll. And I developed myself an ear.

"Whatever I hear, I can play it. My fingers just went that way and I never got lost in one particular vein. If I can hear it, I can play it.

"See, I can get in a church and rock that, I can get in a nightclub and rock that, too. As long as I'm accepted, I'll do my thing."

Slim was singing with his own group, the Gospel Four, when the Selah Jubilee Singers came to Wilson.[3]

He booked the New York–based group to appear at his local church and went down to rehearse the backup band. "And you know, it was something like baseball—the leader brought me from behind the club. I beat him singing his own tunes so good that he elected me as a Selah member!"

The Selahs waited for the country boy to harvest his crop, and then in September 1947, Slim began touring countrywide with the group, continuing for four years.

In 1951 a subsidiary group, the Larks, was formed from the nucleus of the Selahs to sing "rock 'n' roll," and Slim became the leader.[4]

"That lasted, I'd say, about a good four years, and then at that time the whole trend changed. We started drifting apart and I kind of cooled it there for a minute."

In spite of continuing to make records under his own name, Slim made his living driving a truck. "My children were growing up and New York being such a wild, wild city, I said, 'I won't make a move until I see that my children are growing up from under the foot of men.' I worked day and night, even shined

Courtesy of Victor Pearlin.

Courtesy of Victor Pearlin.

shoes for a while, then after they became grown, I said, 'You're on your own, now daddy's going to cool it and relax.'"

In 1957, Slim met his present wife in the church. Their first record together as the Lovers, "Darling It's Wonderful" on Lamp, was a national hit.[5] But before this and even during the period they worked together, Slim had tied himself up with producer Bobby Robinson under several contracts, and his singles appeared on labels like Red Robin, Fire, Fury, and later Enjoy, and under several different names.

He recorded "Number 9 Train" for Fury in late 1958, which sold quite a few copies.[6]

"When I look back in my past," Slim said, "I been wrapped, tied, and tangled with contracts so many times. I even wrote a song with that name, right there in the studio: 'Wrapped, Tied, and Tangled, Head Over Heels in Love'"!

While working with Little Ann, he had a nationwide hit with "It's Too Late" for Fire in 1959. This sold almost 750,000 copies, according to Slim, and gave the couple five years of work on the road.[7]

Little Ann and Tarheel Slim. Courtesy of John Broven.

Mike Leadbitter and Neil Slaven's book *Blues Records 1943–1966* excludes all Tarheel Slim's recordings made after 1959 on the grounds that they are "too commercial." But now [in 1973] the wheel has turned full circle, and the Tarheel man has gone back to the blues he was raised on.

"Have I changed in myself? I hope I haven't. In fact, now I will try some of the things that I did twenty years ago. I believe it will work. Sometimes the musical trend changes, but the individual, I don't think the individual changes really that much.

"If you want to buy something, I must have what you are looking for. Now, if you want to rock, I've got to be able to rock. If you want a spiritual, I've got to be able to do that. Ask me what you want and I'll try to deliver.

"I change with the people—it's what the people want. When I get on the stage, I don't play to suit me. I look around that whole audience and I hear some of 'em over there, they want this groove.

"Now if I can get enough of 'em to go with me, I'm gonna get on the stage and give 'em what they want. 'Cause if I don't I won't be coming back no more next week!"

Little Ann and Tarheel Slim at Bobby Robinson's office, Harlem, 1959. Photo © Jacques Demêtre/
Soul Bag Archives.

NOTES

1. The Trix LP *No Time at All* was eventually released in 1975.

2. According to *Blues: A Regional Experience* by Bob Eagle and Eric S. LeBlanc (Santa Barbara, CA: Praeger, 2013), Bunn is registered with the first name "Allen" in the North Carolina
"Birth and Index" records, whereas his Social Security records and World War II draft card
show him as "Alden."

3. Tarheel Slim sang and played guitar with Thurmon Ruth's Selah Jubilee Singers and various offshoots from 1947 through 1950, recording for labels such as Capitol, Jubilee, Regal, and
Apollo.

4. The Larks scored two *Billboard* R&B hits for Apollo in 1951, with Tarheel Slim as lead
vocalist. "Eyesight to the Blind" made no. 5 and was a cover of Sonny Boy Williamson no. 2's
first record for Trumpet—Williamson later recorded the Larks' flip side, "I Ain't Fattenin' Frogs
for Snakes" (Checker). The second Larks hit, "Little Side Car" (no. 10), is better known as the
blues favorite popularized by Lowell Fulson, "Let Me Ride Your Little Automobile" (Swing
Time) or "Too Many Drivers" (Kent). In the Larks, with Thurmon Ruth and Tarheel Slim, were
Eugene Mumford and David McNeil, who would join Billy Ward's Dominoes; Mumford sang
lead on the Dominoes' big 1957 top 20 pop hits "Star Dust" and "Deep Purple."

5. "Darling It's Wonderful" by the Lovers, with the Ray Ellis Orchestra and Chorus, made no.
48 on *Billboard*'s pop chart and no. 15 R&B in late 1957 on Lamp, the Aladdin subsidiary.

6. Although "Number 9 Train," with Jimmy Spruill on guitar, made noise in the New York
area, it didn't break into the national charts. However, with its flip side, "Wildcat Tamer," it has

become a revered black rocker. Another Tarheel Slim favorite release, recorded earlier in the conflated name of Allen Baum for Bobby and Danny Robinson's Red Robin label in 1953, was "Too Much Competition"/"My Kinda Woman" (with the Larks).

7. "It's Too Late" made no. 20 on *Billboard*'s R&B chart in late summer 1959. It's difficult to quantify the actual sales figures with no formal documentary evidence available. The follow-up, "Lock Me in Your Heart," was a no. 34 hit in the *Cash Box* R&B chart in early 1960.

JOHN BROVEN INTERVIEWS

Billy Bland (1932–2017), Harlem, May 10, 1989. Photo by Paul Harris.

BILLY BLAND

Unpublished interview, Eleanor Barbecue, Harlem,
May 10, 1989

Born in Wilmington, North Carolina, Billy Bland was a versatile singer, adept at doo-wop, rock 'n' roll, R&B, soul, blues, even pop ballads. His biggest hit was "Let the Little Girl Dance" for Hy Weiss's Old Town label in 1960. Bland first started performing in New York about 1954. Among those he worked with were Edna McGriff, Lionel Hampton, Buddy Johnson, Dave Bartholomew, and Mickey Baker. Bland retired from performing and recording in the 1960s and in the 1980s ran a small, wonderful soul food restaurant, Eleanor Barbecue, at 143rd Street and Amsterdam in Harlem, where the pictures here were taken.

This interview with Billy Bland was conducted in very convivial circumstances at his Harlem soul food restaurant—with specialties of barbecued ribs, candied yams, and black-eyed peas. The location was noted in the Les Matthews *Amsterdam News* column in 1981 as "Eleanor Barbecue and crab spot on Amsterdam Ave. at 143rd St." The circumstances for an interview were far from ideal, but Billy kindly agreed to answer random questions into my trusty cassette recorder. An abiding memory is of him singing along to a jukebox stacked full of his own records, playing them even during the questions and answers of the interview. He proved himself to be a natural storyteller with a fine sense of humor. To my knowledge, this is the only lengthy interview conducted with him. This edited version shows that Billy was quite a character on the New York music scene into the 1960s including involvement with the big dance bands, also blues, R&B, and soul artists, local and national. After the interview, he remained in musical retirement and died in 2017.

John Broven: In Carolina did you hear any of the blues singers when you were growing up? As a boy, did you hear any of the local guitar players?

Billy Bland: See, I was a kid and I'd be breaking in stores and windows and stuff. That's back way back. Well see, Buddy Johnson, I met him in Wilmington, North Carolina, when I was a little boy, but I never thought I would ever be able to perform with him. I used to sneak into his dances in a place they called the Barn.

Broven: How did you get started in New York with artists like Buddy Johnson?[1]

Bland: The girl who really gave me my start in show business, Edna McGriff—the girl who made "Heavenly Father" [in 1952—*sings*: "Heavenly father, oh up above ..."].[2] I used to love her records and when I got to New York, she took me to Bermuda with her and I sang with her for awhile. But I wasn't known then, I was just doing shows with her. But once I sang, they took me with them. Whoever I sang around wherever I was, they'd take me with them, that's all. But I worked with so many, so many.

So she took me to Joe Glaser [of the Associated Booking Corporation, New York] and I told him, "I'm Billy Bland," and that Nat King Cole sent me. He welcomed me, and I looked up on the wall and I see Dinah Washington, Nat King Cole, Buddy Johnson, and all the great entertainers.[3] So he put me with Lionel Hampton first, and I was with Lionel Hampton fiddling around for about a month because he was doing jazz. He was a nice leader, but he was singing the wrong kind of music—I can't feel it—and I left him and I started going to the Savoy Ballroom [in Harlem] and I started singing with Nolan Lewis, and then I got with Buddy Johnson and I sang with him for a while.

Broven: Did Buddy invite you to join him?

Bland: Well, I just didn't sing with one person because I didn't wanna be strapped down: Buddy Johnson, Willis Jackson, Illinois Jacquet, anybody. When I was young I was singing, but I just wasn't too serious. I would start off, then I'd quit, I'd start off, then I'd quit—it was the kind of thing that I wasn't interested in at all.

Broven: What sort of songs did you sing with Buddy Johnson?

Bland: "Secret Love" [a 1954 hit—*sings*: "Once I had a secret love, that lived within the heart of me ..." *laughs*].[4] I've forgotten a lot of them now, like I used to do "Those Things Money Can't Buy" by Nat King Cole [from 1947]. But there was two singers and I didn't wanna clash between Nolan Lewis and myself, so I stuck mostly to the ballads. Because Buddy's sister, Ella Johnson, she would let you sing so much and then she would come on, because she was the star of the show. That's about it. 'Cause back in those days songs would just come into your mind, you would sing 'em and you'd forget about 'em. So it's kinda hard wanting me to go back that far.

Broven: What was the routine of a Buddy Johnson show?

Bland: He was good, I mean, he was a helluva musician. Nolan Lewis would come on, then later on Buddy would come on, then the band would come on,

Ella Johnson, Harlem, 1986. Photo by
Paul Harris.

then Nolan Lewis would come on again, then he would come on [also Ella]. But
he wanted me to really stay with them for a long time because I drew a lot of
people, and plus I could sing [*laughs*]. I guess they really wanted me because I
could move, you know, I could really do what I wanna do, you know, and I guess
it went to my head. That's when I started making records [in 1955], then things
changed. After I started making records then I see him a couple of times, then
I kinda found out it wasn't no joke. Show business was a job. He used to get on
my case and tell me to be serious, make rehearsals, stop playing around, and I
just thought it was a joke, but then I got a hit record [in 1960]. Then I had to have
musicians, and I was their boss—then it wasn't no joke, and everything he told
me, then I knew that he told me right. It was hard, but it was nice. Everybody I
worked with has treated me pretty good.

Broven: So did you go on the road with Buddy?

Bland: No, just right here in New York. I never wanted to go on the road with
him. I could have gone on the road with whoever I wanted, but I was a young
boy and I loved New York and I wouldn't go—he asked me—I wouldn't go. I was
young and stupid. I had a hot head, you know. You couldn't put me out in New
York with a horse and a plow once I got here.

[With vocal group music becoming popular, Billy Bland formed the Choco-
late Drops, soon renamed the Bees. "The group included myself, J. D., Bernard
[Ward], and Jimmy," he told Ace Records (UK) researcher Ray Topping in 1987.
Unlikely as it may seem, the group was signed by Fats Domino's A&R man, Dave
Bartholomew, to Imperial Records of Hollywood, and dispatched twice to New
Orleans to record in 1954.]

Bland: So I made "My Ding-a-Ling" [as "Toy Bell"] before [Chuck Berry] made a record, made money with it. I was the first one that made "My Ding-a-Ling," and they took it off the air.[5] I also made "Sunny Side of the Street" for Cosimo Matassa—I made about two good records.

Broven: What was it like recording in Matassa's [J&M] studio in New Orleans?

Bland: Fantastic. Nice. They had the beat.

Broven: They had the beat?

Bland: The beat: This is like the beat that they carried, that's how I copied the beat. This is the New Orleans beat. This is how they played, this is how U. S. Bonds got the beat, this is the same beat he had [*plays a record and demonstrates the beat, talking over the music*]. You can do anything with it. That's why everybody likes Fats Domino, always had the same beat, the music carries the same flavor, it's so easy. This is another one here [*plays another record*].

Broven: How did Dave Bartholomew discover you and the Bees?

Bland: I did a show with the Five Keys, and the leader of the Five Keys got sick one night—Rudy [West] got sick. And I was on the show and I had that tenor lead and Dave saw me there and he heard me sing, and he offered me a recording. Dave Bartholomew came to New York to find me, and he took me back to Cosimo Matassa.

Broven: Where did Bartholomew hear you first of all?

Bland: When he found me in New York. I was in a show at Smalls Paradise, I was a singer at Smalls.[6]

Broven: What was Harlem like in those days, that is the club scene?

Bland: Harlem was all clubs—it wasn't nothin' but clubs. You could work every night. Because I was a known name in those days, you know, I lived as a singer, but my reputation was pretty strong. Wherever I went there was a crowd. And that's how it was, if you had a name, if you could sing, you was big, you know.

Broven: Did you play the Rockland Palace [280 West 155th Street] at all?

Bland: Oh man, I played the Rockland Palace, I played them all. Every place you can name, I been there.

Broven: And how about the Apollo?

Bland: When I was playing the Apollo Theatre, you really had to be a performer. If you made it at the Apollo, you could go any place in the world. Not everybody gives you credit, they just smiling at you and they say you're nice, but back in those days, if you didn't have it . . . it's like playing the Metropolitan Opera House. You were an entertainer at the Apollo Theatre, you could go anywhere when you performed there. In Washington, DC, the Howard Theatre, that would be another bad theater to go in. It was like entertainment back in those days. If you could sing then, what the heck, but if you couldn't sing, they don't wanna hear. You had to work then, now you ain't gotta do nothin' but get up there and pat your foot and talk and you make money. But back in those days you had to sing.

Broven: What artists influenced you?

Bland: Wynonie Harris is a nice entertainer, he's a howlin' entertainer, you know, a shouter. See, he was a legend to me because when I know Wynonie Harris, I wasn't singing—I was a young boy. I used to admire him for the way he dress and the way he sing, but I didn't know anything about him because he was a rocker, you know, he was what you call a "rock house" singer. He's like a volume singer, you know, like loud, strong, and he knows what he was doing, see. And that's how I know about him, I used to admire him—and Roy Brown is on the same kick. "For You My Love," Larry Darnell, they was all in the same, they was the battleground singers together, very strong people.

Back in those days there was competition between singers—at that particular time you had Hank Ballard and the Midnighters, the Clovers. There was a few singers you had out there like the one you mentioned today, he's pretty good, "No More Doggin'," Rosco Gordon, he was pretty heavy, he could move. We had Dinah Washington was singing. It was pretty heavy out there—Louis Jordan and Tiny Bradshaw were out there. These were people that I would go under when I did my shows, you know, I would try to have a little piece of each person in me—that's what got me over. Back in those days it was heavy. Besides Eddie Vinson, you know, Eddie "Cleanhead" Vinson, right? [*sings:* "They call me Mr. Cleanhead head 'cause my head is bald"]. Now he was a helluva entertainer—now he was the best of all. He was a very powerful entertainer, a very powerful singer.

See a lot of people don't seem to understand, anytime you can perform you don't need no act—it's only when you got a weak entertainer he needs a step, he needs something to move, try to trick the people, to draw attention.

[After the Bees disbanded, Bland was introduced by promoter Joe Glaser to Hy Weiss and started to record for the Old Town label in late 1955. Bland's first solo recording was the Bo Diddley–inspired "Chicken in the Basket," with the hambone beat supplied by guitarist Tommy Ace. Next came "Chicken Hop," with Brownie McGhee and Sonny Terry. In 1958, both tracks were leased to Tip Top Records, operated by the Allen Distributing Company of Richmond, Virginia. It's possible that Bland's reissues were inspired by Rosco Gordon's recording of "The Chicken (Dance with You)," which was performed by Gordon in the 1957 movie *Rock Baby Rock It*. Then in late 1959 Bland entered the studio to record a song with potential: "Sweet Thing." Instead, it was the flip side, "Let the Little Girl Dance," that became the hit, at no. 7 on the *Billboard* Hot 100.]

Bland: Old Town did that, it was an accidental recording. Somebody else [Titus Turner] was doing the song in the studio and I was just down there, like

Billy Bland at the jukebox in his Harlem soul food restaurant, May 10, 1989. Photo by Paul Harris. Label courtesy of Victor Pearlin.

I'm here now. And I just got involved in the record and [A&R man] Henry Glover heard me sing. So, the fella that was recording the record [Titus Turner] for Henry Glover, I was showing him how to sing the song.[7] This wasn't my session, but I was showing the other guy how to do the song. Henry Glover switched on [the tape machine], and I'm in the studio singing and they recorded the hell outta me. They recorded me and I don't know I'm recording. That was this track here [*plays* "Let the Little Girl Dance" *on the jukebox*].

[Titus Turner] used to write for Ray Charles.[8] We didn't speak no more! This is Buddy Lucas blowing the horn—I kept singing, so the session, when I started singing, it took off, so the girls that were singing said. Playing the guitar was Mickey Baker. Bass is my bass player, Tommy Ace, and drums, Rod Porter. The girl chorus was the Miller Sisters. This is the side that they pushed [*plays* "Sweet Thing," *the B side*]. That's Mickey "Guitar" Baker playing there. It was a very difficult song. It took me from about nine o'clock to two a.m. You see, you gotta get it all together.

Broven: How many copies did "Let the Little Girl Dance" sell?

Bland: "Let the Little Girl Dance," it made a lot of money, but everybody [in the studio] wanted "Sweet Thing." You see, I wasn't there to make "Let the Little Girl Dance," I was there to do "Sweet Thing" because I had worked on it.

Broven: Did Dave "Baby" Cortez play on many of your records?

Bland: Me and Baby Cortez started out together. We did a thing together called "Whoa Bessie," he was a piano player.[9] We started working together, so basically I went one way, I got a hit record, he went another way, you know. He had a [no. 1] hit record with "The Happy Organ" [with Jimmy Spruill, 1959].

Broven: Did you appear on *American Bandstand*?

Bland: Dick Clark was a very rich man. I liked him, I loved him, but I just didn't wanna be commanded, and Clark was the type to say, "Go here, that's what you wear." Oh hell yeah, I did *American Bandstand*, a lot of the shows—*The Clay Cole Show*—all the shows I've been on. But I wasn't getting paid, you know. I didn't like the TV shows because you didn't get paid.

Broven: Did you enjoy the trappings of success?

Bland: I had a big limousine that was accidentally bought. I wanted a Fleetwood, but they didn't have a Fleetwood Cadillac, they had the limousine. Then a guy said, "Look, Billy, you need a chauffeur." I said, "C'mon man!" He said, "You can't drive this car with a name like you got. Let me chauffeur for you." I said, "Please man, I don't wanna go for that chauffeur stuff." But he spoiled me, he kept talking to me, so in about a week or two I hired him. But he was opening the door, doing all the things for me, and when he stopped doing them, I missed them.

Broven: How did you get on with Hy Weiss?

Bland: Hy Weiss was my father. I missed a lot of shows and he would cover for me. Hey, I was young and stupid, man. I was making money and, like, money didn't mean nothin' to me, you know. Hy Weiss was like a father to me.

[The Old Town follow-ups "You Were Born to Be Loved," then "Harmony" and "My Heart's on Fire," barely breached the Hot 100 as Bland's time as a chart artist was running out. Billy kept up to date with the trend toward soul and continued recording for Weiss until 1963. His final single, "Little Boy Blue," was an estimable cover of the Bobby "Blue" Bland classic. Meanwhile, Billy was still performing.]

Bland: See, I was always working with Ray Charles, Jackie Wilson, James Brown, Otis Redding; everybody. I was with them, you know, so I was like a hot act. I could open a show and I could close them, because I had records myself, you know.[10] Joe Tex, there was very few I didn't work with.

Broven: And you had a dance routine as well, did you?

Bland: If you could perform, if you could sing, you didn't need a stage routine. If you couldn't sing, you needed something to get you over. James Brown ain't never been a singer—he's been an entertainer, but he could scream and make you holler from the way he moved, you know. Otis Redding was never a great singer, but he was a helluva performer. Jerry Butler was a singer, some parts of Jackie Wilson is a singer, but he is mostly a performer. Sam Cooke is a singer, he's not a performer. Arthur Prysock is a singer. Roy Hamilton, he's a singer. Performers they can get over anyway because they can go the singing way, or dancing way, or clowning way, or telling jokes—the entertainers really get over, you know. James Brown has always been a performer, that's why nobody can go up against him. He can go four or five different ways, plus he makes his band not play, but he makes his band perform. That's why when James Brown leads a band, the band can't play for nobody but him because he teaches them how to play James Brown. And when they get behind somebody else they're not as strong as James Brown, and they can't feel it. Chubby Checker is not a singer, he's a performer—he moves around, he can get over and do things. Johnny Mathis is a singer, he stands up and he can sing.

But if a man can perform when he hit the stage, automatically it's over. When I first see James Brown in my life, I went to Florida with "Chicken in the Basket" and I see this little guy—like a little midget—with a big bus, two Cadillacs with one record.[11] And I said, how can a man have one of them big brand new Greyhounds, a big band, people cookin' for him, with one record? So me and Little Willie John at the time was touring, and I said to Little Willie John, "Who the hell can this little dude be?" I said, "We're staying in the cabinette, and this dude is staying in the hotel over there!" They gave us a cabinette, and James Brown had the whole damn hotel, you know. The place filled up with the people, the Palms in Hallandale, Florida.[12] So I told Little Willie John, I said, "Now this fella is not rehearsing." Because I was gonna go over to see him rehearse and see what he was doing. So I told Little Willie John, "You gotta watch this guy because

Billy Bland at his Harlem soul food restaurant, May 10, 1989. Photo by Paul Harris.

something is shaking with him. I'm going [on] first," I said, "I'm gonna do what I gotta do and get on first." This man, they said he was very polished and every-body called him Boss. He was a very quiet dude and to have all that he had, I knew he had to be a pretty powerful guy. When I heard him sing, I said, "There ain't nothin' here, man!" But something else said, "Don't mess with that." So I told Little Willie John, "Let him close the show. There's something funny about this guy—with a bus and two Cadillacs out there—there's something shaking that we ain't seen!" So Willie John said, "I'm gonna put him on second." So I got on first, I did my little "Chicken in the Basket," my two little numbers that I got [probably the B side, "The Fat Man," not the Fats Domino song], and I watched. So I see them take the lights down, then they were sweeping the floor, changing the scenery for this little guy to come on the stage. I said, "What the hell is going on?" you know. So when they said "Billy Bland," the people clapped, because I had a nice little following. Then they said, "Ladies and gentlemen . . ." and all they said was "James . . ." and when they say "James" you thought the world was com-ing to an end! People started moving closer to the stage, I thought what the hell is going on—and all at once this man hit the stage. When he hit the stage you could not see his feet—he danced for thirty minutes before you knew he was up there, and people were screamin' and hollerin'. Hey, I wasn't a woman and I was screamin' too! But he was a performer. And after that when I used to see him, I used to duck him—I used to see him in the street, and I would run from him, you know, because he always got on my case. And we were very good friends.

Broven: So Little Willie John was top of the bill?

Bland: He never got on stage! James Brown . . . nobody can follow James Brown. I always admired him, and I admired Otis Redding because they are hardworking men. They talk about Elvis and these people, man, but I worked with these men. James Brown is a worker. When James Brown is on the stage, people don't go nowhere. They get scared to go to the bathroom, some of them stand there peeing themselves, they don't want to miss him. So when they do talk about Elvis and these people, I think it's a joke. 'Cause Elvis or nobody could touch James Brown. They'd be a fool to go on the stage with him because it would be like a disaster, because he could kill any act.

Broven: And Brown's band was good in those days?

Bland: The band was good. He had three or four bands, man—he'd wear a band out. He couldn't have one band back him up: two drummers. That's how good he was, he was the master, man. I sell crabs out of here [in the restaurant]. When I put James Brown on [the jukebox], I sell more crabs, and people be dancin'. And people in the street, ol' men that know him be twistin' in front of here. He is a genius. Now he is a performer, and Jackie Wilson is next to him. Michael Jackson is a copycat—he is pretty good, but he got most of it off James Brown.

Broven: When did you record with Brownie McGhee and Sonny Terry?[13]

Bland: Well, they was out of my league, they did records with me. But, see, Brownie and Sticks McGhee, they used to be those people that I didn't know anything about. I heard 'em play, but we was in a different category. Remember the guy I did a show with—what's his name? What's the guy's name who got drunk all the time [*impersonates*]?

Broven: Jimmy Reed?

Bland: Jimmy Reed! I never knew he was that powerful. See, Jimmy Reed is the type of entertainer that if you do a show with him, you gotta tie yourself to him, you gotta follow him all over the place, because when it's time to go on the stage, you ain't gonna find him. You find him way down the street by a drugstore. The place is packed full of people but, I'm gonna tell you a secret, Jimmy Reed can be drunk but when he hit the stage, in a minute, "Ladies and Gentlemen . . . Jimmy Reed" [*visual impersonation and laughter*]. And people scream, I say, "Jesus, how can this man make these people go crazy?" He sings "Bright Lights, Big City," have a nice day. I was backstage, I was falling all over the drums, but we couldn't go on behind him—no, you can't follow him. People get hypnotized, Jimmy Reed, people get hypnotized. Wilbert Harrison used to drink millions of gallons of liquor and go on the stage and sing "Kansas City." Come off stage . . .

drunk—on stage . . . sober. So these people like Sticks McGhee, these people are singers, so what they do they do good. You heard the one with the harmonica on the song that I did with the blind guy—Sonny Terry was blind—I did a session with him. You know, he's blowin' the harmonica but, you know, not this talkin' and agitatin'.[14] I've been with a helluva lot of entertainers, I've been in show business thirty-five years, you know, and I've been everywhere. I've been to Israel, that's abroad isn't it? I've been to Australia—kangaroo country. Yes, but I never got to England and Paris.

Broven: Billy, is there anything else you want to say about the future, about what you hope to do in music?

Bland: I dunno, man, I dunno. I'm not gonna work. I enjoyed myself, you know. It's been a great evening—very entertaining.

NOTES

1. Billy Bland told researchers Wayne Jancik and Ray Topping, independently, that he arrived in New York in 1947, but it seems he didn't start performing professionally until around 1954. (In our 1989 interview, he said, "I've been in show business thirty-five years.")

2. Edna McGriff, a largely forgotten figure, had an influential no. 4 R&B *Billboard* hit with "Heavenly Father," backed by Buddy Lucas and his Band of Tomorrow, for Jubilee in spring 1952. Born in Tampa, Florida, on December 16, 1935, the pianist was only sixteen at the time of the recording. She never had another hit and at one time resorted to cutting cover versions for the budget Bell label with Buddy Lucas. She stopped recording after a Capitol release in 1965 and died in Jamaica, New York, in March 1980.

3. The formidable Joe Glaser launched the Associated Booking Corporation in 1940 with Louis Armstrong, who remained ABC's principal client and Glaser's main preoccupation.

4. "Secret Love" was a massive hit for Doris Day (Columbia), topping the *Billboard* pop charts in early 1954.

5. "My Ding-a-Ling" was first recorded by Dave Bartholomew for King in 1952, before the Bees with Billy Bland recorded Bartholomew's song as "Toy Bell" (Imperial) in 1954. Chuck Berry had a huge no. 1 pop hit with "My Ding-a-Ling" (Chess) in 1972, after which Bartholomew and his music publisher successfully fought Berry for the song's copyright.

6. Smalls Paradise was the famous Harlem club located at 2294½ Seventh Avenue. In 1987, Bland told Ray Topping that the Bees "were spotted by Fats Domino while on the same bill." When Domino returned to his New Orleans hometown, he recommended that his A&R man Dave Bartholomew should sign the group to Imperial.

7. "Let the Little Girl Dance" was written by Carl Spencer and Henry Glover. Billy Bland's recording was in fact a reworking of the original 1958 version by Carl Spencer and the Videos on the Manhattan label, out of 1650 Broadway, written by Spencer and Bert Lawrence. While Bland's recording was still climbing the *Billboard* Hot 100 in April 1960, Al Brown and Ray Bryant entered the chart with "Madison" and "Madison Time," respectively, paving the way for Chubby Checker's no. 1 "The Twist" in September 1960, followed by a rash of dance records.

8. Titus Turner (1933–1984) had minor hits with "We Told You Not to Marry" (Glover, 1959)—an answer to "Stagger Lee" hitmaker Lloyd Price's "I'm Gonna Get Married" (both

ABC-Paramount)—and "Sound-Off" (Jamie, 1961). Turner's biggest song successes were "Leave My Kitten Alone" for Little Willie John (1959) and "Sticks and Stones" for Ray Charles (1960).

9. "Whoa Bessie" is an obscure record from 1958 by Dave and Bob on the tiny M&F label. The writers are Dave Clowney—that is, Dave "Baby" Cortez—and Big Bob Kornegay, presumably Dave and Bob. Billy Bland's presence is not readily apparent on the released version.

10. Paul Oliver's all-encompassing book *The Story of the Blues* (London: Barrie and Rockcliff, 1969) has a photo of a playbill for June 24, 1960, at the Howard Theatre, Washington, DC, showing Billy Bland, just coming off his national chart run with "Let the Little Girl Dance," playing below the two headliners Ruth Brown and the Drifters, along with Screamin' Jay Hawkins with Rick Henderson's Band.

11. While Billy Bland was promoting "Chicken in the Basket" on Old Town, James Brown had just released in February 1956 his first single, the big R&B hit "Please, Please, Please" (on Federal, the King subsidiary). Brown obtained the gig at the Palms in Hallandale through Miami record distributor Henry Stone, who had close connections with King Records.

12. The Palms in Hallandale, near Miami, was a hot spot on the chitlin' circuit in the 1950s and 1960s, with popular performers including B. B. King, Guitar Slim, Jackie Wilson, and Sam Cooke.

13. Brownie McGhee and Sonny Terry were accompanists on "Chicken Hop," Billy Bland's second Old Town release (1956). The duo also had two Old Town singles, "Uncle Bud"/"Climbing on Top of the Hill" (1956) and "She Loves So Easy"/"I Need a Woman" (a delayed 1960 release). In 1986, an Ace Records (UK) LP, *Old Town Blues*, vol. 1, featured eleven tracks by Brownie McGhee and Sonny Terry.

14. This is probably a reference to Terry's immersion in the folk-blues scene with McGhee.

16

BILLY BUTLER

Unpublished interview, Lincoln Center, New York,
May 13, 1989

Virtuoso guitarist and a real gentleman, Billy Butler was born in Philadelphia. Comfortable across a variety of styles, especially jazz, blues, R&B, and soul/jazz, his beautifully fluid style graced innumerable albums both as leader and sideman, and many singles. Butler's guitar creations on "Honky Tonk (Part 1 & 2)," cowritten with members of Bill Doggett's combo, are eternal classics and have been copied and learned by countless guitarists to this very day. The artists Butler worked with, Doggett apart, included Sammy Price, King Curtis, Dinah Washington, and many others.

John Broven: Billy, could you tell me when you were born?

Billy Butler: December 15, 1924. In Philadelphia, that's my hometown, I was born and raised there. I'm the only musical one. Neither of my parents played anything or whatever. They weren't into music at all. My two sisters played a little piano, but that's it.

Broven: And what did your parents do?

Butler: My father did mostly janitorial work, like downtown Philadelphia in hotels and stuff like that, but my mother did domestic work. You see, we're talking like the Depression now, we're talking anywhere from '29 on into the early '30s, so there wasn't much work about and, I mean, they had to do whatever they could do. But they did it, they raised us, they were just wonderful. What can I tell you? I wish every kid had parents like I had [*laughs*].

Broven: Billy, how did you become interested in music?

Butler: Oh gee, I don't know. It was just one of those things that starts to grow on you, I guess. I wanted to play and, for some stupid reason, I asked for a violin, I didn't know what it was, you know. My father got one for Christmas, I was eight years old [*laughs*], and I picked the thing up and started using it like a

Billy Butler (1924–1991), the West End, 114th Street, New York, May 16, 1986. Photo by Paul Harris.

guitar, and he handed me the bow and ... oh no! So I took lessons, and I played in the school orchestra at Barratt Junior High School in South Philadelphia.

Broven: So you played in the school band?

Butler: Yeah, I played until I graduated, and then went on to high school, and then I had given it up by that time because I was playing guitar. I started with the guitar at thirteen.

Broven: How did you get your first guitar?

Butler: Well, I saved up some of my lunch money from school, and my mother gave me the other fifty cents to put with it, and I bought a guitar in a pawnshop—that was two dollars and fifty cents. It was hanging in the window, and every day from school I would stop and look in this window. Oh, I am so fascinated, I have got to have that, so I got it—and my sister still has it in Philadelphia.

Broven: What make of guitar was it?

Butler: I have no idea, just a guitar, I don't know what it was, had a hole in the middle [*laughs*], I don't know. Anyway, that was the start of it all, and then from there I just kept fooling with it, and I taught myself. And then, finally somebody decided that they wanted to hear me play in a club, and they sneaked me in—because I was under age. I was only fourteen, fifteen years old, so they had to really sneak me into the club, because at that time you had to be at least eighteen to go in. But I looked a little older than I was because I always had a moustache—I had a moustache from the time I was fourteen—so they didn't know. I worked with a lot of the old-timers. To me they were old-timers at that

Billy Butler, the West End, 114th Street, New York, May 16, 1986. Photo by Paul Harris.

time, guys like thirty, thirty-five years old, forty years old, and they taught me a lot.

Broven: Can you think of some of their names?

Butler: I can't really. Some of the names you might not even know, like Ike Covington, Lee Nelson, my goodness, Henry Lowe, there were so many, and the names don't come back now, Harry Marsh, a drummer.[1]

Broven: What sort of music were they playing?

Butler: Jazz, basically jazz.

Broven: For dancing?

Butler: That's how I really got into jazz, at that particular time, the era that we are talking about. I had so much to reach for, because all of the big bands—and you could distinguish one band from another—they all had their own trademark more or less, their style, their own styles, and we had it quite good. The kids today don't have that, they are pretty much locked into one thing. It's a rock 'n' roll thing or country, and that's it, it doesn't go anywhere else. And they hear pretty much the same type of thing over and over and over again, and the disc jockeys, the media doesn't help, doesn't help at all. They just keep feeding that to them,

I mean, they know nothing about musical history. I went to Europe for the first time in '76, and I went to France, Switzerland, Holland, Germany—I didn't get to London until 1981. I came over with a jazz festival . . . but over there, I mean everybody, they've got libraries with all of this information in them. They teach it in school, little kids like this [*visual description*]. A little fellow in France, I mean, we were in a town called Villeneuve, France, and he came backstage with his parents, seven years old, they couldn't speak any English, but he could. He was translating to them, telling them what I was saying and so forth—and this kid stood there and told me my life story. He told me where I was born. He told me where I went to school. Now I mean, I'm one out of how many million musicians, and [*laughs*] I had never been there before and he told me my entire life story.

Broven: So what was the Philadelphia club scene like when you were starting to play?

Butler: It was very good in those days.

Broven: Can you name some of the clubs?

Butler: I started my first real professional gig was in a club called Murray's Rhythm Bar, which was downtown in the heart of the city. You had like Broad and Market Streets in Philadelphia, around that area, a little club, but nice. That club and a club called Spider Kelly's. And I did some like banquets and weddings and things at a place called Bookbinder's—a very excellent restaurant in Philadelphia [on Walnut Street]. I don't know even if it's still there, but it was marvelous; very good seafood and very good steaks, chops, and that sort of thing. I used to do things there. There were so many clubs. A lot of things to reach for, you know. And of course at that time I had just met Charlie Christian.

Broven: How did you start to play the electric guitar?

Butler: Well, principally because of Charlie, because he was the first one that we heard play real jazz on an electric guitar. Everybody else was playing acoustic guitar, playing jazz, but it was acoustic like Django Reinhardt. But we had some guys from Philadelphia that were absolutely fantastic, great guitarists, a guy called Harry Crafton, Lee Nelson, Harry Pope, Jimmy Shirley, Teddy Walters, I don't know, I can't remember them all.[2] I didn't start with the electric until, oh, I guess it must have been around 1940. Prior to that I was playing acoustic guitar. The solos that I used to record, I'd get in front of the microphone, play the solos—just like Django did—that sort of thing. But after hearing Charlie, I said I've gotta have an amplifier, so I bought an amplifier, put a pickup on the guitar, and went from there.

Broven: And what type of guitar were you playing then?

Butler: The first good guitar I had for that was, I think, an Epiphone. I still have it, it's a 1940 Epiphone Broadway. They went out of business, they sold out to Gibson, so Gibson is now making that guitar again. I have one of the new Epiphones at home, so Gibson is making that again.

Broven: So at this time in the '40s, were you hearing any blues music at all, or was it just purely jazz?

Butler: Yeah, I heard blues, but I wasn't carried away with it. I was never that fascinated with blues. But it's like playing tarantellas [folk dances] for an Italian, you know what I mean, or the hornpipe for an Irishman, you know? So with the blacks, I mean, blues was a native thing. So we didn't find anything that exceptional about it, it wasn't that fascinating—I mean, we liked it of course. So I got to play blues pretty much because of association with different groups, and playing behind different groups and that sort of thing, that's how I started. There were blues singers and such, but no one that you would really know. I mean, some of these, most of these, were local people around Philadelphia, and you wouldn't recognize any of the names, some of them, most of them, are dead, you know.

Broven: Could you just name two or three?

Butler: Well, Pearl Bailey's sister was one, Eura Bailey, I played for her. That was later when I came to New York. Then, a guy who called himself Mr. Blues.

Broven: Wynonie Harris?

Butler: Wynonie Harris! Wynonie Harris, I backed him up, and Guitar Slim. And, oh yeah, Sammy Price. I did a recording of Sammy Price back in 1942. I was called to come over to New York to do the date for Decca Records. Went to Europe in '76, and somebody had the record like it was just made yesterday, a 78 [rpm] record! It was unbelievable, it was glistening like glass, and he put the thing on he says, "Bill, I want you to tell me if you can recognize this guitar player on this record." So he put it on—he wouldn't show me the label or anything, he just put it on the thing. I listened to it. Said, "That's Sammy Price on piano." And then the guitar comes in, plays the blues. I said, "No, I don't recognize him." He said, "What do you think of him?" I said, "He's all right" [laughs]. He said, "That's the recording you made with Sammy Price in 1942." I said, "Oh my goodness, I don't believe this!"

Broven: So that was your first recording?

Butler: That was the first time I did any commercial recording.[3]

Broven: Where did you make the record?

Butler: It was in New York.

Broven: Can you recall anything about playing behind Wynonie Harris?

Butler: Not too much. I did club work with him, basically. Well, I'd say actually almost exclusively at the Baby Grand here in New York, on [319 West] 125th Street, yeah, 125th and St. Nicholas. Yeah, I worked with him there.

Broven: What year was that?

Butler: That was around 1947–48.

Broven: And can you recall who else was in the group at the time?

Butler: Well, at that time, I was in a group called the Harlemaires.[4] We had three fellas and a girl. We were doing stuff like the Modernaires and the Pied Pipers. We were singing, close four-part harmony. Jesse Stone was doing the writing for us. He wrote all of our arrangements, and so we sang with four-part harmony, like the Four Freshmen, that sort of thing, and we played jazz, you know.

Broven: Who else was in the group?

Butler: Chester Slater was the pianist and leader and sang. And Percy Joell, who has passed away, the bass player. And Dottie Smith was the girl, she was the female voice, and she played a thing called a conga drum, looked like a tall tom-tom, and they used brushes on it. Maybe you've seen girls do that? [She was] from Philadelphia. Yes, as a matter of fact the whole group was from South Philly.

Broven: And so you backed Wynonie Harris?

Butler: Yeah. We went into the club as a house group. And then we would play for whatever top vocalist would come in . . . and also doing some singing and dancing.

Broven: What sort of show did Wynonie have then?

Butler: Oh, it was a variety type of thing. We would go on and play a couple of tunes, then we would bring the featured artist on, then they'd come down and we would play some more behind them. There was a supper club also at that time, and while they were eating we would play, nice soft listenable stuff.

Broven: So Wynonie belted out the blues, did he?

Butler: Yeah, yeah, I mean when they would have what they called show time, and . . . people were crazy about him, they were nuts about him. As soon as they would say, "Now, here he is ladies and gentlemen, Mr. Blues: Wynonie Harris!" The women were going nuts there, grabbing for him [*laughs*]. It was a lot of fun.

Broven: Did he open with "Good Rockin' Tonight"?

Butler: Yeah, either that or he would open with something else and he would go into that, he had about two or three different hits that he had at that time—they were riding pretty high for him, oh yes.[5]

You remember the group called the Ravens? With Ricky [Jimmy Ricks], the bass singer, doing bass lead instead of the tenor doing the lead, it was a unique thing. Yeah, we worked with them there. And I'll never forget—this was one of the highlights of my life—Ricky and I used to go some nights, in the intermissions, we would go down to the telephone booth. And I would go in the booth—and you know your voice reverberates in a booth?—and I would sing his parts for him, and he said, "Oh, you got me, you're singing all my stuff." As fate would have it, Ricky got laryngitis, and they came in one night and they didn't know about it until they got to the club, and when they got there, they were without the bass man. So, Maithe Marshall, he was singing tenor with them, Maithe said, "Hey, look, Billy's been going doing the stuff with Ricky, they go down to the phone booth, and Billy knows a lot of the tunes." He said, "Why don't we give it a shot and see what happens?" So I said, "Oh, come on." He said, "Would you mind Billy?" I said, "No, I'll do it for fun, I don't care." So they announced the Ravens to come on—I had played with my group—they announced, "Here are, ladies and gentlemen, the Ravens!" They come on, and I come running behind them, and got up on the stage and grabbed the mic and went [*demonstrates singing song*]. The people went wild, the people went absolutely wild, I don't think they heard the first sixteen bars of the tune, they were just screaming and applauding. And then we went into the other tunes that they had. Yeah, "Ol' Man River." I think I did five tunes.[6] So when they did the second show, of course we repeated those tunes because those were the ones that I knew, I didn't know their entire repertoire, but it was a lot of fun.

Broven: What was the Baby Grand like as a club?

Butler: It was great, terrific place. It was small, wasn't that large, but the food was excellent, and it was a nice club, a very intimate type of club.

Broven: And there was a tiny stage?

Butler: Yeah. The stage wasn't too large, but they had a floor, like a platform that could move out into it, and they would move the tables back for show time. And then they would put that back and then let the people dance if they wanted to a little bit. Not a heck of a lot of room, but everybody had a good time. And it was always crowded.

Broven: How many people did it take?

Butler: About maybe two hundred.

Broven: But it is a very famous Harlem club, isn't it?

Butler: Oh yes, very well known.

Broven: Going back to Wynonie, what was he like as a person?

Butler: Well, I found him . . . some people thought he was obnoxious. Some people found him very tasteless, if I may, because of his demeanor. Well, that was his trademark, you know. "I am the greatest" and "I am Mr. Blues." Always stayed dressed well and stuff, but he had a very gruff manner, especially with females, and not too many people liked that, you know. I didn't care for it myself, really, but I mean he was always nice with me. I always found him to be relatively pleasant when he was away from that atmosphere.

Broven: From the star bit?

Butler: Yeah. You see, whenever there was a crowd, then he would go through this loud talk and, like I said, I didn't particularly care for that, but he never pulled any of that on me, you know. So I go by how I am treated.

Broven: Sure. So he did make quite a few enemies, did he?

Butler: Yes, oh yes, oh yes. It was bound to happen, I mean, it was just one of those things.

Broven: So people wanted to bring him down?

Butler: Yeah, yeah. As I say, it was one of those things when you have that type of veneer. I remember Muhammad Ali had the same problem just after he won the [world heavyweight boxing] championship. I did the recording with him, "I Am the Greatest."[7]

Broven: With Sam Cooke?

Butler: Yeah, Sam Cooke was there, yes. Ali comes in—at that time he was Cassius Clay—he comes into the studio and he looked, he saw me with the guitar, and he comes over. And I said, "Hi, Champ, how you doin'?" And I stood up and shook his hand. His hand swallowed my hand [*laughs*], but it was a thrill for me, you know. And, however, he says, "I wonder if you could show me something on that thing?" I said, "Well, if you want to, sit down." And I gave him my guitar, and then I put his fingers on the strings and showed him what to do—and he sat there and he had a ball. He was like a little kid, like about five years old. And he was one of the nicest guys you ever want to meet. Even after he started this business with "I am the greatest" and all that loud talk on television and you-name-it in the media, you get him all to himself and it's like two different people. One of the nicest people I ever met in my life—that's the truth. And, like I said, it was the same way with Wynonie. Ricky, with the Ravens—I mean, Jimmy Ricks, that was his right name, though everybody called him Ricky. Jimmy was the same way. When he was out, I mean in the public eye, he had that gruff exterior, but you get him like we're sitting here now talking intimately, he was one of the nicest most humble guys you'd ever meet. You'd never hear this [*impersonates Jimmy Ricks's voice and manner of speaking*], you'd never hear that, never [*laughs*].

Broven: So you played a lot in Harlem, did you?

Butler: Quite a bit. But basically most of the stuff that I did in Harlem was at the Baby Grand. Other than that, I did very little in Harlem. Whenever I came over to New York, I was usually in one of the downtown recording studios, or in some hall somewhere, you know, like Webster Hall or one of the larger places downtown like Village Gate, that sort of thing in Greenwich Village. But as far as Harlem was concerned, it was pretty much relegated to the Baby Grand.

Broven: Did you play at the Apollo?

Butler: Yes, I did. I'm sorry, I completely forgot that—I'm glad you mentioned it. Yeah, I played the Apollo, but I was with Reuben Phillips's house band for a while.

Broven: When was that?

Butler: Oh golly, it's back in the '50s. It was before I went with Bill Doggett [in late 1954], it was prior to that I was with the house band. When I went back to the Apollo, I went back with Bill Doggett as a featured artist. The audiences were great because they always had top-name entertainment, you know. I mean they had a lot of the groups that were popular at that time, the Five Keys and the Clovers, [and later] the Coasters. Oh golly, so many, it's hard really to name them all.

Broven: Were there any famous names in the Reuben Phillips band?

Butler: Oh, great question because it was a big band. We had, oh, I dunno, Reuben had twelve or fifteen pieces in the band, and it's hard to say who now. That's a tough one.[8]

Broven: Was it Doc Bagby that you played with?

Butler: Doc Bagby, yes. The trio was Doc Bagby on the organ, his brother Bill Bagby on drums, and myself on guitar.[9]

Broven: You had two releases on Gotham before 1950 as Billy Butler and the Four Stars.

Butler: Yeah. I did a tune called "Pretty Eyes" [in 1949], and a thing, I forget the name of the other tune, a very pretty tune ["Can You Forgive"], the fella who wrote it he was a vibraphonist. But it was "Pretty Eyes" which Peggy Lee recorded later [in 1960]. [The other Gotham 78 was "Too Bad"/"I Made Up My Mind."]

Broven: Who were the Four Stars?

Butler: Let's see, who was in my group? Well, Doc was on piano, Doc Bagby, and Percy Joell was on bass. Let's see, who was on drums. I think it was Charlie Rice, yeah. And let me see, and on saxophone I had a fella named Bob Brown.

Broven: Did you record behind Doc Bagby with the Doc Bagby Trio?

Butler: Yeah, I did a series of things with Doc with the group, that I would sing and he would talk. What would happen was, we would start—they were all ballads—and so he would start, like he would make an introduction then he would come in and talk the lyric, and when he had finished then I would come in and sing the song, you know.

Broven: I didn't know you sang, Billy!

Butler: Oh yeah, I used to sing. I used to do a troubadour thing. I used to come off the stand on my own and walk through the tables with my guitar singing.

Broven: You signed a contract with Gotham's publishing arm, Andrea Music, on February 5, 1949. Presumably you recorded initially around that date or soon after?

Butler: Yeah, right. Sometime in that time slot, it was about then, yeah.

Broven: How did you come to record for Gotham?

Butler: Because Doc Bagby had an affiliation with them. That's how I happened to get into that.

Broven: Right, and so he introduced you to the label owner . . . was it Ivin Ballen?

Butler: Ivin Ballen, that's it, yeah.

Broven: So presumably the sessions were done in Philadelphia?

Butler: Yes.

Broven: At the Gotham studio?

Butler: I don't remember the location, but it was in Philly.

Broven: Who decided what was to be cut at the sessions? Was it up to you or did Ballen tell you what to do?

Butler: Well actually, a couple of the tunes, "Pretty Eyes" and ["Can You Forgive"], were two ballads, that was my own choice. After that then they were telling me what they wanted to use. But first of all, the things with Doc, they were his idea—this talk and then sing—because we started doing those in clubs and they seemed to go pretty well. See, the problem with Gotham was they didn't distribute the records. I don't have to tell you about that, and we had the same problem here in New York with Prestige [in 1969–1971]. They had the same problem, I mean, they would record you, but they put no promotion unless you already were known.

Broven: Did Gotham get local radio airplay?

Butler: Yes.

Broven: But that was about the only promotion you had?

Butler: That was about it, yeah. And I mean, like I said, it was just no real promotion behind it. I mean, the disc jockey picked up the records and decided if he wanted to play them, that sort of thing.

Broven: Did Gotham have any big successes to your knowledge?

Butler: They had a few with Earl Bostic. As a matter of fact, that was their top artist at that time, Earl Bostic.

Broven: How long did you stay with Doc Bagby's group?

Butler: Oh, I stayed with Doc I guess, about three years.[10] Then I packed up and went with Johnny Sparrow, a tenor player out of Baltimore.

Broven: When did you leave Doc?

Butler: I left Doc, I think, sometime in about the end of '53, and I went with Johnny Sparrow and his Bows and Arrows [*laughter*]. How's that for a title! Nice group, nice little jazz group and everything was rehearsed and tight; everything was together, and I enjoyed working with them. I worked with them up until I joined Bill Doggett in '55.

Broven: Let's talk about Bill Doggett then. How did you come to join Bill?

Butler: Well, he asked me to come with him. He had another guitarist with him.

Broven: Was that Bill Jennings?

Butler: Bill Jennings was with him. And Bill left the group, because Bill had quite a few problems. It's no secret, I mean Bill had a narcotic problem, and it just got to be too much, and Bill [Doggett] actually told him that he would appreciate it if he would just go, you know. So he let Bill go, and then he asked me if I would come in. I said, "Sure, why not?" Because I could see this as a chance for me to get into recording, and Bill was very well known at that time. So it worked and, that's about it.

Broven: What was the first record that you cut with Bill?

Butler: The actual first record I don't know because, see, we would go in and do six or eight sides, in a session. So to say which one was actually the first . . . I don't really know.[11]

Broven: Did you make these records at Cincinnati at the King studio?

Butler: Yes, basically we did, because we were traveling and we would stop at Cincinnati—maybe to do a dance—and then we would have a recording session, stay over a day or so, and have a recording session.

Broven: What was the King studio like?

Butler: It was nice. Quite large, and run very well, very efficiently.

Broven: And did they have good equipment?

Butler: Yes, they had excellent equipment. They didn't have like the multi-track things at that particular time, they hadn't gotten into that, eventually they did. But when I first started down there with Bill, they didn't have the ultra-modern stuff. I was always satisfied with what they did. Some, you'll go in with a nice big fat sound but when it comes out on the record it's so thin it sounds like you're playing a ten dollar guitar [*laughs*]. So no, I was always satisfied with the sound.

Broven: And who actually produced the records? Was it Henry Glover?

Butler: Yes.

Broven: Was he a good producer?

Butler: Excellent, excellent. A great mind for producing and putting together a record. He knew what he wanted. Yeah, he was excellent.[12]

Broven: Was he hard in the studio?

Butler: He was a taskmaster but, on the other hand, it wouldn't bother you as long as you kept your mind on what you were doing. You didn't go in there to have a ball or have fun. We went in there to work, and that's what we did, so we got results, you know. If he said, "I'd like to have this," or "I'd like to have that." That's what he got. So we got on fine, we never had a problem.

Broven: Presumably because it's King's own studio, you weren't limited to four titles in three hours . . . you could spend as much time as you wanted?

Butler: No, we weren't limited to the three hours thing. We would just go until they decided that they had what they wanted and we were through.

Broven: And you'd work all through the night and all day and night?

Butler: Well no, we never went over like maybe five hours, you know . . . not all-night or, in the morning and later. Because nobody ever saw the sense in that, I mean, we knew what we wanted to do and we did it.

Broven: OK. Big question: How did "Honky Tonk" come about?

Butler: We went to Lima, Ohio, checked in the hotel. We had a dance there that night—this was sometime in early '56. Clifford Scott [the sax player] called me and said, "Why don't you come down to my room? I've got a fifth of Johnnie Walker, red label [*laughs*], and let's play some." So I went down to his room with my guitar. So we're sitting there, and I'm fooling around with the guitar. I said, "My uncle used to sit out on the back porch and he used to play something like this" [*illustrates a bluesy tune and sound of the bass line*]. And Scotty said, "Keep that going." And he comes in with [*impersonates tune/sound again*]. That's what happened! So Scotty said, "Look, let's pull this on Bill when we go to work!" I said, "OK, why not, let's have some fun." We got to work that night and I said to Bill, "Scotty and I have got something we were fooling around with in the hotel, just play a shuffle." I told Shep Shepherd, the drummer, I said, "Just play a shuffle, but give it to us, we'll start it off and you pick us up." I said, "That OK?" Bill said, "Yeah, fine." And I played that entire guitar solo that you heard on the record, note for note. Now why, I could not tell you to this day, why I remembered that solo note for note, every bit of it, and I played it. So we played it and when we got through, when we ended the thing, the people started to applaud. They wouldn't get off the dance floor, they just continued to stand there and applaud: "More, more, more!" So we did it again. Then we played some other tunes and had an intermission, and when we went back, they started yelling, "We wanna hear that tune." And we didn't even have a name for it, we didn't even know what to call it. So I said to Bill, "What are we gonna call this thing, man?" So he said, "Don't tell me you guys don't have a name for it?" I said, "No, we just got it together." So he said, "How do you like 'Honky Tonk?'" I said "It's as good as any." So when we got back to New York, he [Bill Doggett] set up a recording session with a studio down on Thirty-First Street—King's wasn't there, they used an outside studio.[13] We did eight sides. When we got through the eight sides, Bill said, "Hey, let's do that tune that we did in Ohio, at Lima." He said, "You guys feel like doing it, too?" "Yeah, why not?" So we started to play it, and the engineer said, "What is this, is this an extra tune?"

["Honky Tonk," is a standard known and performed by just about every blues and R&B band in the world. Billy Butler's solo is a virtually perfect composition and is learned by guitarists the world over. Clifford Scott's saxophone parts are just as iconic. The two-part record turned out to be a timeless hit and inspired a rash of rock instrumentals in its immediate aftermath including "Slow Walk" by Sil Austin; "Raunchy" by Bill Justis, Ernie Freeman, and Billy Vaughn; "Walkin' with Mr. Lee" by Lee Allen; "Tequila" by the Champs; "Big Guitar" by Owen Bradley; "The Happy Organ" by Dave "Baby" Cortez; and "Smokie Part 2" by Bill Black's Combo.]

Broven: It must make you feel very proud.

Butler: Ah yeah, yeah, I am. Believe me, I'm quite proud of what has happened with me over my . . . I don't say my accomplishments as such. But it has been wonderful, the response from people, the public, the media, it's been great.

Courtesy of Victor Pearlin.

I mean, because nobody could have ever told me that I was going that far, but it did happen, and it's just wonderful. When I go overseas and I meet people over there, I mean, I certainly never thought I'd ever see in my life. How in the heck do they know me, you know? Who am I? I'm a grain of sand on the beach. It's so marvelous, so wonderful. Now an instrumental, it's very difficult for that to happen [at the time]—an instrumental over a vocals. We pushed Elvis Presley out of first place; he was in second, but we were no. 1, this was in *Billboard* and *Cash Box*.[14] And it stayed up, it stayed up from '56 on. And that record is still selling today—I still get royalty checks.

Broven: In fact, all the band members were credited with the tune, weren't they?

Butler: It was done that way because we didn't know it was gonna be a hit— we did it for fun. We didn't know it was gonna be a hit, so I couldn't say, "Hey, that's my tune, you can't have any of it," or something like that, or Scotty couldn't say it. So Bill said, "Why don't I put everybody's name on it, just in case something should happen with it. And if it doesn't, what the heck! I'll put everybody's name on it." So we said fine. All the band was credited with the song, plus Henry Glover whose name was on the credits until removed later.[15]

Broven: Everyone was happy with that?

Butler: Yeah.

Broven: Were you happy with it?

Butler: Sure, at that time, of course. I've heard more kids play that thing. It's unbelievable, three generations of kids I've heard play that song. It started with the Beach Boys [*laughs*].

Broven: Who was the bass player on "Honky Tonk"?

Butler: Oh gee, I can't remember who played bass on that, isn't that strange [it was Carl Pruitt], because Bill always used a bass on recordings—he never would go with the pedals . . . he didn't like that sound. Wild Bill Davis did, Wild Bill Davis always used the pedals. Well, Bill [Doggett] would use the pedals but he wanted the bass player to play almost the exact same notes that he was playing, which made it pretty hard for the bass player, you know. I was glad I was playing something else [*laughs*]. He was playing upright [string bass] of course, yeah, he wasn't playing the electric Fender.

Broven: And then presumably the record took off, and you went out on the road.

Butler: Yeah, we really started to travel then. Like I said, I got to the place where by '61 I had had it, you know. I'd had six years of that going out, going out and you'd come home, you were home for a week, three or four days, just long enough to get some more clothes, fill your suitcase, and go back out. And I got very tired of that, so I came off in '61.

Broven: Did you have any follow-up records to "Honky Tonk"?

Butler: Oh yeah, too many, too many—they got a fever with that. Every time we'd go to the studio we would have to do something that was based on the "Honky Tonk" principle. And I did tell Bill, I said, "Bill, this is kinda foolish. A hit is a one-time thing, let's do something else, maybe we'll get a hit with something else. I'm not trying to tell you your business, Bill, but on the other hand I think it's a little superfluous really because we've done that." I mean, people don't need to keep hearing the thing, every tune you come out with it's the same, it's got the same [*impersonates tune/sound*]. But he insisted on doing it, so there must have been about five or six.[16]

Broven: Did you get a fair deal from King?

Butler: I think so, all things considered. I mean because, like I said, when the tune was initially done, we didn't know it was gonna be a hit, nobody ever does. So I couldn't say, "Look, man, the tune is a hit, for crying out loud I think

I should get more money." No, because it wasn't that type of thing. I mean, I don't think that anybody gave me a bad deal. I think it was quite fair. It was split evenly between us.

Broven: Did you like King's owner, Syd Nathan?

Butler: Yes, I thought he was a fine man.

Broven: He certainly did well with the company, didn't he?

Butler: Yes, he did. No, I had no complaints at all.

Broven: He really brought King from being a small label to a big independent, didn't he?

Butler: Yeah. And prior to that, Earl Bostic really was his [hit act], because Bostic left Gotham and went with King, and then also Doggett was with King. But Bostic was the one who was putting out the top, the hits more or less.[17] And then when we got "Honky Tonk," of course, we were the top group with King, you know. So that's the way that happened.

Broven: And during your time with Doggett, did you record with anybody else in the studio, or did you just stay with that group?

Butler: Yeah, I did a couple of things. Like when we went to California, I did a couple of things out there at Capitol Tower in Los Angeles. But not a heck of a lot, you know.

Broven: Any well-known records that you recorded behind?

Butler: You remember a thing called "Peppermint Twist"?[18]

Broven: Yes.

Butler: Little Joey Dee. I'm on it, I'm the guitar on that.

Broven: Good lord!

Butler: Yeah, "Peppermint Twist," we did that. We got that together at the Peppermint Lounge here in New York. I was working with his little group there and did it, just for a short while. He asked me did I want to do the date and I said, "Sure." So we did the date, that was it, then came up with a hit with that. Then I did the thing with King Curtis, "Soul Twist."[19]

Broven: Who actually produced that record? Was it Bobby Robinson or Danny Robinson?

Butler: Bobby Robinson, that's right, I had forgotten.

Broven: Was he good in the studio?

Butler: Yeah, he knew what he was doing.

Broven: Bobby has got a very good ear, hasn't he?

Butler: Yeah, yeah. He knew what he was doing.

Broven: Did you play in Curtis's group?

Butler: Yeah, I was with Curtis's group for a while. Soon after I came off the road in '61 I worked with Curtis, I think for about two years.[20]

Broven: Did you play just around New York?

Butler: Basically yes, because I didn't wanna travel anymore. I had had enough of the road. So I worked with Curtis for a couple of years, and then I was getting into the studios.

Broven: What was King Curtis like to play with live?

Butler: Live, a lot of fun, lot of fun—good player, excellent saxophonist. I mean, he had his little faults, here and there, nothing astronomical. I found him to be a nice guy.

Broven: But he had a great group then?

Butler: Ray Lucas on drums, yes, and gee, I can't think who was the bass player.

Broven: Was it Jimmy Lewis?

Butler: Jimmy Lewis! I don't know, why couldn't I think of Jimmy? Jimmy and I have done, over the years, we've done duets—just guitar and bass duets—and we've done clubs and stuff, yeah.

Sammy Price, Billy Butler, and Jimmy Lewis, the West End, 114th Street, New York, May 16, 1986. Photo by Paul Harris.

Broven: Because when we saw you three years ago you were playing with Jimmy and Sammy Price.

Butler: Right, yeah, down at the West End.

Broven: That's it. Is Jimmy still around?

Butler: Oh yeah. Jimmy's still around doing things, he's doing some things on his own, and his wife has been doing a little singing with him, you know. He's still active [at the time].[21]

Broven: What about Dinah Washington?

Butler: She had just married [in 1963] "Night Train" [Dick Lane], the football player, he adopted both of her sons, and she was like madly in love with this guy—and for the first time in her life, she was happy. Dinah had a very turbulent life. So for the first time she was really happy, and then she had this accident. She was on some sort of reducing plan, and she obviously had taken the medication and didn't remember it, and took some more, and it stopped her heart—she had cardiac arrest. And that's how her husband found her on the couch, she had passed away.[22]

Broven: And you played on the *Back to the Blues* Roulette LP?

Butler: Yeah, I was on this. We did it in three days here in New York.

Broven: Dinah was happy with this session, was she?

Butler: Yeah, she was happy. She insisted on being right out in the studio with us. She said, "I'm gonna stay out here with the guys."

Broven: Did you play on any other hit records in the '60s in New York as a session musician?

Butler: It's hard to say. I mean there were some, but I don't remember the names, the titles of the tunes. I know I did some with the Flamingos.

Broven: You didn't play on "I Only Have Eyes for You"?

Butler: I think I did that, yeah.

Broven: Was that you playing that wonderful guitar?

Butler: I don't know how wonderful it was [*laughs*] but yeah, I was on that. Let's see, I did some things with the Coasters too. Also the Drifters, I did some things with them—I did "On Broadway" with them.

Broven: So you must have been quite a fixture in the New York studios?

Butler: Yeah. See I had gotten into it in the '60s up until about '72 or '73 when it started to slow down, the entire studio scene. That's when they were getting very rock 'n' roll oriented.

Broven: What, the rock groups?

Butler: Yeah. And so they were bringing the groups in and having them stay from nine o'clock in the morning until ten o'clock at night, that sort of thing, to get one side. We were knocking out like four or five sides in three hours, three and a half hours. But they decided they wanted to do that, and so that's what happened. So now recording [studio work] hardly exists anymore [in 1989].

Broven: Did you enjoy doing rhythm & blues material, because obviously jazz is your first love?

Butler: Yeah. Well, yeah, I enjoyed it because I did several club dates with Big Joe Turner. Big Joe Turner only sang in one key [*laughs*], the key of C, that's it, and they were playing the blues over and over again in the same key, but we enjoyed it, we enjoyed working with him. And so, I've had some fun with it, and it's been lucrative. I've made a living.

Broven: Having gone through the '60s and into the '70s and the recording scene suddenly ending, what did you do then?

Butler: What I'm doing now, shows. I started getting shows and nightclub work, and that's what I've been doing ever since.

Broven: Can you name some of the shows you've played in?

Butler: Well, I did a show called *Ballroom* with Dorothy Loudon and Richard Gardenia at the Majestic Theatre [Broadway, 1978]. At St. James I did *The 1940's Radio Hour* [Broadway, 1979] and also we did *My One and Only* there with Tommy Tune and Twiggy [1983]. And in '73 I went and did *Don't Bother Me, I Can't Cope* that was at the Edison Theatre, I did that for about two and a half years. Then I've done—I'm sort of skipping around trying to remember these things—I did an Israeli musical. The entire troupe came over from Israel to do it, and we did it at the old Helen Hayes Theater called *To Live Another Summer* [Broadway, 1971]. It was very much like *Don't Bother Me, I Can't Cope* except *Cope* was a black show, and this was an Israeli musical, but the format was almost the same—it was uncanny how similar they were. I did that, we did that for about a year, then they all had to leave. That's the only reason we closed it down—all of the actors were in the Israeli army. And I did the black version of *Guys and Dolls!* with Robert Guillaume [Broadway Theatre, 1976].

Broven: And so recording has almost stopped now [in 1989], has it?

Butler: Yeah, there's not very much around. I mean, first of all, one of the big deterrents is the advent of the electronic keyboards and the synthesizers. I mean, they can do everything. So one guy can go into the studio and sound like twenty—the only difference is, it's an electronic sound. And you don't have to be that trained to know what you are hearing, and a lot of people are annoyed about it. They are saying that they'd rather hear the live musician with the acoustic instrument, you know. The electronics, they are getting too much of it in the commercials, in recordings, even they're taking it into the clubs and it really doesn't make it. They've really fouled up the industry, I'll tell you.

Broven: Going back, did you have any records, any albums, in your own name Billy?

Butler: Yeah. I had four from Prestige Records [1969–1971]. The first one I did was called *This Is Billy Butler!* That was the introductory album. I had two fellas that are no longer with us: Rudy Collins on drums—he just passed away about six or eight months ago—and Bobby Bushnell on bass who died about five or six years ago. And, let's see who else, Ernie Hayes on piano and Houston Person on tenor sax. That was my first album, and then I did one—it had a picture of a girl on the front—*Guitar Soul!* it was called. Then the third album was called *Yesterday, Today and Tomorrow*—it had a picture of me on the front, needing a shave [*laughs*]. I had two other great guitar players with me, one passed away: Everett Barksdale, he had cancer. With Bill [Suyker], I had three guitars [on two tracks]. One tune in particular was a tune of mine called "Evening Dreams" and I wanted a three-guitar thing on there, and so I did like a guitar section. So I did that with them [also on "The Butler Did It"]. The last album, the cover had a picture of me on the cover, and it was almost like a violet haze over the thing. The title tune was the title of the album [*Night Life*]. I did that, and I did an album for Galt MacDermot, he did the music for *Hair*—he was the composer of all the music for the show. And we did another show called *Via Galactica* but it didn't last.

Broven: Everett played on a lot of rhythm & blues sessions, didn't he?

Butler: Not a heck of a lot. He did more of the straight commercial type of stuff. He didn't do too much blues.

Broven: Those Prestige records, were they blues or jazz?

Butler: A little mixture, a mixture of a little of these. The A&R man, Bob Porter, he's an excellent A&R man. Well, anyway, he was working for Prestige at that time, and he has since set up with station WBGO, a jazz station they have now in Newark. However, he had some ideas. He wanted me to do a lot more blues than I did, and I told him, "I am not a blues guitarist, I'd like to mix it up." He said, "OK, I'm not gonna insist with you." So I said, "Yeah, I'd rather mix it up, I don't wanna do one thing, and particularly I don't wanna sit there and play blues for a whole hour. I don't see that."

Broven: Your wife [Marion Wise Butler, who died June 1990] is a lovely songwriter.

Butler: She got hurt, oh about six and a half years ago. We would do a session here and a session there, something like that, or a demonstration record or something, you know. She knows what she's doing. She's a very lovable person.

NOTES

1. It has not been possible to verify these Philadelphia musicians, but they deserve a phonetic name check pending confirmation.

2. In this case, it has been possible to confirm the names of Harry Crafton, Jimmy Shirley, and Teddy Walters.

3. Sam Price and his Texas Bluesicians recorded for Decca in January 20, 1942, but the guitarist is listed in discographies as William Lewis. However, Price and Billy Butler did accompany Albinia Jones for Decca in 1947, with healthy rations of Butler's guitar on "Papa Tree Top Blues."

4. The Harlemaires had only the sixth Atlantic release in June 1948 with "If You Mean What You Say"/"Rose of the Rio Grande." *Billboard* reviewed "Rio Grande" positively, describing it as "jump cleffing of oldie smoothly and rhythmically done, with two vocal bebop breaks giving up-to-the-minute flavor." Alas, the top side was called "a draggy pop performance." The group also backed Wynonie Harris on two Aladdin releases: "Ghost of a Chance"/"Big City Blues" (released September 1947) and "Hard Ridin' Mama"/"You Got to Get Yourself a Job, Girl"

(February 1948). At our interview, Butler did not refer to the Aladdin recording session, and I was not aware of it at the time.

5. Wynonie Harris had two *Billboard* R&B no. 1 hits in 1948–1949 for King with "Good Rockin' Tonight" and "All She Wants to Do Is Rock."

6. The Ravens, with bass singer Jimmy "Ricky" Ricks, had a run of *Billboard* R&B hits in 1948 for National, including "Write Me a Letter" (no. 5), "Ol' Man River" (no. 10), "Send For Me if You Need Me" (no. 4), and "It's Too Soon to Know" (no. 11).

7. The Cassius Clay single "I Am the Greatest"/"Stand by Me" (Columbia) just failed to break into the *Billboard* Hot 100 in March and April 1964, at no. 113 and no. 102, respectively. He had just beaten Sonny Liston for the world heavyweight boxing championship on February 25, 1964, in Miami Beach.

8. The Reuben Phillips band at the Apollo is not at all well documented. Later, in 1962, Billy Butler played guitar on the Phillips *Big Bad Band at the Apollo* LP for Ascot, the United Artists subsidiary. Phillips blew alto saxophone with James Powell in an eleven-strong horn section, with Emile Russell (drums).

9. Philadelphia-born Harold "Doc" Bagby was a pianist/organist who became A&R man at Gotham Records and had a minor hit in 1957 with "Dumplin's" (OKeh).

10. Interestingly, in *Billboard*, December 8, 1951, it was announced that Jimmy Thomas, pianist, had "formed a foursome for Philadelphia's newly opened Blue Note with Shep Shepherd, arranger with Gotham Records on drums, Percy Joell formerly of the Original Harlemaires on bass, and Billy Butler for guitar pickings." Shepherd would later play with Butler in Bill Doggett's combo and cowrite "Honky Tonk."

11. *The King Labels: A Discography*, compiled by Michel Ruppli with assistance from Bill Daniels (Westport, CT: Greenwood Press, 1985), shows that the first Billy Butler sessions with Bill Doggett were held on March 23 and 28, 1955. One of the ensuing King singles, "True Blue," was a Doggett-Butler cowrite.

12. Born on May 21, 1921, in Hot Springs, Arkansas, Henry Glover was hired as a record producer by Syd Nathan of King Records in late 1948 after playing trumpet with Buddy Johnson, Tiny Bradshaw, and Lucky Millinder. Not only did Glover record jump blues and R&B for King but he also produced hillbilly and country artists, too. His biggest successes for the label were "Blues Stay Away from Me" by the Delmore Brothers (1949), "Fever" by Little Willie John, and, of course, "Honky Tonk" by Bill Doggett (both 1956). After leaving King under a payola cloud, in 1959 he started up his Glover label (including Titus Turner and Larry Dale) in conjunction with Hy Weiss of Old Town Records, for which label he produced Billy Bland's "Let the Little Girl Dance," a *Billboard* top 10 hit in 1960. After joining Morris Levy's Roulette outfit, Glover scored two no. 1 pop hits: "Peppermint Twist" by Joey Dee and the Starliters (early 1962) and "Easier Said Than Done" by the Essex (summer 1963). He also recorded for Roulette Sarah Vaughan, Dinah Washington, Wynonie Harris, and Louisiana Red (whose *The Lowdown Back Porch Blues* album from 1963 was much lauded at the time). In 1975, Glover produced *The Muddy Waters Woodstock Album* (Chess), which won a Grammy. Among Glover's songwriting successes—as well as "Blues Stay Away from Me," "Peppermint Twist," and "Let the Little Girl Dance"—were "Seven Nights to Rock" (Moon Mullican), "Lovin' Machine" (Wynonie Harris), "Annie Had a Baby" (the Midnighters), "Drown in My Own Tears" (Ray Charles), and "California Sun" (the Rivieras). He died in St. Albans, New York, on April 7, 1991, at age sixty-nine.

13. "Honky Tonk" was recorded on June 16, 1956, at Beltone Studios, 4 West Thirty-First Street, located in the Hotel Wolcott. Only four cuts are noted for this session in the standard discographies. The full story of the "Honky Tonk" session is included in John Broven's *Record*

Makers and Breakers: Voices of the Independent Rock 'n' Roll Pioneers (Urbana: University of Illinois Press, 2009).

14. While "Honky Tonk (Part 1 & 2)" made no. 1 on the *Billboard* R&B chart on August 25, 1956, it stalled at no. 2 on the Top 100 in an incredible twenty-nine-week stay, halted only by Elvis Presley's massive back-to-back no. 1, "Hound Dog"/"Don't Be Cruel." "Honky Tonk" also made no. 2 on the *Cash Box* pop chart.

15. The "Honky Tonk" writer credits on the record label read: Doggett-Shepherd-Scott-Butler, originally published by Billace Music of Long Island City. Henry Glover came into the picture when he received a credit for the lyrics of the song's vocal version by Tommy Brown, also on King (see Library of Congress Register of Copyrights).

16. Among the Bill Doggett recordings in the "Honky Tonk" groove were "Slow Walk," "Ram-Bunk-Shush," "Hold It," and "Smokie (Part 2)," good records all.

17. Alto saxophonist Earl Bostic had one R&B hit for Gotham, "Temptation" (no. 10, 1948), but scored big with "Sleep" (no. 6, 1951) and especially "Flamingo" (no. 1, 1952) when he signed to King.

18. "Peppermint Twist (Part 1)" by Joey Dee and the Starliters (Roulette), cowritten by Henry Glover, was one of the biggest records of the twist craze, making no. 1 on the *Billboard* pop chart in early 1962.

19. "Soul Twist" by King Curtis was a surprise no. 17 *Billboard* pop hit and no. 1 R&B hit on Bobby and Danny Robinson's Enjoy label in spring 1962.

20. Billy Butler also recorded extensively on King Curtis's Capitol sessions during 1962–1965, mainly at Capitol Records Studio, 151 West Forty-Sixth Street, New York. Other noted session men included Jimmy Lewis (bass) and Ray Lucas (drums), along with Cornell Dupree and Eric Gale (guitars), Ernie Hayes (keyboards), and Paul Griffin (piano). The biggest King Curtis Capitol hit was "Soul Serenade" (*Billboard* no. 51 pop, no. 20 R&B, 1964), written by Curtis and Luther Dixon and covered successfully in 1968 by Willie Mitchell on Hi of Memphis.

21. Jimmy Lewis (1918–2000) was a regular call as a bassist in the New York studios. Among the many artists he recorded with were Count Basie, Sam Cooke, Otis Redding, King Curtis, Willis Jackson, the Modern Jazz Quartet, Horace Silver, John Hammond Jr., and Billy Butler.

22. Footballer Dick "Night Train" Lane married Dinah Washington in July 1963, but she died soon after from a drug overdose at their home in Detroit.

Rose Marie McCoy (1922–2015). Photo courtesy of Richard Tapp.

17

ROSE MARIE MCCOY

Rose Marie McCoy—birth name Rose Marie Hinton—was born on April 19, 1922, in Oneida, Arkansas. Originally planning on a singing career, she moved to New York in 1942. Eventually she became a prolific songwriter, beginning in 1952. An early presence in New York's famous songwriting and publishing landmark Brill Building, she wrote hit songs for Big Maybelle, Faye Adams, Ruth Brown, Nat King Cole, Nappy Brown, Elvis Presley, and many others, for awhile in partnership with Charlie Singleton.

Whenever you saw her, she always had a smile on her face and a twinkle in her eye. It was easy to imagine her successfully pitching songs in the vibrant atmosphere of 1950s and 1960s New York. As a woman songwriter in a male-dominated industry, she paved the way for New York greats such as Carole King and Ellie Greenwich.

This updated, edited chapter with my new endnotes was first published in *Juke Blues* in 1992, based on 1989 and 1992 interviews. In 2014, Arlene Corsano wrote a biography, *Thought We Were Writing the Blues but They Called It Rock 'n' Roll: The Life and Music of Rose Marie McCoy* (Tenafly, NJ: ArleneChristine).

"ALMOST EVERY STATION WOULD BE
PLAYING A SINGLETON-MCCOY TUNE"

When I was a little girl in Arkansas, you never heard of this, Oneida, Arkansas, I used to write poems, songs, and I thought that you paid people to sing your songs. I didn't know you got paid! I was willing to really pay somebody, and when I told my brother-in-law about it, he lived in Memphis, Tennessee, he said, "No, you get paid." We used to go up to Memphis to see [the bands of] Erskine Hawkins, Duke Ellington, Jimmy Lunceford, people like that.

I sang in school and had instruction on the piano and guitar. Then I played piano in the local church and sang in the choir. I knew I wanted to be a singer, but I wasn't thinking about writing then. So then I came to New York in 1942 and I wrote this one song, "After All." I was singing with the Dixieaires before they went on Arthur Godfrey's show, and they recorded that song on [Queen,

1946] with Muriel Gaines—her husband [Lee] was singing with the Delta Rhythm Boys. Earl Bostic was going to record it on the Gotham label, that was Sam Goody's label at the time. And then I was waiting to get rich, and when I got my first check it was eighteen bucks, so I quit writing for money. But then about [six] years went by, but I still wrote for myself.

I had a day job working in a Chinese hand laundry but I worked every weekend in nightclubs, and then I used to go travel around singing in Canada and Detroit and come back. The showcases included the Apollo Theatre in Harlem, the Cobra Club in Greenwich Village, the Flame Show Bar in Detroit, the Basin Street in Toronto, and the Café St.-Michel and Club Montmartre in Montreal. I did everything, ballads, everything, mix it up, you know? Then a friend of mine, Mamie Watts, who wrote "Well Alright, Okay, You Win," came up and said, "I'm gonna get you out of this laundry," and she brought me down and I sang and they recorded me.

Courtesy of Victor Pearlin.

[On March 1, 1952, *Billboard* announced that "Wheeler Records, the latest R&B firm, has Leroy Kirkland, formerly of Savoy Records, as A&R director for the label. The firm has signed Alberta Hunter, Eddie Durham, Danny (Run Joe) Taylor, Rose-Marie McCory [*sic*], [and] Eddie Banks and the Tune Blenders, and has five platters set for release next week."[1]]

That was a good record on Wheeler ["Cheatin' Blues"/"Georgie Boy Blues"]. Every time Leroy Kirkland, that used to do all the arranging round here—he passed away in [1988]—every time he had a session, I'd say, "All of my songs you record, I'll put your name on them." You know? So I always got two or three songs from him, Little Esther Phillips, Savannah Churchill, almost everybody he did arrangements for. That's how I got my Big Maybelle record. I wrote "Gabbin' Blues" for Big Maybelle and I talked on that record.

Rose Marie McCoy and
Charlie Singleton. Photo
courtesy of the *Juke Blues*
archive.

["Gabbin' Blues" is a female version of "The Dozens." *Billboard*, December 6, 1952, in a rare misjudgment, noted that "Big Maybelle vents her scorn on a catty female who gabs away on this talk-sing disking. It doesn't come off, tho', and the excitement is all on the other side ('Rain Down Rain' on OKeh)."]

I went to Canada, when I came back I had a [no. 3 *Billboard* R&B] hit. And so Danny Fisher of Fisher Music said, "I want to introduce you to Charlie Single-ton,"[2] so I told Mamie [Watts], she said, "Oh, you see that guy down there smiling all the time?" And I had already spoken to him unknowingly. They introduced me, teamed us up, but I had had a lot of songs recorded before I met him.

When Charlie and I started writing together [in 1953], we were based in the Brill Building on [1619] Broadway where Fisher Music had offices. We used to write songs in Beefsteak Charlie's, that's a big restaurant chain now. We used to come in there at six o'clock in the morning and we had a booth and we could write in there. We would buy a glass of wine for thirty cents and we would sip on it. And they would take our phone calls and all the big publishers used to come there and hear our songs.

Then Louis Jordan was in the same hotel that I was in Detroit. And I showed him this song, I guess you know about that one, it was called "If I Had Any Sense I'd Go Back Home." And he took the song, it was just on a piece of paper, and when he came to New York he was going to record, he said, "I'm going to record that song." So I went into the studio with him, he didn't record that song that day. So then Charlie said, "Louis Jordan is not gonna do that song. Why don't we rewrite it for Ruth Brown?" And I said, "No, I can't do that!" But we rewrote it up-tempo and Ruth Brown recorded it [as "If I Had Any Sense" for Atlantic in November 1953]. And then I go up to 125th Street and I met Louis Jordan, who said, "McCoy, you know I did that thing today [for Aladdin]?" And I said, "Wha-a-at?" I said, "Oo-oo-oo-oh, I thank you." And now I'm gonna die! Anyway, I had two out at the same time, one slow [Jordan] and one fast [Brown].[3] I almost got a bad reputation behind that, I felt awful. Most of the [disc jockeys] were playing it at the same time. But they let me get away with it 'cause I guess I was new.

[Louis Jordan gave this song the sensitive treatment it merited. It was featured in the musical *Five Guys Named Moe*, which opened in the West End, London, in 1990 and on Broadway in 1992. The Singleton-McCoy team scored a no. 1 *Billboard* R&B hit in fall 1954 with Faye Adams's "Hurts Me to My Heart"(Herald), published by Bill Buchanan's Monument Music company, followed immediately by another no. 1 R&B, "Mambo Baby" by Ruth Brown (Atlantic).[4]]

Both of us contributed to the lyrics and melody. At the restaurant we used to remember the melody and we'd go sing it right off a yellow piece of paper. In fact we sang "Mambo Baby" for Georgia Gibbs [a Mercury cover version] off the piece of paper. You know, we used to say, "If they let us get to them, we'll get the record." And it was true. Every time we'd sing one, we'd get the record. And Georgia Gibbs would say, "Whatever are you bringing to me next on a piece of toilet paper?" Ruth Brown had a hit with "Mambo Baby" on Atlantic Records, that was M&M music publishers. We were aware of the mambo craze in 1954— we just sort of kept up. You know, like if something was happening, we did it to stay in the vein of what was happening. That was one of the advantages, I guess, of being downtown here.

We used to go up to Atlantic Records on [234] West Fifty-Sixth Street and sing songs for them, 'cause we used to write a lot of stuff up there for Ruth Brown, Joe Turner, and almost everybody that recorded out of there. At that time it was like an open door down here, you could just walk in with a song on a piece of paper, you know? I was aware of the controversy over rude R&B songs. Once I wrote a song, "I Know Which Side My Bread Is Buttered On," if I think about it I'd die, it was really clean compared to what's coming out now. And Ahmet Ertegun and Jerry Wexler who was at Atlantic, they said, "Oh, Rose Marie, you can't get away with that." And that's why I didn't try with it, like I felt so embarrassed, I felt terrible.

And then they heard me singing and they recorded me. It was so easy then compared to now. I was recorded on Atlantic [on March 10, 1954] for their subsidiary, Cat. One was "True Love" and the other one was "Down Here" [the single was "Dippin' in My Business"/"Down Here"]. We had like studio musicians but they were all like musicians we used down here to record. Atlantic used to record up there in their office, I guess you know about that? Push all the desks back, then they had a little cubby hole where they had a [tape machine]. Twenty-three pieces being shoved in there, playing—I don't know how they did that. All those hits, you know, Ray Charles, Ruth Brown and Joe Turner, the Clovers.

Courtesy of Victor Pearlin.

And, you know, I'm sick about that because they asked me when they moved up to [157 West] Fifty-Seventh Street [in 1956] to come up there with them. They said, "We know you want to have your own publishing firm. We'll go along with you, splitting the publishing." And I said, "No, you all know it's too far up here." I sure am sick about that! Now they're millionaires. I went over to see Ahmet Ertegun I guess about six months ago [late 1988]. I guess out of curiosity he wanted to see what I was doing and he told me to come on and I went over there. I saw this fabulous big office. And Ahmet said, "I bet you're dreaming." But he's just as sweet as he ever was but, boy, he's made.[5]

In 1955 I won a BMI award for "Don't Be Angry" by Nappy Brown. Freddy Mendelsohn from Savoy brought Nappy up to my house—I lived in the Bronx then. And he brought him up there and said, "Help this boy with this song." And that was his melody and his gimmick, you know: "So-la-la-la-la-la." I thought that was nothing. And everybody at the session said, "That's a hit!" and I said, "Boy, everybody's crazy. That ain't nothin'." And sure enough it was like we got three records on that [gimmick] but it was one of those things. [Herman] Lubinsky [of Savoy Records] had it.

I also wrote "Piddily Patter Patter" for Nappy Brown. That was a trend thing, like you follow a trend, like "my heart goes piddily patter." That was like you get a little hook, where I think "Tweedlee Dee" would give you the idea to write a thing like that. Patti Page did [it as] "(My Heart Goes) Piddily Patter Patter." I met her when I was in [photographer] James Kriegsmann's [studio] one day having my picture made. And I had "Little by Little," Nappy Brown did that.[6]

[McCoy and Singleton wrote prolifically for Savoy Records at this time. Along with Nappy Brown, the artists included Little Jimmy Scott, Varetta Dillard,

Courtesy of John Broven.

Larry Darnell, and Little Esther. However, the reputation of the songwriting team soared when they wrote "If I May" for the iconic Nat King Cole on the prestigious Capitol label of Hollywood, and the song earned a BMI award in 1955. On *The Nat King Cole Story* album, Cole recalled, "This was one of my first attempts at a transition into a rock 'n' roll beat, or whatever you want to call it. We originally made it with a vocal group called the Four Knights."[7]]

A little later in 1957 Charlie and I wrote "My Personal Possession" for [Cole], that was on the other side of "Send for Me."[8] I had "personal property," but Charlie changed it to "possession" 'cause he was a very experienced writer.[9] And that's how . . . we just collaborated. We were right here in this building, 1650 Broadway, when we wrote. We were in the Roosevelt Music offices.[10]

[The Singleton-McCoy team had one of their songs, "Tryin' to Get to You," recorded by Elvis Presley in 1956. Although it was buried at the time by Presley's "Hound Dog," it has become a favorite Presley track via reissues through the decades.]

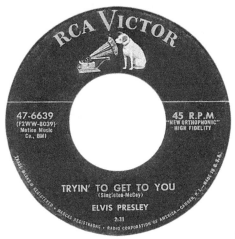

Courtesy of Victor Pearlin.

They said we were really lucky to have him [record our song]. 'Cause "Tryin'
to Get to You," we produced a group called the Eagles [originally in 1954]. Not
the [country rock] Eagles that you know about but a little black group out
of Washington [DC]. And Elvis bought the record in Memphis and came up
here, and he said, "I don't care what y'all want me to sing, I want to sing this
song." The Eagles was on Mercury, that was Bob Shad. He used to be the A&R
man over there, and he let us get acts and produce them and do the whole
thing. Then there was a second one by Elvis, "I Beg of You" [cowritten with
Savoy Records arranger Kelly Owens]. And you know, I almost had the title of
a movie. They even sent me all the papers, but at the last minute they changed
it to *Loving You* [1957]. That was close, boy. Oo-oo-oh, I still have the stationery and things. It's to give us checks for this picture. Only if I take it to the
bank everybody'd go crazy. Oh well, that was the good old days. Once I rode
in a plane with Elvis from Memphis. He got off in Nashville, and I was coming
to New York. I knew that was him but I didn't say anything 'cause I'm not like
that. Anyway, I don't bother people, you know? I always figure that they want
to be left alone, but I'm really sorry now 'cause I really would have liked to have
had that autograph. I was so silly then. At first I didn't understand Elvis, but
you know when I really started to appreciate him? After I saw him on stage,
there was something very . . . I don't know what you'd call that . . . spiritual
about that guy. Most of the big stars are like that, though. Big, big stars like
Michael Jackson and people like that, there's something else there other than
just a good voice. In fact, you don't have to have a good voice.

Charlie Singleton and I stopped writing together around '56, '57. And then
we tried again. It was like all of a sudden we didn't write together any more. We
tried, too. It's funny but it was like it was something broken there in between. I'm
sorry. I wish I had been writing with him on straight into the '90s.

I don't think you can say there is a "typical" Singleton-McCoy song. We wrote country & western and pop songs besides the rhythm & blues numbers. We didn't have any common thread, I would say. You keep up to date and also you write. I think it's a spiritual thing with me when I write a song. It sort of writes itself, I don't really take credit for it. It's like I don't believe I'm really that smart. It sort of comes, you know, like it's a gift. Sometimes it comes easily and quickly, sometimes I write and I have a hard time. If you write a nice ballad or something, it sort of takes it out of you. You know, like it's kind of what I'm writing about myself. 'Cause I write some things about myself and sometimes I'm like a basket case.

No, we didn't aim for teenage themes, which I think was a mistake. And when I hear songs like "Da Doo Ron Ron" [the Crystals, 1963] and "The Book of Love" [the Monotones, 1958], I wish we had did that 'cause we could have did that easier than what we did. And look at that song, "[Who Wrote the] Book of Love."[11] It's the theme song of that *Newlywed Game* [on TV]. You can imagine how much that writer's gonna make. And we just thought that was so silly, we wouldn't write a song like that. Mind you, we did "Piddily Patter"!

[Before they split, Rose Marie and Charlie recorded as an R&B duet for RCA Victor on "Don't Call the Wagon"/"Toodle Loo Tennessee" (1956). However, any ambitions McCoy may have had as a recording artist were still strictly secondary to her career as a songwriter, even though she went on to record for Coral (1958) and Brunswick (1977).]

In 1957 James Brown recorded one of my songs. I bet you've never heard that one, it's called "That Dood It" [for Real McCoy Music], that's a funny song. Sometimes I can't believe I wrote that lyric, it's a comedy, really. It's like this guy was going to get some gold, I don't even remember, but it was very clever. I was surprised when I heard it. A couple of years ago I played the record and I said, "Boy, I wrote that?" "That dood it" is the hook. I was on the staff of King Records at the time as a writer, producer, and they were trying to get some of their money back. I think I wrote that with Rudy Toombs, yeah.

[Rudolph Toombs was a noted songwriter from Monroe, Louisiana, who penned many songs, particularly for artists on the Atlantic and Aladdin labels. Among his big R&B songwriting hits were "Teardrops from My Eyes" and "5-10-15 Hours" by Ruth Brown, "One Mint Julep" by the Clovers, and "One Scotch, One Bourbon, One Beer" by Amos Milburn. Toombs was tragically murdered in Harlem in 1962.]

And James Brown was up there at King. Little Willie John, he did a lot of my songs, including "Letter from My Darling" [May 1956].[12] And the guy that wrote and sang "The Twist," Hank Ballard, and Otis Williams and the Charms, I used to write for all them because I was on the staff then and they used to take me down to Cincinnati to do a lot of them 'cause they had a studio down there, too. And that's how that happened, through Henry Glover. He was vice president, that was up here on Fifty-Fourth Street. So they put me on the staff and so every time anybody recorded, they always had a song. King Records boss Syd Nathan was like a nice Lubinsky. I liked Lubinsky, too, like you couldn't help but like him, it was just that he was a character, you know? But Syd was very close to Lubinsky about everything.

Around this time I wrote a lot of songs for Brook Benton. Roy Hamilton had got sick and they thought he wasn't going to be able to sing no more. So Marv Holtzman, the head of Columbia [Epic division], had me over there. He said, "Rose Marie, you're going to make this boy another Roy Hamilton." And he had me to write a song for him ["All My Love Belongs to You" with Leroy Kirkland, late 1956], and they brought him over to my house in Teaneck, New Jersey, and we rehearsed him over there in my basement. And every time he'd record, he would do one or two of my songs [for OKeh]. And then I used to use him for demos. And all those songs he did of mine, none of them were hits. Then when Clyde [Otis] went to Mercury, Clyde took me over there—Brook had this demo "It's Just a Matter of Time." And he said, "Rosie, I'm going to make this one demo for you, but after this I won't be making any more demos because I have me a hit." That was "It's Just a Matter of Time" [released in December 1958]. And he played me the dub. "Boy, I hope you're right," you know?

But after that he got real big, although that was over at Mercury, I didn't go over there.[13] But Clyde Otis recorded a song of mine called "Please, Please Make It Easy" with Brook [released in November 1964]. That was when he was on his way down, which never made it, and that was a good record, too. And that was one of those sessions I didn't go to. Clyde said, "He almost didn't do it." You know, if you're there and they know you and they like you, they'll do it anyway. But if you're not there, a lot of times they get thrown out, like they don't have to worry about your feelings. But Clyde said, "Man, you can do the song." He was having like a problem, little places, said, "I don't think I'll do that song." But they was happy eventually. Brook started writing a lot of songs with Clyde. The whole thing started right on a stool in this building [1650 Broadway]. They tied up with Raleigh Music [and Eden and Play], but I think Clyde ended up having the catalog back.

[Then in 1961 came "It's Gonna Work Out Fine" by Ike and Tina Turner on Juggy Murray's New York–based Sue label, which was a home for quality R&B.]

Joe Seneca wrote that with me.[14] I brought him downtown to the recording studio as a writer [for King]. He went on writing on his own and did very well with "Talk to Me" [by Little Willie John]. He was a good writer.

That was Mickey Baker talking on "It's Gonna Work Out Fine," and that was Sylvia playing the guitar. She paid for that session, because they recorded it. She loved that song; everybody turned that song down. At home I've got boxes of songs I started and song publishers have turned down before I had my own publishing career. Anyway, I had said to Sylvia, "Oh, you won't like that, don't nobody like that song." She said, "Let me hear it." And I sang about four lines and she said, "This is a hit!" I said, "Boy, she's crazy." So then she stopped everything and brought us to RCA Victor, and Hugo and Luigi.[15] They knew me and they didn't want to hurt my feelings, they didn't like it either. They just smiled and she got mad, she said, "Y'all didn't like "Love Is Strange." And so [Mickey and Sylvia] recorded it and then it didn't come out.[16]

So to prove a point, Sylvia was singing at the Apollo Theatre with Ike and Tina Turner and she taught it to them. And she called me and said, "Rose, come up here. You've got a smash!" So I thought, "Oh God, here she goes with her song again. Is she crazy?" So I go up there and then Ike brings Tina in and sits her down in the chair by me, and says, "Sing that song for that girl!" And she sang like her life depended on it, with no music, she sang just like you hear it on the record. But Tina, boy, I can't get over that girl. And she didn't talk. She wouldn't say nothing, she looked so pretty. Then Ike said, "All right, you can go now." And she went back to her room. So I said, "Gee whiz, I've got to go out and see this show. If this girl can sing like this without any music . . ." And I was really delighted I did because she was so great. Oh boy. I'm so happy for her, really making it big like she is. But Sylvia said, "Why don't you go to the session?" I said, "No, I've got to go." I didn't have nowhere to go, I just thought she was crazy. It was like a little session, you know, you go through it, whatever. And they got Mickey and her playing the guitar and that's Mickey talking. Knowing Mickey, he does probably most [of the guitar] of what you hear, but I'm pretty sure that knowing Ike they had to let him play. You know, he had something about him that you respected. In the little time I talked to him, I knew you had to let him be a part of it 'cause it was his thing.

Then the record came out, it was in California, it was just playing like mad before it got here. All of a sudden it started playing here. And Sylvia was really sick because she knew it was a hit and she wanted to do it, she just did it with Ike and Tina Turner to prove a point. And boy, that was something because here Ike and Tina got to be big stars because of that song.

Linda Ronstadt and James Taylor did that in [1982]—that was in her *Get Closer* album.

Actually Juggy Murray, of Sue Records, had asked me to write a song for [Tina] and I never wrote it, never took it there. He gave me a tape of her to write some songs for her, coming out of St. Louis I think, and it was the same girl.

[Somehow McCoy's songs of relishable sentiment were too sweet and innocent for the soul era, but artists like Frankie Lymon still approached her for new material. In his case, she gave him "Don't Let Up" when he was in good spirits on the very night before he overdosed and died in February 1968. McCoy had one more fling as a recording artist when she cut the melodic disco-styled "I Do the Best I Can with What I Got" for Brunswick in 1977. Songwriting remained her breadwinner, but throughout her career she had constant battles for royalty entitlements in a catalog of more than six hundred recorded songs.]

I started off in publishing being associated with BMI and went to ASCAP [the American Society of Composers, Authors, and Publishers] at a point, but now I'm back into BMI. Oh, we got cheated out of a hell of a lot. That song by Big Maybelle, "Gabbin' Blues," I never got a penny. Not one penny. Now we can't even find out who's the publisher. Oh, it's terrible. Like, I have five songs on that [Epic reissue] album,[17] and one publisher paid me for that out of that album. That was Fisher Music, they were very honest. But all those other publishers, "Gabbin' Blues," I never got one cent. See, they keep selling the publishing firm to another company, and then you don't know who even has it.

It's pathetic what happened to all of us down here. Atlantic were honest as publishers, they had a firm called Progressive. They used to pay us fair, like money that I didn't even thought I had. But Savoy were terrible, they were pitiful. I had so many songs over there. Little Jimmy Scott, he recorded I don't know how many songs of mine. Lubinsky just didn't pay nobody. But we figured that we would get an advance, we got more money from him than anybody because of that advance. There were lawyers that wanted us to sue him and I didn't want to get a reputation of suing. The lawyers wanted to take the case free, but I said, "No."

You have to be careful of breach of copyright. Like you might have heard [Charles Wright and] the Watts 103rd Street Rhythm Band, "Love Land" [Warner Bros.]? Well, that was my song and Luther Dixon's. We wrote that and Al Hibbler recorded it [Decca, 1958], slow song, and years later [in 1970] I heard this song and I said, "Boy, somebody took the whole song."[18] But I still wasn't sure and I was doing some work with Jimmy Mundy, the arranger, and I played Al Hibbler's record and he said, "That's your song." And I said, "I thought it sounded like it." So Luther flew up here from Florida, he said, "Do you know we've got a song in the top 10?" I said, "We have?" And he said, "Love Land."

Quite recently we had a big lawsuit over "Tryin' to Get to You." I could really do detective work and I'd go around to the record stores and copy out all the [release] numbers. So I started pinning that down and I got a good lawyer and we got a good, pretty good settlement. Charlie [Singleton] was very ill then and he said, "Take the money." It was a good thing, though, because Bob Shad died [in 1985] shortly after we got the money.[19]

Today [in 1992], I have my publishing firm here in New York and I do a lot of different things: I do commercials, Coca-Cola commercials, and I manage and produce . . . get kids into movies. I keep active doing personal things because I really am not too ambitious any more. But I write all the time. That's funny, I write gospel, too: Caravans, Shirley Caesar, Dorothy Norwood, kind of message songs, you know. Sometimes I write songs like that and I don't show them to anybody unless they ask me. I'm not a pusher any more, like I used to be. And yet I find myself doing just as much because other people are so ambitious.

I still get royalties from the old songs, sure. It's really hard down here now. These artists and these groups, everybody's coming in with everything finished—the master, the song, you know . . . But I never sold a song [copyright], I would never do that, no.

I didn't have any problems being a woman in the music business. Looking back, I thought it was so easy and I just thought it was gonna go on forever. You know? I must say we were really lucky, 'cause we used to have so many songs [recorded]. And whenever we used to turn the dial on the radio, almost every station would be playing a Singleton-McCoy tune.

NOTES

1. Rose Marie McCoy's Wheeler single was an accomplished debut in the raunchy female style popularized by Dinah Washington, Julia Lee, and Little Esther. Wheeler Records was owned by Harriet Wheeler and operated out of 1585 Broadway, New York, during 1952. She ran the Hartness School of Music for veterans under the GI Bill.

2. Charlie Singleton, the songwriter, was born on September 17, 1913, in Jacksonville, Florida, and died on December 12, 1985, in Florida. He should not be confused with the bandleader and saxophonist of the same name from the New York area who recorded for labels such as Apollo, Decca, and Atlas.

3. Ruth Brown's version of "If I Had Any Sense," credited to Singleton-McCoy, was released in April 1954 by Atlantic, while Louis Jordan's "If I Had Any Sense I'd Go Back Home," credited to McCoy only, was released a little later in August 1954 by Aladdin.

4. Singleton-McCoy's "Mambo Baby" by Ruth Brown (Atlantic) knocked the songwriters' "Hurts Me to My Heart" by Faye Adams (Herald) from the top spot on *Billboard*'s R&B chart on November 20, 1954. This meant that the songwriting pair held the no. 1 R&B spot for six weeks consecutively at that time.

5. Ahmet Ertegun was born in Istanbul, Turkey, on July 31, 1923, and died in New York on December 14, 2006.

6. McCoy had three hit songs in quick succession for Nappy Brown on Savoy: "Don't Be Angry" (cowritten with Brown), no. 25 *Billboard* pop, no. 2 R&B, early summer 1955; "Piddily Patter Patter" (with Charlie Singleton), no. 10 R&B, summer 1955; and "Little by Little" (with Kelly Owens), no. 57 pop, early 1957. The sheet music for "Piddily Patter Patter" showed a photo of established star Patti Page, even though her cover version on Mercury did not chart. It was a symbol of how New York's music publishing community of the time, with its Tin Pan Alley roots, was adverse to R&B and black artists. Interestingly, the sheet music photograph of Page was credited to James Kriegsmann, noted studio photographer of New York artists, as McCoy related.

7. Notes to *The Nat King Cole Story* by Leonard Feather (Capitol CDS 79 5129 2).

8. It was a dream ticket for songwriters and music publishers to have the B side of a big hit single, as the royalty rate was the same as for an A side. In this case, Nat King Cole's "Send for Me" made no. 6 in the *Billboard* pop chart in 1957 and stayed on the charts for twenty-seven weeks. However, "My Personal Possession" stirred up action in its own right and hit no. 21 pop.

9. Charlie Singleton's greatest moment came in 1966 when he cowrote Frank Sinatra's international no. 1 smash hit, "Strangers in the Night," with Bert Kaempfert and Eddie Snyder.

10. Roosevelt Music was founded by Hal Fine in 1954, and its writers included Otis Blackwell, Jesse Stone, and Charlie Singleton. Around 1956 Roosevelt Music pitched many Singleton-McCoy compositions to the hot Modern outfit in Hollywood, some of which were recorded by the Jacks, Jesse Belvin, and Dolly Cooper. Roosevelt was sold to Columbia Pictures in 1969.

11. "Book of Love" by the Monotones (Mascot, then Argo, 1958) is just one in a series of big hit records in the rock 'n' roll era that are not widely appreciated for their New York roots. Others include "Over the Mountain, Across the Sea" by Johnnie and Joe (Chess, 1957); "Maybe" by the Chantels (End, 1958); "Will You Love Me Tomorrow" and "Dedicated to the One I Love" by the Shirelles (Scepter, both 1961); "Daddy's Home" by Shep and the Limelites (Hull, 1961); "Sally, Go 'Round the Roses" by the Jaynetts (Tuff, 1963); and "Hi-Heel Sneakers" by Tommy Tucker (Checker, 1964). Interestingly, record women Bea Kaslin (Mascot and Hull), Florence Greenberg (Scepter), and Zell Sanders were involved with all these hits except for those by the Chantels and Tucker. See the appendix for chart details.

12. "Letter from My Darling" by Little Willie John (King) was a no. 10 *Billboard* R&B hit in summer 1956. It was the B side of his famous "Fever" (no. 1 R&B, no. 24 pop).

13. "It's Just a Matter of Time" (Mercury) became Brook Benton's breakthrough hit in 1959 (no. 3 pop, no. 1 R&B). Benton's producer, Clyde Otis, was a good friend of Rose Marie McCoy, and they lived in the same town of Teaneck, New Jersey.

14. Originally "It's Gonna Work Out Fine" was credited to Joe Seneca and James Lee (Leland James Gillette), but that was changed to Rose Marie McCoy and Sylvia McKinney before settling down to Rose Marie McCoy and Joe Seneca. Ike and Tina Turner's Sue recording of the song made no. 14 on the *Billboard* pop chart, no. 2 R&B, in late summer 1961.

15. Producers Hugo and Luigi (Hugo Peretti and Luigi Creatore) had big success at RCA Victor with Sam Cooke in the early 1960s.

16. Mickey and Sylvia's RCA Victor version of "It's Gonna Work Out Fine" was produced by Hugo and Luigi on September 26, 1960, and was released eventually by Bear Family (Germany) in 1990.

17. *Big Maybelle: The OKeh Sessions* includes "Gabbin' Blues" and four other Rose Marie McCoy cowrites (Epic double LP, 1983).

18. "Love Land" by Charles Wright and the Watts 103rd Street Rhythm Band (Warner Bros.) was a *Billboard* hit (no. 16 pop, no. 23 R&B) in 1970. The song was credited to Don Trotter–Charles Wright. The Al Hibbler 1958 Decca version was credited to "James Lee–Barney Williams."

19. Record man Bob Shad, who owned the Sittin' In With, Time, and Shad labels among others and was also an A&R man at Mercury Records, was born on February 12, 1919, in New York and died on March 13, 1985, in California.

18

DOC POMUS

Mostly unpublished interview, Vintage Restaurant,
New York, May 18, 1989

Jerome Solon "Doc" Pomus was born in Brooklyn, New York. Afflicted with polio at age six, that did not stop him from pursuing his dream to become a blues shouter in the style of his idol, Big Joe Turner. Before gaining fame as a songwriter, Pomus performed mostly around the New York area as well as making a number of jump blues recordings from the late 1940s into the mid-1950s. An inductee into the Rock and Roll Hall of Fame, Pomus wrote hundreds of songs including classics such as "Save the Last Dance for Me," "A Teenager in Love," and "Lonely Avenue." Artists who recorded his songs include Ray Charles, Elvis Presley, Dr. John, B. B. King, and many others. Doc, latterly confined to a wheelchair, was a gregarious, super-friendly person who seemed to know everybody in the business, including record collectors, and loved discussing music history, as this interview shows.

Doc Pomus: [*discussing the Apollo Theatre amateur night*] They would have the regular show plus the amateur night. The amateur night was spectacular. The amateur would walk up on the stage, he would touch the Tree of Hope, the tree that was on one side of the stage for good luck, and the amateurs were from the very worst to the very best, and when an amateur was very bad, Porto Rico,[1] this gentleman who wore the most garish type of attire, came up and yanked him off stage with an actual hook. Now the audience overacted always. If they liked an act they screamed and if they didn't like an act they screamed. And the band was always a wonderful band, and it was like a thing to do on Wednesday nights. You could come down to the Apollo. Now at the time Harlem was an absolute safe place. I used to park my convertible in front of the theater and there was never a problem at all.

John Broven: Did any big artists ever come out of the Apollo's amateur night?

Doc Pomus (1925–1991) with Rose Marie McCoy at the Lone Star Roadhouse, New York, May 8, 1989. Photo by Paul Harris.

Pomus: I understand Ella Fitzgerald came out of there. Sarah Vaughan, many, many of the big jazz acts came out of the Apollo.

Broven: Can you tell us about the heyday of New York's Fifty-Second Street and the clubs into the early 1950s?

Pomus: There was this long row of jazz clubs on Fifty-Second Street between Fifth Avenue and Eighth Avenue. Among the clubs that were featured were the Onyx, Three Deuces, Jimmy Ryan's. They all had the best jazz musicians and jazz was so featured. At one club, Kelly's Stables, they would put on a show where instead of a singer you would have a great jazz star like Coleman Hawkins, or a Pete Brown would get up and do his three songs backed by an orchestra, and then he would get down. Instead of a singer they'd have a saxophone. Now you could go club to club and you might see at one club you'd see Art Tatum, the next club you'd see Billie Holiday and the next club you'd see Milt Jackson. And in those days when people went out, they would always get dressed up. Not only would they get dressed up but people got along with each other and there were no racial problems, at least I wasn't aware of any. Blacks and whites went to clubs. There was no such thing as a club that was all black or all white.

Broven: And the music was jazz and rhythm & blues?

Pomus: The music was jazz, rhythm & blues. In Brooklyn there was at least forty clubs that had entertainment. Black types of entertainment and then you had Fifty-Second Street, then you had Harlem with an enormous amount of clubs. The Baby Grand on 125th Street, which by the way is still in existence [in

1986], was the main club in Harlem and they featured always a great blues singer like a Joe Turner. They would have a shake dancer, which was like a stripper, and then they would have very often a popular singer and an emcee. For many, many years Nipsey Russell, who became so well known in the States, he emceed at the Baby Grand. And then you had a variation of that kind of show at many other clubs in Harlem.

Broven: Nipsey was a comedian?

Pomus: Yes, a comedian and an emcee. Very classic who became a very big what we call a variety actor in the States, who we call a variety actor.

Pomus: [*discussing New York record labels*] Originally I knew Herb Abramson and Tommy Dowd from National Records. In fact National Records was the record company that recorded the first song of mine by Gatemouth Moore—it was a song called "Love Doctor Blues" [in 1946].[2] But, anyway, I met Herb Abramson and Tommy Dowd. Herb Abramson was the A&R man at National Records and Tommy Dowd was the engineer—they were really kings of blues and rhythm & blues, producers and engineers. Then they brought their expertise into Atlantic Records and I'm sure that everything that Ahmet Ertegun and Jerry Wexler learned they learned from Herb Abramson and Tommy Dowd.

Broven: Could you tell us about some of the other early guys like Joe Davis, who was primarily a music publisher.

Pomus: Joe Davis I never knew. Otis Blackwell I remember used to have some sort of relationship with Joe Davis [with Jay-Dee Records]. I just knew Joe Davis as a guy who made the rhythm & blues records very early in the '40s [including country bluesman Gabriel Brown for Davis's Beacon label].

Broven: Were his labels very popular?

Pomus: Not really too popular then. But when you say by popular, popular is a strange term, because when we say popular today, we mean records that really sell, but he probably had some records that were popular with the small segment of the population but it was not as popular say as an Apollo or Savoy record. They were both popular in terms of doing that kind of music, which at that time was called race music.

Broven: Could you tell us something about Savoy and Apollo?

Pomus: Apollo Records was owned by a woman, Bess Berman, and she was a very tough kind of lady and everybody was kind of terrified of being in the room with her because she seemed a very strong, very aggressive woman. Savoy Records was owned by Herman Lubinsky, who was a character out of Newark, New Jersey. His A&R man was a guy, Teddy Reig, who I used to see periodically until his death [in 1984].[3] Teddy was a big, heavy guy, used to hang out and go to all the black clubs. He was stoned most of the time but later on in life he kind of settled down. Lubinsky was a tough businessman. I know when I did sessions with him I had a lot of problems getting paid.

Broven: Of the New York labels in the '40s, which were the most influential would you say?

Pomus: I think Apollo was a very influential label. I was really fortunate recording for them because they had people like Wynonie Harris. They also had great gospel singers on the label [including Mahalia Jackson and the Roberta Martin Singers]. Then later on I used to see a label called Gotham. The reason why I mentioned Gotham is because I remember I used to get my Cousin Joe records on Gotham.⁴ And there were a lot of little jazz labels that came to me that used to record people like Charlie Parker and Dizzy Gillespie.⁵ I only knew these labels really as a collector because I always considered myself in those days to be more of a collector who incidentally made records himself.

Broven: Could you tell me about Smalls Paradise [on Seventh Avenue, Harlem]?

Pomus: Well, you know that was a club that I never knew very well. See, first of all I would know the clubs usually that I worked and that was a club I never worked. Usually I would know a club by having appeared there or once in a while I would wander off to Manhattan, but you must realize that there were so many clubs that I worked at in Brooklyn and in New Jersey, and some in Connecticut, that I very seldom had the opportunity to go to Manhattan. I would just go there once a week, if I wasn't working, to go to the Apollo. So the ones I knew of [in Harlem] were the Palm Cafe [125th Street], Jimmy's Chicken Shack [148th Street], one or two others, and the Baby Grand. So although I knew of Smalls Paradise, it just so happened I never spent any time there.

Broven: OK. Was Lenox Avenue bubbling in those days?

Pomus: Oh, absolutely. Lenox Avenue, 123rd, there were clubs all over the place, an excitement you know, a real excitement in those clubs. I guess today they call it energy and vibes and that's what you felt: great energy, great vibes in all the clubs. Very exciting. I guess the band got sent by the crowd, the crowd got sent by the band.

Broven: What about the Savoy Ballroom [at 596 Lenox, between 140th and 141st Streets]?

Pomus: Well I'll tell you, it's very interesting. One of the reasons I was discouraged from spending time as a boy because there was a long flight of steps to get there. Usually if I didn't have to go into a place that had a lot of steps I would never go in there unless I was working, so I'd never worked at Savoy. And so I never had any occasion to go there because of the long flight of steps. It was difficult for me to get around to places.

Broven: Sure, but it had a good reputation?

Pomus: A phenomenal reputation. In fact there was a group in there called the Lindy Hoppers, which was a great group of dancers that always was there dancing in the place, usually with groups like the Savoy Sultans, a group that featured a great alto player, Rudy Williams.

Broven: Buddy Johnson used to play up there.

Pomus: Yes. They had the larger bands, the house bands, like Buddy Johnson who featured Red Prysock very often on tenor, and Arthur Prysock used to sing with the band and Ella Johnson.

Broven: Doc, can you tell me something about the history of the black disc jockey, because it seems to me that early on black music wasn't really heard on the radio until say the late '40s, early '50s?

Pomus: The first two black disc jockeys I knew were Tommy Smalls and Willie Bryant. Now, Willie Bryant, I think he was just a very popular black emcee and consequently became a well-known person in Harlem, so it seemed natural that he would be a personality to have his own show, and he played records and also had a number of sponsors and he would talk in between records. But now the derivation of the black disc jockey, I imagine it was just to serve the needs of the community where the black people never had a disc jockey to listen to. Where the first black disc jockey was, I have no idea. I've heard about B. B. King being a disc jockey originally [at WDIA, Memphis]. I would think that because there was such a large black community that wanted to hear music they would feel more in tune to a black person playing the records, and also he would know more about the records than any white person.

Broven: Could you tell us a bit about the disc jockey scene in New York in the late '40s and early '50s?

Pomus: There were three great disc jockeys that would spin that kind of music. One was Symphony Sid Torin, who mostly specialized in jazz. He was a very influential jazz disc jockey in New York, and I hung around him a lot—a great guy. In the end he died broken in Florida somewhere. I understand three people came to his funeral. He was very popular in New York. He was one of those hipsters that hung around Fifty-Second Street, a great guy. Then there was Willie Bryant, the great black emcee [at the Apollo Theatre], and a nice white guy by the name of Ray Carroll. They had a show together, it was called Willie and Ray.[6]

Broven: Yes, and another one was Alan Freed. Was he really as influential as the books say?

Pomus: A great guy. Let me tell you a couple quick stories about Alan. Not long before he died, he had nothing left. He was absolutely broke, and he owned a piece of property in Palm Beach, and he came into Al & Dick's [Steak House], which was a hangout for music people on [151] West Fifty-Fourth Street. He came over to me one night and said, "How are you doing, Doc"? I said, "Great."

He said, "I've got this place in Palm Beach, I'm buying it" . . . that's all he had left. He said, "Why don't you stay there for a while." He handed me the key. That's the way he was, absolutely. Now let me explain something about the payola. Every guy was on payola, but the difference between Alan Freed and the others was that he wouldn't play a record unless he liked it. Those other guys would play anything, and they made him the scapegoat for a lot of reasons. I think that he didn't play ball with certain people in New York, so they made him the scapegoat. But he was no better or worse than the other people, any other disc jockey in the country that played that kind of music. The only difference was Alan really helped people, and also he knew a lot about the music—he had great instincts. To me it was sad, and as I said he wouldn't play a record unless he liked it.

Broven: And do you think that he was really responsible for rock 'n' roll, as the people are saying?

Pomus: I would think that if there is one disc jockey who would be responsible, that he was the guy. And I tell you, the bottom line was he really loved the music. Just like I hated Murray Kaufman as a person, right, but he really loved that music, you know. Murray the K and Alan, if they weren't disc jockeys, they'd be hanging out at all those joints, and that was what was great about those guys. And then there was the Dr. Jive show on WWRL, New York.

Broven: That was Tommy Smalls.

Pomus: Tommy Smalls was a good friend of mine. In fact when Tommy first came here from Atlanta where he had been a well-known disc jockey, and he had become popular over here, he decided to take shows around to different local clubs. Tommy and I had a thing where we had a show that we took around and

Celebrity Club, Freeport, Long Island, 1960, with a Tarheel Slim and Little Ann window poster for Saturday–Sunday, April 9–10. Photo courtesy of the Freeport Historical Society and Museum.

had Jimmy Scott[7] singing and myself singing and Tommy being the emcee, we had a shake dancer. We worked a lot of local clubs in Long Island [such as the Celebrity Club, Freeport] and Brooklyn and also one or two up in Harlem. I don't remember the places in Harlem we worked, maybe Jimmy's Chicken Shack.[8]

Broven: And you were just singing blues?

Pomus: Yes, right. I think that at that time I was like probably the only white person who had an act composed of singing the blues. I didn't play an instrument yet. It was really strange in those days, I took advantage. There were people doing that all over the country but not going around, so it didn't seem like there was anything very peculiar about it to me. Only later on did I realize there was a uniqueness about it.

Broven: How in fact did you become interested in the blues?

Pomus: Well, very early in life I used to catch what we called remote broadcasts in radio. Late at night I would get broadcasts from jazz stations. And I would listen to Pete Brown, Coleman Hawkins. There were programs from Kelly's Stables and every once in a while a blues singer would sing a few songs and it vaguely titillated me. But the real thing happened when I heard a Joe Turner record, "Piney Brown Blues," and I was hooked from then on.[9] I wasn't hooked on the blues so much as being hooked on Joe Turner, and naturally because he was a blues singer I got involved in the blues. And the first time I ever appeared anywhere I just wandered in a club, I was about seventeen years old, and the owner was giving me one of these eyes that meant he wanted you to leave because I wasn't spending any money. And I told him I was a singer and he made me get up and sing with the band. And I knew one song, "Piney Brown Blues," and that was my singing career. Then I would go into clubs. Then I wrote another blues, then I learned "Jelly, Jelly," then I had a repertoire of three songs. And the incredible thing was that the band was led by Frankie Newton, the great trumpet player. The first band I ever sang with was a great, great jazz band. And soon afterward whenever Frankie got a ballroom date, a dance to play, he used me as a vocalist. Only in retrospect did I realize how phenomenal this was at such an early age to be singing with people like Frankie Newton. Then again I never knew this was unique. I thought maybe there was people like this all over the place. Then I worked in a club around the corner. This first place was George's on Seventh Avenue. And then I started running jam sessions at a little place around the corner from there called the Pied Piper [on Barrow Street] and I started working there occasionally. While I was there one night Leonard Feather [the noted English-born jazz writer and songwriter] came in and heard me and got me a recording date. And that was the first session I did [about 1948].

Broven: Which company was that for?

Pomus: Apollo Records.[10]

Broven: Later on, how did the transition from rhythm & blues to rock 'n' roll happen?

Pomus: I think what happened, white people were not buying records that much and [the record companies] were trying to boost record sales. And also they decided they're going to have a new market by getting records that young kids would buy because the black music, black records, were bought not by young kids. They were bought by older black people. The white music wasn't being bought by everybody, but I think the record [companies] ... the moguls, the smart people finally realized what you had to do, you had to have music that would get the kids in the store, 'cause they had buying power and they developed the kind of music that the kids bought. But I think it all started because the white record industry was really bothered. The first records I ever heard that were of that nature were Frankie Lymon [and the Teenagers'] first hit [in 1956], "Why Do Fools Fall in Love,"[11] and I heard that on a disc jockey show one night. It was a show here called *The Milkman's Matinee* [WNEW Radio]. It was a popular all-night program, by a guy by the name of Stan Shaw. I was working in a club called the Musicale that had a few hours of sponsored time on the show,[12] and it was located on West Seventieth Street [off Broadway]. So we'd go over [to the radio station] and I heard his record "Why Do Fools Fall in Love." The first time I heard the record I hated it. It sounded so unmusical to me, and then I heard it again, and I heard it again, and by the third or fourth time I really started liking it. And then I heard Elvis Presley, a record of Elvis Presley's, "Mystery Train" [on Sun] that was on the jukebox at this place I worked at, and that was the first time I heard it. It sounded like some guy come out of the swamps. It really sounded great to me. And then when I saw him on the Dorsey Brothers' TV show [*Stage Show*, January 28, 1956], it was just astonishing to me. He had impressed me almost as much as any singer I'd ever heard for the first time.[13]

Broven: How did you get into songwriting?

Pomus: Well, I always thought of myself primarily as a singer. Now I used to write material for myself, I didn't write material for blues singers. I was encouraged early in my life to write material by Herb Abramson, who was the president of Atlantic Records at that time,[14] and I would write for a lot of Atlantic acts like Ruth Brown, LaVern Baker, all the big Atlantic acts, Joe Turner especially. And really I would make this extra money to help support my singing act, because I never made much money out of singing. There was a kid [Mort Shuman, Doc's future song collaborator] who was dating a cousin of mine [Neysha], and I saw that he was a very talented kid. He used to trail me on my gigs, and I realized if I was going to make money with songwriting, the way to do it is to write a lot of songs. So I said I want to break in a young kid. This young kid, who is musically talented, maybe we'd write together, and this way I'd be able to write a lot of songs and make money as a songwriter. Now mind you, I always had a reputation as a rhythm & blues songwriter, but there's not much money there. My Joe Turner records were always on the charts. I think they would sell ten or fifteen thousand records, that's all what they called race records would sell.

Broven: What records were those, Doc?

Pomus: With Joe Turner I had "Don't You Cry," "Still in Love" [both 1952], then I had the other side of "Corrine, Corrina," which was called "Boogie Woogie Country Girl" [1956]. What had happened with that song, a guy wrote the lead sheet for me and I gave him 15 percent of the song to write the lead sheet, which I regret later because I could've made all the money on it.

Broven: Who did you give the 15 percent to?

Pomus: Fifteen percent? I gave it to the piano player who worked for me at the time, Reginald Ashby, so I used to do that. You'd always do that with songs. I don't know, it's like one of the poems to a poet; it's one of the songs to a songwriter, so I've given away pieces of songs down the line. Sometimes I lived to regret it, you know, but then again there's the generosity of other songwriters. For instance I have a third of the song, "Young Blood" [by the Coasters, 1957], and I don't think I really wrote it. I think that Jerry [Leiber] and Mike [Stoller] probably wrote three-quarters of the song. I had, maybe a concept, that's all I had. They were so generous, but that's the way we were all toward each other, you know.

Broven: "Boogie Woogie Country Girl" was such a great song. Could you tell me what gave you the inspiration to write that?

Courtesy of Victor Pearlin.

Pomus: I have no idea. First of all, it was so many years ago. Well, it's just I always liked that kind of music, and it just seemed to fit Joe—I was writing it specifically for Joe Turner. And that it was just the type of song I had written that he'd be able to do so well. The funny story about that with Joe was always Joe

A MESS OF BLUES

Words and Music by DOC POMUS and MORT SHUMAN

As recorded by
Elvis Presley
on RCA Victor

Price
60c
(in U. S. A.)

Elvis Presley Music, Inc.
Sole Selling Agent:
Hill and Range Songs, Inc.
1619 Broadway, New York 19, N. Y.

Courtesy of
Victor Pearlin.

never remembered the lyrics, so I kidded him up until his death about when-ever he was working anywhere I'd always request "Boogie Woogie Country Girl" to crack him up. There was always too many lyrics in there.

Broven: What about some of the songs you wrote for LaVern Baker?

Pomus: Well, one for LaVern Baker was "My Happiness Forever," which was a minor rhythm & blues hit [no. 13, *Billboard* R&B, 1956]. I wrote for LaVern Baker an answer song to "Little Sister" [which was an Elvis Presley no. 5 *Billboard* pop hit, 1961], titled "Hey, Memphis."

Broven: Another classic song of yours was "Lonely Avenue."

Pomus: Yeah, that I wrote for Ray [Charles on Atlantic]. That's one of my favorite songs, that and "A Mess of Blues" that I wrote for Presley.[15] But you know, I think that a songwriter in a certain way is always partial to the songs he wrote by himself, so "Lonely Avenue" I wrote by myself, and I'm very partial to that [no. 6, *Billboard* R&B, 1956].

Broven: Did you get the tune from one of the gospel songs … it sounds very gospel based?

Pomus: I've always listened to gospel music so much. I remember writing the song for a fact on a bridge coming back from New York to Brooklyn, and I remember, I was about to get married, and my future wife [Willi Burke, a Broadway actress] and I put it down on tape and I gave it to Ray that way. But the thing that's interesting to me about that was the fact that whenever I made a new song for Ray, Ray always wanted me to do the demo. But those were the only songs that I wrote that I made the demos of, except earlier. Now I have the original demo of "Lonely Avenue" where I was writing it. When I got to my apartment I put it into a tape recorder and we—my wife and I—did it. But I have the tape. You know it's one of those live tapes. To listen to it, it's so weird. You know, it's like another world to me.

Broven: Then you got lined up with Mort Shuman.[16]

Pomus: Yeah, he was this young fellow. For years he sat in the room while I wrote, and I give him a piece of every song while he was in the room. And as the years went by, he contributed more and more, and after about three years I made him a full partner. At first he was getting like 10, 15 percent, then I raised him up to half: 50 percent.

Broven: I suppose one of your biggest songs was "Save the Last Dance for Me" [1960]?

Pomus: Yeah, that was the Drifters on Atlantic. And when the record came out, that was on the other side. I had both sides of the record when it came out. I think the other side was "Nobody But Me," which was the song that they ran with. "Save the Last Dance for Me" wasn't the A side. It started to catch on in a couple of areas, but what had happened was that Dick Clark [on *American*

UK release, courtesy of John Broven.

Bandstand], when he heard it, Dick Clark said they were on the wrong side, to turn it over—and "Save the Last Dance for Me" became the play [no. 1, *Billboard* pop and R&B]. Otherwise it would have never been played.

Broven: How did you come to write for Elvis Presley?

Pomus: Well, the [publishing] firm I was contracted to [Hill & Range, owned by Julian and Jean Aberbach] also had two firms with Elvis Presley. One was Elvis Presley Music and the other was Gladys Music, so because we were under contract with the firm, we were given the opportunity to write for Elvis Presley. Now let me explain what the opportunity means. It means that when he was doing a movie, we were shown a script. But this doesn't mean that we were automatically in the movie. Also, we were told when he had a recording session coming up, and probably it was five hundred to a thousand songs sent in for each session, and sometimes we'd get lucky. But it was never because we were under contract with the firm that we were automatically going to get an Elvis Presley record. And also another thing—the only person that looked at the material was Elvis. He made all the final decisions except his movie material, then it was in conjunction with the producer of the movie. Most people think that [Colonel Tom] Parker had something to do with the music, and he was never involved in nothing. It was all Elvis. One time we got really lucky was, we got "Little Sister" and "His Latest Flame." That happened because we were told that he had a session coming up and he needed material immediately. So we had these songs that Bobby Darin had recorded unsuccessfully. He tried to record on the West Coast so we were on the coast at the time. And when Darin did record them and we sent them right over to Nashville, and Presley recorded them and it was just dumb luck—and we had "Little Sister" and "His Latest Flame." We had them back-to-back and they both made top 10. It was just dumb luck.[17]

Broven: And the royalties are still coming in?

Pomus: Oh, absolutely. The Presley royalties decrease with each year, but the first two or three years after he died [in 1977] they were enormous.[18] You see, the fascinating thing is that the [mechanical] royalty rates and the performance rates have increased so much in recent years that a songwriter makes so much more money today then he made twenty or thirty years ago, so consequently I guarantee you I'll make more money on the songs of mine today then when they were recorded.[19] Fortunately some of them are hits again, you know, but it's incredible.

Broven: One thing that always fascinated me in the late '50s is the way people talked about million-selling records, and I just wonder how many of those records actually sold a million? In other words, what were the accounting practices like? Were they very accurate?

Pomus: We've heard about two sets of books [*laughs*]. That was the thing that they always talked of—the one set that was the real royalties, and the one set that was shown to the public. I remember I had wonderful instances. I wrote a song called "Your Other Love" that was recorded by a group, the Flamingos [no. 54, *Billboard* pop, on End, 1960]. We also wrote the other side of the record ["Lovers Gotta Cry"]. Now when it was royalty statement time we got paid one amount for one side and a different amount for the other side. So the fellow who had the record company, George Goldner [of the Gee, End, Gone, and Red Bird labels], who, by the way, was a fantastic character. I'm speaking to Goldner, and I said, "George, what would you do if a record company records both sides of a song and they pay you royalties on one side for one figure and a different set for the other side?" He said, "I'd sue them." I said, "I'm going to sue you, George," and he cracked up. He was a great character. I used to love George, I had so much fun with him.

Broven: Can you tell me some of your other famous rhythm & blues songs . . . your personal favorites?

Pomus: Well, my personal favorites are not necessarily the hits, I'll just tell you that. But I like "Save the Last Dance for Me," and I like "Sweets for My Sweet," that was originally recorded by the Drifters [later by the Searchers]. And I think the Andy Williams song, "Can't Get Used to Losing You" [no. 2, *Billboard* pop, 1963], is kind of an interesting song. I always liked "Little Sister," and I always especially liked "A Mess of Blues" that Presley recorded. You know, it's strange, I find it's so hard for me to remember these songs. "A Teenager in Love" I liked because it was a concept I had about young people really tortured when they were in love. You know the interesting thing about "A Teenager in Love"? We were guests of the British recording industry when "A Teenager in Love" came out because there were three records in the top 10 in England of the same song: Marty Wilde, there was the Dion and the Belmonts' record, and there was another one by Craig Douglas, and that had never happened before.[20] So we were their guests, and we had a good time in England that time, and I got very friendly with Marty Wilde, and also very friendly with [guitarist] Joe Brown at that time. And so those are some of my favorite songs. I like "Hushabye" [by the Mystics, Laurie, 1959, no. 20, *Billboard* pop], too. I always like songs that end up being exactly what I try to make them. That's why to me they're not necessarily hits, they're songs. I like the Joe Turner record "Still in Love" very much, that was exactly what I wanted. "Lonely Avenue" I liked because that was exactly what I wanted it to be, you know. And there were a few songs like that. Most of the time it's all coming from inside you, so they're all yours, different parts of you that you portray at the time. But always some of them you feel more closely attuned to.[21]

Broven: Do you write the lyrics and the music?

Pomus: Primarily the lyrics in recent years. In those days I used to write the words and music. Today I think you could say I write all the lyrics and I structure a lot of the melodies, but in the old days when I wrote with Shuman, I would say he wrote 25 percent of the lyrics and I wrote 25 percent of the melodies. That's about the way we did it at the time.

Broven: Could you tell us a little about Leiber and Stoller when they first came to town [in 1957]?

Pomus: Well, they were the most helpful people in the world. First of all they were real geniuses, I mean they put comedic ideas into pop songs. I thought they were phenomenal—also they were very helpful to me. As a songwriter they gave me a lot of hints, and also they were great comrades. When we worked with them on records, it was always wonderful because Jerry and Mike always structured the arrangements for the arranger as well. A lot of arrangers took complete credit. And then I would sit with [Leiber and Stoller]. Sometimes they were telling the arranger what to write for the horn parts, what to write for the rhythm section—they were just marvelous. They were two of the greatest that I ever encountered. Not only that but wonderful, intelligent guys who I'm still very friendly with these days.

Broven: But they also called on some very, very good session musicians, like King Curtis.

Pomus: A fact that's unbeknown to most people, I had my own band and Curtis was my saxophone player for a long time. Curtis and Mickey Baker were both in my band, and I believe I gave Curtis his first session with Atlantic Records. And Mickey Baker, I recommended him to Atlantic Records. But King Curtis, his first session with Atlantic was a session we did with a group called the Tibbs Brothers [Andrew and Kenneth]. Two great, great singers. It was on Atco, a subsidiary of Atlantic.[22]

Broven: What did you think of King Curtis and Mickey Baker as musicians?

Pomus: Unbelievable. Not just good, unbelievable. I knew Mickey Baker at first because he was studying with the guitar player I used to work with, and the guitar player I used to work with was raving about this guy. Eventually I started working with him, and he was great even then. For a fact, I think that Mickey and King Curtis's first recording date was on a session. I've heard contrary reports, but I'm pretty sure they said it was their first date. It was on a label [production company] called Flaps and it was a guy [Lexy "Flap" Hanford] who owned an after-hours club called Flap's on 158th Street. So he called his label After Hours. And the session we did on After Hours [in 1954], Mickey played guitar and Curtis played tenor. Those guys were phenomenal. They were just unbelievable. Even though King Curtis's sound was a little different in those days, it evolved into that thing they called "chicken scratch" later, but he always was a great, great saxophone player, just as Mickey was a great guitar player.

Broven: Were they easy to work with in the studio?

Pomus: The session I did with them was very easy. I don't know how they were later on, but I thought they were great, a lot of fun. Great guys to work with, and I never had a problem with them.

Broven: They came up with ideas?

Pomus: Oh, they were very innovative. Curtis was less innovative because Curtis, in those days, was more reserved, but Mickey was very innovative. Mickey always had ideas. I remember them that way. Mickey was in France but he was here about a year ago [about 1985]. We spent time together, and I knew Curtis up until the time he was murdered [in 1971]. Curtis was killed in my neighborhood. He had some kind of altercation in front of a piece of property. Up until the time he died we were friends.

Broven: What were the major New York recording studios in the '50s?

Pomus: Well, Atlantic had their own studio [first at 234 West Fifty-Sixth Street (1951–1956), followed by 157 West Fifty-Seventh Street]. Then there was, in the '50s, there was one studio called Bell Sound that was the principle studio [at West Forty-Sixth Street and Eighth Avenue (mid-late 1950s), then 237 West Fifty-Fourth and Eighth]. And then there was Dick Charles [Recording Service at 729 Seventh Avenue]. There was a studio that we used, and the demos were out of a studio called Associated [at 723 Seventh Avenue]. But the blues sessions we used to do in a studio called Beltone at the Hotel Wolcott. That's where a lot of blues sessions went on at Beltone, wherever that was [4 West Thirty-First Street]. I figure it's now defunct. But they all used to use that. It had a real kind of funky sound. And when we started recording, you made it right on the record, and all you were allowed was a false start. Could you imagine how phenomenal those singers were to make hits that way? [People today] can't believe it that people made hits that way. I never knew anything about records, so I never made really good records, you know. Some of those guys, like [Joe] Turner, I don't know how they did that. It was incredible. And there was no such thing as an A&R man then. I remember when we were recording, there was a guy at Apollo [Records] who was in charge of the sessions, a saxophone player, Jerry Jerome. And he'd come in at the beginning of the session and he said, "Well, you guys, everybody showed up" and make you sign the slip and then he'd say, "You guys know what you're doing" and leave. It was us and the engineer. It was always like that. I remember I never had a bona fide A&R man in the studio.

Broven: Just to bring us up to date, what are you doing now?

Pomus: Dr. John and I produced and wrote an album with Jimmy Witherspoon [*Midnight Lady Called the Blues*, Muse Records, 1986]. In fact 'Spoon called me up yesterday specifically to say that this is the first time he's ever acquired an album where the material is specifically written for him. Dr. John and I wrote for the last several years; we wrote a lot of material for B. B. King [notably for the 1981 MCA LP *There Must Be a Better World Somewhere*], and I wrote some material with Kenny Hirsch, Johnny Adams, and Irma Thomas.

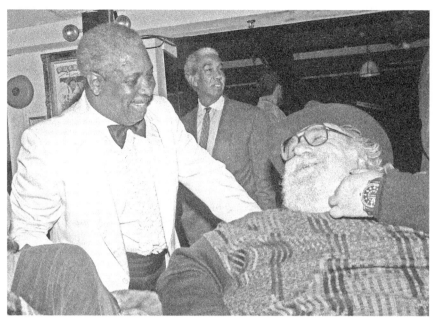

Doc Pomus (r.) with drummer Panama Francis at the Lone Star Roadhouse, New York, May 8, 1989. Photo by Paul Harris.

Courtesy of Victor Pearlin.

Mac [Rebennack], that's Dr. John, we also wrote some material for Johnny Adams. Then I just wrote a song ["One More Time"] for Easter Seals [formerly the National Society for Crippled Children] that Ray Charles did on a telethon.

Broven: Great. And you're still keeping very much close to the New York blues scene?

Pomus: Oh yeah. Thank God I make enough money that I don't have to reach out, you know, drive myself crazy. I mean the world did bring me enough money, so I try to do projects that intrigue me, and usually they're blues projects or something like that. I'm still active, I go out. I'm still hanging around the clubs, the same thing I did all my life, only now I can afford to pay the bills.

[Short extracts from this interview appeared in John Broven's *Record Makers and Breakers: Voices of the Independent Rock 'n' Roll Pioneers* (Urbana: University of Illinois Press, 2009), used with permission. Included in the book are details of Pomus's short flirtation with label ownership with R n B Records in 1958.]

NOTES

1. Porto Rico was a character created by an Apollo Theatre stagehand, Norman Miller.

2. Dwight "Gatemouth" Moore recorded "Love Doctor Blues" with the Tiny Grimes Swingtet for National on October 25, 1946.

3. Teddy Reig, a hustling A&R man who produced many jazz stars including Charlie Parker, Count Basie, and Miles Davis—mainly for Savoy, Roost, and Roulette—was born on November 23, 1918, in New York and died on September 29, 1984, in Teaneck, New Jersey.

4. Gotham Records was founded by Sam Goody in New York in 1946 but was acquired by Philadelphia's Ballen Record Company, headed by Ivin Ballen, at the start of 1948, and it lasted until 1956. The label's most popular artist was alto saxophonist Earl Bostic. Still, Gotham was mainly a gospel label, while its primary country blues artists were Dan Pickett from Alabama and Doug Quattlebaum from South Carolina. The Ballen family also ran a thriving pressing plant business, which became Disc Makers, while Goody was known as a notorious retail record discounter who would live to see the growth of a huge record chain bearing his name.

5. Among the New York independent record labels releasing jazz in the 1940s were Commodore, Savoy, Apollo, Blue Note, National, Manor, Guild, Musicraft, and Sittin' In With.

6. On October 23, 1948, *Billboard* ran this news brief: "The Doc Pomus blues-styled 'Alley' commercial on Willie Bryant and Ray Carroll's WHOM late show became so popular that Apollo Records has cut a full-length version with Pomus warbling." See also note 10 below.

7. Little Jimmy Scott (1925–2014) was a sensitive jazz-blues balladeer who recorded for Roost, Coral, Savoy, and King in the 1950s, and also Tangerine in 1962. His career was revived after he sang at Pomus's funeral in 1991.

8. With regard to black clubs he played, Pomus wrote in his own liner notes for the LP *It's Great to Be Young and in Love* (Whiskey, Women, and . . . , Sweden) that he performed at "the Verona, Paul's Cafe and the Baby Grand in Brooklyn; the Celebrity Club in Freeport, Long Island; the Club Harlem in New Jersey [Atlantic City]; and another New Jersey venue known as Murphy's [Elizabethtown]."

9. "Piney Brown Blues" was recorded by Joe Turner and his Fly Cats, featuring Hot Lips Page (trumpet) and Pete Johnson (piano), for Decca on November 11, 1940. Pomus would have been an impressionable fifteen years old at the time.

10. Doc Pomus had two singles released by Apollo in 1948: "Blues in the Red"/"Blues without Booze" and "Naggin' Wife Blues"/"Alley Alley Blues." The accompaniment was provided by alto saxophonist Tab Smith and his Band, with Taft Jordan (trumpet) and Leonard Feather (piano). Pomus also recorded as a blues shouter in the Joe Turner style for Savoy, Baronet (Denmark), Selmer, Derby, Chess, Coral, After Hours, and Dawn (as Doc Palmer) through 1955 before concentrating on songwriting. Regrettably, it is not known how the 1950 release on the Chess label, which had only just started at the time, came about. In the liner notes to *Send*

for the Doctor (Whiskey, Women, and . . . , Sweden), Pomus said: "The Chess people came to New York to record me. I don't remember the details as to how I got that session. . . . I think it was Rex Stewart's session." Pomus did tell Dan Kochakian, the magazine editor for *Whiskey, Women, and . . .* , after which the Swedish label was named, that he was proud to record for Chess before Chuck Berry.

11. "Why Do Fools Fall in Love" by the Teenagers featuring Frankie Lymon broke into the *Billboard* Top 100 chart on February 11, 1956, on George Goldner's Gee label. It made no. 6 in a twenty-one-week stay, and hit no. 1 R&B. The record opened doors for many teenage vocal groups in the pop field. It also proved to be an inspiration for the Doc Pomus–Mort Shuman smash, "A Teenager in Love," by Dion and the Belmonts (Laurie, 1959). See note 20 below.

12. Also in the notes to the *It's Great to Be Young and in Love* LP (see note 8), Pomus described the Club Musicale in great detail, including its owners Sandy Messina and Morty Jay. On weekends, "it was jazz and low-down blues with an audience of aficionados" listening to a band that featured Mickey Baker (guitar), King Curtis (tenor sax), and Jimmy Lewis (bass).

13. On that broadcast of *Stage Show*, Elvis Presley sang "Shake, Rattle and Roll" and "Flip Flop and Fly" (two songs associated with Doc Pomus's hero Joe Turner), and Ray Charles's "I Got a Woman."

14. Herb Abramson launched Atlantic Records with Ahmet Ertegun in January 1948, and sold his interest under a cloud in December 1958. He formed the Blaze, Triumph, and Festival labels without real success but fared better with his A-1 Sound Studios, where he produced Tommy Tucker's influential hit "Hi-Heel Sneakers" (Checker, 1964).

15. "A Mess of Blues" was a 1960 *Billboard* pop hit for Elvis Presley, but the song's earnings were considerably enhanced as it was the B side of the blockbuster no. 1 hit, "It's Now or Never."

16. Mort Shuman was born on November 12, 1938, in Brooklyn and died on November 2, 1991, in London, shortly after Pomus died. Shuman had moved to Europe in the mid-1960s and lived in Paris.

17. "(Marie's the Name) His Latest Flame"/"Little Sister" by Elvis Presley made no. 4 and no. 5, respectively, on the *Billboard* pop chart. Other big Presley songs written by Pomus-Shuman were "Surrender" (no. 1, 1961) and "Viva Las Vegas" (no. 29, 1964).

18. Royalty income generally, not only for the astonishingly strong Presley sales that still continue, picked up considerably when songs started to be reissued all over again on compact disc from the mid-1980s, helped by increased royalty rates (see note 19 below).

19. From 1909 to 1978, the US mechanical royalty remained static at 2 cents per song, regardless of new listening formats, with the royalty split 50–50 between songwriter(s) and the music publisher. After the 1978 Copyright Act, a system for royalty rate hearings was established, with the current rate being 9.1 cents per song.

20. In the *New Musical Express* (UK) charts, "A Teenager in Love" was a multiple-artist hit in 1959 with releases by Marty Wilde (no. 2, Philips), Craig Douglas (no. 13, Top Rank), and Dion and the Belmonts (no. 28, London). In the United States, Dion's original version made no. 5 on the *Billboard* pop chart on Laurie.

21. Other famous recordings of Pomus-Shuman songs, not discussed in the text, include "Turn Me Loose" and "Hound Dog Man" by Fabian (Chancellor, 1959), "Go, Jimmy, Go" by Jimmy Clanton (Ace, 1959), and "This Magic Moment" by the Drifters (Atlantic, 1960). The songwriters' partnership ended in the mid-1960s.

22. The Tibbs Brothers' 1956 Atco single "I'm Going Crazy"/"(Wake Up) Miss Rip Van Winkle" featured Pomus-Shuman songs on both sides.

PAUL HARRIS
PHOTO PORTFOLIO

———————

19

LEGENDS OF NEW YORK CITY

Text by Richard Tapp and John Broven

CHAMPION JACK DUPREE

It's fair to say that Champion Jack Dupree is seen primarily as a link to New Orleans's old-time barrelhouse piano tradition, not to New York blues. Indeed, his recording of "Junker Blues" (OKeh, 1941) directly inspired Fats Domino's unforgettable Crescent City debut hit, "The Fat Man" (1950). Yet Dupree lived in New York at the peak of his creative career through the 1940s and 1950s, recording for labels such as Joe Davis, Apollo, Red Robin, King, Vik, and Atlantic. His greatest moment on record came with *Blues from the Gutter* (Atlantic, 1958), an audacious drug concept album enhanced by Larry Dale's sensational guitar work. From 1960, Dupree started a new life and career in Europe. His performances at the piano, laced with his trademark irreverent humor, were well received by the European audiences of the day.

For many years Dupree lived in a brownstone behind Harlem's Apollo Theatre. A neighbor was Brownie McGhee, who was influenced by Blind Boy Fuller's Piedmont blues and, like Dupree, is better known for his original roots music than as a New York blues exponent—and later, of course, as a folk-blues guitarist with harmonica player Sonny Terry. Dupree and McGhee accompanied each other in the 1940s and early 1950s. For all their subsequent fame, they deserve to be better recognized as pioneering New York bluesmen. (JB)

PANAMA FRANCIS

David "Panama" Francis was an outstanding drummer renowned for laying down a rhythm that dancers loved. He was New York's equivalent of Earl Palmer, the superb New Orleans and West Coast studio drummer. Born in Miami in

Champion Jack Dupree (1909 [passport] or 1910 [probable]–1992), 100 Club, London, May 29, 1990. Photo by Paul Harris.

Panama Francis (1918–2001), Lone Star Roadhouse, New York, May 8, 1989. Photo by Paul Harris.

1918, Francis moved to New York twenty years later. In the glory days of swing he played in the bands of Lucky Millinder, Cab Calloway, and Slim Gaillard, but in 1952 Francis went freelance and became an in-demand session drummer. He played on countless sessions, many of which produced R&B-pop hits such as "Drown in My Own Tears" and "Hallelujah I Love Her So" by Ray Charles, "C. C. Rider" by Chuck Willis, and "I Cried a Tear" by LaVern Baker; there was also the rock 'n' roll of Bobby Darin's "Splish Splash" and "Queen of the Hop." Among the many other artists to benefit from his driving drum work were Faye Adams, Big Maybelle, Wilbert Harrison, Screamin' Jay Hawkins, Louisiana Red, Brownie McGhee, Sam Price, and Joe Turner. In 1979, Francis formed the Savoy Sultans, whose aim was to re-create the jumping swinging style of music that was so popular at Harlem's Savoy Ballroom in the 1930s. (RT)

BUDDY JOHNSON ORCHESTRA ALUMNI

Arthur Prysock

Arthur Prysock first came to prominence as the featured ballad singer in Buddy Johnson's blues-based swinging dance band. More than any other, his orchestra was able to capture "the fancy of both uptown New York and down-home South Carolina," to quote leading authority Bob Porter. Prysock was born in Spartan-burg, South Carolina, in 1924, but in 1943 he was living in Hartford, Connecticut, where Buddy Johnson discovered him. Modeling himself on his hero, Billy Eckstine, Prysock had a part-time gig singing in one of the city's clubs, but after a successful audition he became Johnson's male vocalist, making his Apollo Theatre debut in 1944. With his matinee-idol looks and silky voice, Arthur was soon a heartthrob with "the ladies in the house," while his smooth delivery on "They All Say I'm the Biggest Fool" was to give Johnson a top 10 "race" chart hit in 1946. After eight successful years with Johnson, Prysock left the band and went on to enjoy fruitful years as a solo artist. For many of these years, he was signed to Hy Weiss's Old Town label, where several small R&B hit singles resulted from 1960 through 1977 as well as a raft of albums ranging from MOR ballads to jazz with the Count Basie Orchestra. (RT)

Purvis Henson

Tenor saxophonist Purvis Henson was born in Itta Bena, Mississippi, in 1917. B. B. King was born in the same town and was taught by Purvis's uncle, Luther Henson, at Elkhorn School in nearby Kilmichael. By the early 1940s, Purvis was

(L. to r.), Harold "Geezil" Minerve (1922–1992); Arthur Prysock (1924–1997); and Purvis Henson (1917–1997), Searington, Long Island, May 9, 1989. Photo by Paul Harris.

leading his own large dance band, playing New York venues and the chitlin' circuit. However, after having to call time on this venture, in 1946 Henson joined Buddy Johnson's outfit. The sax player eventually became Buddy's assistant band manager and musical director, and he stayed with Johnson until the band was wound up at the end of the 1950s. Henson's rasping sax solos can be heard to particularly good effect on Buddy and Ella Johnson's mid-1950s Mercury recordings pitched at the teenage rock 'n' roll market. (RT)

Geezil Minerve

Alto saxophonist Harold "Geezil" Minerve was raised in Florida, having been born in Cuba in 1922. He is reported to have played with Ida Cox early in his music career before moving to New Orleans, where he worked as a freelance musician. Minerve then enjoyed stints with both Clarence Love's and Ernie Fields's bands before joining Buddy Johnson's New York–based outfit in 1949. He stayed with Johnson until 1957 and can be heard on the band's later Decca sessions as well as some of the Mercury recordings that followed. Geezil is also the credited vocalist on two of Johnson's Decca sides. After leaving Buddy, Minerve worked with Ray Charles, Arthur Prysock—one-time Buddy Johnson vocalist—and then Duke Ellington from 1971 to 1974. (RT)

Rosetta Reitz, feminist and founder of Rosetta Records (1924–2008), New York, May 19, 1986. Photo by Paul Harris.

ROSETTA REITZ

Rosetta Reitz was a prominent feminist who championed the contribution of women performers to jazz and blues, primarily concentrating on artists who were active in the pre–World War II era. Born in 1924 in Utica, New York, she settled in Manhattan in the mid-1940s, where she enjoyed a varied career, including contributing to the *Village Voice*. In 1979 Reitz formed her own label, Rosetta Records, to showcase artists about whom she felt passionately. Eighteen LPs resulted with tracks dubbed from pristine 78s both from her own collection and from those of friends; several albums were compilations in a series under the banner "Independent Women's Blues."

The catalog was given fulsome praise in 1989 by *New Musical Express* (UK) journalist and archivist Fred Dellar, when saluting the label's tenth anniversary: "Reitz has produced not only a personal statement but also the finest series of pre-rock sides ever devoted to female music makers. These days the names of Billie Holiday, Bessie Smith, and Josephine Baker are revered as black music legends but Reitz reminds us that this is just the tip of the iceberg. Her glorious Ethel Waters compilation proves the point." Citing Julia Lee, the International Sweethearts of Rhythm, and Sister Rosetta Tharpe, Dellar concluded: "Thanks to the Rosetta label, the work of these [women] and the likes of the trumpet-playing Valaida [Snow], 'Yas Yas Girl' Merline Johnson, 'Real Gone Gal' Nellie Lutcher, and boogie empress Hazel Scott, continues to surface." (RT)

Jerry Wexler, retired partner, Atlantic Records (1917–2008), New York, May 21, 1986. Photo by Paul Harris.

JERRY WEXLER

Jerry Wexler was a partner and producer from 1953 to 1975 at New York's Atlantic Records, about the most successful independent label ever. He oversaw the label's growth, with cofounders Ahmet Ertegun and Herb and Miriam Abramson, in the blues, rhythm & blues, rock 'n' roll, jazz, soul, and early rock markets through to the inevitable corporate takeover. Wexler started off as a music journalist with *Billboard* and helped popularize the term "rhythm & blues" in 1949 to replace the term "race" music. The star Atlantic names roll off the tongue: Ruth Brown, the Clovers, Joe Turner, Clyde McPhatter and the Drifters, Ray Charles, the Coasters, Bobby Darin, and later Solomon Burke and Otis Redding, all enhanced by Tom Dowd's innovative work at the studio control board.

The accompanying photograph was taken in 1986 at Wexler's apartment near Central Park, where he readily greeted Paul Harris and me as representatives of recently launched *Juke Blues* magazine. As we left, Wex handed me an LP box set, *East Memphis Music: 81 Hits from the Stax Era*, which he inscribed: "To John Broven: Fan, appreciator, and keeper of the faith—always." My pride resounds to this day.

Later, I was to interview him at his delightful East Hampton home and by telephone for my book *Record Makers and Breakers: Voices of the Independent Rock 'n' Roll Pioneers*. I noted in 2005 that "his mind is as sharp as ever at 88."

Baby Grand club, Harlem, 1986. Photo by Paul Harris.

Along with his track record, hip streetwise demeanor, colorful vocabulary, and erudition, he was literally the perfect interviewee to discuss the history and mechanics of the old-style independent record industry. (JB)

BABY GRAND CLUB

In the late 1940s and for very many years thereafter, the Baby Grand was one of the top music nightspots in Harlem. Open for business in November 1946, it was located at 319 West 125th Street, close to Eighth Avenue, near Bobby Robinson's record shop and just a block from the Apollo Theatre. There was also a Baby Grand in Brooklyn; both were owned by the Krulick brothers, with Jack Krulick being the sibling most associated with the Harlem nitery. It was an intimate integrated club that seated about two hundred people, and had a reputation for serving excellent food while patrons were entertained by a show that usually included a variety act and an exotic dancer as well as the billed singer. Jimmy Scott enjoyed a residency at the Baby Grand in 1947, and Doc Pomus, another who performed there in the early days, confirmed that Krulick sought to bring in top blues artists such as Jimmy Witherspoon, Joe Turner, and Wynonie Harris. Indeed, guitarist Billy Butler recalled backing Harris at the club around 1947–1948, when Billy was in a group called the Harlemaires. Lee Magid, a hustling A&R man and talent scout, told how he was so knocked out by Al Hibbler at the Baby Grand, he took him to Decca Records to cut "Unchained Melody," a no. 1 R&B hit in April 1955.

In the early 1950s, the club hosted DJs Willie Bryant and Ray Carroll, who spun records from the front window for their late-night rhythm & blues radio

Smalls Paradise, Harlem, 1986. Photo by Paul Harris.

show on station WHOM. Bryant was a Harlem personality and emcee at the Apollo, but the one most associated with the Baby Grand was comedian Nipsey Russell, who enjoyed a near-twenty year tenure at the club. Former Old Town artist Ruth McFadden sang there in the 1960s, and she confirmed that Nipsey, billed as "Harlem's Son of Fun," was a huge attraction, telling jokes that had the audience rolling in laughter. She added, "Folks came to the club knowing no matter who was on the bill, they were probably going to see Nipsey Russell, no extra charge. The Baby Grand was famous, a must-visit if you came to New York. Knowing you might be entertained by Nipsey was a huge draw!"

Alas, as with so many of the Harlem nightspots, the years took their toll, and the club closed its doors in 1989, with a Radio Shack outlet taking over the site. (RT)

Sources include Arnold Shaw, *Honkers and Shouters: The Golden Years of Rhythm & Blues* (New York: Collier, 1978). With thanks to Marv Goldberg.

SMALLS PARADISE CLUB

Smalls Paradise—sometimes known as Small's Paradise or Smalls' Paradise— was a nightclub at 2294½ Seventh Avenue at 135th Street, opened there in 1925 by Ed Smalls. At the time it was the only one of the famed Harlem nightspots to be black owned. The house band for the first ten years was led by Charlie Johnson, and in the early 1930s a young Billie Holiday was to fail her audition at Smalls for Johnson, this being Billie's first attempt at a career as a professional singer. In 1945 the club was the setting for the movie *It Happened in Harlem*, a musical comedy. Then in late 1955 Ed Smalls sold the club to Tommy Smalls (no relation), a popular disc jockey known as Dr. Jive, who was soon broadcasting his WWRL radio program from the club. However, by the late 1950s the club was struggling and was bought by basketball star Wilt Chamberlain, who renamed it Big Wilt's Smalls Paradise. Chamberlain changed the emphasis from jazz to rhythm & blues, and in the early 1960s the club was famous for its Tuesday night twist parties. One of the regular artists to feature was King Curtis—his third Atco LP, *Live at Small's Paradise*, was recorded there in 1966. However, by 1983 the club was known as New Smalls Paradise after becoming a disco venue. It finally fell vacant about 1986. (RT)

APOLLO THEATRE

The Apollo Theatre is located in the heart of Harlem on famed 125th Street (253 West 125th Street). Previously a burlesque showplace, the theater was christened the 125th Street Apollo Theatre in 1934 and blossomed when Frank Schiffman took over the venue the following year. Although big names like Billie Holiday and Count Basie appeared at the Apollo in the 1930s and 1940s, for the best part of two decades Schiffman kept largely to the tried-and-tested variety format, which appealed to the everyday black populace of Harlem. It wasn't until the appearance of Sonny Til and the Orioles in 1949 that Schiffman was prompted to change his approach. Overwhelmed by the response to the group, he gradually moved the weekly shows away from the variety format so that, by the mid-1950s, all-music rhythm & blues revues had become the usual offering. By this time, Frank Schiffman's son, Bobby, was managing the Apollo on a day-to-day basis. From the rock 'n' roll era through to soul's golden age, most of the great black stars appeared there: Ray Charles, Ruth Brown, Jackie Wilson, Marvin Gaye, and Joe Tex, to name just a few. However, pride of place goes to James Brown, who smashed attendance records at the Apollo while his album *Live at the Apollo*, recorded in 1962 for King Records, flew off the shelves. For many years, Reuben Phillips led the resident orchestra.

The top names in jazz and gospel also featured regularly at the theater, but blues artists only rarely. Frank Schiffman didn't care for the lifestyle of some blues musicians and thought that the subject matter of some of the songs "wasn't right" for a family theater. However, Bobby Schiffman was more accommodating, and, with the wider acceptance of the blues in the 1960s, the Apollo did feature "Blues Nights" billing leading names such as Bobby "Blue" Bland, John Lee Hooker, Muddy Waters, and especially B. B. King, who was always a top attraction at the Apollo.

Apollo Theatre, Harlem, 1986. Photo by Paul Harris.

Bobby Schiffman closed the theater in 1976. By then it was struggling financially, not helped by drugs and crime in the neighborhood. The theater reopened in 1978 under new ownership and was then taken over by Inner City Broadcasting in 1981. The venue was designated a cultural landmark two years later. The future of the Apollo was secured when it was purchased by the state of New York in 1991 and run by the nonprofit Apollo Theater Foundation with a mission to promote "concerts, performing arts, education, and community outreach programs." The theater still holds its fabled amateur night every Wednesday along with regular shows, and is a prime tourist attraction. (RT)

Source: Ted Fox, *Showtime at the Apollo* (New York: Holt, Rinehart and Winston, 1983).

GOODBYE TO A FRIEND

20

ANDREW "A. J." JOHNSON

Favorite drummer for many of New York's bluesmen.

Tragically passed away in 1996, simply sitting in his car, waiting for alternate side of the street parking one evening in New York City. He was born in 1958 and raised in Harlem.

A great musician and a great friend.

The Blue Frog, the Bronx, 1993.

APPENDIX

RECOMMENDED RECORDINGS

Such is the timespan and variety of New York blues recordings that "best of" lists must always be subjective. With this caveat in mind, we wish to give a broad picture of an underrated blues scene by listing Larry Simon's choices, country blues from Bruce Bastin and Chris Bentley, and a "golden age" selection from John Broven, Mike Gilroy, and Richard Tapp, along with selections from other artists featured in this book.

Larry Simon

Blues from the Gutter, Champion Jack Dupree with Ennis Lowery (Larry Dale), guitar (Atlantic, 1958).
The Blues Ain't Nothin' but a Good Man Feelin' Bad, Sammy Price and His Bluesicians featuring Doc Horse (Kapp, 1962).
Big City Blues, John Hammond with Billy Butler and Jimmy Spruill, guitars (Vanguard, 1964).
Muddy Waters "Live" (at Mr. Kelly's) featuring Paul Oscher, harmonica (Chess, 1971).
"No More Doggin'," Roscoe Gordon (RPM, 1952) (launch of *Rosco's Rhythm*).
"Honky Tonk (Parts 1 and 2)," Bill Doggett featuring Billy Butler, guitar (King, 1956).
"South of France Blues" (based on "Blues After Hours"), Mickey Baker with Coleman Hawkins (YouTube, 1962).
"Sit Right Here," Rosco Gordon with ska musicians featuring Roland Alphonso and Lester Sterling of the Skatalites (private recording available at larrysimon-music.com, 1995).
The Fire/Fury Records Story (Capricorn, 2-CD box set, 1993).
Hy Weiss Presents Old Town Records (Ace, London, 2-CD set, 2003).
Scratch 'n Twist: The Wild Jimmy Spruill Story (Night Train, CD, 2005).
Honkin', Shakin' & Slidin', Noble "Thin Man" Watts featuring June Bateman (Jasmine UK, CD, 2019).

Country Blues: Bruce Bastin and Chris Bentley

"Step It Up and Go," Blind Boy Fuller (Vocalion, 1940).
"West Kinney Street Blues," Skoodle-Dum-Doo and Sheffield (Manor, 1943).
"Dices! Dices!," Big Boy Ellis (Lenox, 1945).
"Johnson Street Boogie Woogie," Champion Jack Dupree (Davis, 1945).
"Shake Your Stuff," Little Boy Fuller (Richard Trice) (Savoy, 1946).
"Quincey Avenue Boogie," Sonny Boy and Lonnie (Continental, 1947).
"Worried Man Blues," Alec Seward (the Blues Boys) (Super Disc, 1947).

"Shake That Thing," Ralph Willis (Signature, 1949).
"Too Much Competition," Allen Baum (Tarheel Slim) (Red Robin, 1953).
"Bad Hangover," Square Walton (RCA Victor, 1953).
"Christina," Brownie McGhee (Harlem, 1954).
"One of These Days," Emright (Holman) (Scatt, early 1960s).

Golden Age: John Broven, Mike Gilroy, and Richard Tapp

"My Fault," Brownie McGhee (Savoy, 1948).
"Drinkin' Wine Spo-Dee-O-Dee," "Stick" McGhee (Atlantic, 1949).
"The Huckle-Buck," Paul Williams (Savoy, 1949).
"The Guy with a '45'," Allen Bunn (Tarheel Slim) (Apollo, 1952).
"I'm Just Your Fool," Buddy Johnson Orchestra with Ella Johnson (Mercury, 1953).
"Shame, Shame, Shame," Paul Williams Orchestra with Larry Dale (Jax, 1953).
"Slow Down Baby," Bob Gaddy (Harlem, 1955).
"No Good Lover," Mickey and Sylvia with Washboard Bill (Groove, 1956).
"Love Is Strange"/"I'm Going Home," Mickey and Sylvia (Groove, 1956).
"Number 9 Train"/"Wildcat Tamer," Tarheel Slim (Fury, 1958).
"Till the Day I Die," Bob Gaddy (Old Town, 1959).
"Kansas City"/"Listen, My Darling," Wilbert Harrison (Fury, 1959).
"After Hours Blues," Hal Paige (Fury, 1959).
"Hard Grind," Jimmy Spruill (Fire, 1959).
"Believe Me, Darling," June Bateman (Fury, 1960).
"Your Evil Thoughts"/"I'm a Good Man but a Poor Man," Lee Roy Little (Cee-Jay, 1960).
"Mind on Loving," Little Danny ("Run Joe" Taylor) (Sharp, 1960).
"Picking Cotton," Little Red Walters (Le Sage, 1960).
"Soul Twist," King Curtis with Billy Butler (Enjoy, 1962).
"New York City Blues," Larry Dale with Bob Gaddy and Jimmy Spruill (Juke Blues, 1987).

Other Artists Featured in New York City Blues

Billy Bland with Brownie McGhee and Sonny Terry, "Chicken Hop" (Old Town, 1956).
Reverend Gary Davis, "Say No to the Devil" (from Prestige Bluesville LP, 1962).
Dr. Horse, "Jack, That Cat Was Clean" (Fire, 1962).
Panama Francis, "Hallelujah I Love Her So" (Ray Charles, Atlantic, 1956).
Larry Johnson with Hank Adkins, "Four Women Blues" (from Prestige LP, 1966).
Bob Malenky with Sonny Terry, "One Woman Man" (from Blue Labor LP, 1974).
Victoria Spivey and Lonnie Johnson, "Idle Hours" (from Prestige Bluesville LP, 1961).
Tarheel Slim and Little Ann, "Security" (Fire, 1960).

Songs

Rose Marie McCoy, *Very Truly Yours: The Songs of . . .* (including her own recordings) (Jasmine UK, 2-CD set, 2016).
Doc Pomus, *Singer and Songwriter* (including his own recordings) (Jasmine UK, 2-CD set, 2012).

Please note these recommendations are a guide only to the depth and breadth of the New York blues sound. Many of the recordings are quoted in the text, but not all. A surprising number of tracks are available to hear, including on Amazon Prime Music, Apple Music, Pandora, Spotify, and especially YouTube. To view the original record labels, with wonderful artwork and a wealth of fascinating data, visit www.45cat.com, www.discogs.com, and www.popsike.com. At the time of publication, Ace Records (London) is preparing a tie-in *New York City Blues* CD.

BIOGRAPHICAL DATA, COMPILED BY JOHN BROVEN

Artists

Faye Adams, May 22, 1923 (Newark, NJ)–possibly November 2, 2016 (probably Englewood, NJ)

Clarence Ashe, December 18, 1945 (possibly Fitzpatrick, AL)–May 1, 2009 (possibly Bronx, NY)

Mickey Baker (McHouston Baker, also of Mickey and Sylvia), October 15, 1925 (Louisville, KY)–November 27, 2012 (France)

June Bateman (Batemon), November 17, 1939 (Schulenberg, TX)–February 16, 2016 (DeLand, FL)

Brook Benton (Benjamin Peay), September 19, 1931 (Lugoff, SC)–April 9, 1988 (Queens, NY)

Otis Blackwell, February 2, 1932 (Brooklyn, NY)–May 6, 2002 (Nashville, TN)

Billy Bland, April 5, 1932 (Wilmington, NC)–March 22, 2017 (New York, NY)

Al Brown, May 22, 1929 (Fairmont, WV)–March 19, 2009 (Randallstown, MD)

Maxine Brown, August 18, 1938 (Kingstree, SC)–

Nappy Brown (Napoleon Brown Culp), October 12, 1929 (Charlotte, NC)–September 20, 2008 (Charlotte, NC)

Ruth Brown, January 12, 1928 (Portsmouth, VA)–November 17, 2006 (Henderson, NV)

Al Browne, March 6, 1918 (New York, NY)–April 30, 1996 (Brooklyn, NY)

Billy Butler, December 15, 1924 (Philadelphia, PA)–March 20, 1991 (Teaneck, NJ)

Ray Charles (Robinson), September 23, 1930 (Albany, GA)–June 10, 2004 (Beverly Hills, CA)

Dave "Baby" Cortez (Clowney), August 13, 1938 (Detroit, MI)–

Cousin Leroy (Asbell/Rozier), September 30, 1925 (Chester, GA)–February 26, 2008 (New York, NY)

Larry Dale (Ennis Lowery), January 7, 1923 (Hungerford, TX)–May 19, 2010 (Bronx, NY)

Leroy Dallas, December 24, 1909 (Mobile, AL)–September 1967 (Brooklyn, NY)

Reverend Gary Davis, April 30, 1896 (Laurens County, SC)–May 5, 1972 (Hammonton, NJ)

Bill Dicey, May 25, 1936 (Annapolis MD)–March 17, 1993 (Rock Hall, MD)

Ola Dixon, February 14, 1943 (Marion, SC)–

Bill Doggett, February 16, 1916 (Philadelphia, PA)–November 13, 1996 (New York, NY)

"Champion" Jack Dupree, July 23, 1909 (passport)/July 4, 1910 (probable) (New Orleans, LA)–January 21, 1992 (Germany)

Wilbert "Big Chief" Ellis, November 10, 1914 (Birmingham, AL)–December 20, 1977 (Birmingham, AL)

David "Panama" Francis, December 21, 1918 (Miami, FL)–November 13, 2001 (Orlando, FL)

Blind Boy Fuller (Fulton Allen), July 10, 1904 (Wadesboro, NC)–February 13, 1941 (Durham, NC)

Bob Gaddy, February 4, 1924 (Vivian, WV)–July 24, 1997 (Bronx, NY)

Rosco (Roscoe) Gordon, April 10, 1928 (Memphis, TN)–July 11, 2002 (Queens, NY)

Lloyd "Tiny" Grimes, July 7, 1911 (Newport News, VA)–March 4, 1989 (New York, NY)

Adam Gussow, April 3, 1958 (New York, NY)–

John Hammond Jr., November 13, 1942 (New York, NY)–

Roy "C" Hammond, August 3, 1939 (Newington, GA)–September 16, 2020 (Allendale County, SC)

Wynonie Harris, August 24, 1915 (Omaha, NE)–June 14, 1969 (Los Angeles, CA)

Wilbert Harrison, January 5, 1929 (Charlotte, NC)–October 26, 1994 (Spencer, NC)

Joe Haywood, June 12, 1939 (Cowpens, SC)–November 14, 1996 (Spartanburg, SC)

Purvis Henson, April 20, 1917 (Itta Bena, MS)–March 14, 1997 (probably New York, NY)

Andrew "A. J." Johnson, 1958–1996 (New York, NY)

Buddy Johnson (Woodrow Johnson), January 10, 1915 (nr. Darlington, SC)–February 9, 1977
    (New York, NY)

Ellamae "Ella" Johnson, June 22, 1917 (nr. Darlington, SC)–February 16, 2004 (New York, NY)

Larry Johnson, May 15, 1938 (Wrightsville, GA)–August 6, 2016 (Harlem, NY)

King Curtis (Ousley), February 7, 1934 (Fort Worth, TX)–August 13, 1971 (New York, NY)

Marie Knight, June 1, 1920 (Attapulgus, GA)–August 30, 2009 (New York, NY)

Lead Belly (Huddie William Ledbetter), January 23, 1888 (nr. Mooringsport, LA)–December 6,
    1949 (New York, NY)

Bobby Lewis, February 9, 1925 (Indianapolis, IN)–April 28, 2020 (Newark, NJ)

Jimmy Lewis, April 11, 1918 (Nashville TN)–2000 (New York, NY)

Little Ann (Anna Sandford), 1935–2004

Little Buster (Forehand), September 28, 1942 (Hertford, NC)–May 11, 2006 (Hempstead, NY)

Louisiana Red (Iverson Minter), March 23, 1932 (Bessemer, AL)–February 20, 2012 (Germany)

Frankie Lymon, September 30, 1942 (Harlem, NY)–February 27, 1968 (Harlem, NY)

Sterling Magee (Mr. Satan), May 20, 1936 (Mount Olive, MS)–September 6, 2020 (Gulfport, FL)

Bob Malenky, March 3, 1943 (Brooklyn, NY)–

Rose Marie McCoy, April 19, 1922 (Oneida, AR)–January 20, 2015 (Champaign, IL)

Ruth McFadden, July 31, 1938 (Charleston, SC)–

Brownie McGhee (Walter Brown McGhee), November 30, 1915 (Knoxville, TN)–February 16,
    1996 (Oakland, CA)

Sticks "Stick" McGhee (Granville McGhee), March 23, 1918 (Knoxville, TN)–August 15, 1961
    (Bronx, NY)

Edna McGriff, December 16, 1935 (Tampa, FL)–March 1980 (Jamaica, NY)

Clyde McPhatter, November 15, 1932 (nr. Durham, NC)–June 13, 1972 (Bronx, NY)

Harold "Geezil" Minerve, January 3, 1922 (Cuba)–June 4, 1992 (probably New York, NY)

Paul Oscher, February 26, 1947 (Brooklyn, NY)–April 18, 2021 (Austin, TX)

Charles "Honeyboy" Otis, November 7, 1932 (probably New Orleans, LA)–October 6, 2015
    (probably New York, NY)

Al Pittman (Dr. Horse), September 17, 1917 (Vienna, GA)–April 28, 2003 (New York, NY)

Tom Pomposello, July 17, 1949 (Long Island, NY)–January 25, 1999 (nr. Kingston, NY)

Jerome "Doc" Pomus (Felder), June 27, 1925 (Brooklyn, NY)–March 14, 1991 (New York, NY)

Lloyd Price, March 9, 1933 (Kenner, LA)–May 3, 2021 (New Rochelle, NY)

Sammy Price, October 6, 1908 (Honey Grove, TX)–April 14, 1992 (New York, NY)

Arthur Prysock, January 1, 1924 (Spartanburg, SC)–June 21, 1997 (Bermuda)

Wilburt "Red" Prysock, February 2, 1926 (Greensboro, NC)–July 19, 1993 (Chicago, IL)

Walter "Little Red Walter" Rhodes, September 4, 1939 (Beaufort, NC)–July 4, 1990
    (Rockingham, NC)

Nehemiah "Riff" Ruffin, May 24, 1920 (Windsor, NC)–February 1991 (Hopewell, VA)

Alonzo Scales, September 16, 1923 (Madison, NC)–June 26, 1975 (probably Brooklyn, NY)

"Big" Al Sears, February 21, 1910 (Macomb, IL)–March 23, 1990 (St. Albans, NY)

Alec Seward, March 16, 1901 (nr. Blanks Tavern, VA)–May 11, 1972 (New York, NY)

Larry Simon, January 4, 1956 (Brooklyn, NY)–

Charlie Singleton, September 17, 1913 (Jacksonville, FL)–December 12, 1985 (Florida)

"Wild" Jimmy Spruill, June 8, 1934 (Washington, NC)–February 3, 1996 (Fayetteville, NC)

Sugar Blue (James Joshua "Jimmie" Whiting), December 16, 1949 (Harlem, NY)–

Tarheel Slim (Allen Rathel Bunn), September 24, 1923 (Bailey, NC)–August 21, 1977 (Bronx, NY)

Sam "The Man" Taylor, July 12, 1916 (Lexington, TN)–October 5, 1990 (possibly Westchester County, NY)

Sonny Terry (Saunders Terrell), October 24, 1911 (Greensboro, GA)–March 11, 1986 (Mineola, NY)

Rudolph "Rudy" Toombs, 1914 (Monroe, LA)–November 8, 1962 (New York, NY)

"Big" Joe Turner, May 18, 1911 (Kansas City, MO)–November 24, 1985 (Inglewood, CA)

Titus Turner, May 1, 1933 (Atlanta, GA)–September 13, 1984 (Atlanta, GA)

Charles Walker, July 26, 1922 (Macon, GA)–June 24, 1975 (New York)

Washboard Bill (William Cooke), July 4, 1905 (Sanford, FL)–April 27, 2003 (West Palm Beach, FL)

Dinah Washington, August 29, 1924 (Tuscaloosa, AL)–December 14, 1963 (Detroit, MI)

Justine "Baby" Washington, November 13, 1940 (Bamberg, SC)–

Noble "Thin Man" Watts, February 17, 1926 (DeLand, FL)–August 24, 2004 (DeLand, FL)

Josh White, February 11, 1914 (Greenville, SC)–September 5, 1969 (Manhasset, NY)

Charles Melvin "Cootie" Williams, July 10, 1911 (Mobile, AL)–September 15, 1985 (New York, NY)

Paul "Hucklebuck" Williams, July 13, 1915 (Lewisburg, TN)–September 14, 2002 (Englewood, NJ)

Ralph Willis, about October 1909 (possibly Irvin, GA)–June 11, 1957 (New York, NY)

Industry Personalities

Herb Abramson, November 16, 1916 (Brooklyn, NY)–November 9, 1999 (Las Vegas, NV)

Miriam Abramson (Bienstock), January 4, 1923 (Brooklyn, NY)–March 21, 2015 (New York, NY)

Moses "Moe" Asch, December 2, 1905 (Warsaw, Poland)–October 19, 1986 (New York, NY)

Bessie "Bess" Berman, July 14, 1902 (New York, NY)–August 8, 1968 (unknown)

Jerry Blaine, December 31, 1910 (Allenwood, NJ)–March 3, 1973 (Long Island, NY)

Ruth Bowen, September 13, 1924 (Danville, VA)–April 21, 2009 (New York, NY)

Dick Clark, November 30, 1929 (Bronxville, NY)–April 18, 2012 (Santa Monica, CA)

Joe Davis, October 6, 1896 (New York, NY)–September 3, 1978 (Louisville, KY)

Luther Dixon, August 7, 1931 (Jacksonville, FL)–October 22, 2009 (Jacksonville, FL)

Tom Dowd, October 20, 1925 (New York, NY)–October 27, 2002 (Aventura, FL)

Ahmet Ertegun, July 31, 1923 (Istanbul, Turkey)–December 14, 2006 (New York, NY)

Aldon "Alan" Freed, December 21, 1921 (Windber, PA)–January 20, 1965 (Palm Springs, CA)

Milt Gabler, May 20, 1911 (Harlem, NY)–July 20, 2001 (New York, NY)

Henry Glover, May 21, 1921 (Hot Springs, AR)–April 7, 1991 (Queens, NY)

George Goldner (Jacob Goldman), February 9, 1917 (New York, NY)–April 15, 1970 (Turtle Bay, NY)

Florence Greenberg, September 16, 1913 (New York, NY)–November 2, 1995 (Hackensack, NJ)

John Hammond II, December 15, 1910 (New York, NY)–July 10, 1987 (New York, NY)

Leroy Kirkland, February 10, 1904 (South Carolina)–April 6, 1988 (New York, NY)

Leonard Kunstadt, May 15, 1925 (Brooklyn, NY)–April 23, 1996 (New York, NY)

Jerry Leiber, April 25, 1933 (Baltimore, MD)–August 22, 2011 (Los Angeles, CA)

Moishe "Morris" Levy, August 27, 1927 (Bronx, NY)–May 21, 1990 (Ghent, NY)

Herman Lubinsky, August 30, 1896 (Bradford, CT)–March 16, 1974 (Glen Ridge, NJ)

Lee Magid, April 6, 1926 (New York, NY)–March 31, 2007 (Los Angeles, CA)

Fred Mendelsohn, May 16, 1917 (New York, NY)–April 28, 2000 (Palm Beach County, FL)

Henry "Juggy" Murray Jr., November 24, 1922 (Charleston, SC)–January 20, 2005 (New York, NY)

Clyde Otis, September 11, 1924 (Carson, MS)–January 8, 2008 (Englewood, NJ)

Bob Porter, June 20, 1940 (Wellesley, MA)–April 10, 2021 (Northvale, NJ)

Sol Rabinowitz, April 26, 1924 (Bronx, NY)–March 16, 2013 (Cary, NC)

Rosetta Reitz, September 28, 1924 (Utica, NY)–November 1, 2008 (New York, NY)

Bobby Robinson (Morgan Robinson), April 16, 1917 (Union, SC)–January 7, 2011 (Harlem, NY)

Danny Robinson, June 23, 1929 (Union, SC)–April 17, 1996 (Bronx, NY)

Zell "Zelma" Sanders, 1922–1976 (possibly Bronx, NY)

Marshall Sehorn, June 25, 1934 (Concord, NC)–December 5, 2006 (New Orleans, LA)

Bob Shad (Abraham Shadrinsky), February 12, 1919 (New York)–March 13, 1985 (Beverly Hills, CA)

Morty Shad (Morton Shadrinsky), September 14, 1915 (Brooklyn, NY)–August 3, 1993 (Miami-Dade County, FL)

Abraham "Al" Silver, January 9, 1914 (Providence, RI)–March 4, 1992 (Fort Lauderdale, FL)

Victoria Spivey, October 15, 1906 (Houston, TX)–October 3, 1976 (New York, NY)

Mike Stoller, March 13, 1933 (Belle Harbor, NY)–

Sylvia Vanderpool/Robinson, May 29, 1935 (New York, NY)–September 29, 2011 (Secaucus, NJ)

Hyman "Hy" Weiss, February 12, 1923 (Romania)–March 20, 2007 (Englewood, NJ)

Samuel "Sam" Weiss, September 19, 1925 (Bronx, NY)–March 19, 2008 (Boca Raton, FL)

Gerald "Jerry" Wexler, January 10, 1917 (Bronx, NY)–August 15, 2008 (Sarasota, FL)

Paul Winley, July 10, 1934 (Washington, DC)–

Notes

1. This summary, as of September 30, 2020, relates mainly to individuals covered in the text and is not deemed to be a definitive listing.

2. While every attempt has been made to ensure that correct information has been filed, there is always a possibility of inaccurate data being handed down. That said, any amendments will be warmly received.

3. With grateful thanks to Bob Eagle and Eric S. LeBlanc, *Blues: A Regional Experience* (Santa Barbara, CA: Praeger, 2013). Also John Broven, *Record Makers and Breakers: Voices of the Independent Rock 'n' Roll Pioneers* (Urbana: University of Illinois Press, 2009).

TOP NEW YORK BLUES AND R&B HITS, 1944-1965
COMPILED BY JOHN BROVEN

Important *Billboard/Cash Box* New York-Related Chart Records, 1954-1964

BB pop	CB pop	BB R&B	
1	1	1	Kansas City—Wilbert Harrison (Fury, 1959)
1	1	1	Stagger Lee—Lloyd Price (ABC-Paramount, 1959)

BB pop	CB pop	BB R&B	
1	1	1	Save the Last Dance for Me—The Drifters (Atlantic, 1960)
1	1	1	Tossin' and Turnin'—Bobby Lewis (Beltone, 1961)
1	1	1	Easier Said Than Done—The Essex (Roulette, 1963)
1	1	2	Will You Love Me Tomorrow—The Shirelles (Scepter, 1961)
1	1	5	The Happy Organ—Dave "Baby" Cortez (Clock, 1959)
2	2	1	Honky Tonk (Parts 1 & 2)—Bill Doggett (King, 1956)
2	3	4	Daddy's Home—Shep and the Limelites (Hull, 1961)
2	3	4	Sally, Go 'Round the Roses—The Jaynetts (Tuff, 1963)
3	3	2	Dedicated to the One I Love—The Shirelles (Scepter, 1961)
3	6	1	My True Story—The Jive Five (Beltone, 1961)
4	7	2	Tears on My Pillow—Little Anthony and the Imperials (End, 1958)
5	1*	2	Sh-Boom—The Chords (Cat, 1954) (linked to the Crew-Cuts version)
5	2	1	Baby (You Got What It Takes)—Dinah Washington and Brook Benton (Mercury, 1960)
5	7	3	Book of Love—The Monotones (Mascot/Argo, 1958)
6	2	1	Why Do Fools Fall Fool in Love—Frankie Lymon and the Teenagers (Gee, 1956)
7	5	1	A Rockin' Good Way—Dinah Washington and Brook Benton (Mercury, 1960)
7	8	1	Ya Ya—Lee Dorsey (Fury, 1961)
7	10	11	Let the Little Girl Dance—Billy Bland (Old Town, 1960)
8	22	3	Over the Mountain, Across the Sea—Johnnie and Joe (J&S/Chess, 1957)
11	7	1	Love Is Strange—Mickey and Sylvia (Groove, 1957)
11	10	1	Hi-Heel Sneakers—Tommy Tucker (Checker, 1964)
11	10	3	I Only Have Eyes for You—The Flamingos (End, 1960)
11	12	3	So Fine—The Fiestas (Old Town, 1959)
14	21	2	It's Gonna Work Out Fine—Ike and Tina Turner (Sue, 1961)
15	19	2	Maybe—The Chantels (End, 1958)
17	7	2	Twist and Shout—The Isley Brothers (Wand, 1962)
17	14	1	Soul Twist—King Curtis (Enjoy, 1960)
19	15	2	All in My Mind—Maxine Brown (Nomar, 1960)
19	17	3	Letter Full of Tears—Gladys Knight and the Pips (Fury, 1962)
20	16	4	I Need Your Loving—Don Gardner and Dee Dee Ford (Fire, 1962)
22	21	12	Wiggle Wobble—Les Cooper (Everlast, 1962)
23	14	14	The Madison—Al Brown's Tunetoppers (Amy, 1960)
25	9	2	Don't Be Angry—Nappy Brown (Savoy, 1955)
32	58	12	We Belong Together—Robert and Johnny (Old Town, 1958)
38	34	1	Fannie Mae—Buster Brown (Fire, 1960)
44	–	–	Hard Times (The Slop)—Noble "Thin Man" Watts (Baton, 1957)
45	–	15	Every Beat of My Heart—Gladys Knight and the Pips (Fury, 1961)
48	–	15	Darling It's Wonderful—The Lovers (Lamp, 1957)

Other New York-Related *Billboard* race/R&B no. 1 discs, 1944-1963 (selective)

When My Man Comes Home—Buddy Johnson (Decca, 1944)
Hamp's Boogie Woogie—Lionel Hampton (Decca, 1944)

Who Threw the Whiskey in the Well—Lucky Millinder and Wynonie Harris (Decca, 1945)
Caldonia—Louis Jordan (Decca, 1945)
Hey! Ba-Ba-Re-Bop—Lionel Hampton (Decca, 1946)
Choo Choo Ch'Boogie—Louis Jordan (Decca, 1946)
Ain't Nobody Here But Us Chickens—Louis Jordan (Decca, 1947)
Good Rockin' Tonight—Wynonie Harris (King, 1948)
Corn Bread—Hal Singer (Savoy, 1948)
It's Too Soon to Know—The Orioles (Jubilee, 1948)
The Huckle-Buck—Paul Williams (Savoy, 1949)
Saturday Night Fish Fry—Louis Jordan (Decca, 1949)
Teardrops from My Eyes—Ruth Brown (Atlantic, 1950)
Don't You Know I Love You—The Clovers (Atlantic, 1951)
Fool, Fool, Fool—The Clovers (Atlantic, 1951)
Flamingo—Earl Bostic (King, 1951)
Booted—Roscoe Gordon (Chess, RPM, 1952)
Ting-a-Ling—The Clovers (Atlantic, 1952)
(Mama) He Treats Your Daughter Mean—Ruth Brown (Atlantic, 1953)
Crying in the Chapel—The Orioles (Jubilee, 1953)
Shake a Hand—Faye Adams (Herald, 1953)
Money Honey—Clyde McPhatter and the Drifters (Atlantic, 1953)
Shake, Rattle and Roll—Joe Turner (Atlantic, 1954)
Hurts Me to My Heart—Faye Adams (Herald, 1954)
Mambo Baby—Ruth Brown (Atlantic, 1954)
Unchained Melody—Roy Hamilton/Al Hibbler (Epic/Decca, 1955)
Fever—Little Willie John (King, 1956)
Jim Dandy—LaVern Baker (Atlantic, 1957)
Young Blood/Searchin'—The Coasters (Atco, 1957)
C. C. Rider—Chuck Willis (Atlantic, 1957)
Mr. Lee—The Bobbettes (Atlantic, 1957)
Yakety Yak—The Coasters (Atco, 1958)
What Am I Living For—Chuck Willis (Atlantic, 1958)
It's Just a Matter of Time—Brook Benton (Mercury, 1959)
What'd I Say (Part 1)—Ray Charles (Atlantic, 1959)
There's Something on Your Mind (Part 2)—Bobby Marchan (Fire, 1960)
Stand by Me—Ben E. King (Atco, 1961)
Baby Workout—Jackie Wilson (Brunswick, 1963)

Other Significant New York-Related R&B Chart Hits, 1948-1965

BB	CB	
R&B	R&B	(from 1960)
2	–	My Fault—Brownie McGhee (Savoy, 1948)
2	–	Drinkin' Wine Spo-Dee-O-Dee—"Stick" McGhee (Atlantic, 1949)
2	–	No More Doggin'—Roscoe Gordon (RPM, 1952)
2	–	Don't Let Go—Roy Hamilton (Epic, 1958)
2	5	Just a Little Bit—Rosco Gordon (Vee-Jay, 1960)
2	27	Sticks and Stones—Ray Charles (ABC-Paramount, 1960)
3	–	Gabbin' Blues—Big Maybelle (OKeh, 1953)
4	–	Heavenly Father—Edna McGriff (Jubilee, 1952)

BB R&B	CB R&B	(from 1960)
5	–	Eyesight to the Blind—The Larks (Apollo, 1951)
5	–	I Didn't Sleep a Wink Last Night—Arthur Prysock (Decca, 1952)
6	–	Lonely Avenue—Ray Charles (Atlantic, 1956)
10	–	Little Side Car—The Larks (Apollo, 1951)
10	–	Are You Satisfied?—Ann Cole (Baton, 1956)
11	9	It's Too Late, Baby Too Late—Arthur Prysock (Old Town, 1965)
14	11	Shotgun Wedding—Roy "C" [Hammond] (Black Hawk, 1965)
15	–	The Sky Is Crying—Elmore James (Fire, 1960)
19	–	Sugar Babe—Buster Brown (Fire, 1962)
20	–	It's Too Late—Tarheel Slim and Little Ann (Fire, 1960)
25	9	It Hurts Me Too—Elmore James (Enjoy, 1965)
39	39	Trouble I've Had—Clarence Ashe (J&S/Chess, 1964)
–	26	Mojo Hand—Lightnin' Hopkins (Fire, 1961)
–	34	Lock Me in Your Heart—Tarheel Slim and Little Ann (Fire, 1960)

Notes

1. Many of these singles are referenced in the text.

2. The data is based on year-by-year chart positions, not actual sales figures.

3. As of March 12, 1960, the *Cash Box* R&B chart ("Hot Top 50 across the Nation") was merged with the Top 100 pop chart, but a "Top 50 in R&B Locations" chart was fully reinstated on December 17, 1960.

Sources

The *Billboard* and *Cash Box* pop and R&B charts, by way of:

Albert, George, and Frank Hoffman. *The Cash Box Black Contemporary Singles Charts, 1960–1984*. Metuchen, NJ: Scarecrow Press, 1986.

Hoffman, Frank. *The Cash Box Singles Charts, 1950–1981*. Metuchen, NJ: Scarecrow Press, 1983.

Whitburn, Joel. *Top Pop Singles, 1955–2012*. Menomonee Falls, WI: Record Research, 2013.

Whitburn, Joel. *Hot R&B Songs, 1942–2010*. Menomonee Falls, WI: Record Research, 2010.

BIBLIOGRAPHY (SELECTIVE)

Books

Bastin, Bruce. *Red River Blues: The Blues Tradition in the Southeast*. Urbana: University of Illinois Press, 1986.

Bastin, Bruce, with Kip Lornell. *The Melody Man: Joe Davis and the New York Music Scene, 1916–1978*. Jackson: University Press of Mississippi, 2012.

Bernholm, Jonas. *Soul Music Odyssey 1968*. 2nd ed. Toronto: York University Pressbooks, 2019.

Broven, John. *Record Makers and Breakers: Voices of the Independent Rock 'n' Roll Pioneers*. Urbana: University of Illinois Press, 2009.

Broven, John. *Rhythm and Blues in New Orleans*. 3rd ed. Gretna, LA: Pelican, 2016.

Brown, Ruth, with Andrew Yule. *Miss Rhythm: The Autobiography of Ruth Brown, Rhythm & Blues Legend*. New York: Penguin, 1996.

Carlin, Richard. *Godfather of the Music Business: Morris Levy*. Jackson: University Press of Mississippi, 2016.

Charters, Samuel B. *The Country Blues*. New York: Rinehart, 1959.

Charters, Samuel B., and Leonard Kunstadt. *Jazz: A History of the New York Scene*. Garden City, NY: Doubleday, 1962.

Cohn, Lawrence. *Nothing But the Blues: The Music and the Musicians*. New York: Abbeville Press, 1993.

Collins, Tony. *Rock Mr. Blues: The Life and Music of Wynonie Harris*. Milford, NH: Big Nickel, 1995.

Corsano, Arlene. *Thought We Were Writing the Blues: But They Called It Rock & Roll*. Tenafly, NJ: ArleneChristine, 2014.

Cosgrove, Stuart. *Harlem 69: The Future of Soul*. Edinburgh: Polygon, 2019.

Dachs, David. *Anything Goes: The World of Popular Music*. Indianapolis: Bobbs-Merrill, 1964.

Demêtre, Jacques, and Marcel Chauvard. *Voyage au Pays du Blues: Land of the Blues*. Paris: Clarb/Soul Bag, 1994.

Eagle, Bob, and Eric S. LeBlanc. *Blues: A Regional Experience*. Santa Barbara, CA: Praeger, 2013.

Emerson, Ken. *Always Magic in the Air: The Bomp and Brilliance of the Brill Building Era*. New York: Viking Penguin, 2005.

Ertegun, Ahmet, et al. *"What'd I Say": The Atlantic Story, 50 Years of Music*. New York: Welcome Rain, 2001.

Fox, Ted. *Showtime at the Apollo*. New York: Holt, Rinehart and Winston, 1983.

Franz, Steve. *The Amazing Secret History of Elmore James*. St. Louis: BlueSource Publications, 2003.

Gart, Galen. *ARLD: The American Record Label Directory and Dating Guide, 1940–1959*. Milford, NH: Big Nickel, 1989.

Gart, Galen. *First Pressings: The History of Rhythm & Blues, 1948–1959*. 12 vols. Milford, NH: Big Nickel, 1986–2002.

Gillett, Charlie. *Making Tracks: The History of Atlantic Records*. St. Albans, Herts., England: Panther Books, 1975.

Goldsmith, Peter D. *Making People's Music: Moe Asch and Folkways Records*. Washington, DC: Smithsonian Institution Press, 1998.

Govenar, Alan. *Lightnin' Hopkins: His Life and Blues*. Chicago: Chicago Review Press, 2010.

Gussow, Adam. *Mr. Satan's Apprentice*. Minneapolis: University of Minnesota Press, 2009.

Halberstadt, Alex. *Lonely Avenue: The Unlikely Life and Times of Doc Pomus*. Philadelphia: Da Capo Press, 2007.

Harris, Sheldon. *Blues Who's Who: A Biographical Dictionary of Blues Singers*. New Rochelle, NY: Arlington House, 1979.

Jackson, John A. *American Bandstand: Dick Clark and the Making of a Rock 'n' Roll Empire*. New York: Oxford University Press, 1997.

Jackson, John A. *Big Beat Heat: Alan Freed and the Early Years of Rock & Roll*. New York: Schirmer Books, 1991.

Josephson, Barney, and Terry Trilling-Josephson. *Cafe Society: The Wrong Place for the Right People*. Urbana: University of Illinois Press, 2009.

Kernfeld, Barry, ed. *The New Grove Dictionary of Jazz*. New York: St. Martin's Press, 1996.

Leiber, Jerry, and Mike Stoller, with David Ritz. *Hound Dog: The Leiber and Stoller Autobiography*. New York: Simon and Schuster, 2009.

McNutt, Randy. *Too Hot to Handle: An Illustrated Encyclopedia of American Recording Studios of the Twentieth Century*. Hamilton, OH: HHP Books, 2001.

Porter, Bob. *Soul Jazz: Jazz in the Black Community, 1945–1975*. Bloomington, IN: Xlibris, 2016.

Porterfield, Nolan. *Last Cavalier: The Life and Times of John A. Lomax, 1867–1948*. Urbana: University of Illinois Press, 1996.

Reig, Teddy, with Edward Berger. *Reminiscing in Tempo: The Life and Times of a Jazz Hustler*. Metuchen, NJ: Scarecrow Press, 1990.

Rolontz, Robert. *How to Get Your Song Recorded*. New York: Watson-Guptill, 1963.

Schiffman, Jack. *Harlem Heyday: A Pictorial History of Modern Black Show Business and the Apollo Theatre*. Buffalo: Prometheus Books, 1984.

Schiffman, Jack. *Uptown: The Story of Harlem's Apollo Theatre*. New York: Cowles, 1971.

Shaw, Arnold. *52nd Street: The Street of Jazz*. New York: Da Capo Press, 1977.

Shaw, Arnold. *Honkers and Shouters: The Golden Years of Rhythm & Blues*. New York: Collier, 1978.

Simons, David. *Studio Stories: How the Great New York Records Were Made*. San Francisco: Backbeat Books, 2004.

Toop, David. *The Rap Attack: African Jive to New York Hip Hop*. London: Pluto Press, 1984.

Wexler, Jerry, and David Ritz. *Rhythm and the Blues: A Life in American Music*. New York: Alfred A. Knopf, 1993.

Wilmer, Val. *Mama Said There'd Be Days Like This: My Life in the Jazz World*. London: Women's Press, 1989.

Zack, Ian. *Say No to the Devil: The Life and Musical Genius of Rev. Gary Davis*. Chicago: University of Chicago Press. 2015.

Charts, Discographical

Albert, George, and Frank Hoffman. *The Cash Box Black Contemporary Singles Charts, 1960–1984*. Metuchen, NJ: Scarecrow Press, 1986.

Fancourt, Les, and Bob McGrath. *The Blues Discography, 1943–1970: The Classic Years*. 3rd ed. West Vancouver, BC, Canada: Eyeball Productions, 2019.

Ferlingere, Robert D. *A Discography of Rhythm & Blues and Rock 'n' Roll Vocal Groups, 1945 to 1965*. 3rd ed. Jackson, CA: Effendee Trust, 1999.

Ford, Robert, and Bob McGrath. *The Blues Discography, 1971–2000: The Later Years*. West Vancouver, BC, Canada: Eyeball Productions, 2011.

Godrich, John, and Robert M. W. Dixon. *Blues and Gospel Records, 1902–1942*. London: Storyville, 1969.

Gonzalez, Fernando L. *Disco-File*. 3rd ed. Self-published, 2008.

Hoffman, Frank. *The Cash Box Singles Charts, 1950–1981*. Metuchen, NJ: Scarecrow Press, 1983.

Jepsen, Jurgen. *Jazz Records, 1942–1962*. Copenhagen. Nordisk Tidsskrift Forlag, 1963.

Leadbitter, Mike, Leslie Fancourt, and Paul Pelletier. *Blues Records, 1943 to 1970*. Vol. 2: *L to Z*. London: Record Information Services, 1994.

Leadbitter, Mike, and Neil Slaven. *Blues Records, 1943 to 1970*. Vol. 1: *A to K*. London: Record Information Services, 1987.

McGrath, Bob. *The R&B Indies*. 2nd ed. 4 vols. West Vancouver, BC, Canada: Eyeball Productions, 2005–2007.

Ruppli, Michel. *Atlantic Records: A Discography*. Westport, CT: Greenwood Press, 1979.

Ruppli, Michel. *The King Labels: A Discography*. Westport, CT: Greenwood Press, 1985.

Whitburn, Joel. *Hot R&B Songs, 1942–2010*. Menomonee Falls, WI: Record Research, 2010.

Whitburn, Joel. *Pop Memories, 1890–1954: The History of American Popular Music*. Menomonee Falls, WI: Record Research, 1986.

Whitburn, Joel. *Top Pop Singles, 1955–2012*. Menomonee Falls, WI: Record Research, 2013.

Magazines and Newspapers

The principle magazines consulted were *Billboard, Cash Box, American Music Magazine, Blues Unlimited, Blues & Rhythm, Juke Blues, Living Blues, Now Dig This*, and *Record Research/ Blues Research*.

CONTRIBUTORS

Photo by Nancy Radloff.

LARRY SIMON

Born in 1956, Larry Simon, guitarist and composer from Brooklyn, New York, has recorded and toured with many jazz and blues artists including Big Jay McNeely, George Coleman, the Skatalites, Bob Gaddy, Larry Dale, Jimmy Spruill, and others. As a composer he has written extensively for dance, film, and theater. Additionally, Simon has worked for many years collaborating with poets, including Robert Pinsky, Ed Sanders, and John Sinclair.

Larry also lived in Portsmouth, New Hampshire, for a number of years. While there, he created the still-ongoing Beat Night series, featuring music and spoken word. In 2004 he founded Jazzmouth, the Seacoast Poetry and Jazz Festival, of which he was the artistic director and producer.

Starting in the late 1970s, Simon became very active in the downtown New York City experimental music scene, having composed and performed some of the earliest minimalist music for electric guitar. He was also a vital part of the "punk/funk" scene working with musicians such as Lester Bowie, Julius Hemphill, David Sanborn, John Zorn, Henry Threadgill, and Phillip Wilson in seminal NYC clubs such as CBGB, Hurrah's, the Lone Star Cafe, and Tier 3. Simon was a member of composer La Monte Young's ensemble as well as Gamelan Son of Lion.

Larry has written for the *Millennium Film Journal*, *Ear Magazine*, the *Portsmouth Herald*, and *Spotlight Magazine*. His most recent recording is *The Dream Keeper* (with David Amram and Eric Mingus), featuring the poetry of Langston Hughes with music.

For rare and unreleased audio tracks, additional photos, and more go to Larry Simon's website: www.larrysimon-music.com.

Photo by Diane Wattecamps.

JOHN BROVEN

After contributing to the first issue of *Blues Unlimited*, founded in 1963 in England by Mike Leadbitter and Simon Napier, John Broven briefly became a coeditor of that influential international magazine in the mid-1970s before cofounding *Juke Blues* magazine in 1985 with Cilla Huggins and Bez Turner. Broven retired from a career in bank management to serve as a consultant from 1991 to 2006 at Ace Records of London, being involved in up to 250 CD reissues, many from leading independent labels such as Atlantic, Excello, Imperial, King, Modern, and Specialty.

He is author of the award-winning *Rhythm and Blues in New Orleans* (originally *Walking to New Orleans* [1974, updated 2016]); *South to Louisiana: The Music of the Cajun Bayous* (1983, updated 2019); and *Record Makers and Breakers:*

Voices of the Independent Rock 'n' Roll Pioneers (2009). Through the years, Broven has made contributions to other books, periodicals, LPs, and CDs, including Ace and Bear Family box sets.

He helped launch in 2013 the Cosimo Code website (www.cosimocode.com) with Red Kelly and John Ridley to document the 1960s and 1970s recordings from the New Orleans studios of famed engineer Cosimo Matassa.

In 1995, Broven married Shelley Galehouse King—whose father, Clark Galehouse, founded Golden Crest Records and the Shelley Products pressing plant—and relocated from England to Long Island, where he still manages the family's music legacy. Living near New York, he was able to augment interviews conducted during trips to the Big Apple in the 1980s. All his taped interviews and research papers are lodged at the Library of Congress in Culpeper, Virginia. For more, go to his website at www.johnbroven.com.

ROBERT SCHAFFER

Robert Schaffer, from Bensonhurst, Brooklyn, is a photographer and writer whose images have been in *Time Out* and *Cosmopolitan*'s Japanese edition. His photos have been used on CDs for Gamelan Son of Lion, the DownTown Ensemble, Larry Simon, Linda Dunn, and others.

VAL WILMER

In the blurb to her acclaimed 1989 autobiography, *Mama Said There'd Be Days Like This*, Val Wilmer, of London, is described as "an internationally acknowledged writer and photographer—a woman with great stories to tell. She brings vividly to life her encounters with the known and unknown artists who created new forms as music as a means of recording black people's history. Her journeys to Africa, Harlem, and rural Mississippi . . . were part of her quest to establish herself as a professional jazz commentator."

She has written for *Melody Maker*, *DownBeat*, *Juke Blues*, the *Wire*, and the *Guardian*. Her other books include *The Face of Black Music* and *As Serious As Your Life*, and her photographs are in major collections including the Victoria and Albert Museum (London), the National Portrait Gallery (London), and the Schomburg Center for Research in Black Culture (New York).

We are honored that she has chosen to join our team with first-hand features on Victoria Spivey, Larry Johnson, and Tarheel Slim from 1970s New York, also contributing telling examples of her astute photographic work.

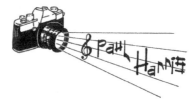

PAUL HARRIS

Since 1977, Paul Harris has been photographing music-related events, especially blues, R&B, rock 'n' roll, and soul, plus those uniquely Louisiana genres Cajun, zydeco, and swamp pop. When his grandfather was a boy living in Kennington, London, he is said to have played a piano loaded onto a horse-drawn cart while Charlie Chaplin danced in the road for pennies! That grandfather went on to become a photographer with a studio in Kennington. In due course, Paul's mother worked in a film-processing establishment, and a camera was always to hand. Hence, Paul's love of music and photography may have been instilled by his forebears.

Paul has visited many locations during his photographic career, his trips to New York being among his favorites. There, in the company of John Broven and Richard Tapp, he photographed many of the local personalities who appear in this book. Paul's images have graced vinyl albums, CDs, DVDs, books, and many magazines including *Juke Blues, Blues & Rhythm, Now Dig This, Vintage Rock*, and *Tales from the Woods* (all UK); *American Music Magazine* and *Jefferson* (Sweden); and *Living Blues* (US). He is a provider of music-related photographs to Getty Images.

Very sadly, Paul died on April 12, 2021, at age eighty, just before the publication of this book.

RICHARD "DICKIE" TAPP

Along with many of his contemporaries, Richard Tapp's lifelong love affair with blues and rhythm & blues started with the British blues boom of the early 1960s. This was when ears were opened to "the real thing," as a succession of iconic American blues artists visited English shores and their records became more widely available. The blues remained Tapp's passion in subsequent years as he continued to both listen to and read about the genre, particularly in *Blues Unlimited*. In 1985, he joined the *Juke Blues* team on the magazine's launch that year, as a reviewer and then writing the occasional article, while making research trips to New York. However, with the demise of that esteemed publication, he joined

American Music Magazine of Sweden, where he has researched and contributed major features including those on Faye Adams and Buddy Johnson.

Marie Knight, another subject of Tapp's research, is an artist who crossed the divide between the blues and the "hidden" world of gospel referenced by John Broven in his introduction. Her later years were devoted to the church as she fulfilled her life as a minister at a Harlem storefront church, the Gates of Prayer, on 145th Street. Her fine legacy of both gospel and secular recordings testifies to the array of supreme talent to be found in New York.

INDEX

CPSIA information can be obtained
at www.ICGtesting.com
Printed in the USA
BVHW031046240921
617467BV00007B/75